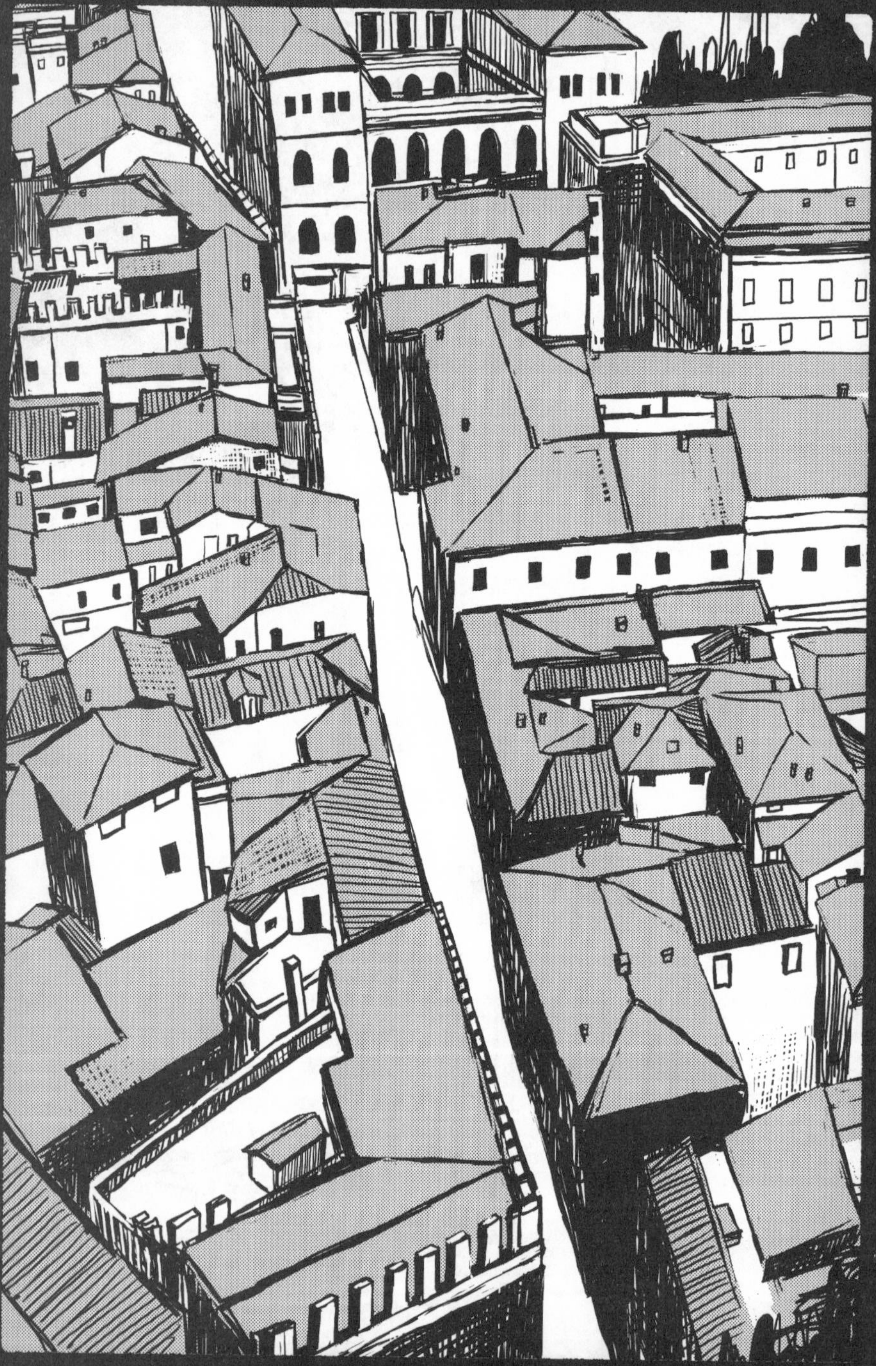

In a city...

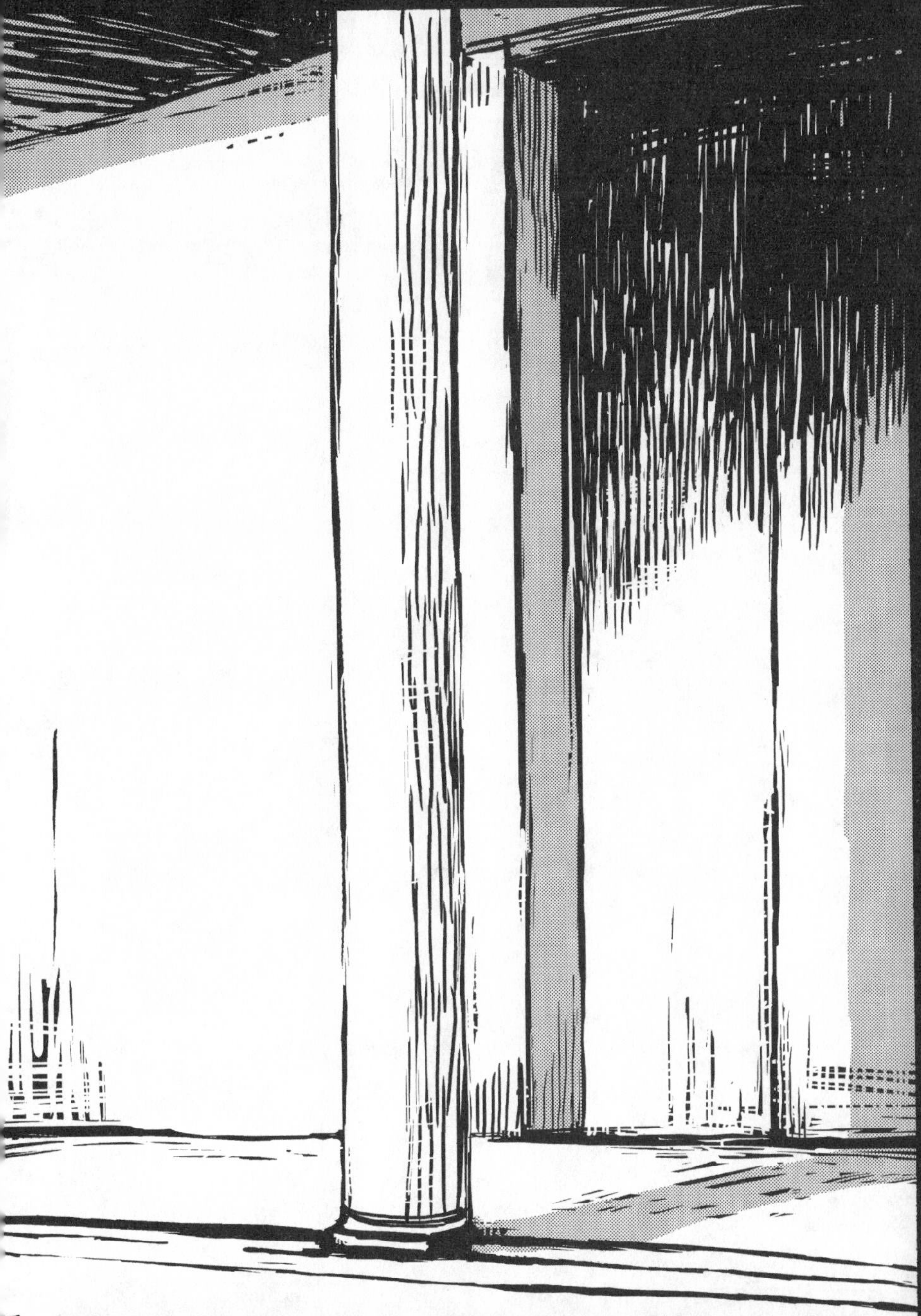

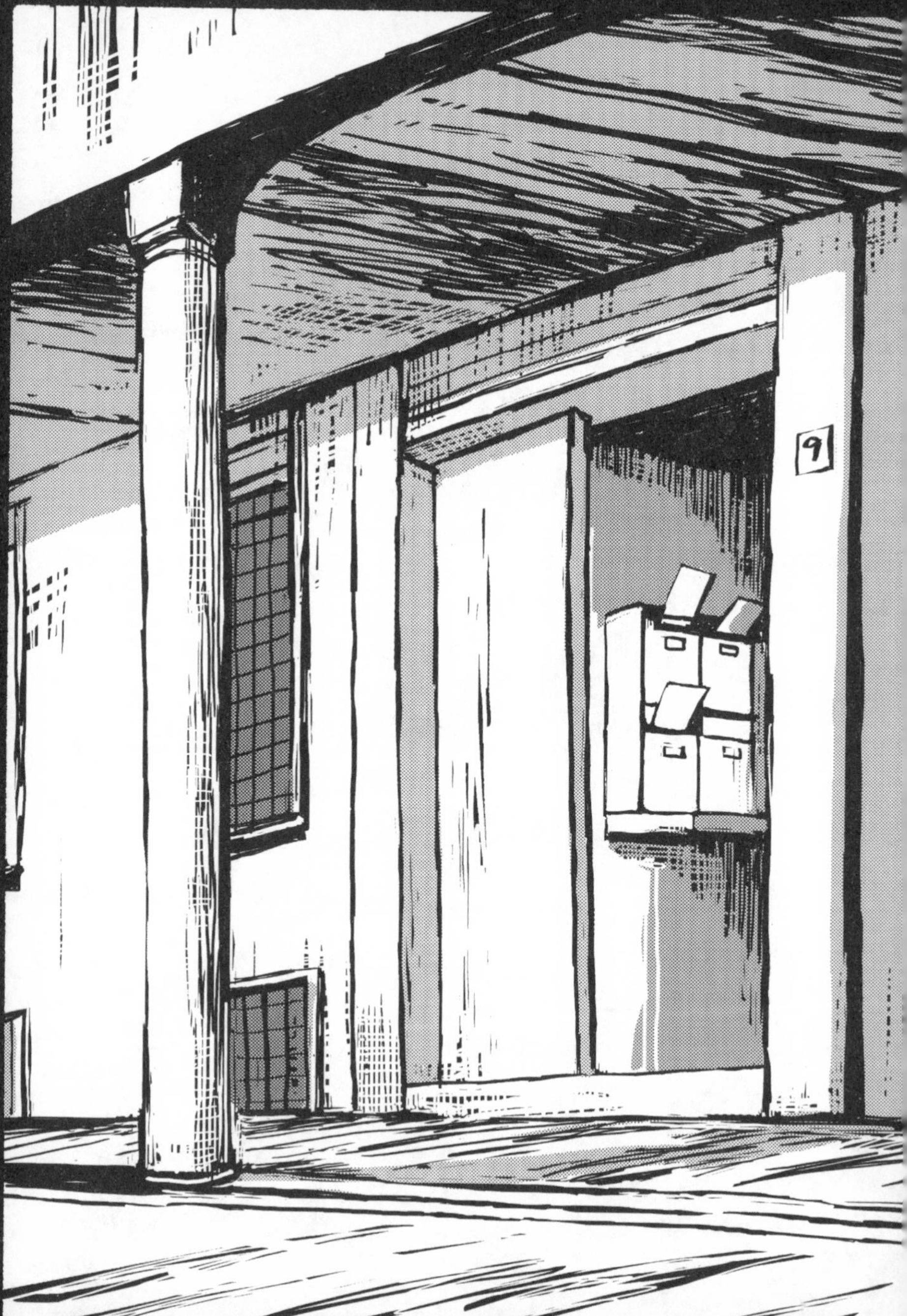
9

Beyond a portico...

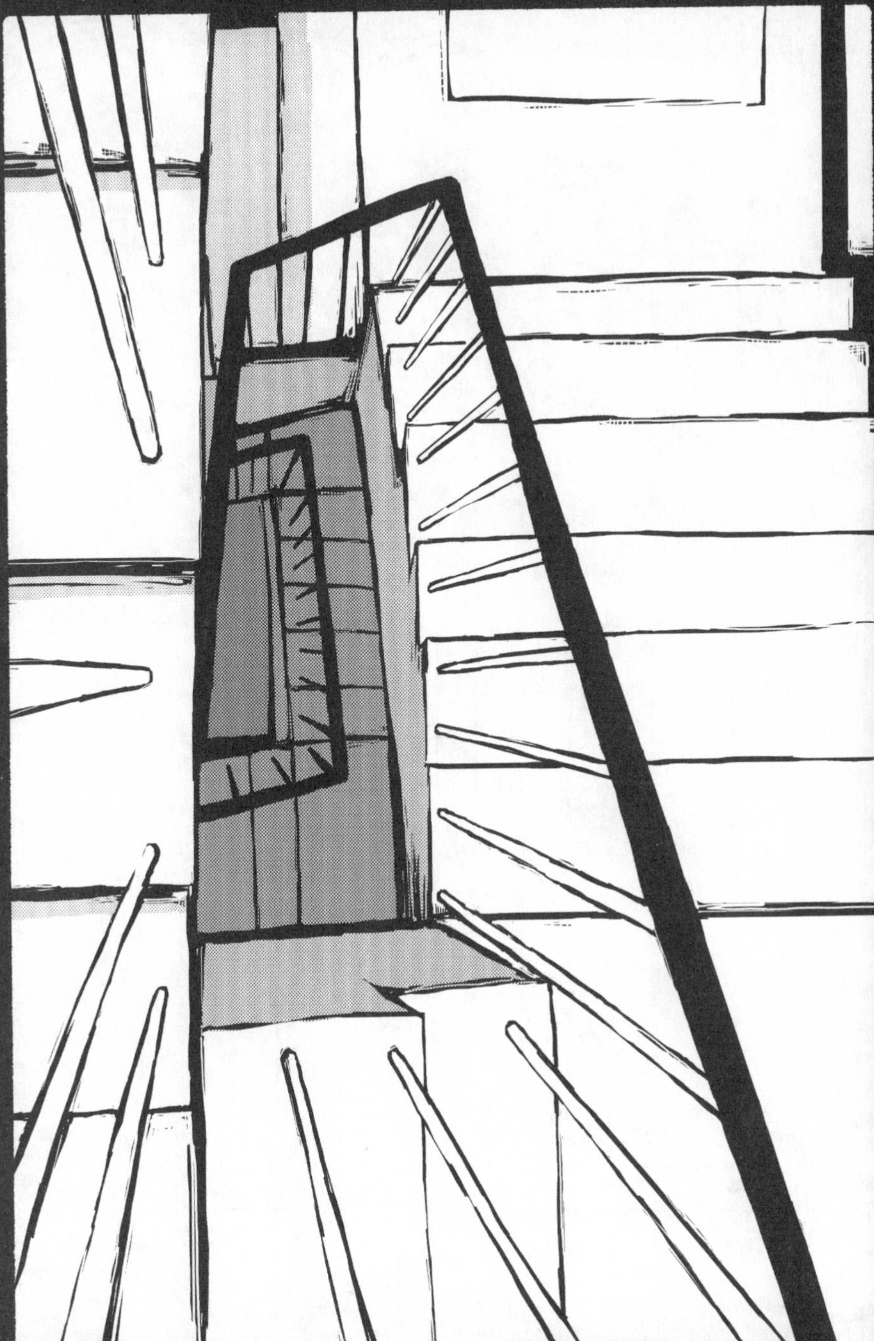

Up some stairs...

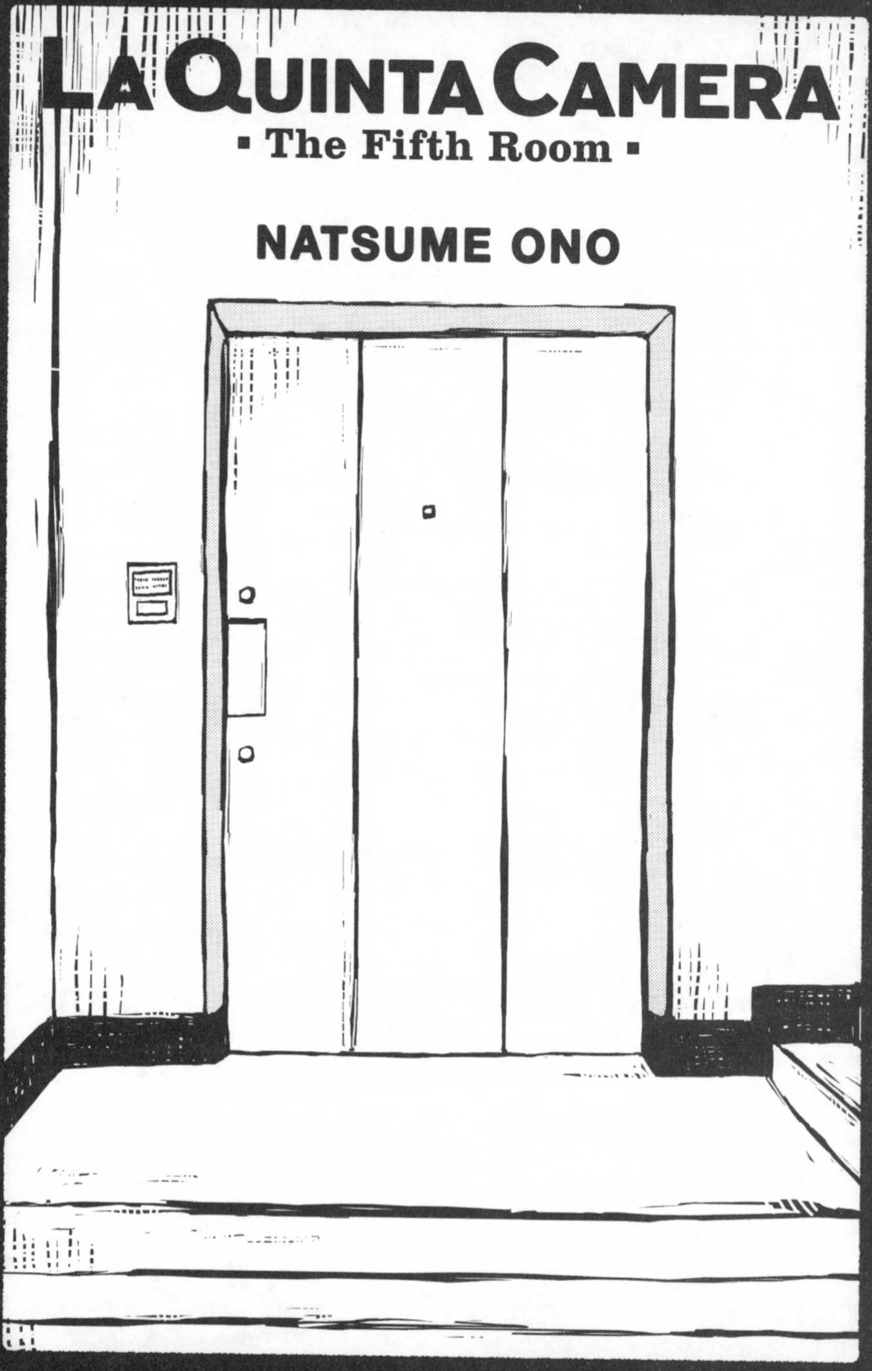
LA QUINTA CAMERA
▪ The Fifth Room ▪
NATSUME ONO

Here, our story unfolds.

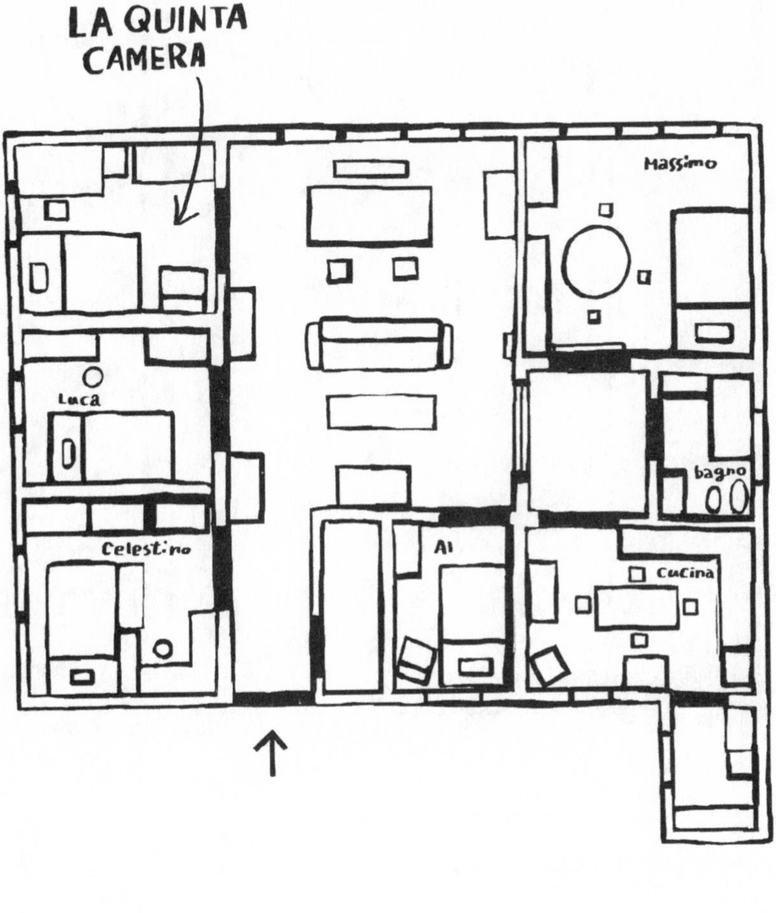
LA QUINTA CAMERA
Massimo
Luca
bagno
Celestino
Al
Cucina

La Quinta Camera
Camera

▪ The Fifth Room ▪

Contents

LA QUINTA CAMERA
Capitolo 1

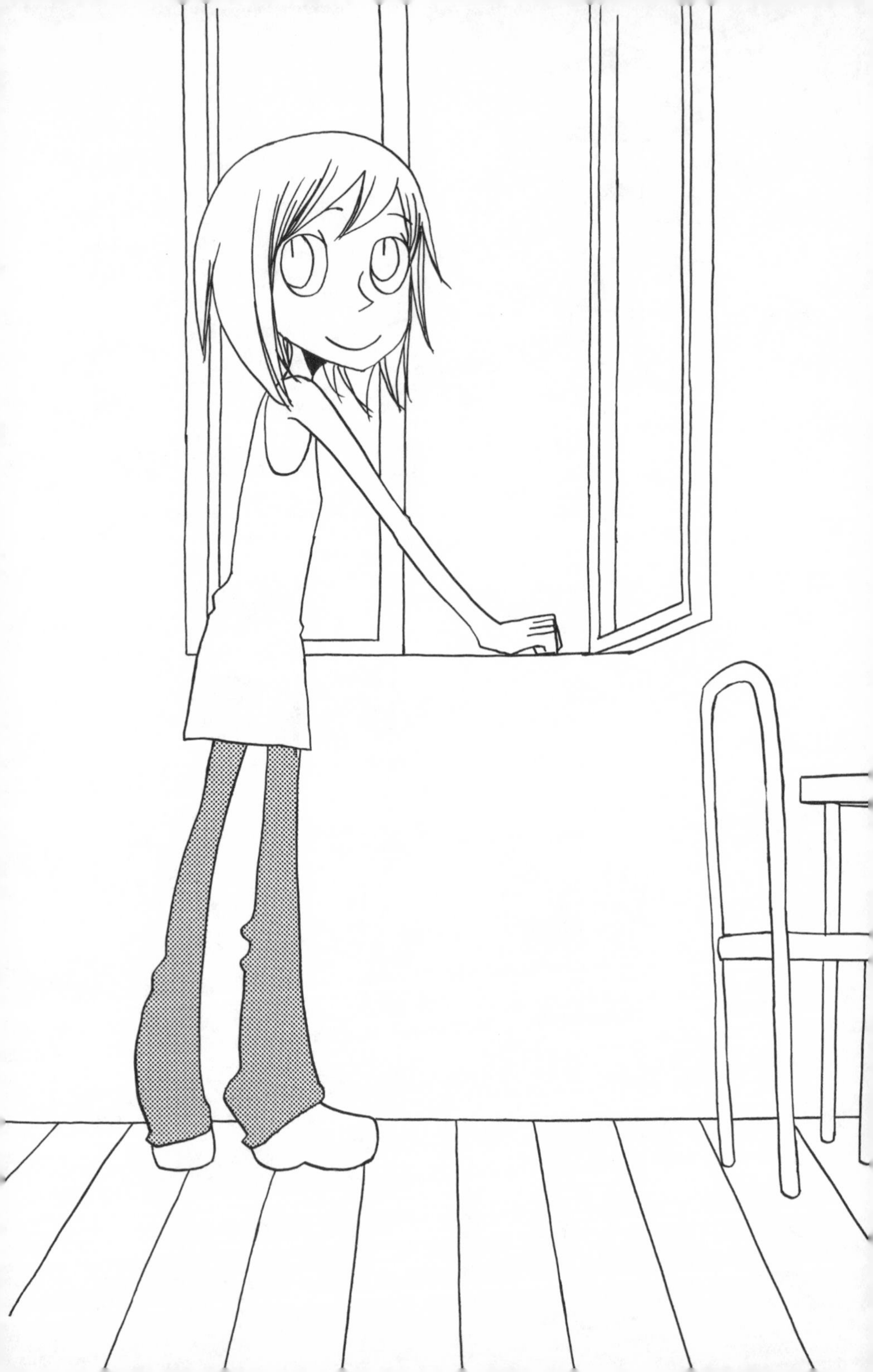

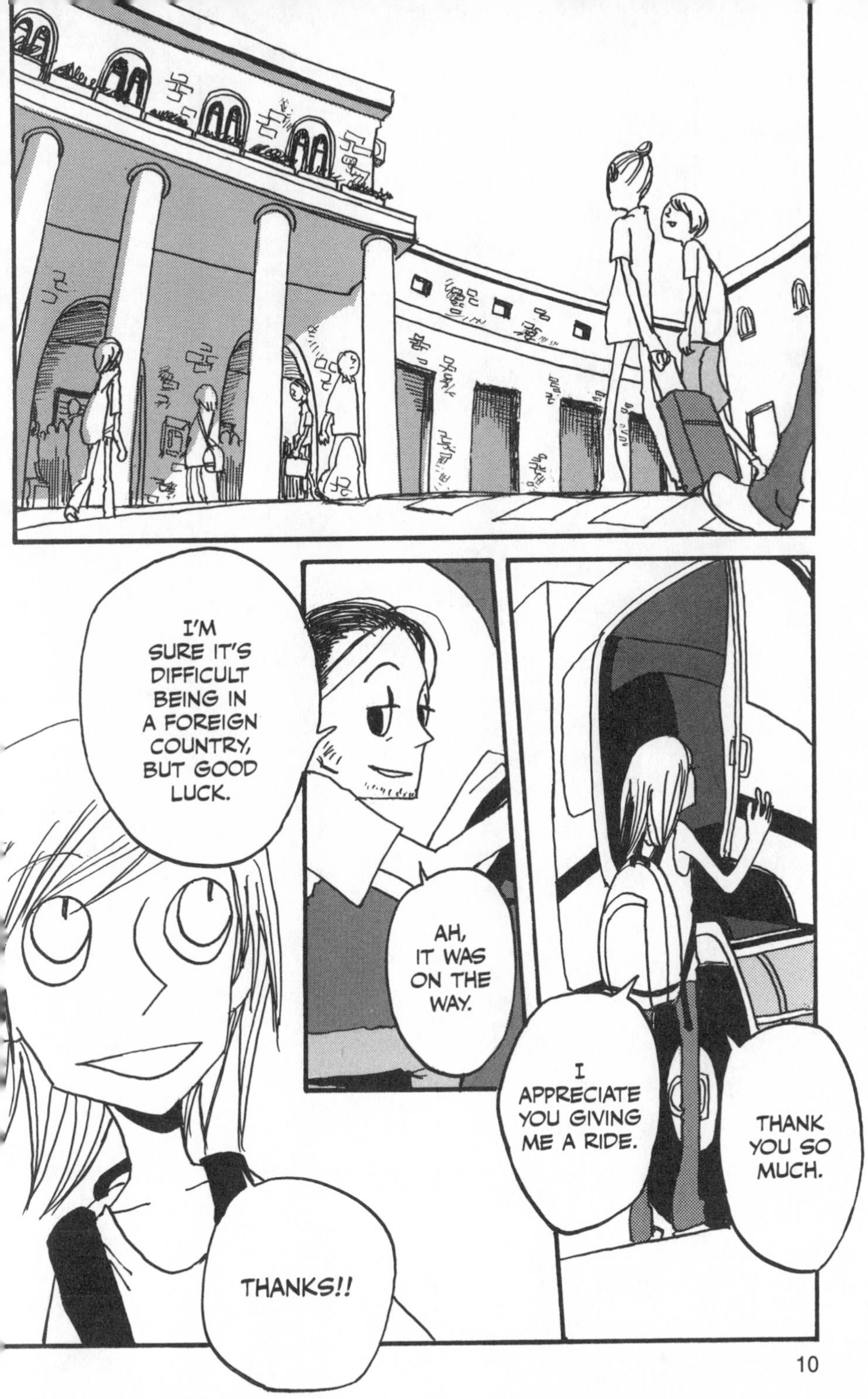
THANK YOU SO MUCH.
I APPRECIATE YOU GIVING ME A RIDE.
AH, IT WAS ON THE WAY.
I'M SURE IT'S DIFFICULT BEING IN A FOREIGN COUNTRY, BUT GOOD LUCK.
THANKS!!

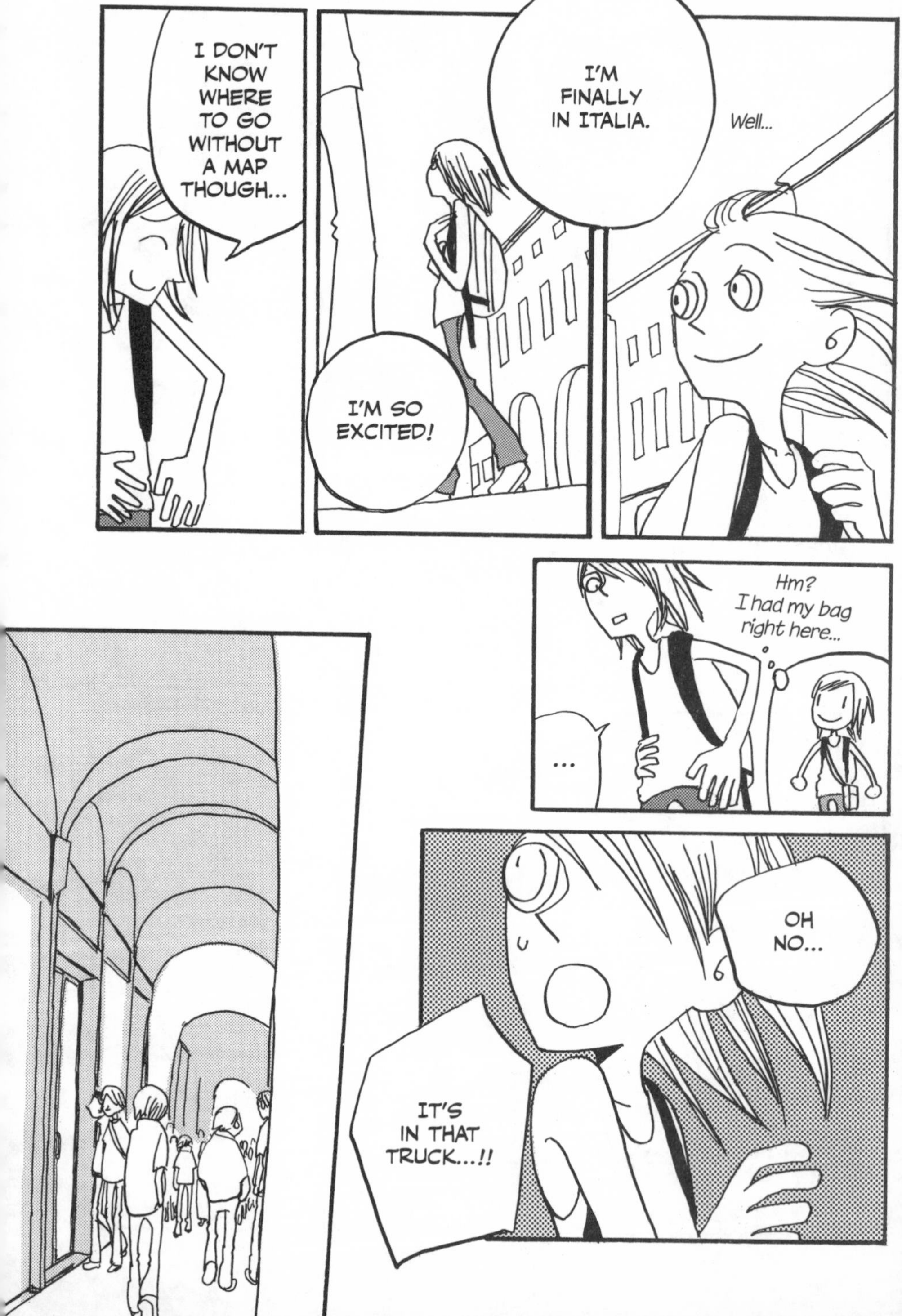
Well...
I'M FINALLY IN ITALIA.
I'M SO EXCITED!
I DON'T KNOW WHERE TO GO WITHOUT A MAP THOUGH...
Hm? I had my bag right here...
...
OH NO...
IT'S IN THAT TRUCK...!!

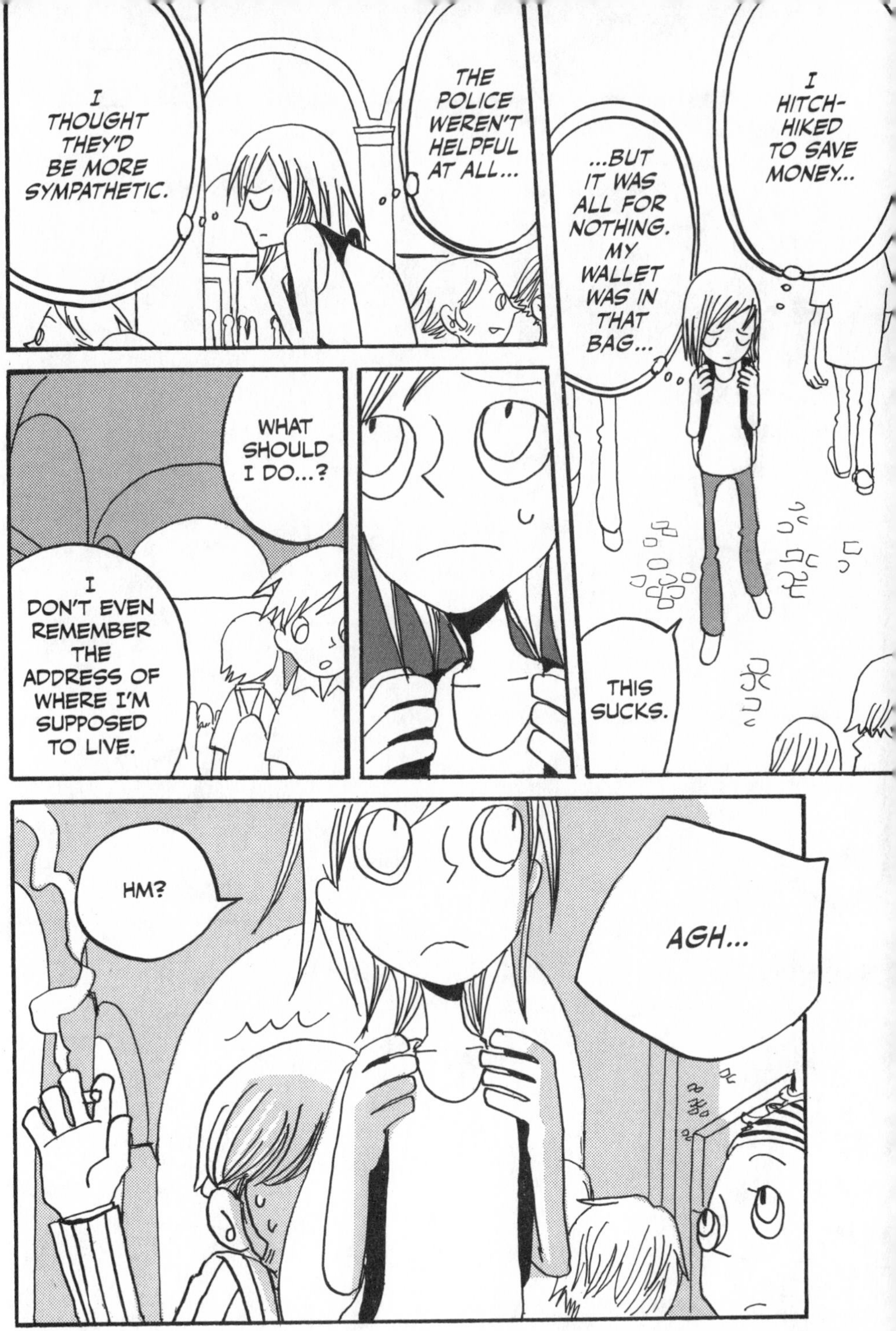

I HITCH-HIKED TO SAVE MONEY...
...BUT IT WAS ALL FOR NOTHING. MY WALLET WAS IN THAT BAG...
THIS SUCKS.
THE POLICE WEREN'T HELPFUL AT ALL...
I THOUGHT THEY'D BE MORE SYMPATHETIC.
WHAT SHOULD I DO...?
I DON'T EVEN REMEMBER THE ADDRESS OF WHERE I'M SUPPOSED TO LIVE.
AGH...
HM?

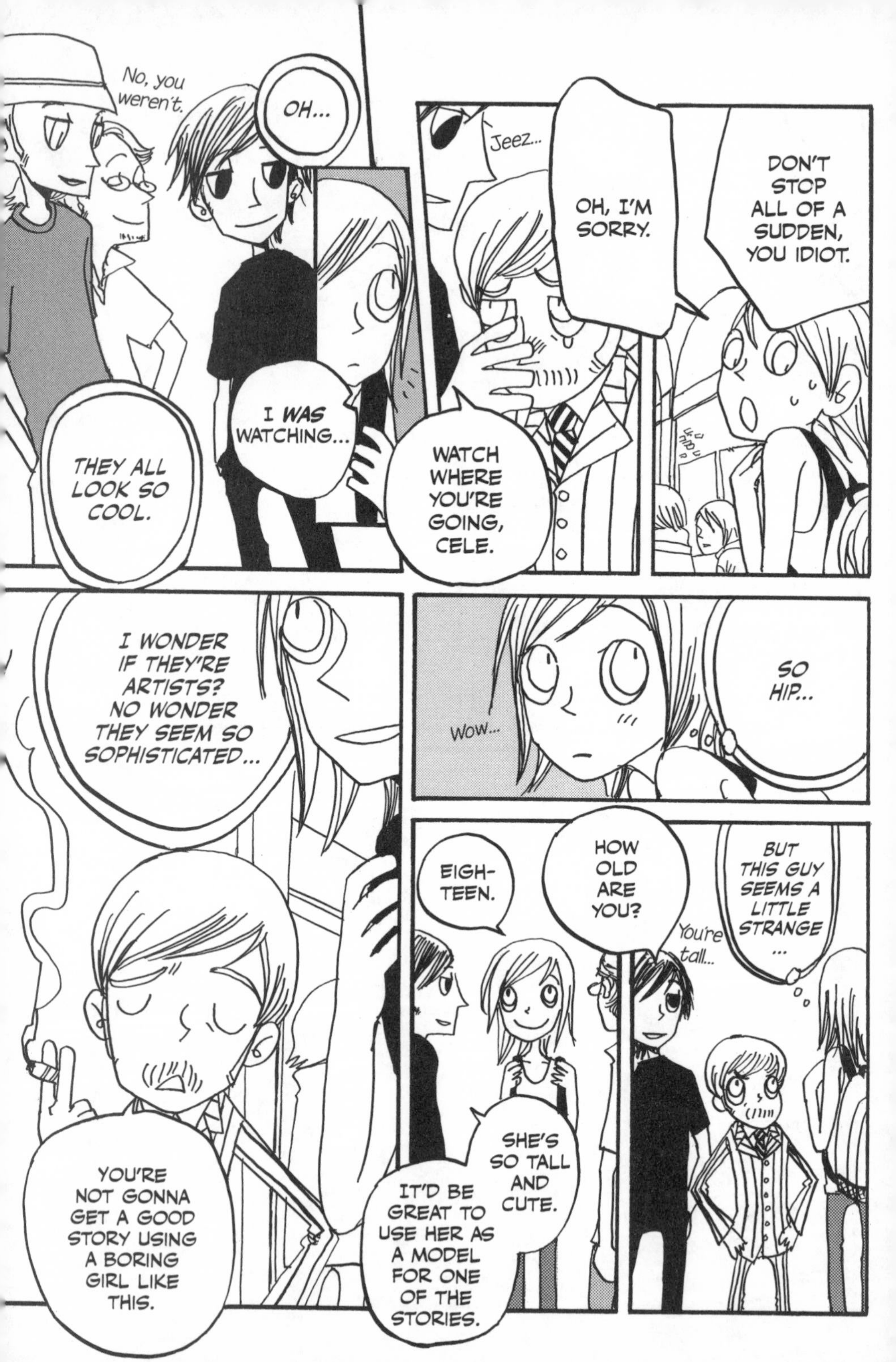
DON'T STOP ALL OF A SUDDEN, YOU IDIOT.
OH, I'M SORRY.
Jeez...
WATCH WHERE YOU'RE GOING, CELE.
OH...
No, you weren't.
I *WAS* WATCHING...
THEY ALL LOOK SO COOL.
SO HIP...
Wow...
BUT THIS GUY SEEMS A LITTLE STRANGE ...
You're tall...
HOW OLD ARE YOU?
EIGH-TEEN.
I WONDER IF THEY'RE ARTISTS? NO WONDER THEY SEEM SO SOPHISTICATED...
SHE'S SO TALL AND CUTE.
IT'D BE GREAT TO USE HER AS A MODEL FOR ONE OF THE STORIES.
YOU'RE NOT GONNA GET A GOOD STORY USING A BORING GIRL LIKE THIS.

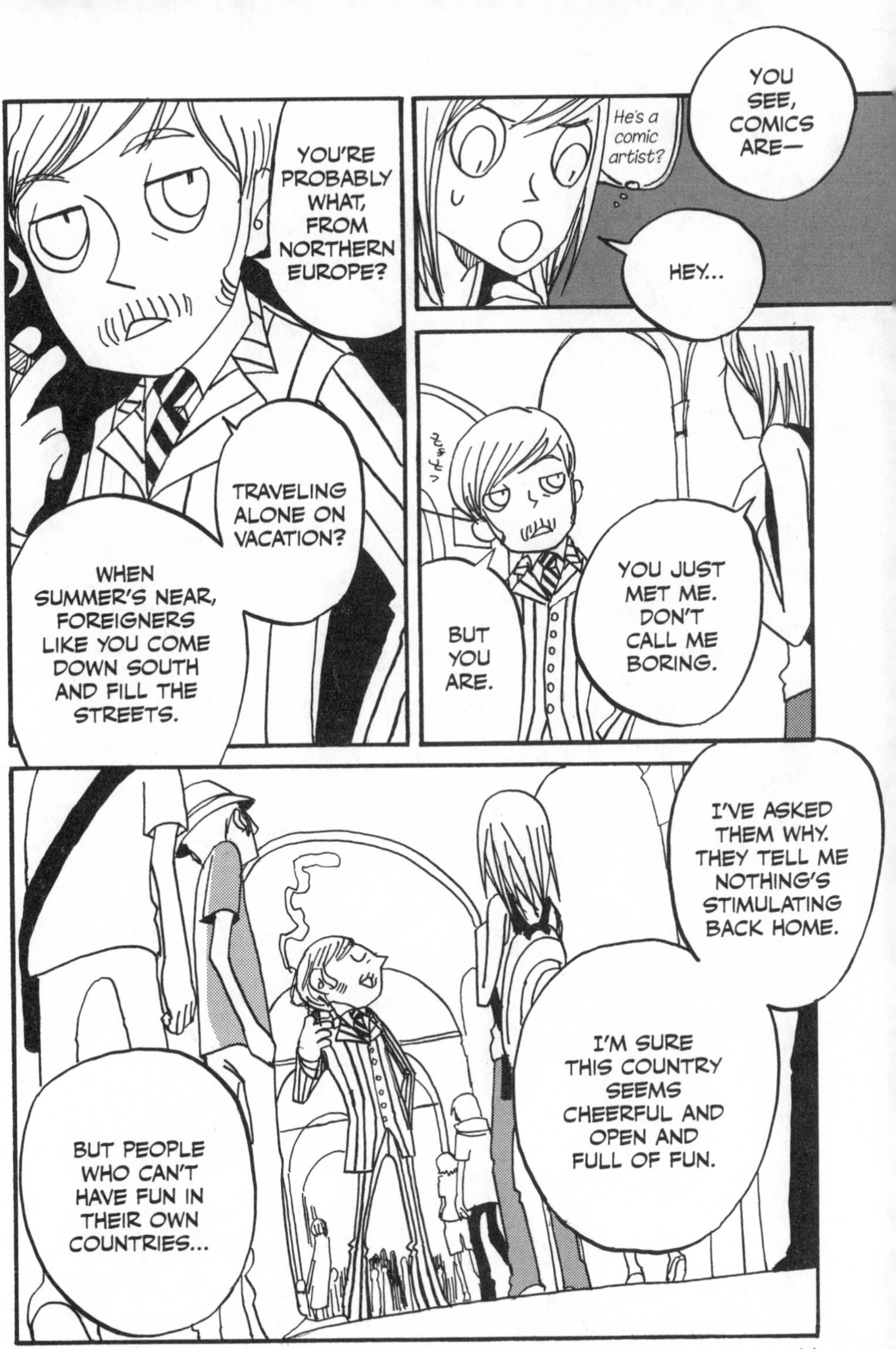
YOU SEE, COMICS ARE—
He's a comic artist?
HEY...
YOU JUST MET ME. DON'T CALL ME BORING.
BUT YOU ARE.
YOU'RE PROBABLY WHAT, FROM NORTHERN EUROPE?
TRAVELING ALONE ON VACATION?
WHEN SUMMER'S NEAR, FOREIGNERS LIKE YOU COME DOWN SOUTH AND FILL THE STREETS.
I'VE ASKED THEM WHY. THEY TELL ME NOTHING'S STIMULATING BACK HOME.
I'M SURE THIS COUNTRY SEEMS CHEERFUL AND OPEN AND FULL OF FUN.
BUT PEOPLE WHO CAN'T HAVE FUN IN THEIR OWN COUNTRIES...

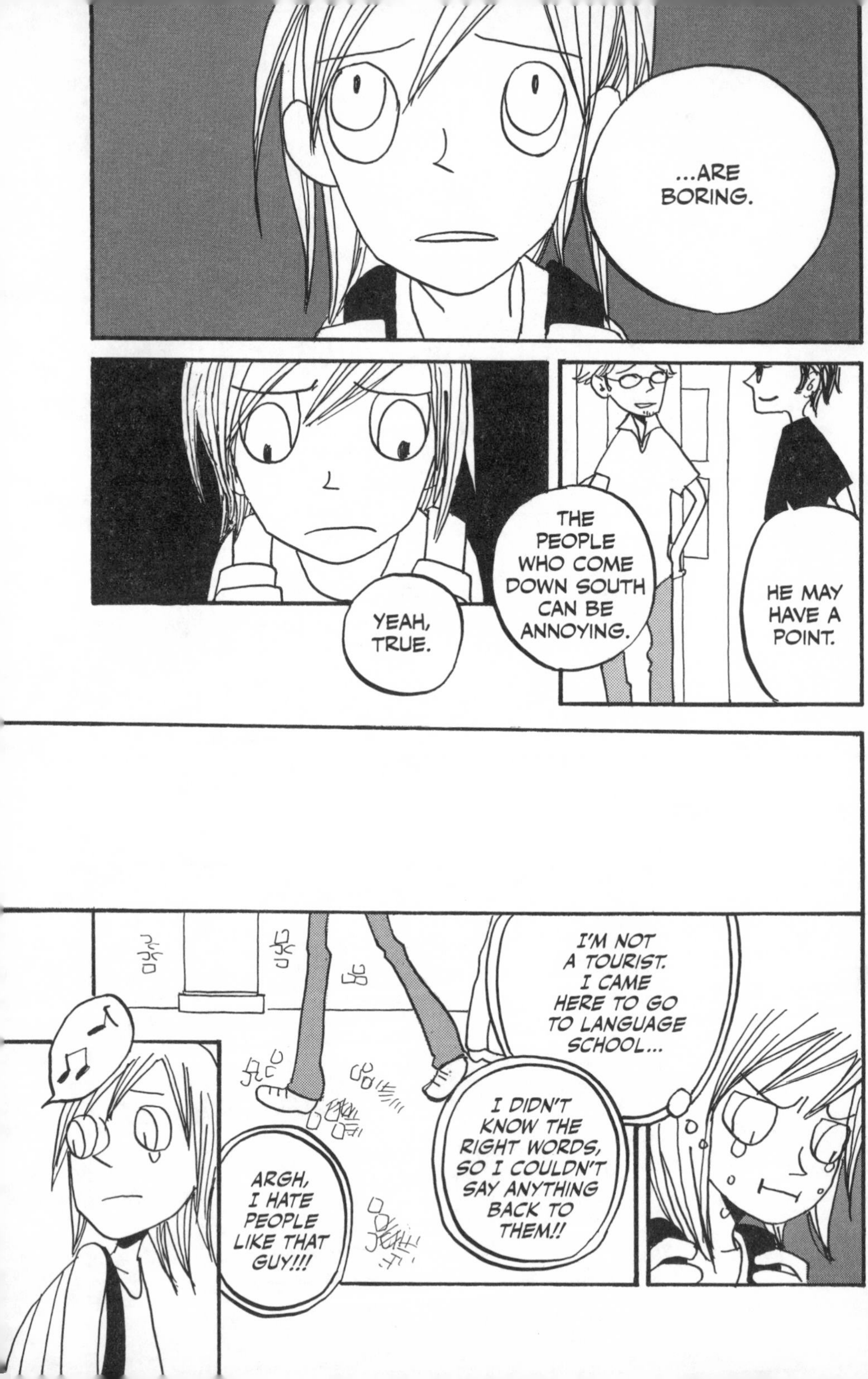
...ARE BORING.
HE MAY HAVE A POINT.
THE PEOPLE WHO COME DOWN SOUTH CAN BE ANNOYING.
YEAH, TRUE.
I'M NOT A TOURIST. I CAME HERE TO GO TO LANGUAGE SCHOOL...
I DIDN'T KNOW THE RIGHT WORDS, SO I COULDN'T SAY ANYTHING BACK TO THEM!!
ARGH, I HATE PEOPLE LIKE THAT GUY!!!

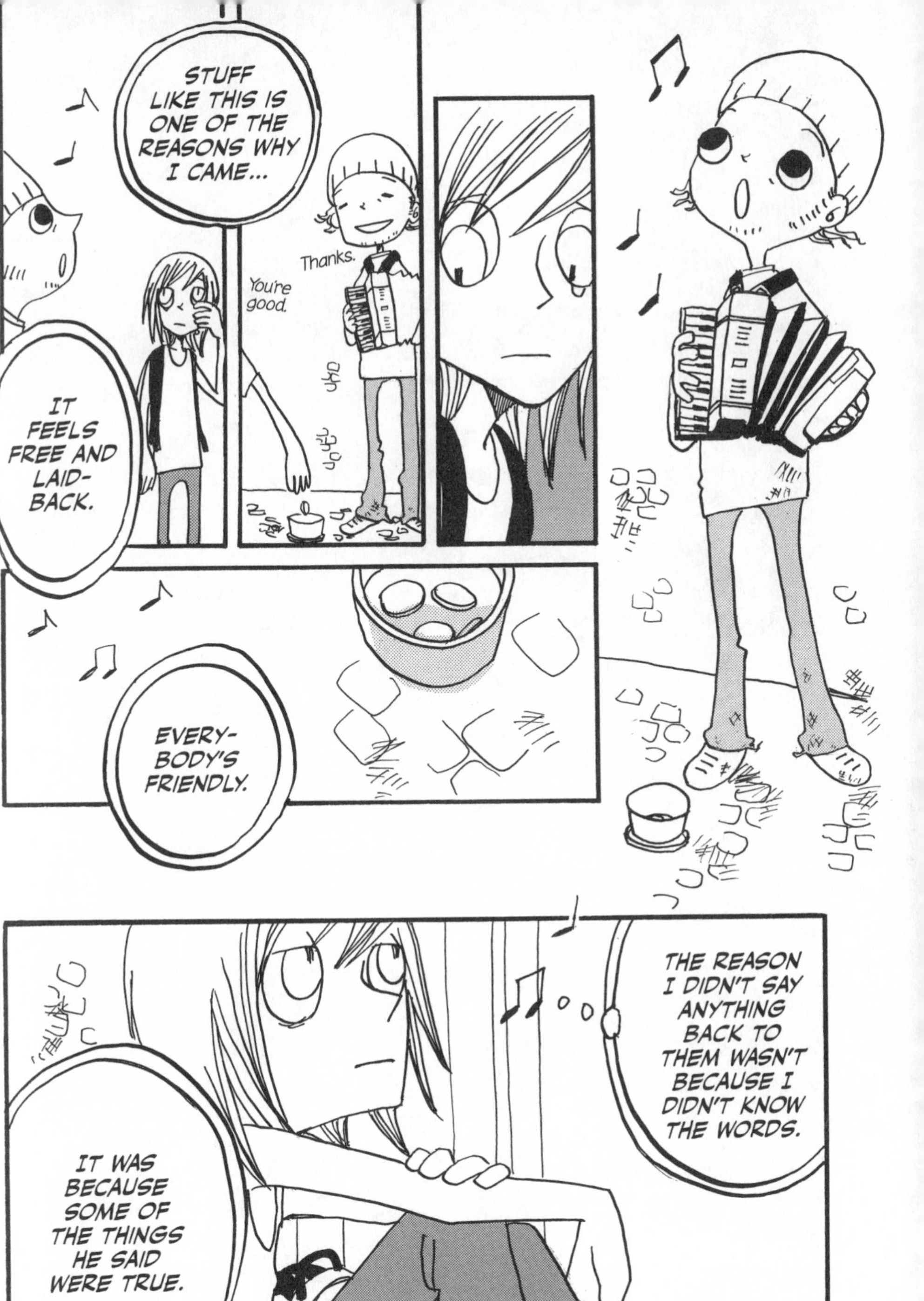

STUFF LIKE THIS IS ONE OF THE REASONS WHY I CAME...
Thanks.
You're good.
IT FEELS FREE AND LAID-BACK.
EVERY-BODY'S FRIENDLY.
THE REASON I DIDN'T SAY ANYTHING BACK TO THEM WASN'T BECAUSE I DIDN'T KNOW THE WORDS.
IT WAS BECAUSE SOME OF THE THINGS HE SAID WERE TRUE.

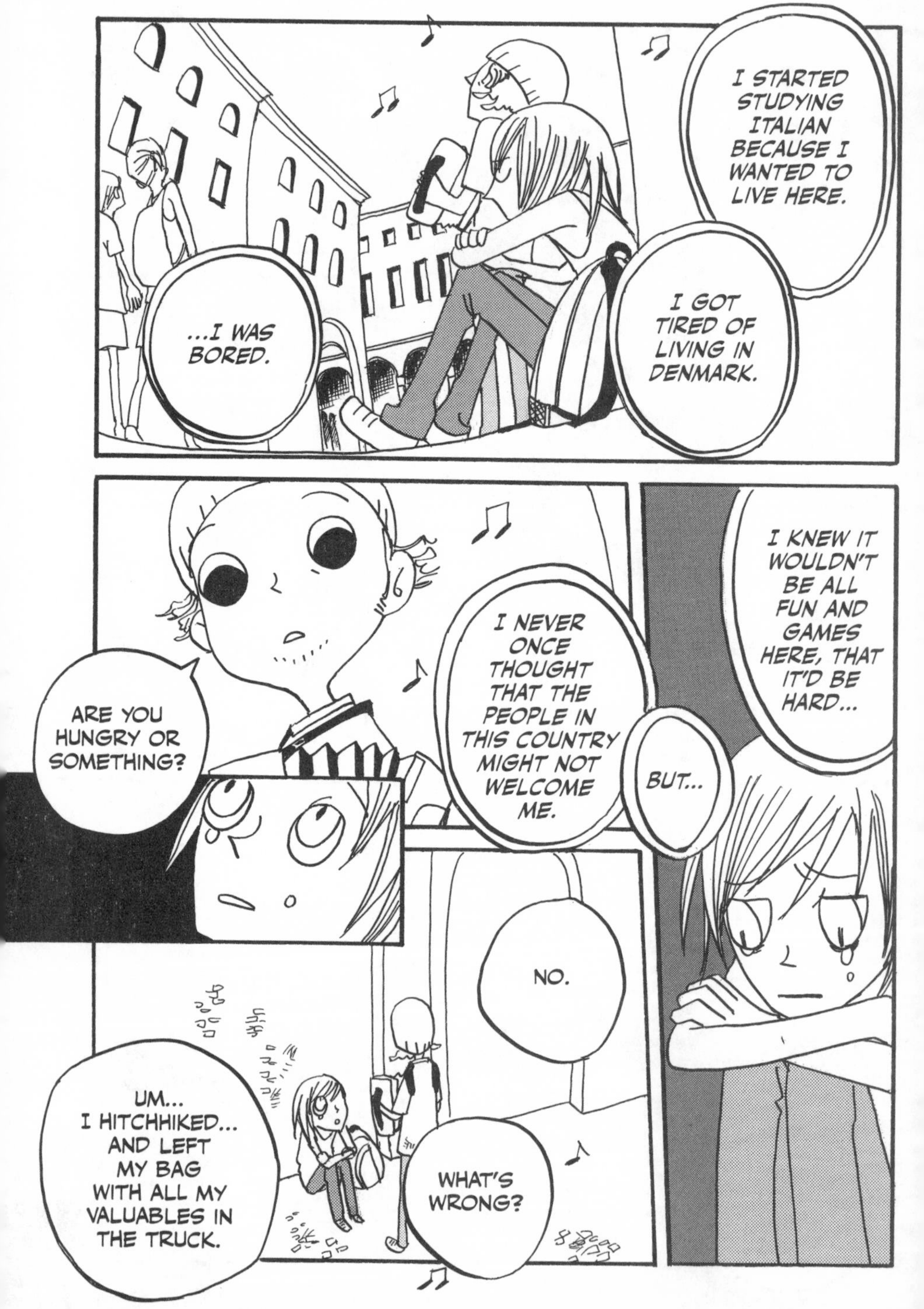
I STARTED STUDYING ITALIAN BECAUSE I WANTED TO LIVE HERE.
I GOT TIRED OF LIVING IN DENMARK.
...I WAS BORED.
I KNEW IT WOULDN'T BE ALL FUN AND GAMES HERE, THAT IT'D BE HARD...
BUT...
I NEVER ONCE THOUGHT THAT THE PEOPLE IN THIS COUNTRY MIGHT NOT WELCOME ME.
ARE YOU HUNGRY OR SOMETHING?
NO.
WHAT'S WRONG?
UM... I HITCHHIKED... AND LEFT MY BAG WITH ALL MY VALUABLES IN THE TRUCK.

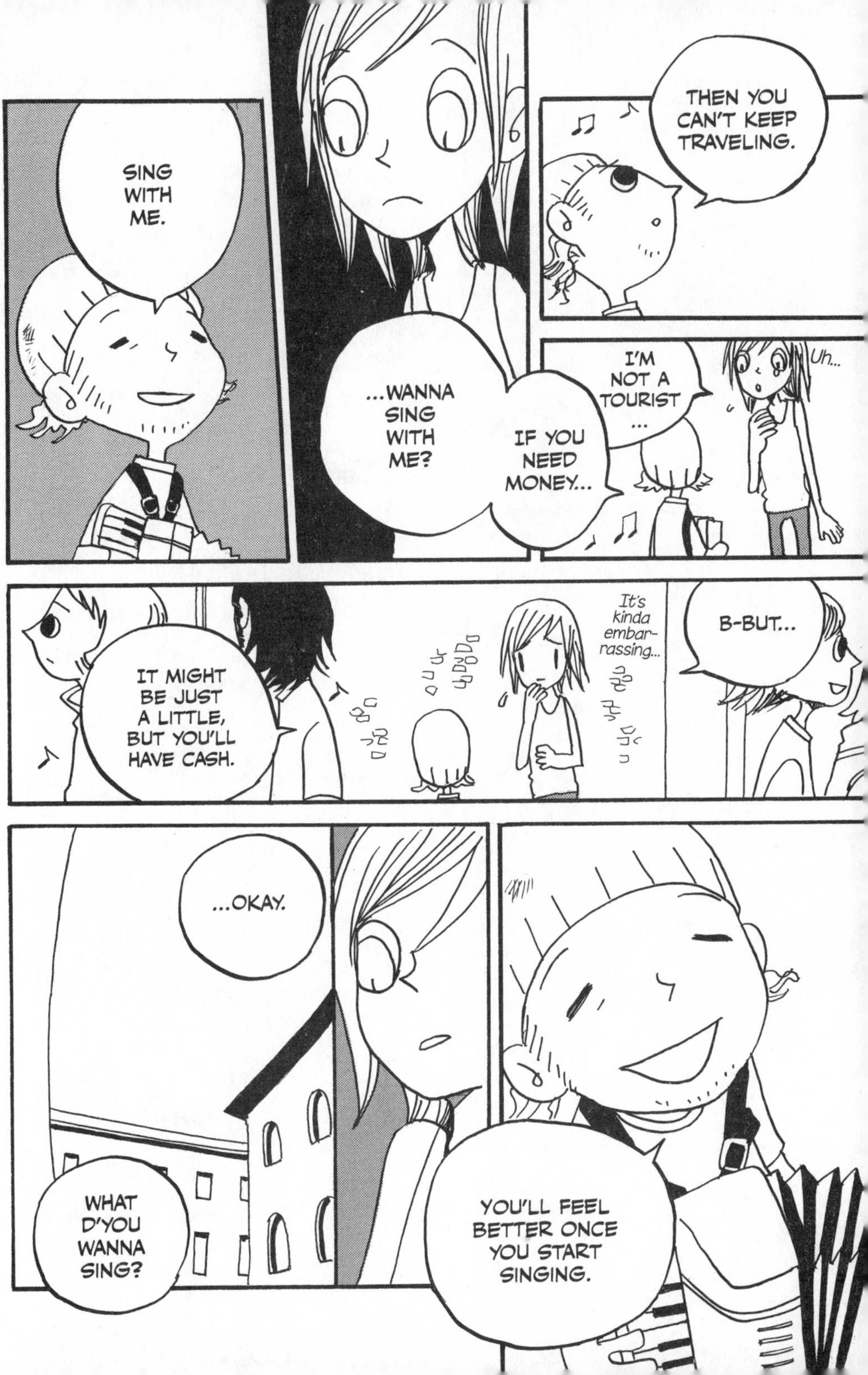
THEN YOU CAN'T KEEP TRAVELING.
Uh...
I'M NOT A TOURIST ...
IF YOU NEED MONEY...
...WANNA SING WITH ME?
SING WITH ME.
B-BUT...
It's kinda embarrassing...
IT MIGHT BE JUST A LITTLE, BUT YOU'LL HAVE CASH.
YOU'LL FEEL BETTER ONCE YOU START SINGING.
...OKAY.
WHAT D'YOU WANNA SING?

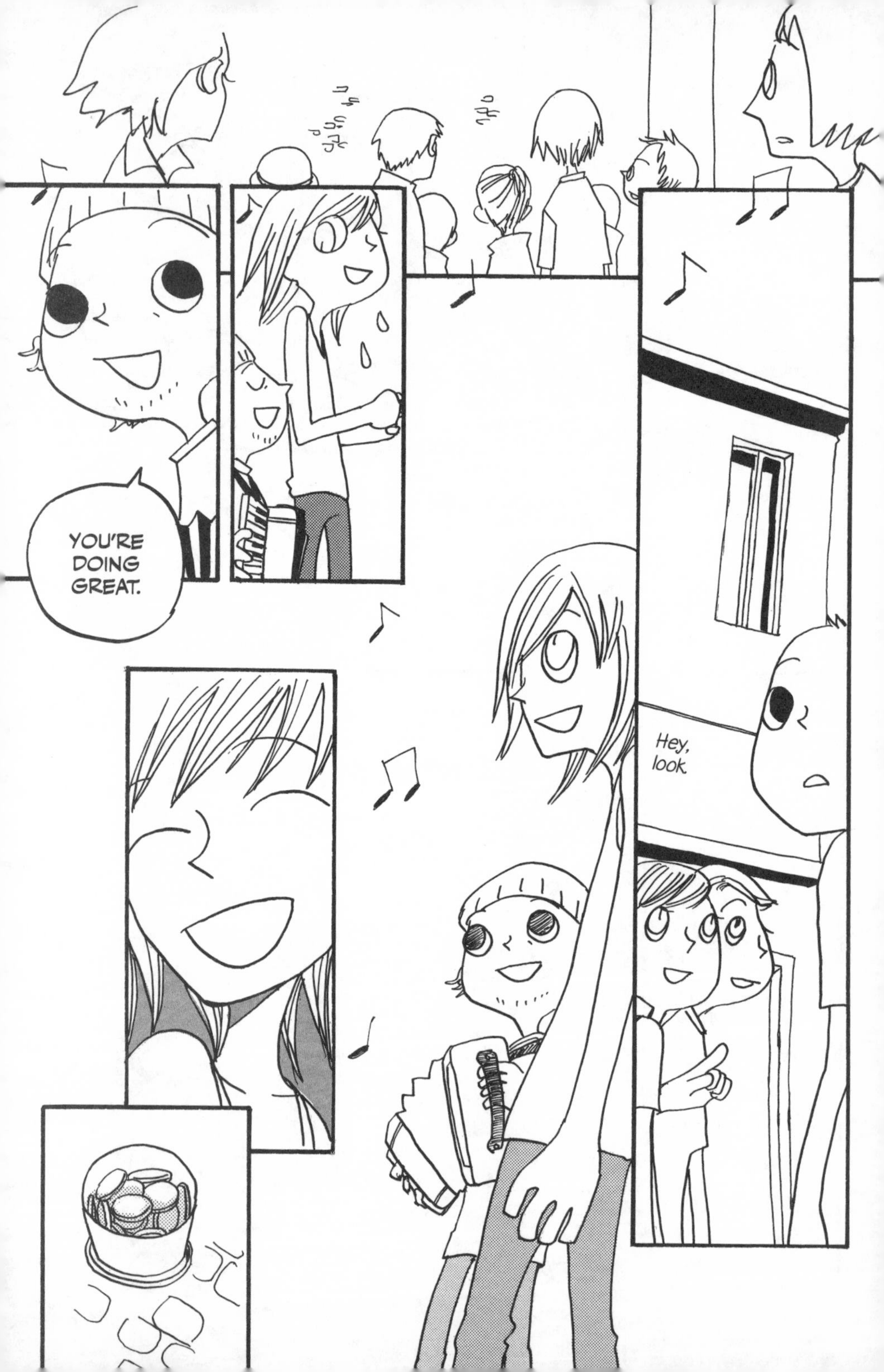
Hey, look.
YOU'RE DOING GREAT.

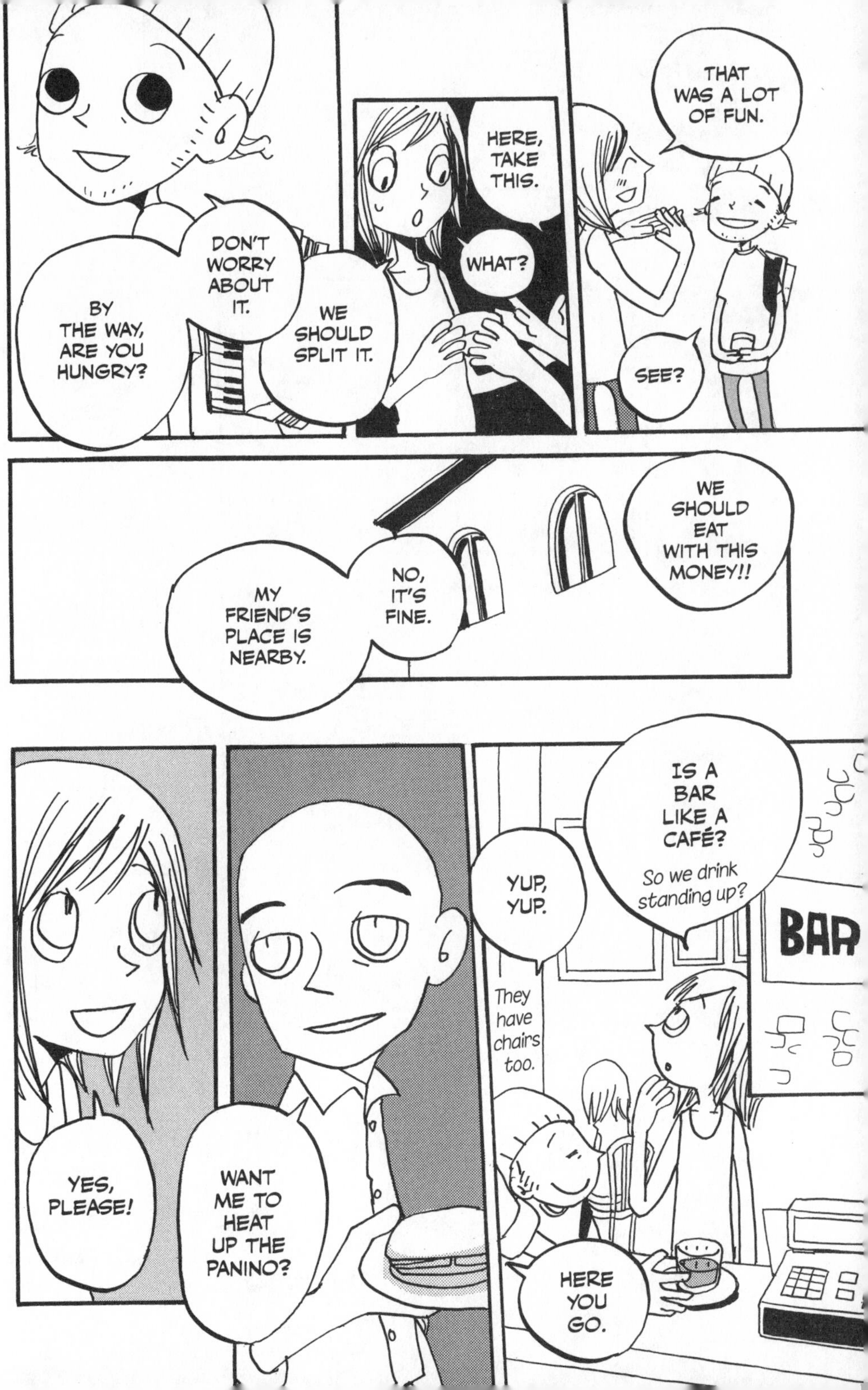
THAT WAS A LOT OF FUN.
SEE?
HERE, TAKE THIS.
WHAT?
WE SHOULD SPLIT IT.
DON'T WORRY ABOUT IT.
BY THE WAY, ARE YOU HUNGRY?
WE SHOULD EAT WITH THIS MONEY!!
NO, IT'S FINE.
MY FRIEND'S PLACE IS NEARBY.
IS A BAR LIKE A CAFÉ? So we drink standing up?
YUP, YUP.
They have chairs too.
BAR
HERE YOU GO.
WANT ME TO HEAT UP THE PANINO?
YES, PLEASE!

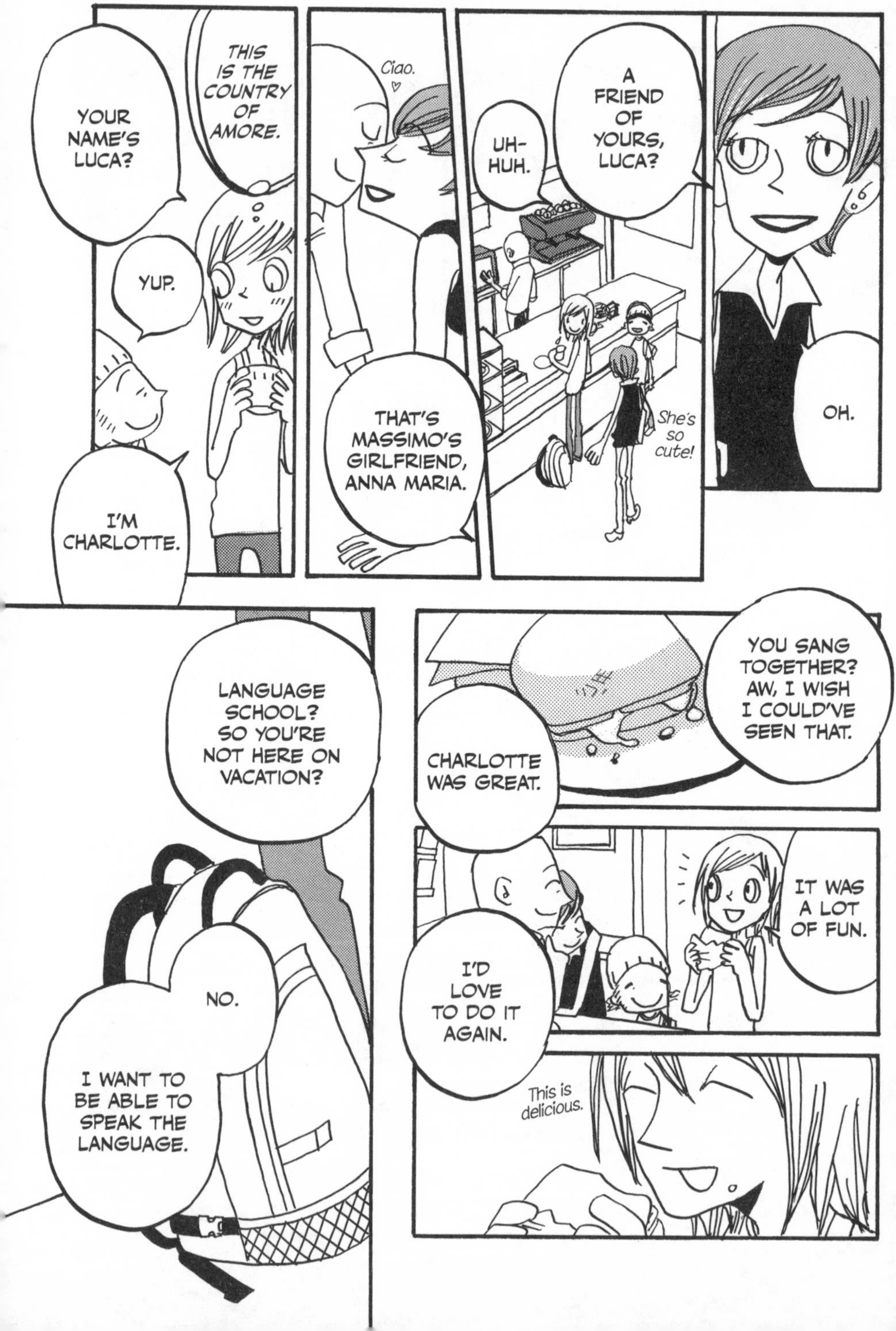
OH.
A FRIEND OF YOURS, LUCA?
UH-HUH.
She's so cute!
Ciao.
THAT'S MASSIMO'S GIRLFRIEND, ANNA MARIA.
THIS IS THE COUNTRY OF AMORE.
YOUR NAME'S LUCA?
YUP.
I'M CHARLOTTE.
YOU SANG TOGETHER? AW, I WISH I COULD'VE SEEN THAT.
CHARLOTTE WAS GREAT.
IT WAS A LOT OF FUN.
I'D LOVE TO DO IT AGAIN.
This is delicious.
LANGUAGE SCHOOL? SO YOU'RE NOT HERE ON VACATION?
NO.
I WANT TO BE ABLE TO SPEAK THE LANGUAGE.

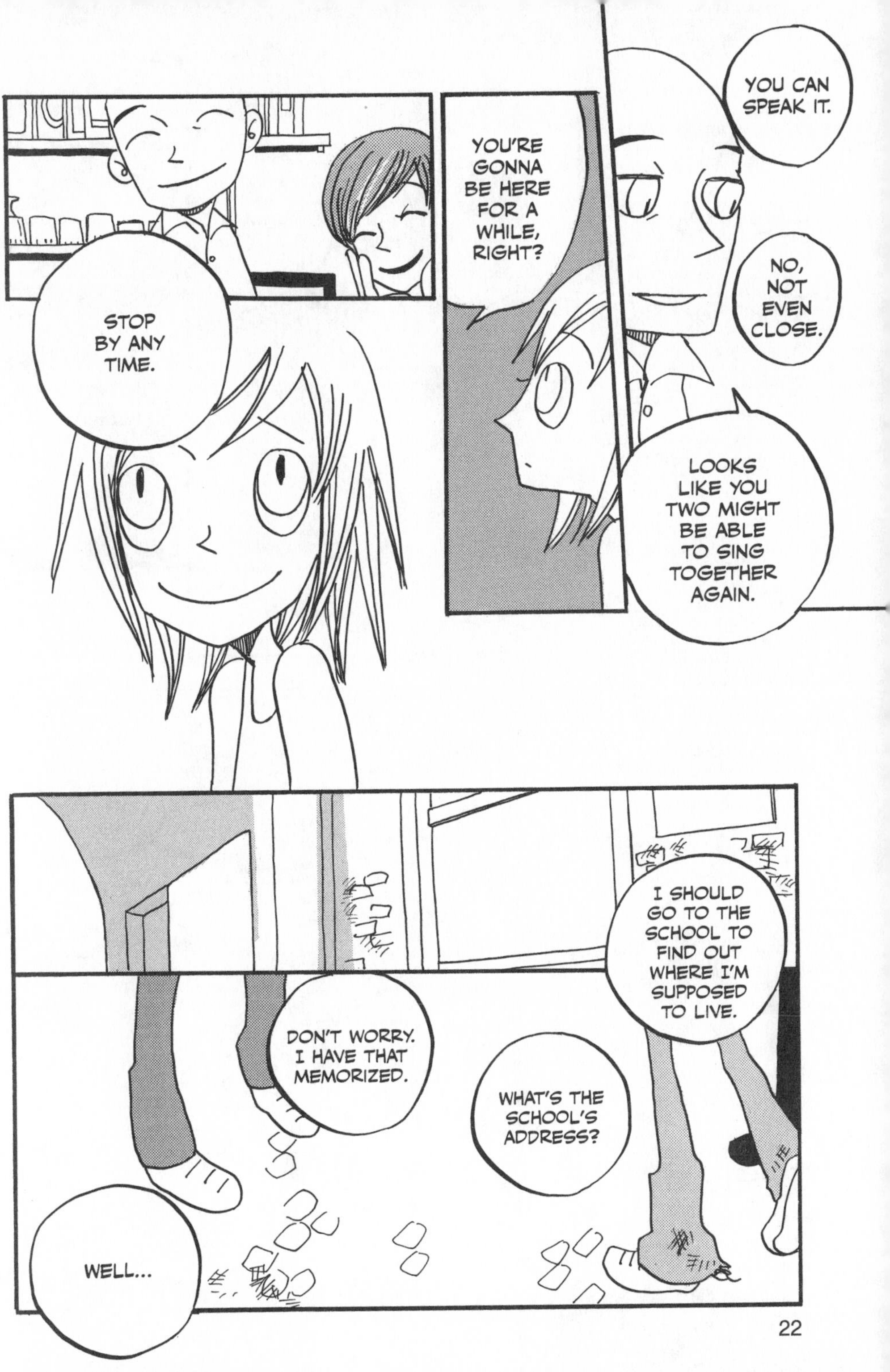
YOU CAN SPEAK IT.
NO, NOT EVEN CLOSE.
LOOKS LIKE YOU TWO MIGHT BE ABLE TO SING TOGETHER AGAIN.
YOU'RE GONNA BE HERE FOR A WHILE, RIGHT?
STOP BY ANY TIME.
I SHOULD GO TO THE SCHOOL TO FIND OUT WHERE I'M SUPPOSED TO LIVE.
WHAT'S THE SCHOOL'S ADDRESS?
DON'T WORRY. I HAVE THAT MEMORIZED.
WELL...

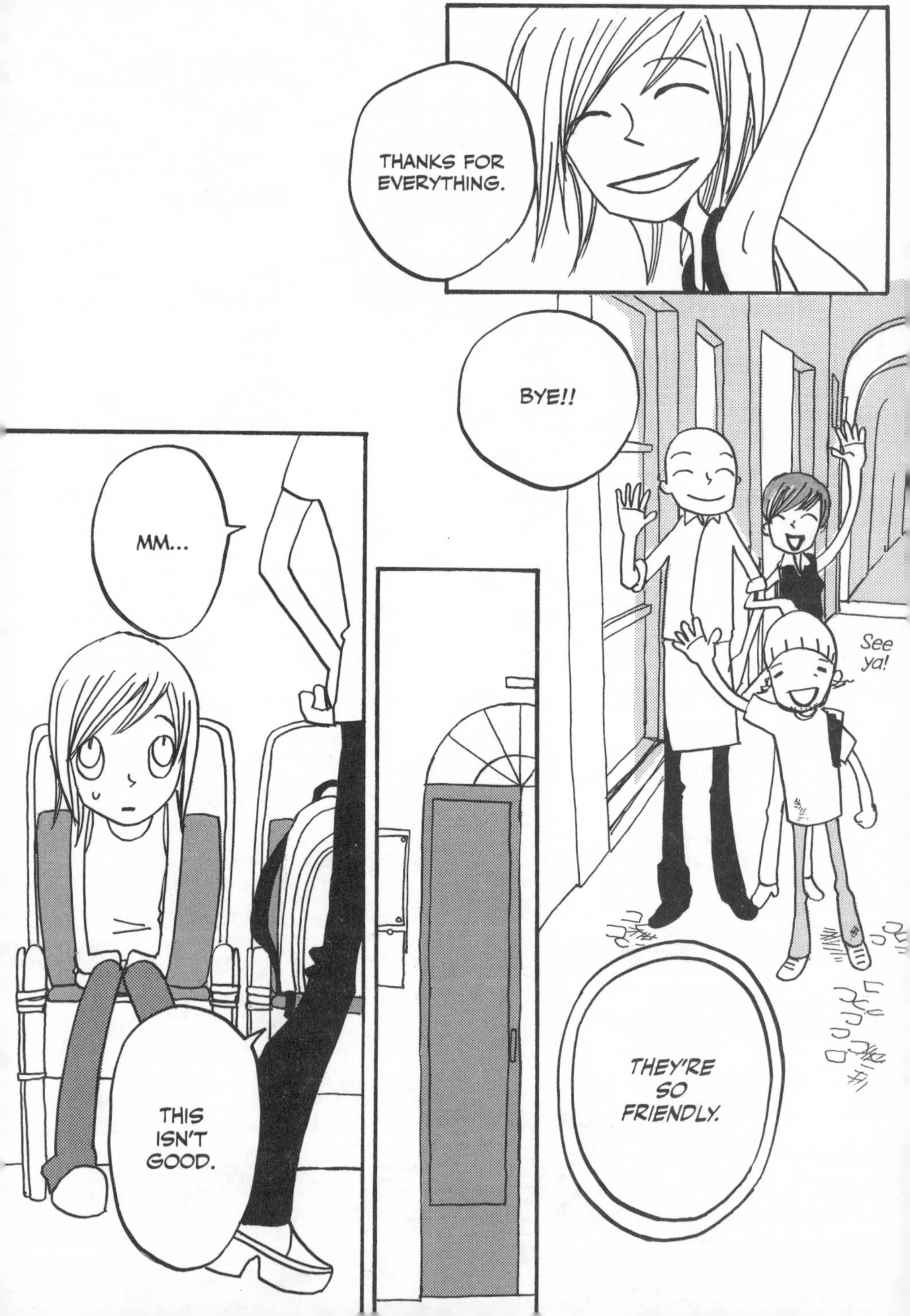
THANKS FOR EVERYTHING.
BYE!!
See ya!
THEY'RE SO FRIENDLY.
MM...
THIS ISN'T GOOD.

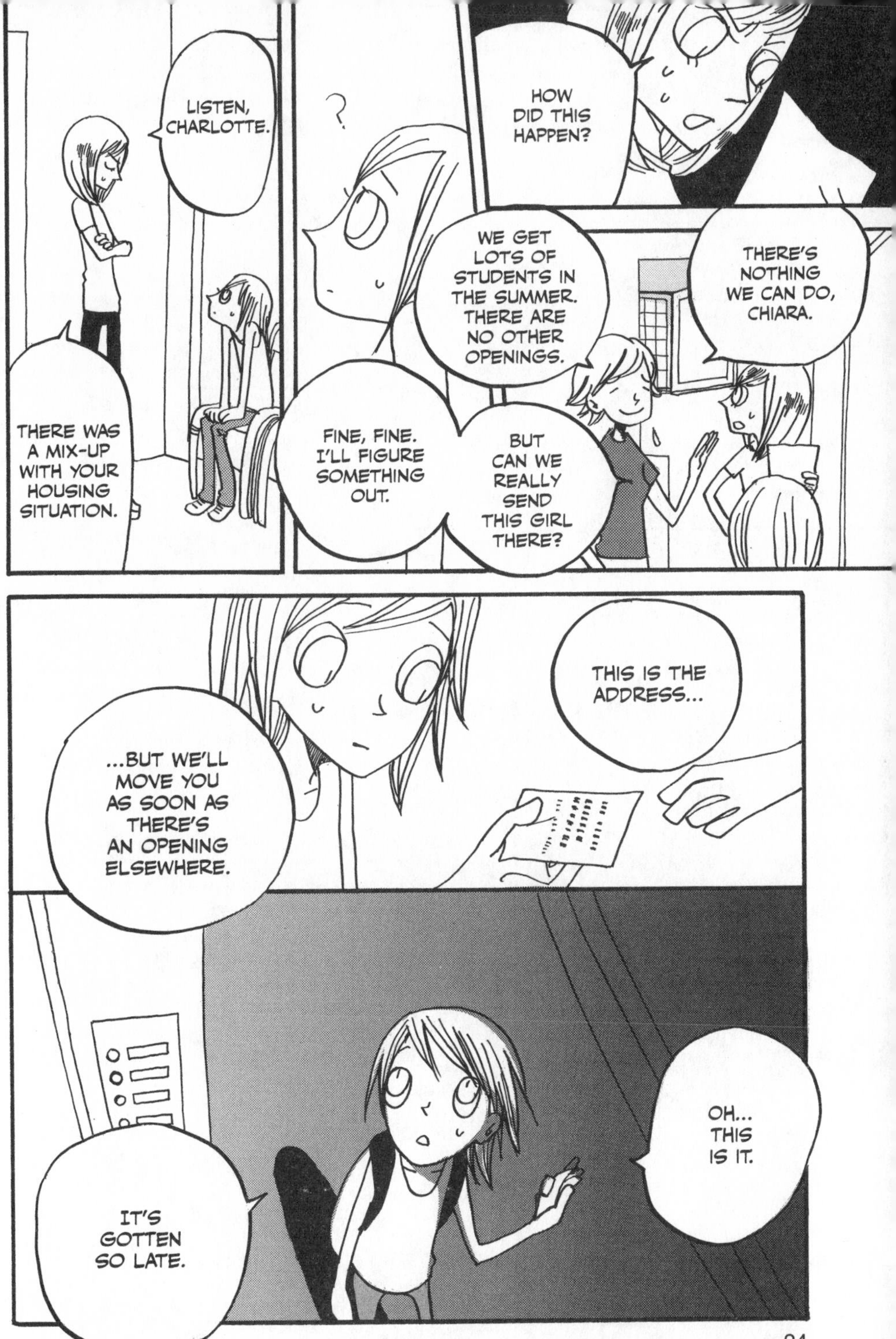
HOW DID THIS HAPPEN?
THERE'S NOTHING WE CAN DO, CHIARA.
WE GET LOTS OF STUDENTS IN THE SUMMER. THERE ARE NO OTHER OPENINGS.
BUT CAN WE REALLY SEND THIS GIRL THERE?
FINE, FINE. I'LL FIGURE SOMETHING OUT.
?
LISTEN, CHARLOTTE.
THERE WAS A MIX-UP WITH YOUR HOUSING SITUATION.
THIS IS THE ADDRESS...
...BUT WE'LL MOVE YOU AS SOON AS THERE'S AN OPENING ELSEWHERE.
OH... THIS IS IT.
IT'S GOTTEN SO LATE.

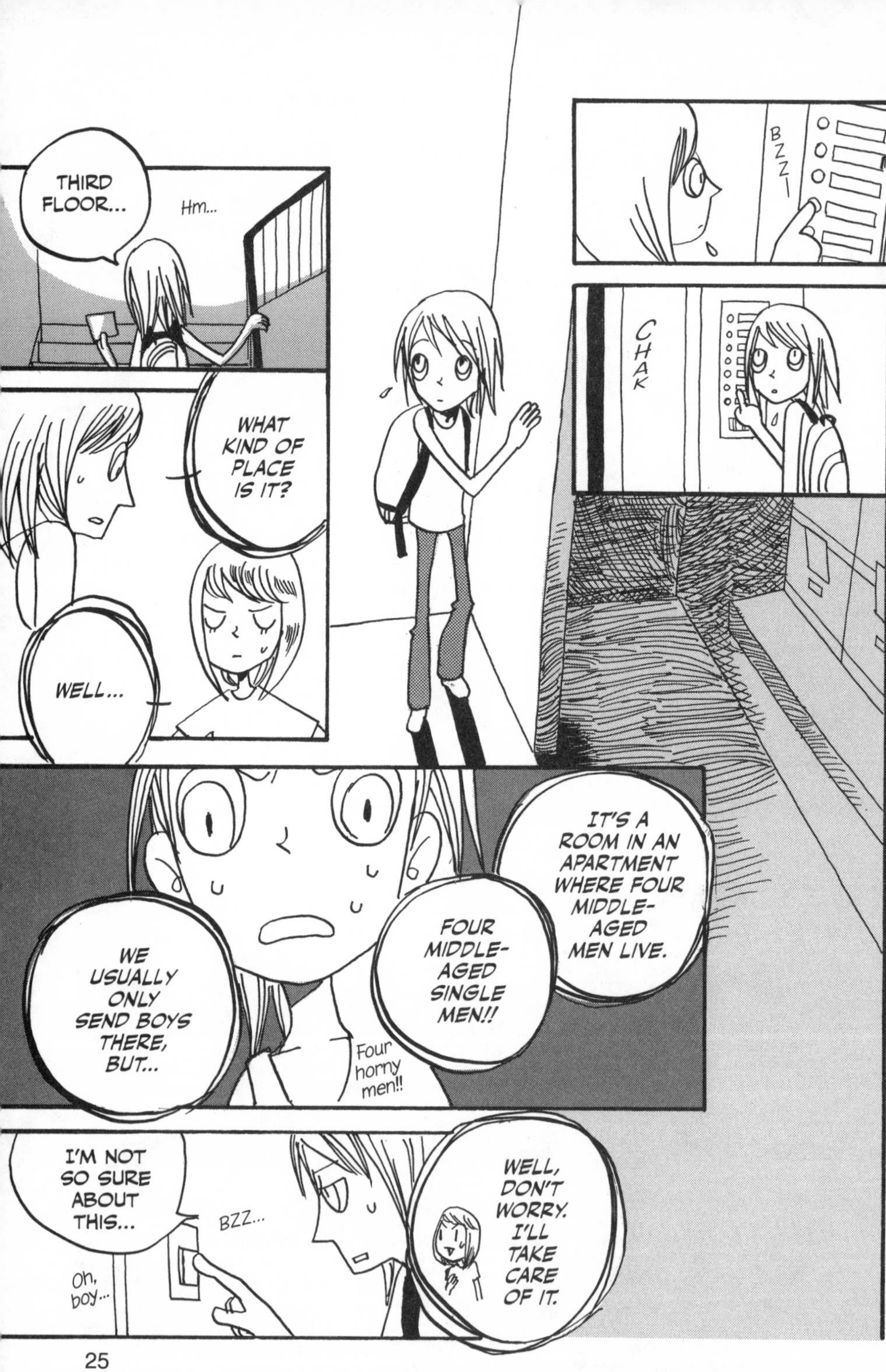
BZZ
CHAK
THIRD FLOOR...
Hm...
WHAT KIND OF PLACE IS IT?
WELL...
IT'S A ROOM IN AN APARTMENT WHERE FOUR MIDDLE-AGED MEN LIVE.
FOUR MIDDLE-AGED SINGLE MEN!!
Four horny men!!
WE USUALLY ONLY SEND BOYS THERE, BUT...
WELL, DON'T WORRY. I'LL TAKE CARE OF IT.
BZZ...
I'M NOT SO SURE ABOUT THIS...
Oh, boy...

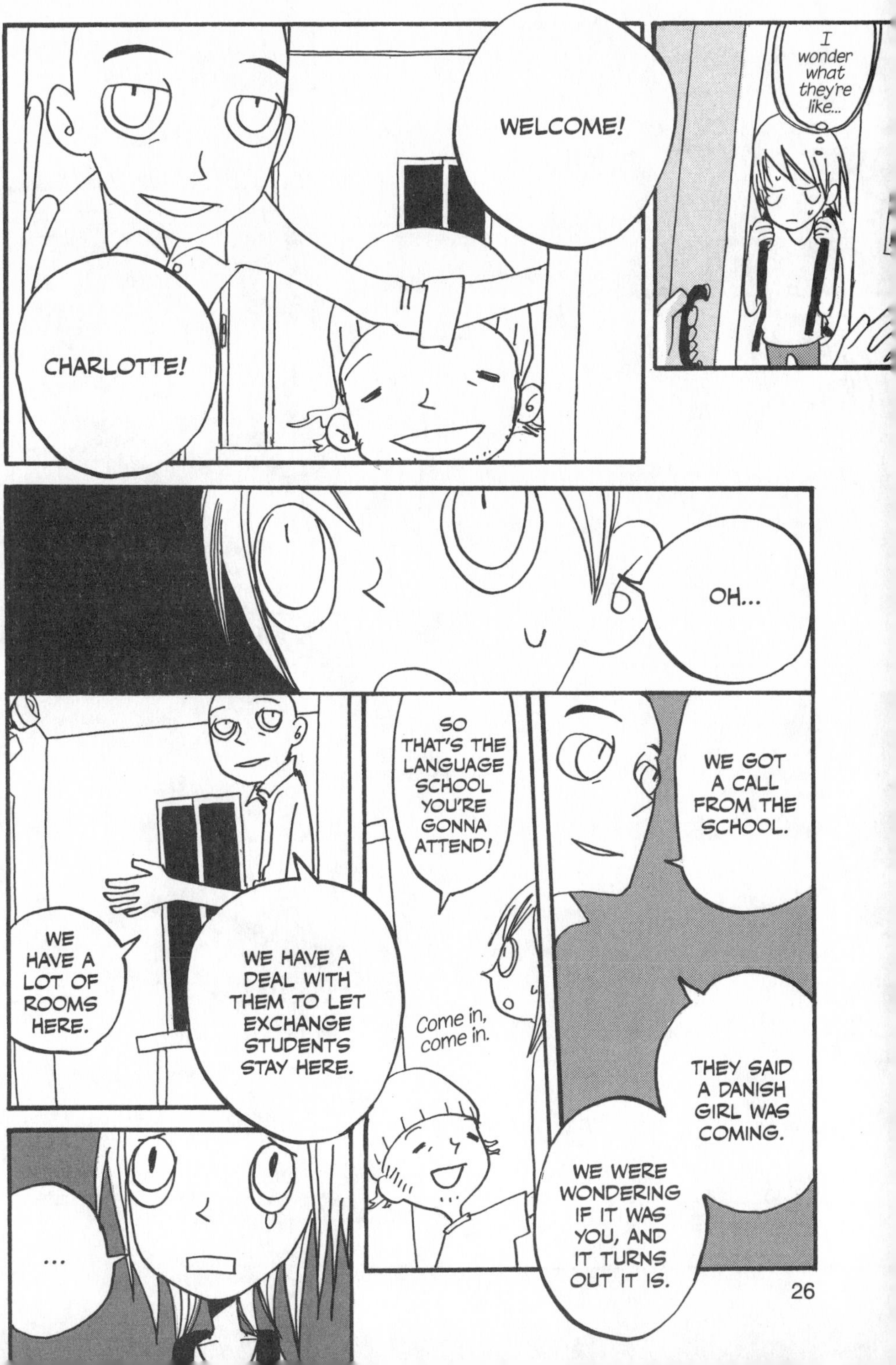
I wonder what they're like...
WELCOME!
CHARLOTTE!
OH...
WE GOT A CALL FROM THE SCHOOL.
THEY SAID A DANISH GIRL WAS COMING.
WE WERE WONDERING IF IT WAS YOU, AND IT TURNS OUT IT IS.
SO THAT'S THE LANGUAGE SCHOOL YOU'RE GONNA ATTEND!
Come in, come in.
WE HAVE A DEAL WITH THEM TO LET EXCHANGE STUDENTS STAY HERE.
WE HAVE A LOT OF ROOMS HERE.
...

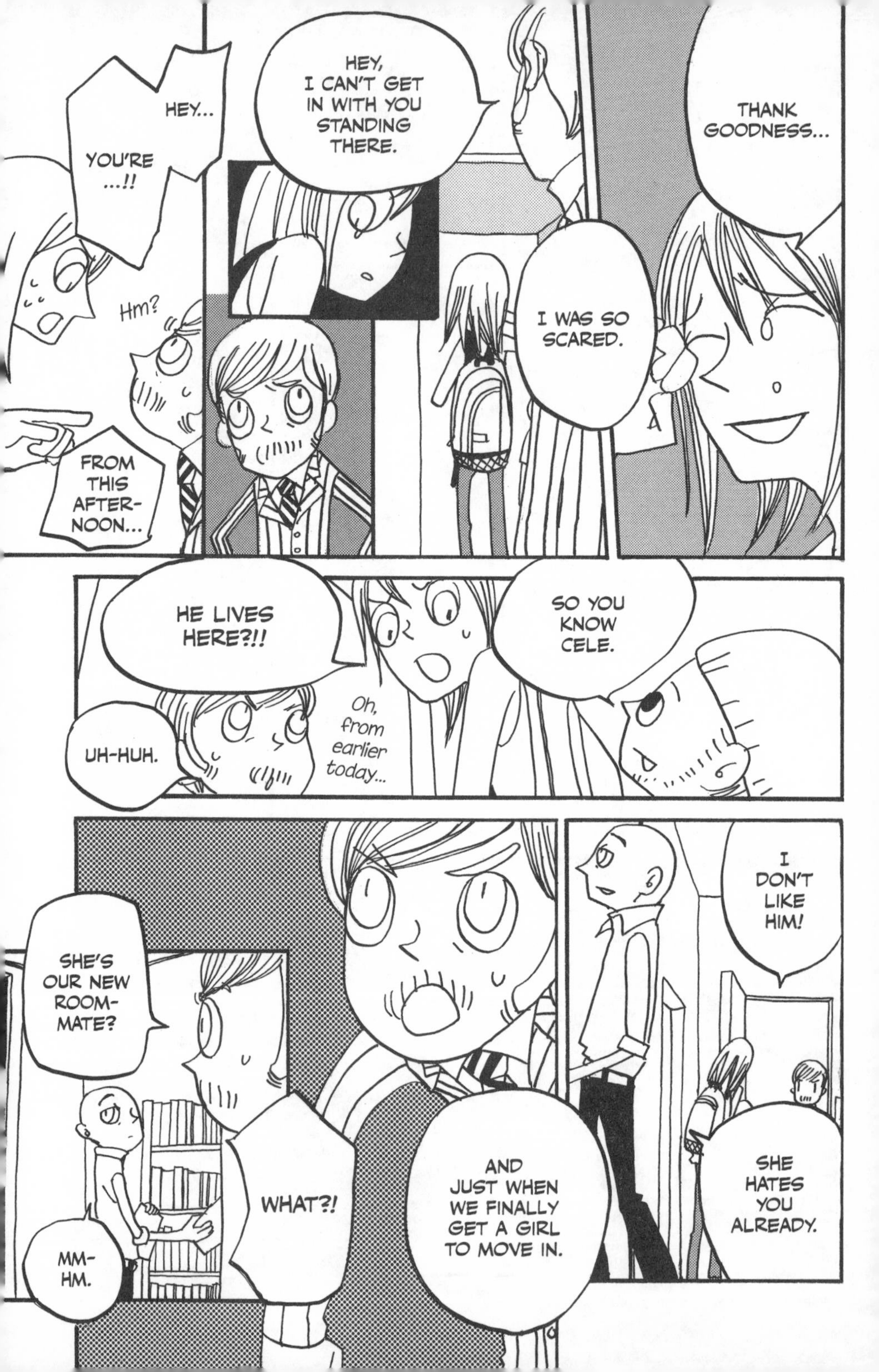
THANK GOODNESS...
I WAS SO SCARED.
HEY, I CAN'T GET IN WITH YOU STANDING THERE.
HEY...
YOU'RE ...!!
Hm?
FROM THIS AFTER-NOON...
SO YOU KNOW CELE.
Oh, from earlier today...
HE LIVES HERE?!!
UH-HUH.
I DON'T LIKE HIM!
SHE HATES YOU ALREADY.
AND JUST WHEN WE FINALLY GET A GIRL TO MOVE IN.
WHAT?!
SHE'S OUR NEW ROOM-MATE?
MM-HM.

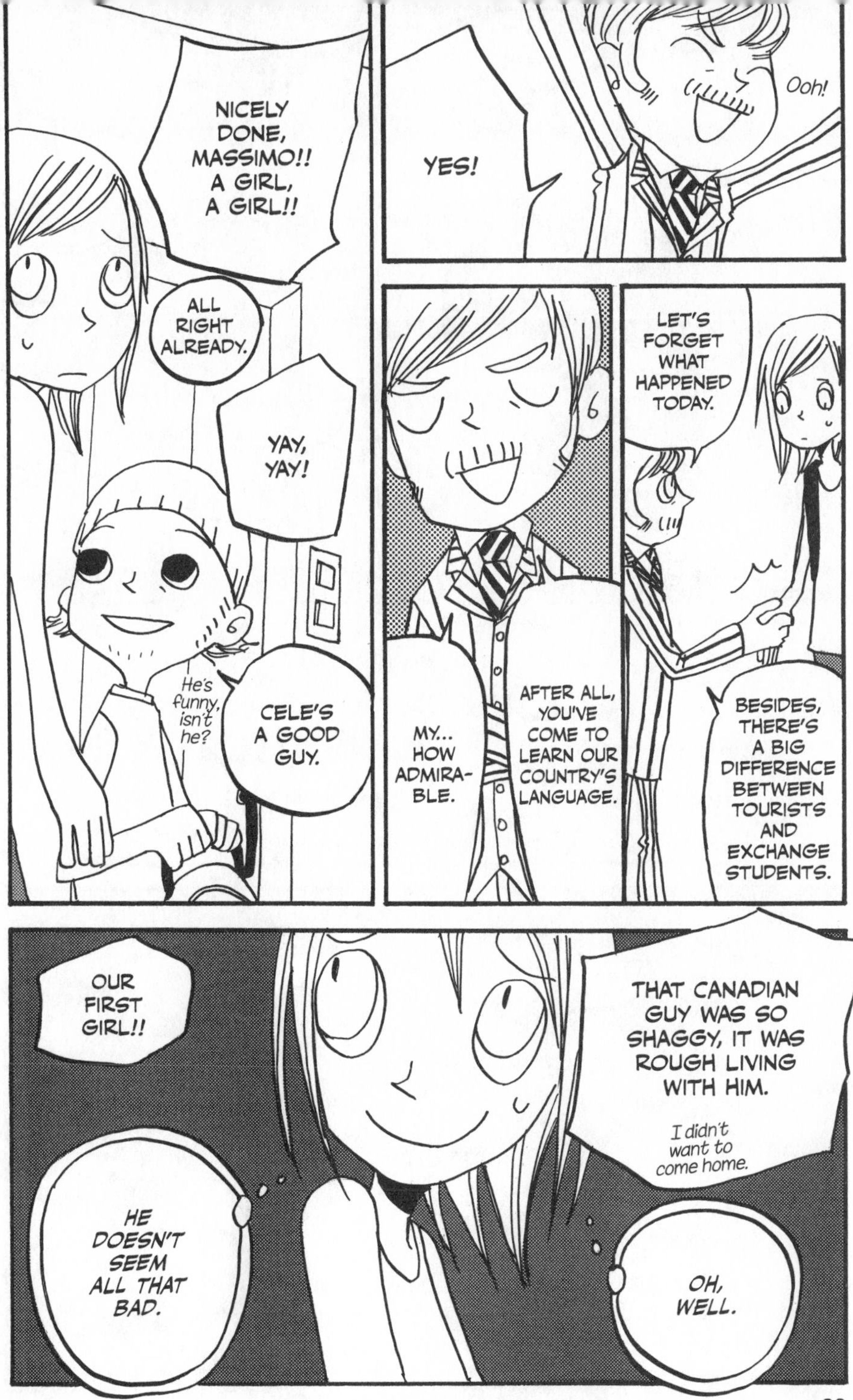
YES!
Ooh!
LET'S FORGET WHAT HAPPENED TODAY.
BESIDES, THERE'S A BIG DIFFERENCE BETWEEN TOURISTS AND EXCHANGE STUDENTS.
AFTER ALL, YOU'VE COME TO LEARN OUR COUNTRY'S LANGUAGE.
MY... HOW ADMIRA-BLE.
NICELY DONE, MASSIMO!! A GIRL, A GIRL!!
ALL RIGHT ALREADY.
YAY, YAY!
CELE'S A GOOD GUY.
He's funny, isn't he?
THAT CANADIAN GUY WAS SO SHAGGY, IT WAS ROUGH LIVING WITH HIM.
I didn't want to come home.
OUR FIRST GIRL!!
OH, WELL.
HE DOESN'T SEEM ALL THAT BAD.

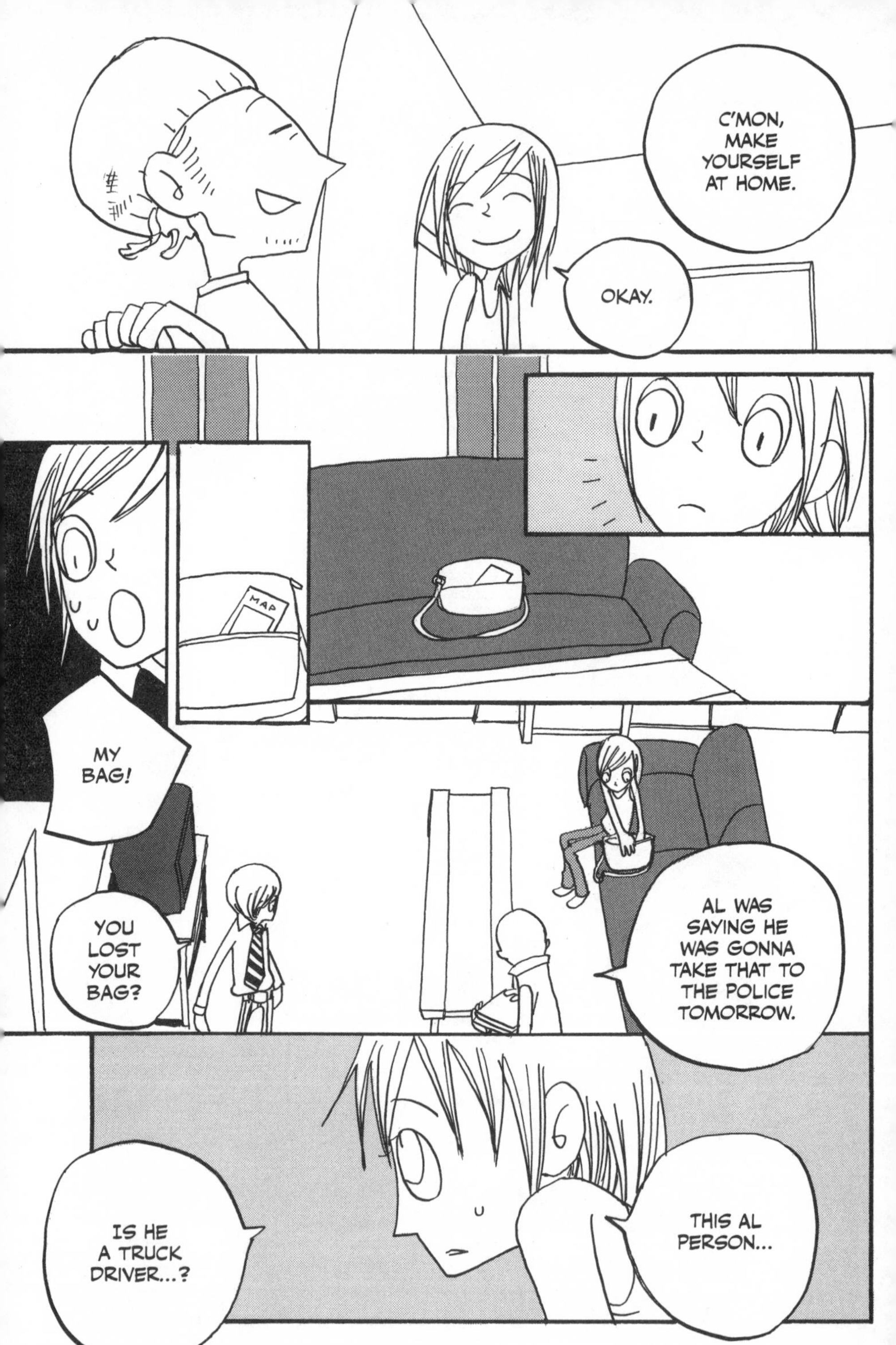
C'MON, MAKE YOURSELF AT HOME.
OKAY.
MY BAG!
MAP
AL WAS SAYING HE WAS GONNA TAKE THAT TO THE POLICE TOMORROW.
YOU LOST YOUR BAG?
THIS AL PERSON...
IS HE A TRUCK DRIVER...?

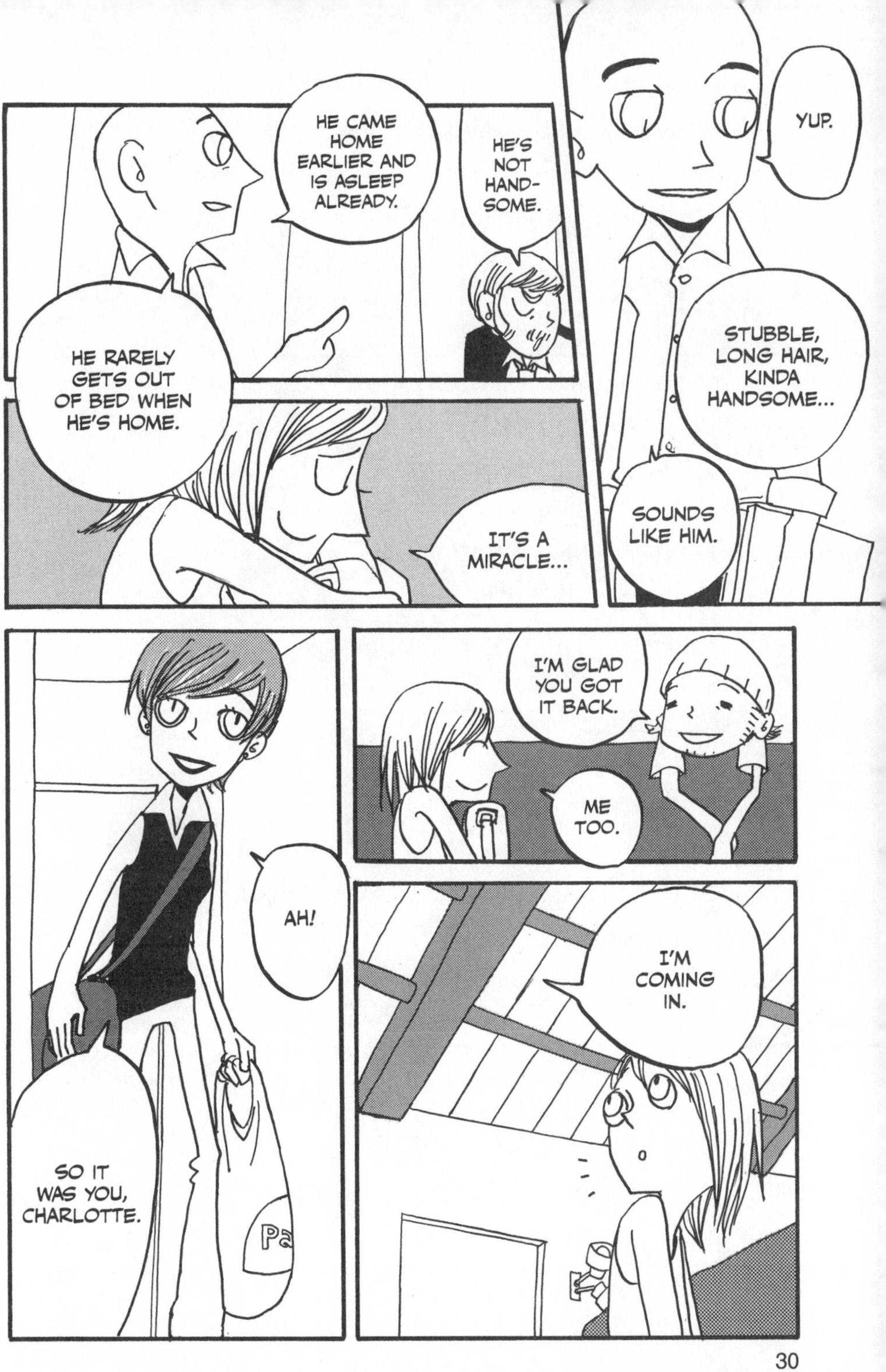
YUP.
STUBBLE, LONG HAIR, KINDA HANDSOME...
SOUNDS LIKE HIM.
HE CAME HOME EARLIER AND IS ASLEEP ALREADY.
HE'S NOT HAND-SOME.
HE RARELY GETS OUT OF BED WHEN HE'S HOME.
IT'S A MIRACLE...
I'M GLAD YOU GOT IT BACK.
ME TOO.
I'M COMING IN.
AH!
SO IT WAS YOU, CHARLOTTE.

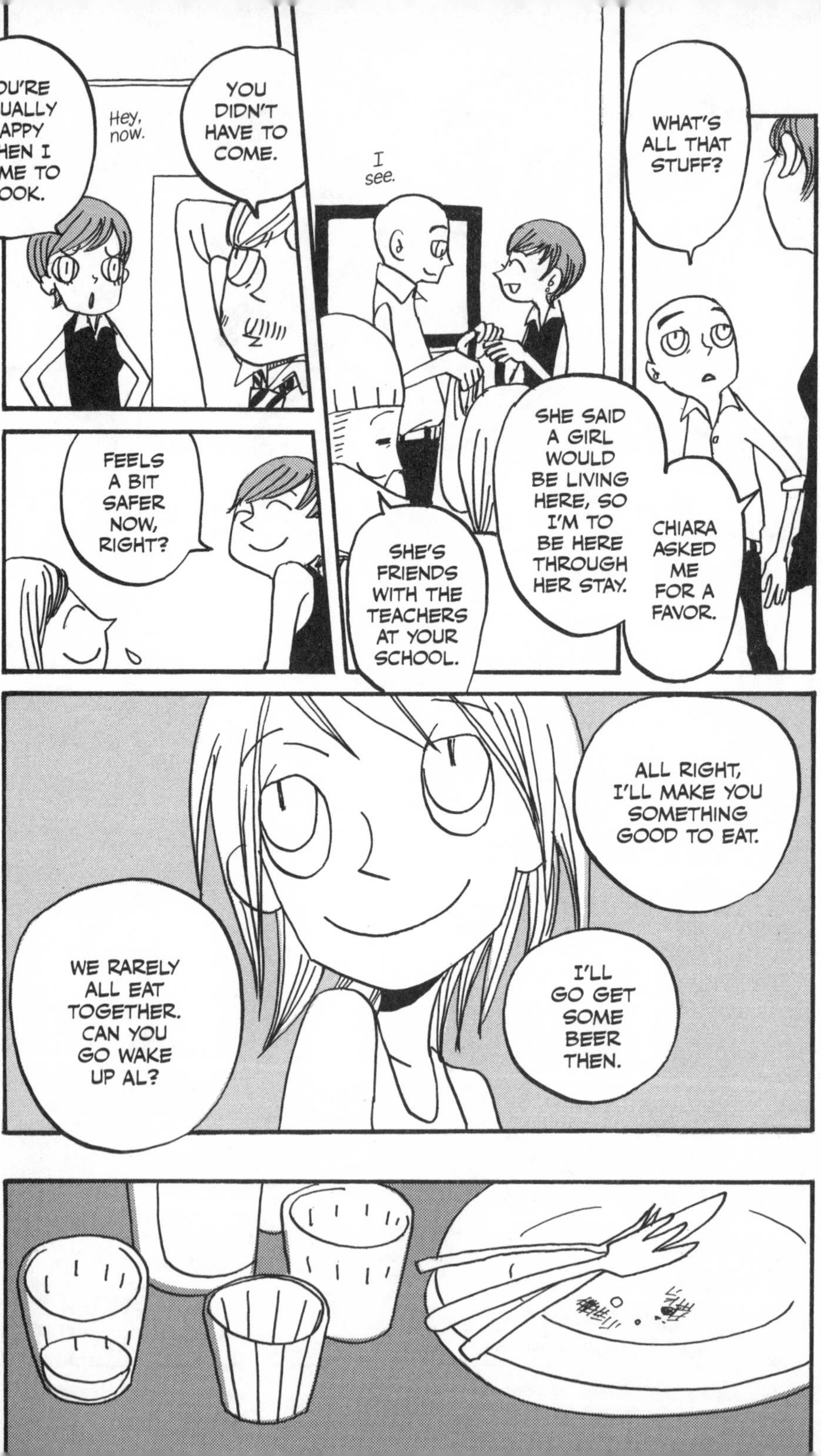
WHAT'S ALL THAT STUFF?
CHIARA ASKED ME FOR A FAVOR.
SHE SAID A GIRL WOULD BE LIVING HERE, SO I'M TO BE HERE THROUGH HER STAY.
SHE'S FRIENDS WITH THE TEACHERS AT YOUR SCHOOL.
I see.
YOU DIDN'T HAVE TO COME.
Hey, now.
YOU'RE USUALLY HAPPY WHEN I COME TO COOK.
FEELS A BIT SAFER NOW, RIGHT?
ALL RIGHT, I'LL MAKE YOU SOMETHING GOOD TO EAT.
I'LL GO GET SOME BEER THEN.
WE RARELY ALL EAT TOGETHER. CAN YOU GO WAKE UP AL?

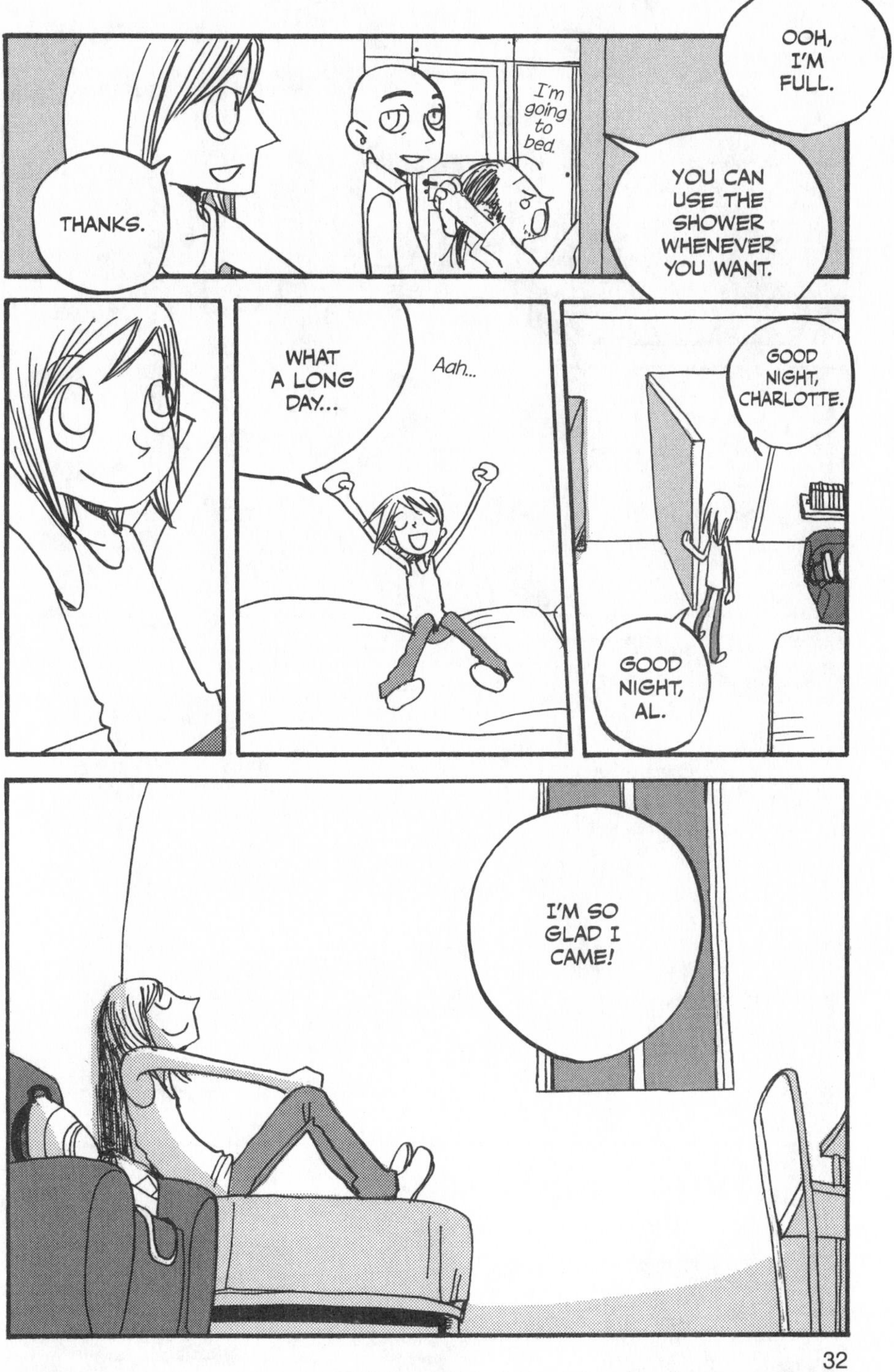
OOH, I'M FULL.
YOU CAN USE THE SHOWER WHENEVER YOU WANT.
I'm going to bed.
THANKS.
GOOD NIGHT, CHARLOTTE.
GOOD NIGHT, AL.
Aah...
WHAT A LONG DAY...
I'M SO GLAD I CAME!

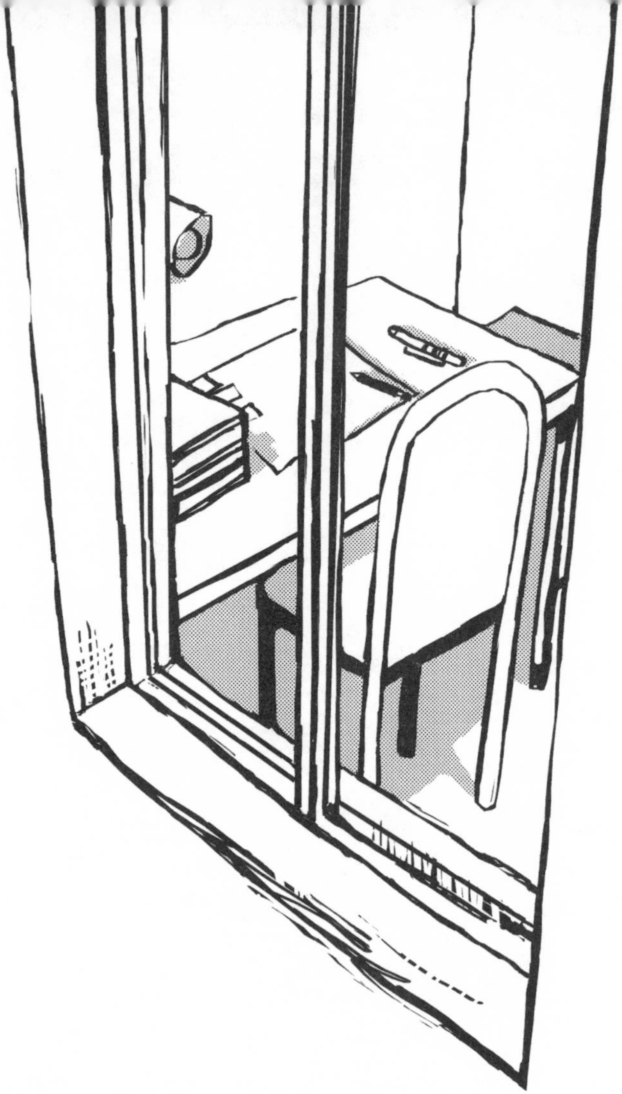

La Quinta Camera
Capitolo 1

LA QUINTA CAMERA

Capitolo 2

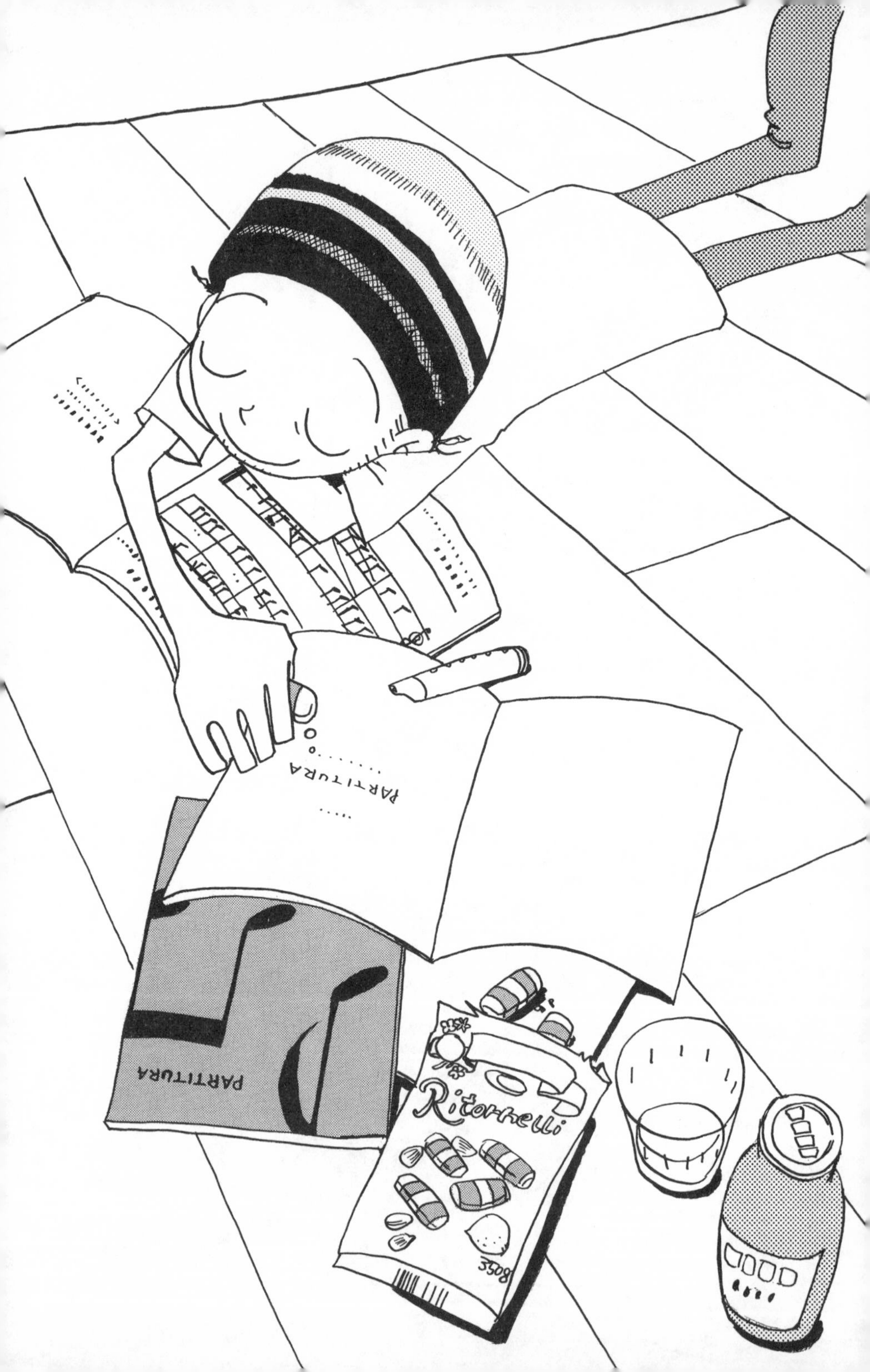
PARTITURA
PARTITURA
Ritornelli
350g

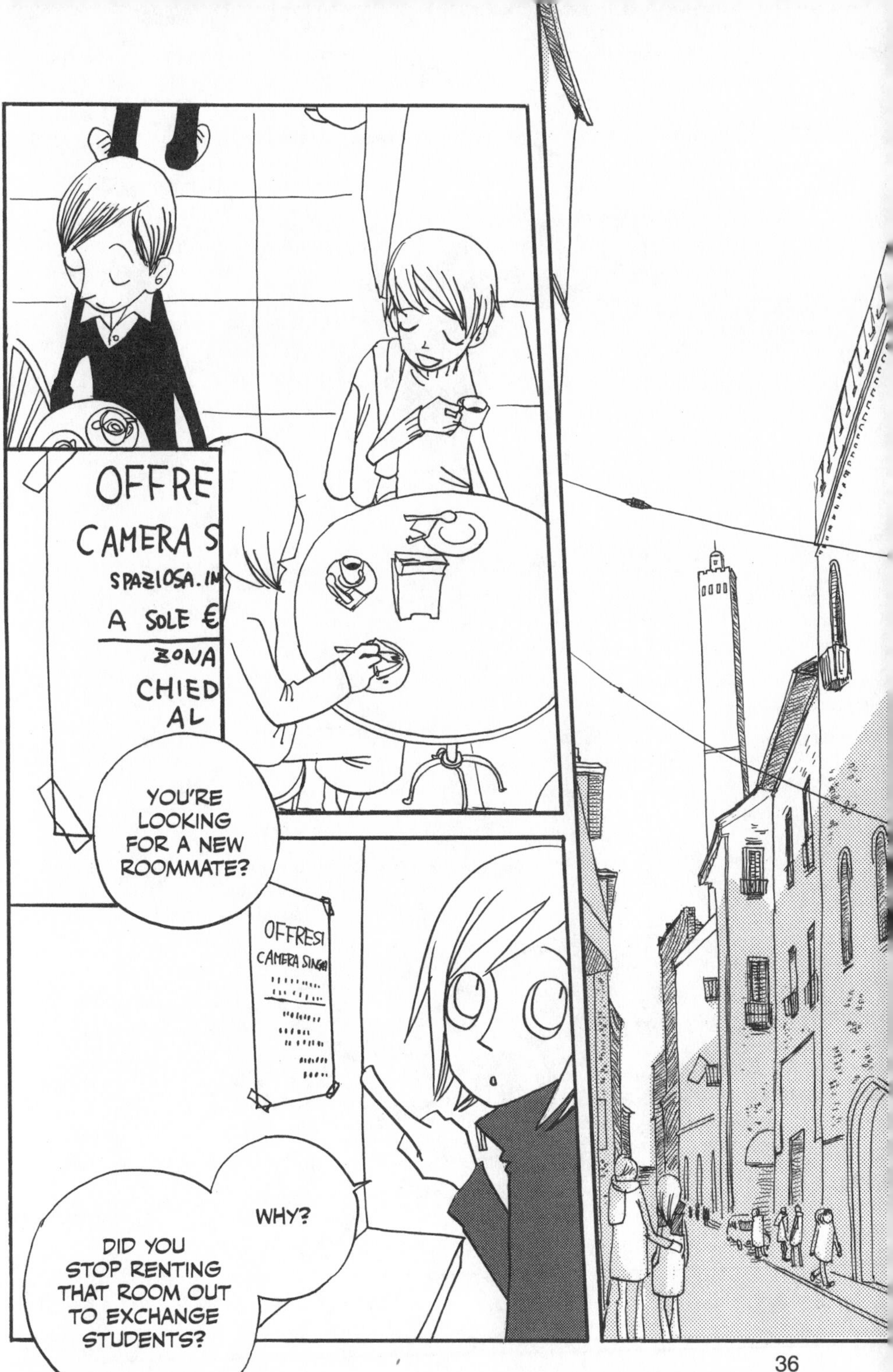
OFFRE
CAMERA S
SPAZIOSA.IM
A SOLE €
ZONA
CHIED
AL
YOU'RE LOOKING FOR A NEW ROOMMATE?
OFFRESI
WHY?
DID YOU STOP RENTING THAT ROOM OUT TO EXCHANGE STUDENTS?

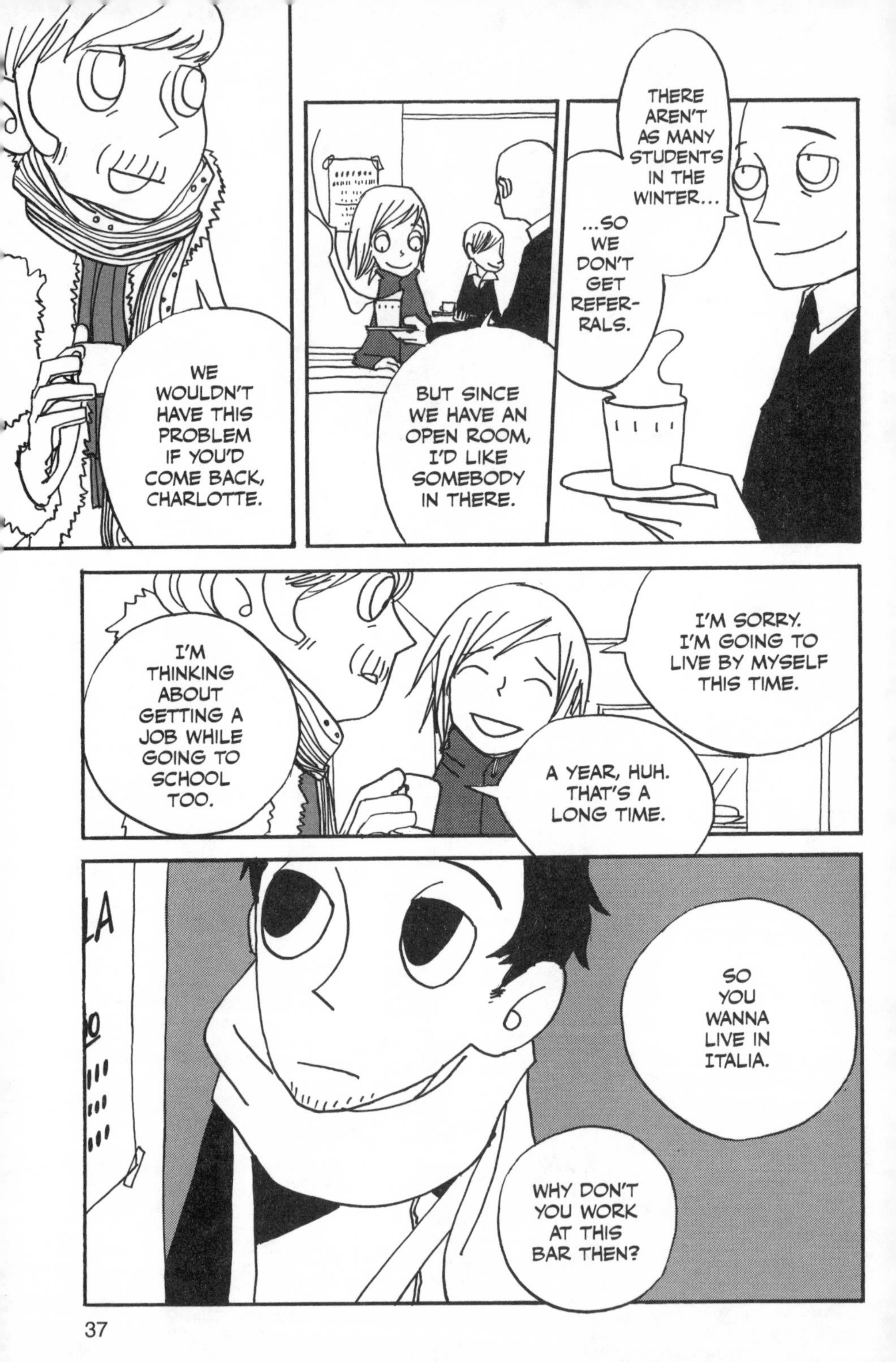
THERE AREN'T AS MANY STUDENTS IN THE WINTER...
...SO WE DON'T GET REFER-RALS.
BUT SINCE WE HAVE AN OPEN ROOM, I'D LIKE SOMEBODY IN THERE.
WE WOULDN'T HAVE THIS PROBLEM IF YOU'D COME BACK, CHARLOTTE.
I'M SORRY. I'M GOING TO LIVE BY MYSELF THIS TIME.
A YEAR, HUH. THAT'S A LONG TIME.
I'M THINKING ABOUT GETTING A JOB WHILE GOING TO SCHOOL TOO.
SO YOU WANNA LIVE IN ITALIA.
WHY DON'T YOU WORK AT THIS BAR THEN?

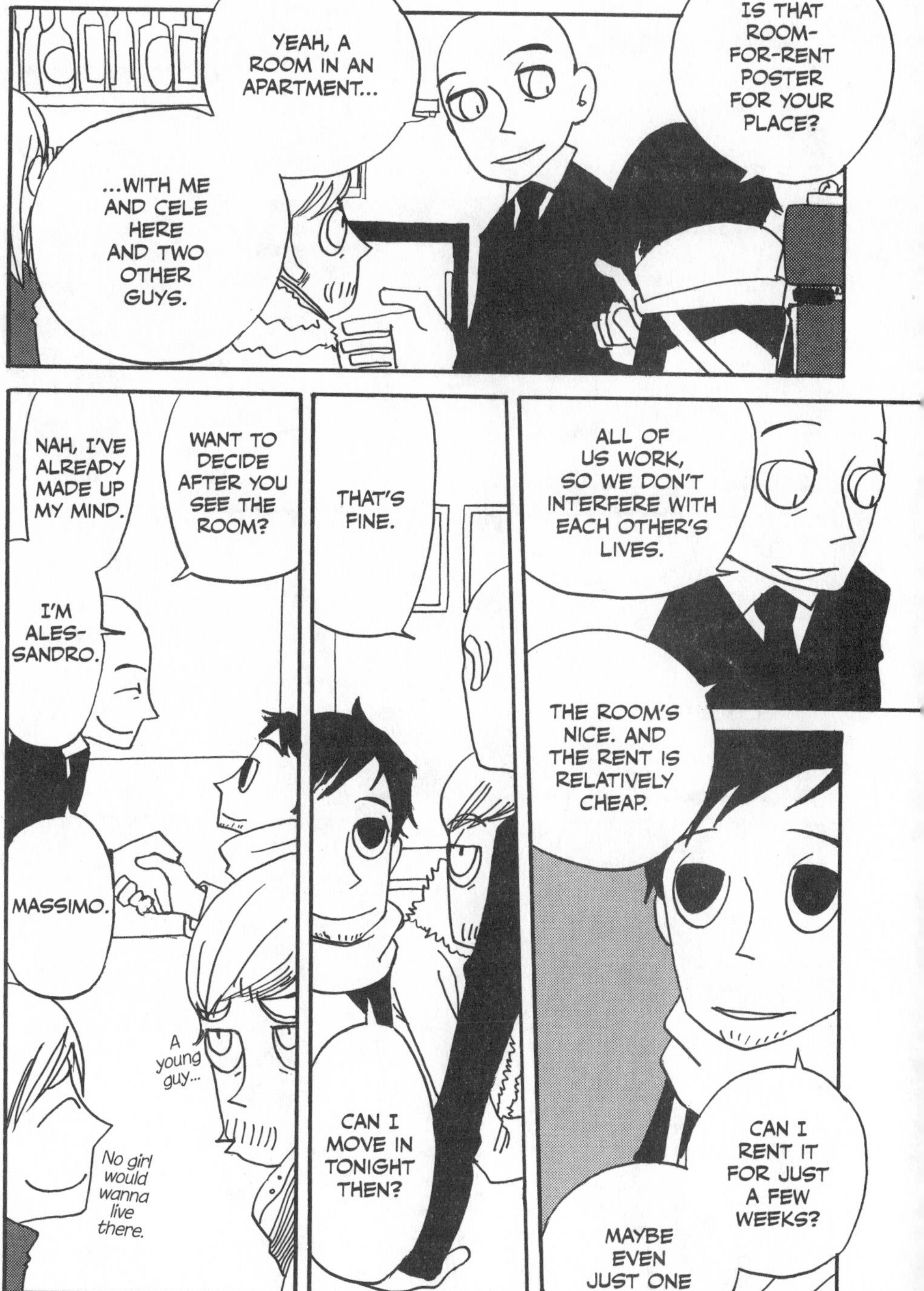
IS THAT ROOM-FOR-RENT POSTER FOR YOUR PLACE?
YEAH, A ROOM IN AN APARTMENT...
...WITH ME AND CELE HERE AND TWO OTHER GUYS.
ALL OF US WORK, SO WE DON'T INTERFERE WITH EACH OTHER'S LIVES.
THE ROOM'S NICE. AND THE RENT IS RELATIVELY CHEAP.
CAN I RENT IT FOR JUST A FEW WEEKS?
MAYBE EVEN JUST ONE WEEK.
THAT'S FINE.
CAN I MOVE IN TONIGHT THEN?
WANT TO DECIDE AFTER YOU SEE THE ROOM?
NAH, I'VE ALREADY MADE UP MY MIND.
I'M ALES-SANDRO.
MASSIMO.
A young guy...
No girl would wanna live there.

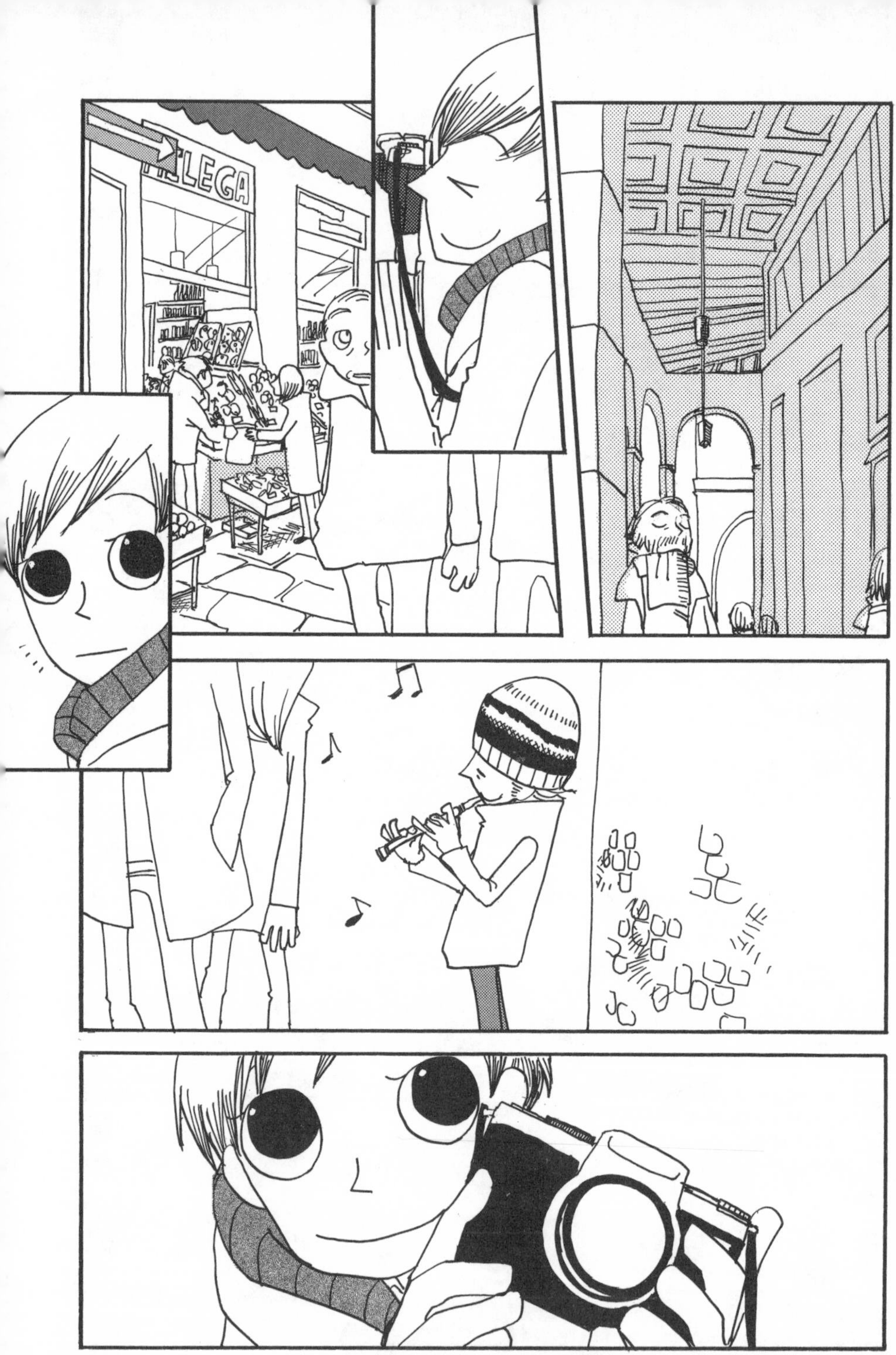
LEGA

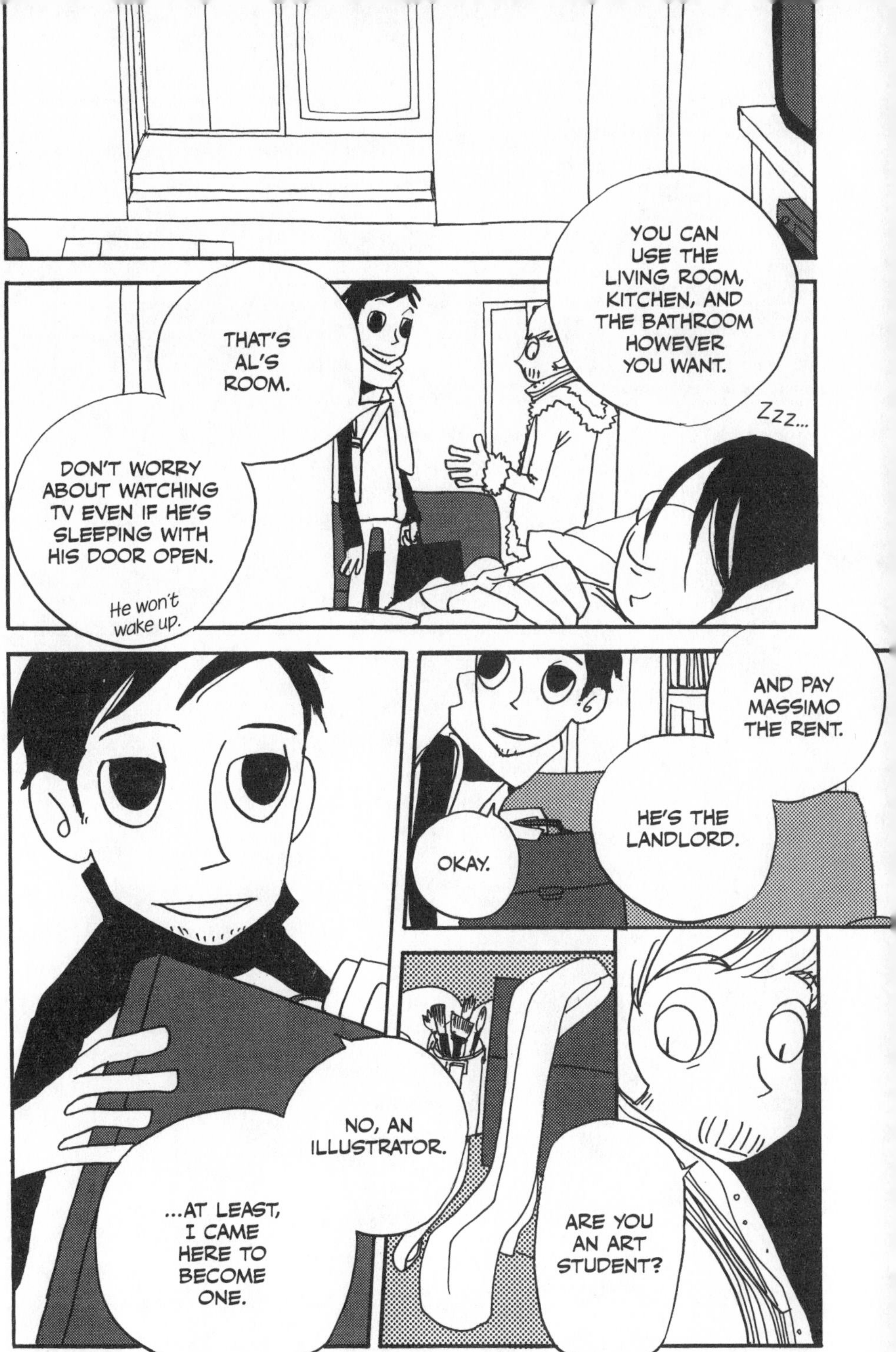
YOU CAN USE THE LIVING ROOM, KITCHEN, AND THE BATHROOM HOWEVER YOU WANT.
THAT'S AL'S ROOM.
Zzz...
DON'T WORRY ABOUT WATCHING TV EVEN IF HE'S SLEEPING WITH HIS DOOR OPEN.
He won't wake up.
AND PAY MASSIMO THE RENT.
HE'S THE LANDLORD.
OKAY.
ARE YOU AN ART STUDENT?
NO, AN ILLUSTRATOR.
...AT LEAST, I CAME HERE TO BECOME ONE.

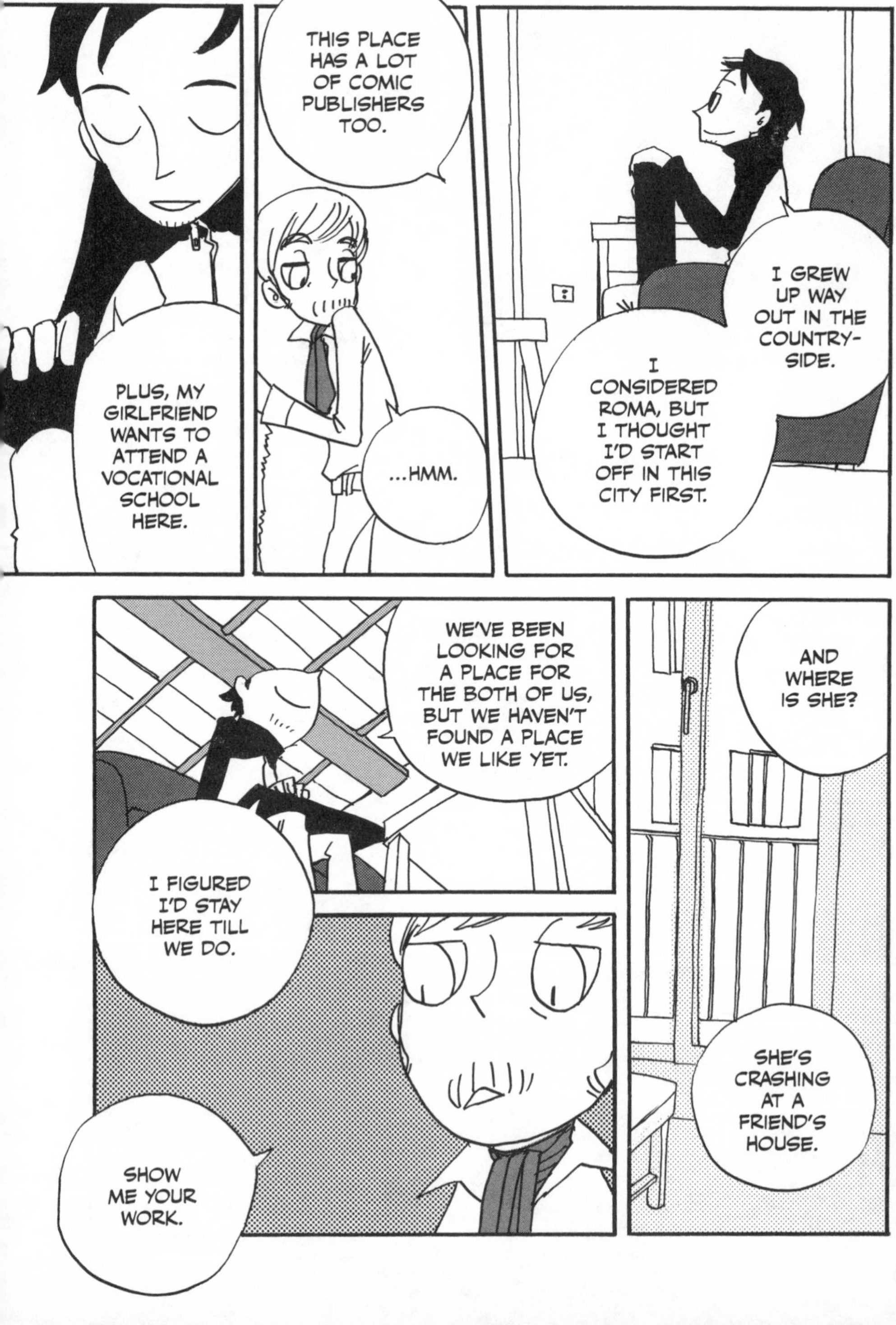
I GREW UP WAY OUT IN THE COUNTRY-SIDE.
I CONSIDERED ROMA, BUT I THOUGHT I'D START OFF IN THIS CITY FIRST.
THIS PLACE HAS A LOT OF COMIC PUBLISHERS TOO.
...HMM.
PLUS, MY GIRLFRIEND WANTS TO ATTEND A VOCATIONAL SCHOOL HERE.
AND WHERE IS SHE?
SHE'S CRASHING AT A FRIEND'S HOUSE.
WE'VE BEEN LOOKING FOR A PLACE FOR THE BOTH OF US, BUT WE HAVEN'T FOUND A PLACE WE LIKE YET.
I FIGURED I'D STAY HERE TILL WE DO.
SHOW ME YOUR WORK.

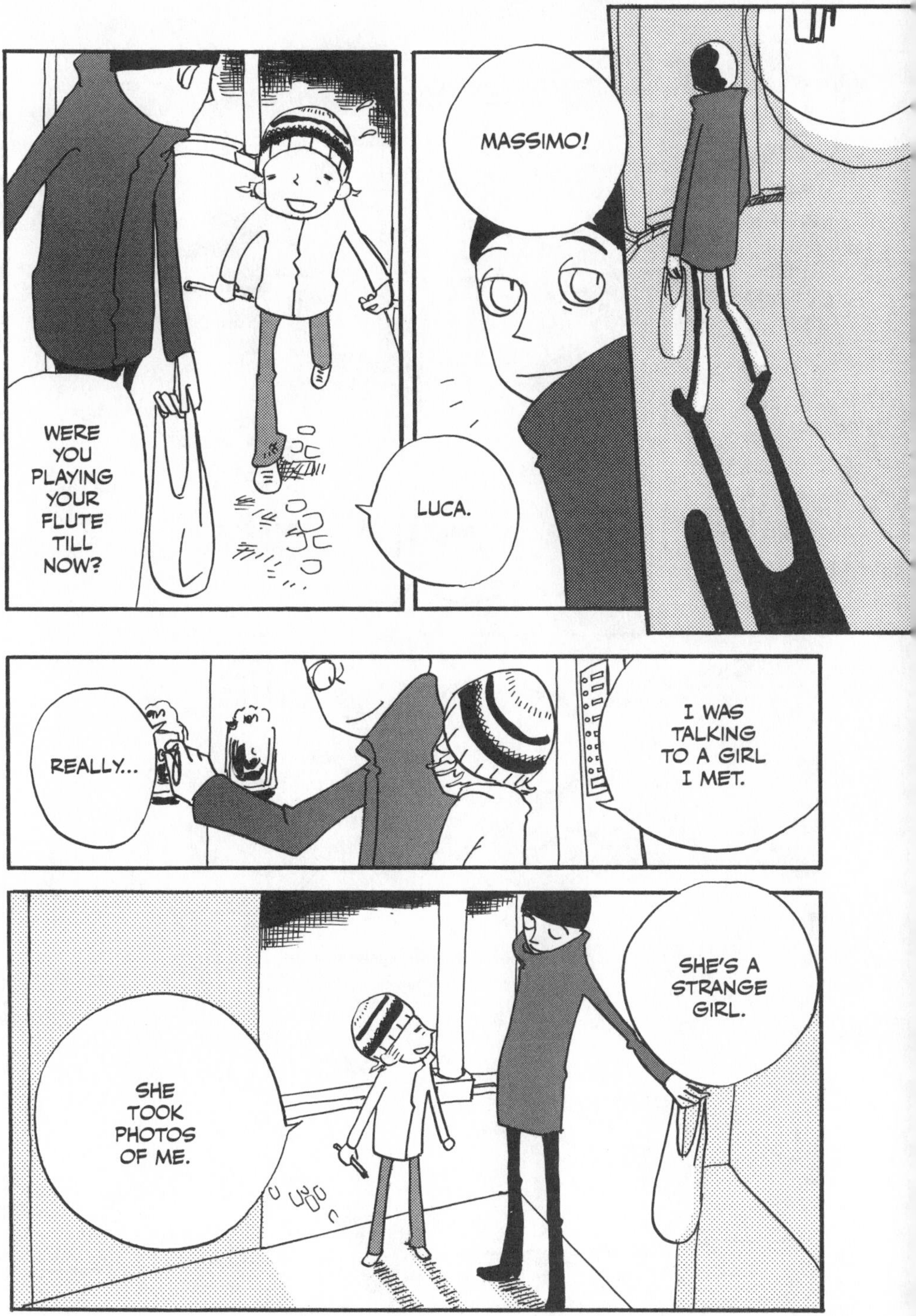
MASSIMO!
LUCA.
WERE YOU PLAYING YOUR FLUTE TILL NOW?
I WAS TALKING TO A GIRL I MET.
REALLY...
SHE'S A STRANGE GIRL.
SHE TOOK PHOTOS OF ME.

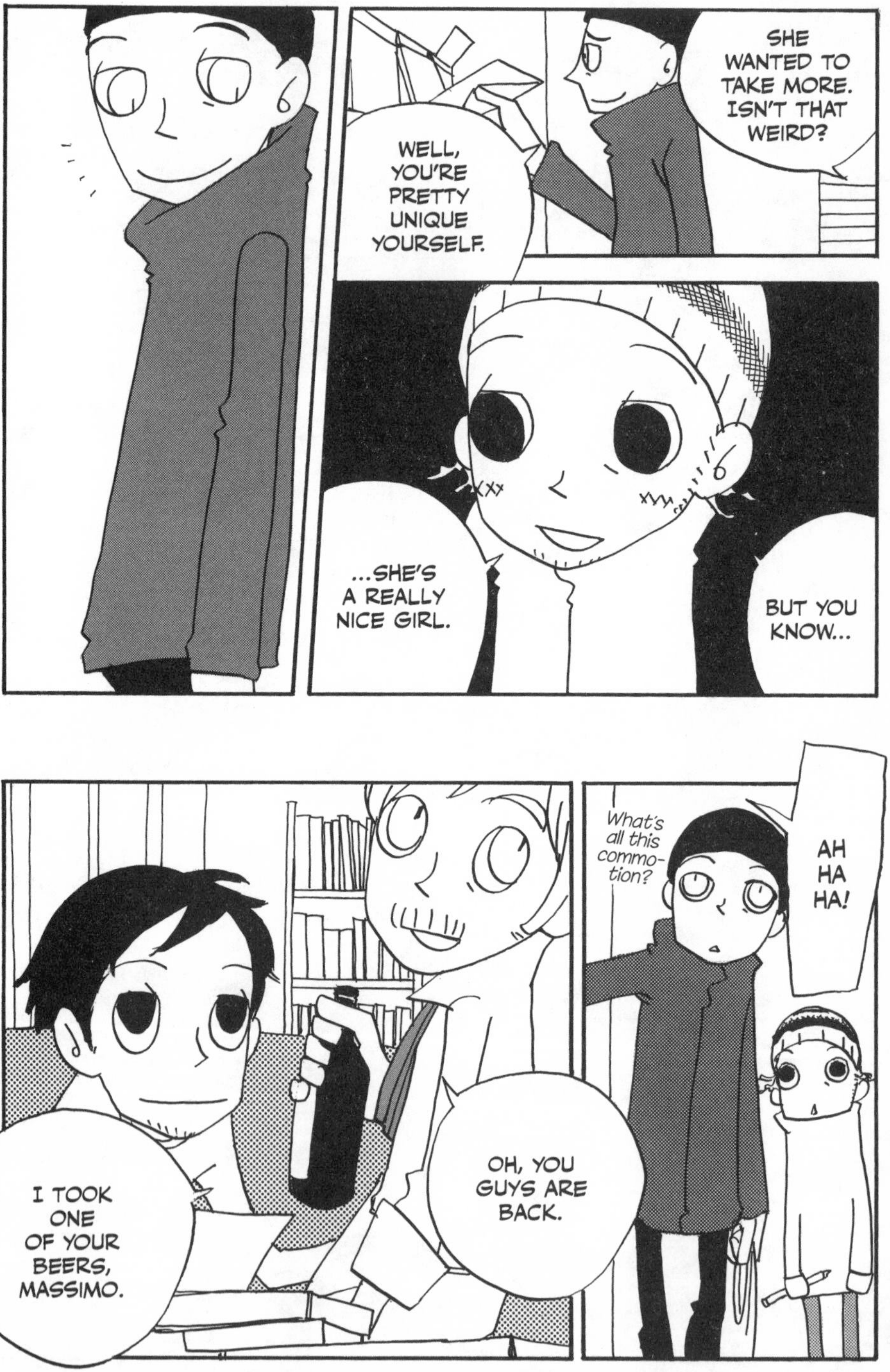
SHE WANTED TO TAKE MORE. ISN'T THAT WEIRD?
WELL, YOU'RE PRETTY UNIQUE YOURSELF.
BUT YOU KNOW...
...SHE'S A REALLY NICE GIRL.
AH HA HA!
What's all this commotion?
OH, YOU GUYS ARE BACK.
I TOOK ONE OF YOUR BEERS, MASSIMO.

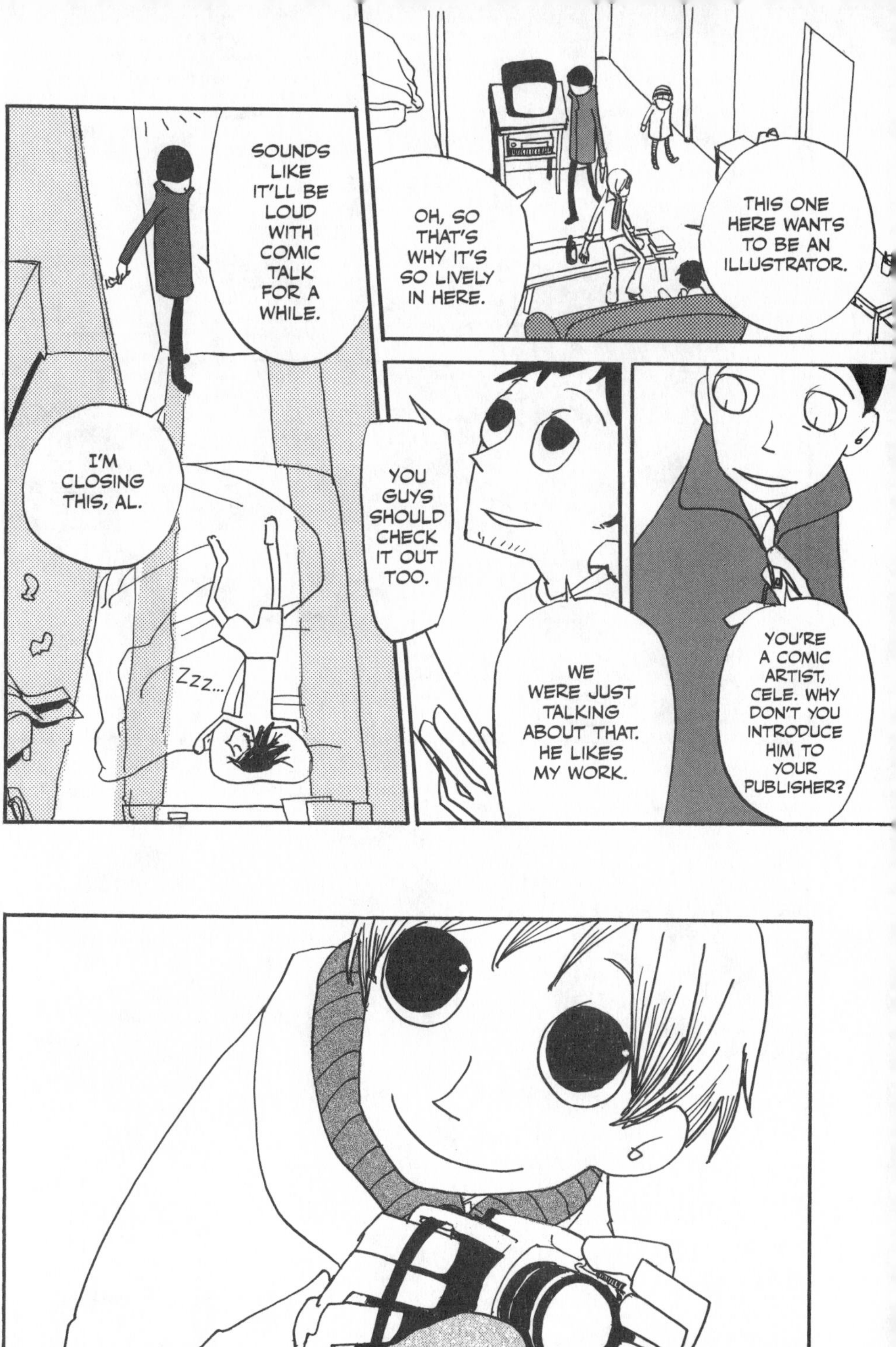
THIS ONE HERE WANTS TO BE AN ILLUSTRATOR.
OH, SO THAT'S WHY IT'S SO LIVELY IN HERE.
YOU'RE A COMIC ARTIST, CELE. WHY DON'T YOU INTRODUCE HIM TO YOUR PUBLISHER?
WE WERE JUST TALKING ABOUT THAT. HE LIKES MY WORK.
YOU GUYS SHOULD CHECK IT OUT TOO.
SOUNDS LIKE IT'LL BE LOUD WITH COMIC TALK FOR A WHILE.
I'M CLOSING THIS, AL.
Zzz...

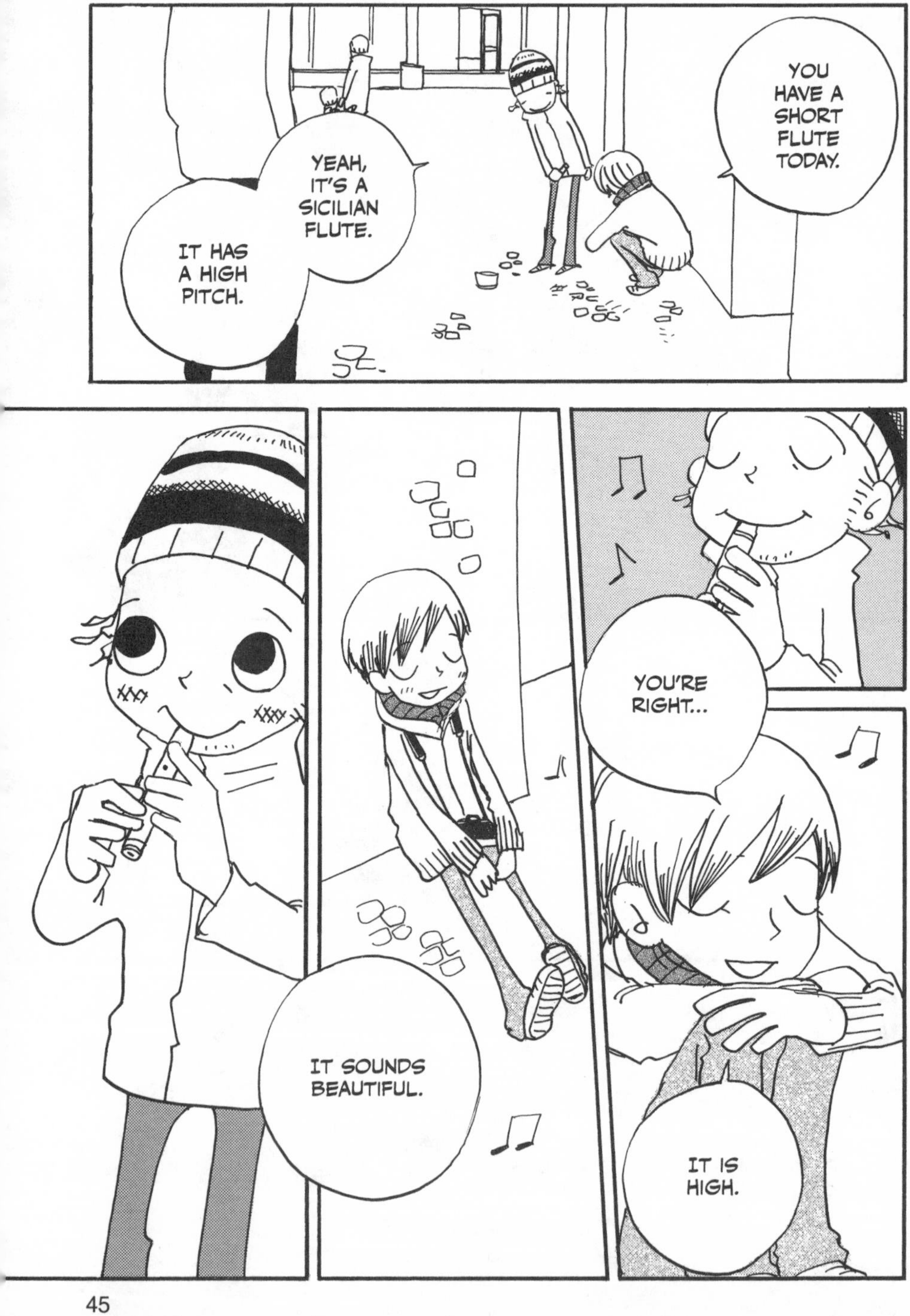

YOU HAVE A SHORT FLUTE TODAY.
YEAH, IT'S A SICILIAN FLUTE.
IT HAS A HIGH PITCH.
YOU'RE RIGHT...
IT IS HIGH.
IT SOUNDS BEAUTIFUL.

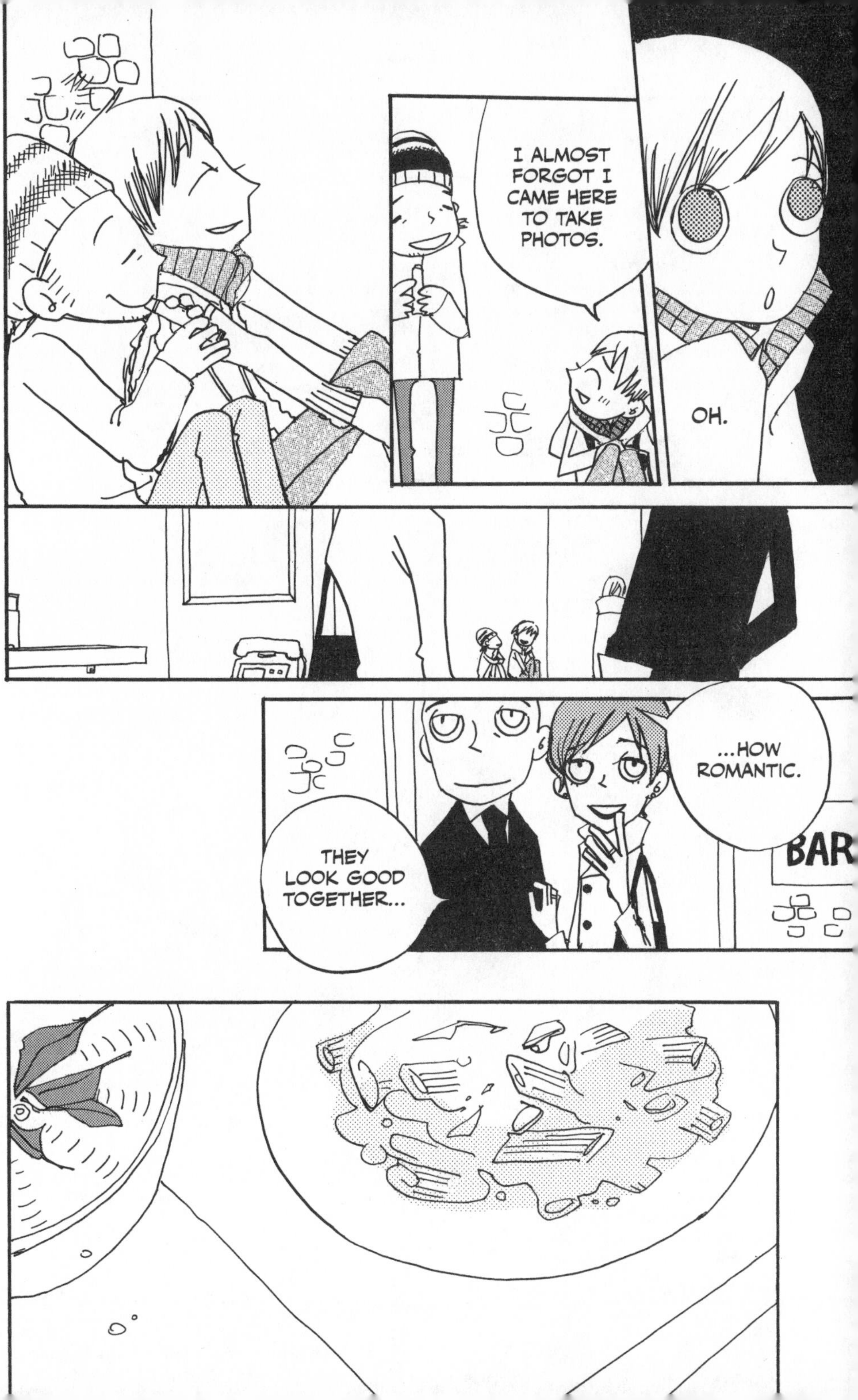
OH.
I ALMOST FORGOT I CAME HERE TO TAKE PHOTOS.
...HOW ROMANTIC.
BAR
THEY LOOK GOOD TOGETHER...

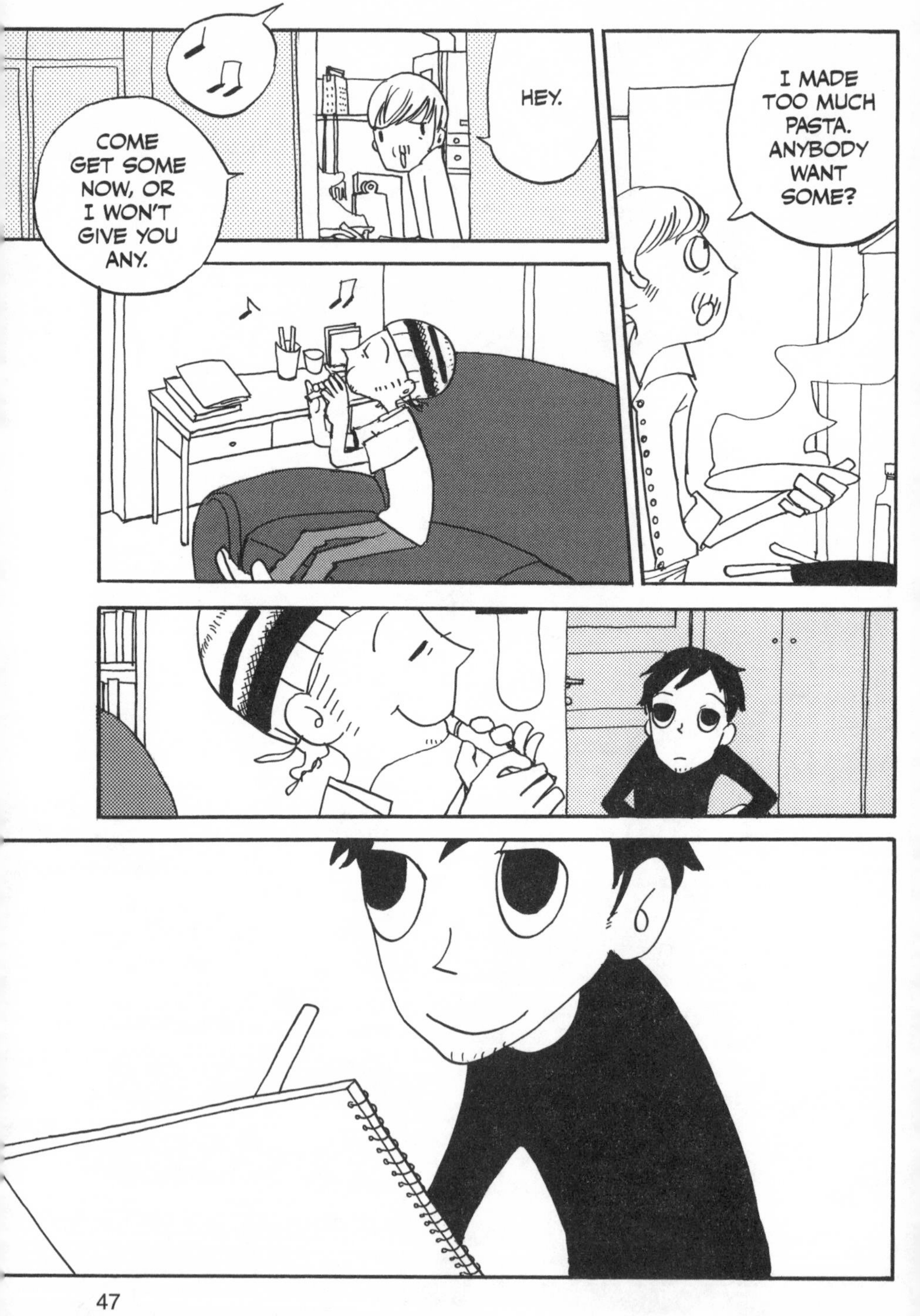
I MADE TOO MUCH PASTA. ANYBODY WANT SOME?
HEY.
COME GET SOME NOW, OR I WON'T GIVE YOU ANY.

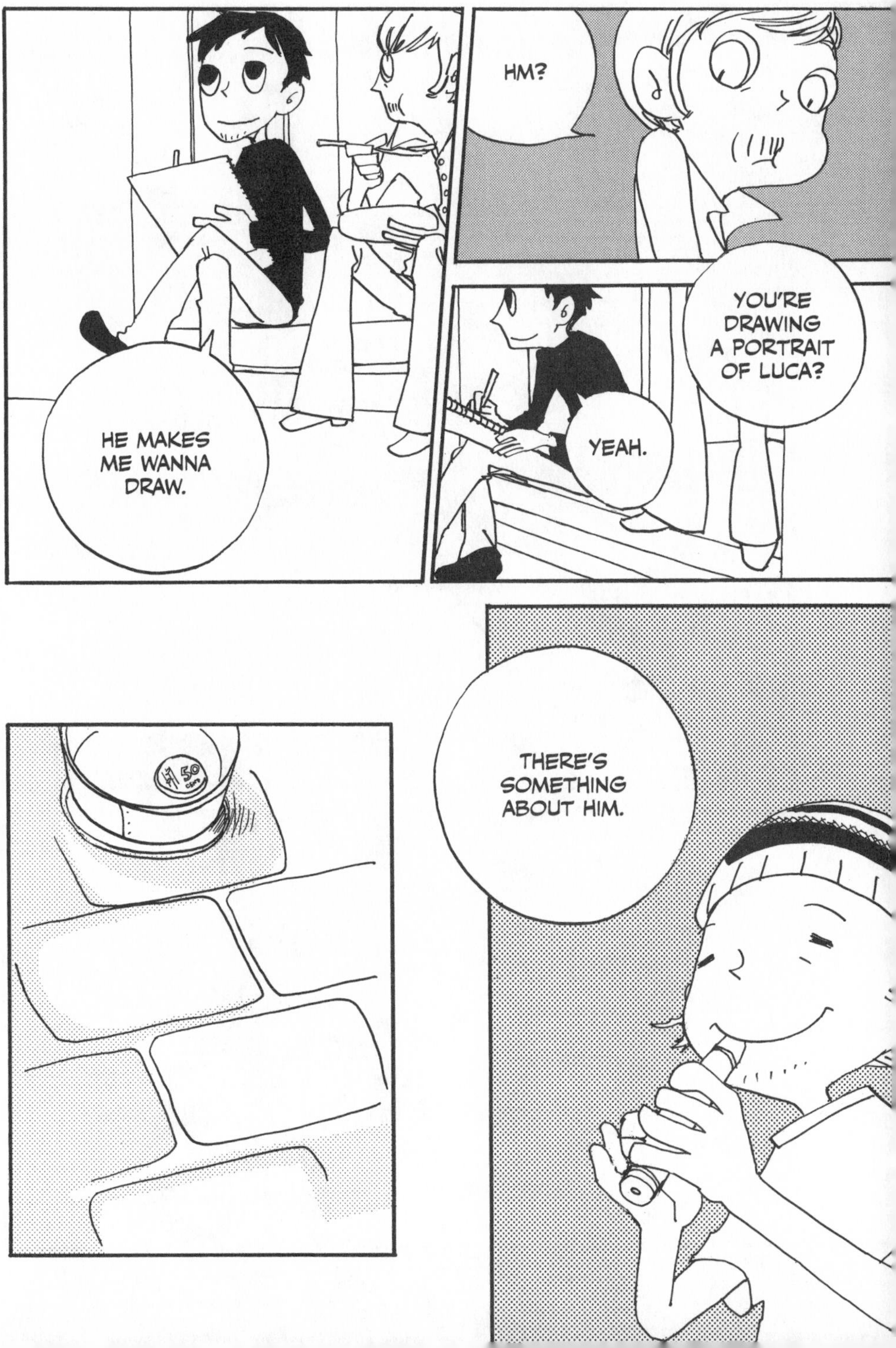
HM?
YOU'RE DRAWING A PORTRAIT OF LUCA?
YEAH.
HE MAKES ME WANNA DRAW.
THERE'S SOMETHING ABOUT HIM.

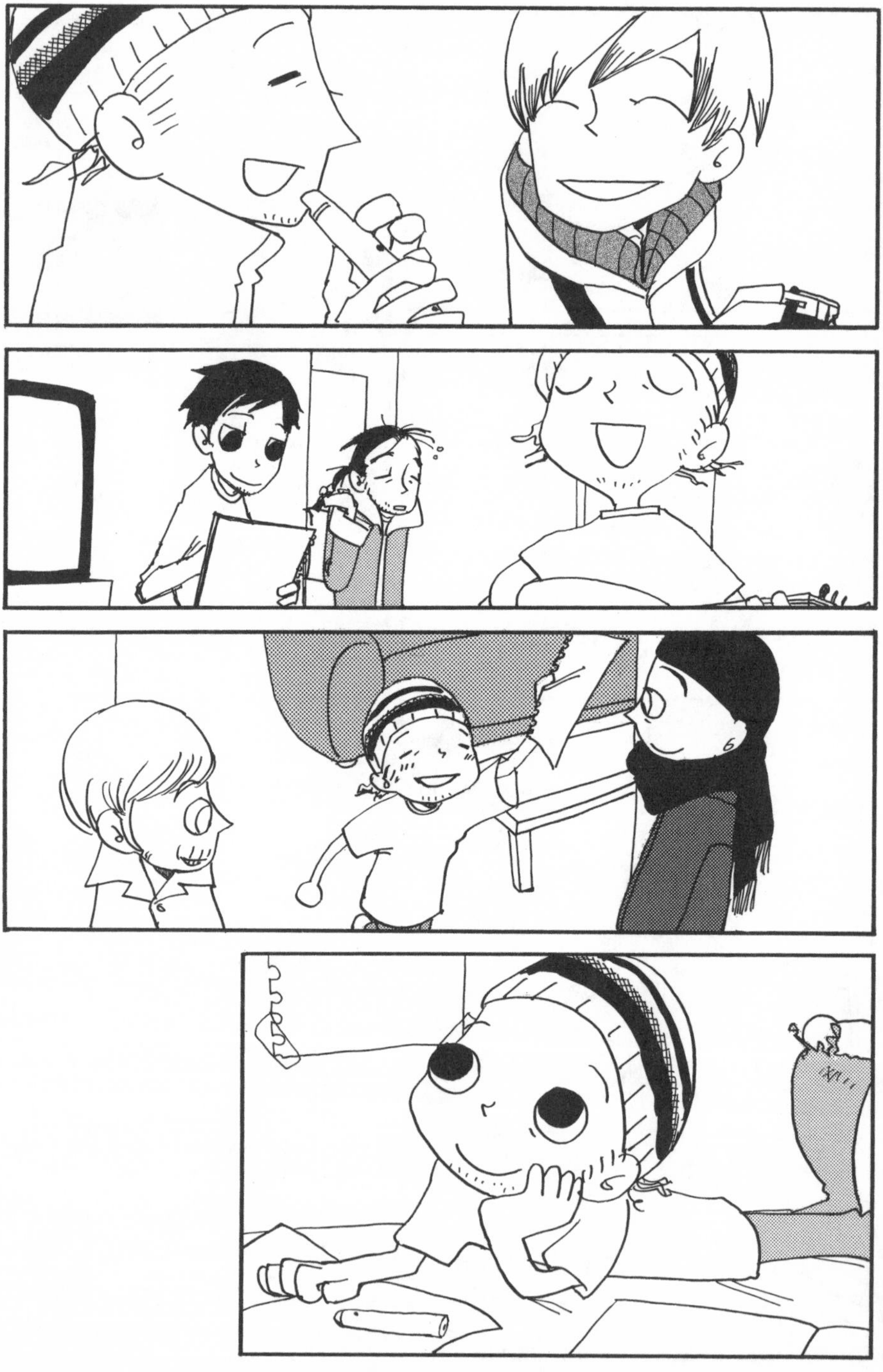

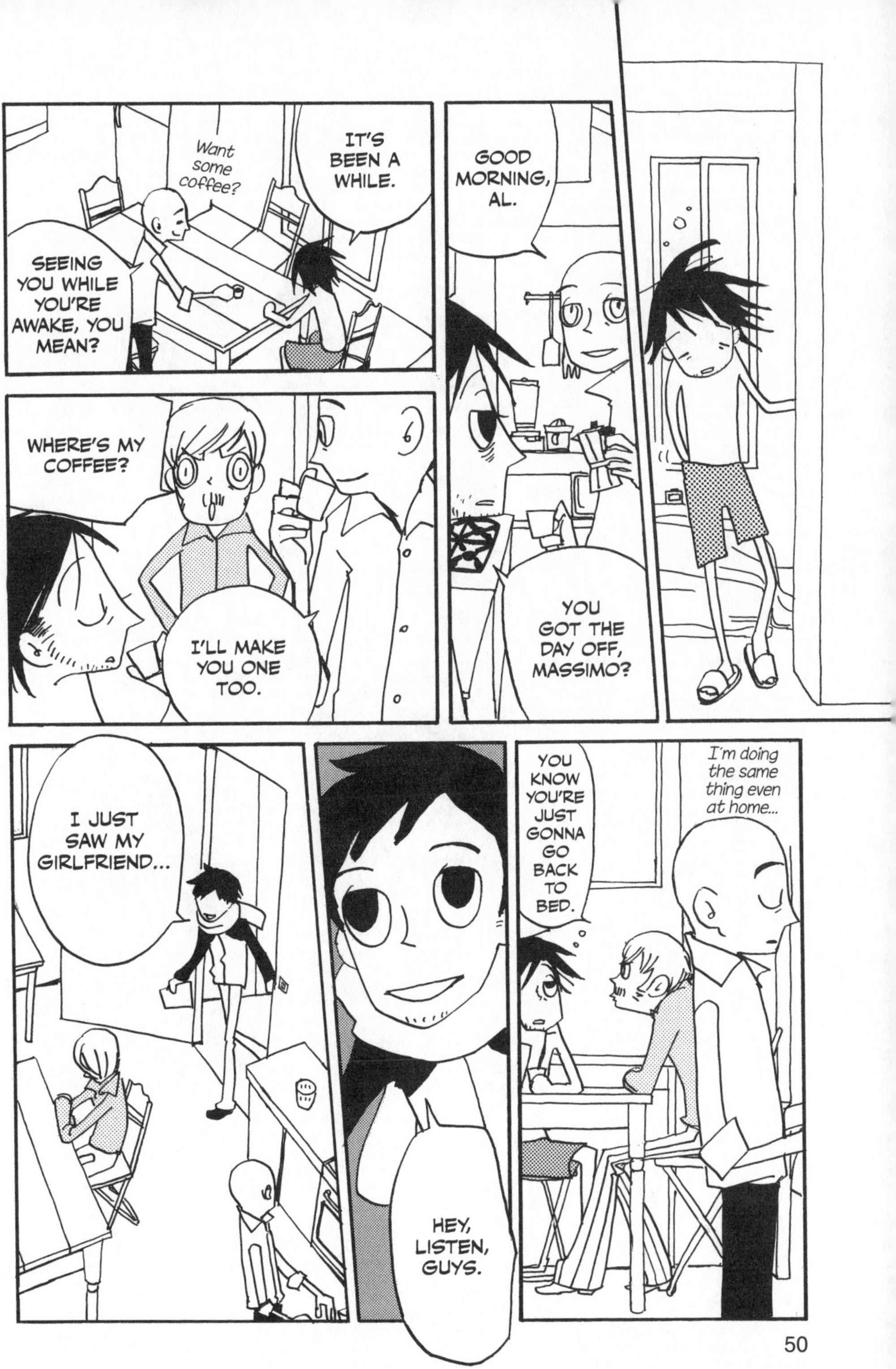
GOOD MORNING, AL.
YOU GOT THE DAY OFF, MASSIMO?
IT'S BEEN A WHILE.
Want some coffee?
SEEING YOU WHILE YOU'RE AWAKE, YOU MEAN?
WHERE'S MY COFFEE?
I'LL MAKE YOU ONE TOO.
I'm doing the same thing even at home...
YOU KNOW YOU'RE JUST GONNA GO BACK TO BED.
HEY, LISTEN, GUYS.
I JUST SAW MY GIRLFRIEND...

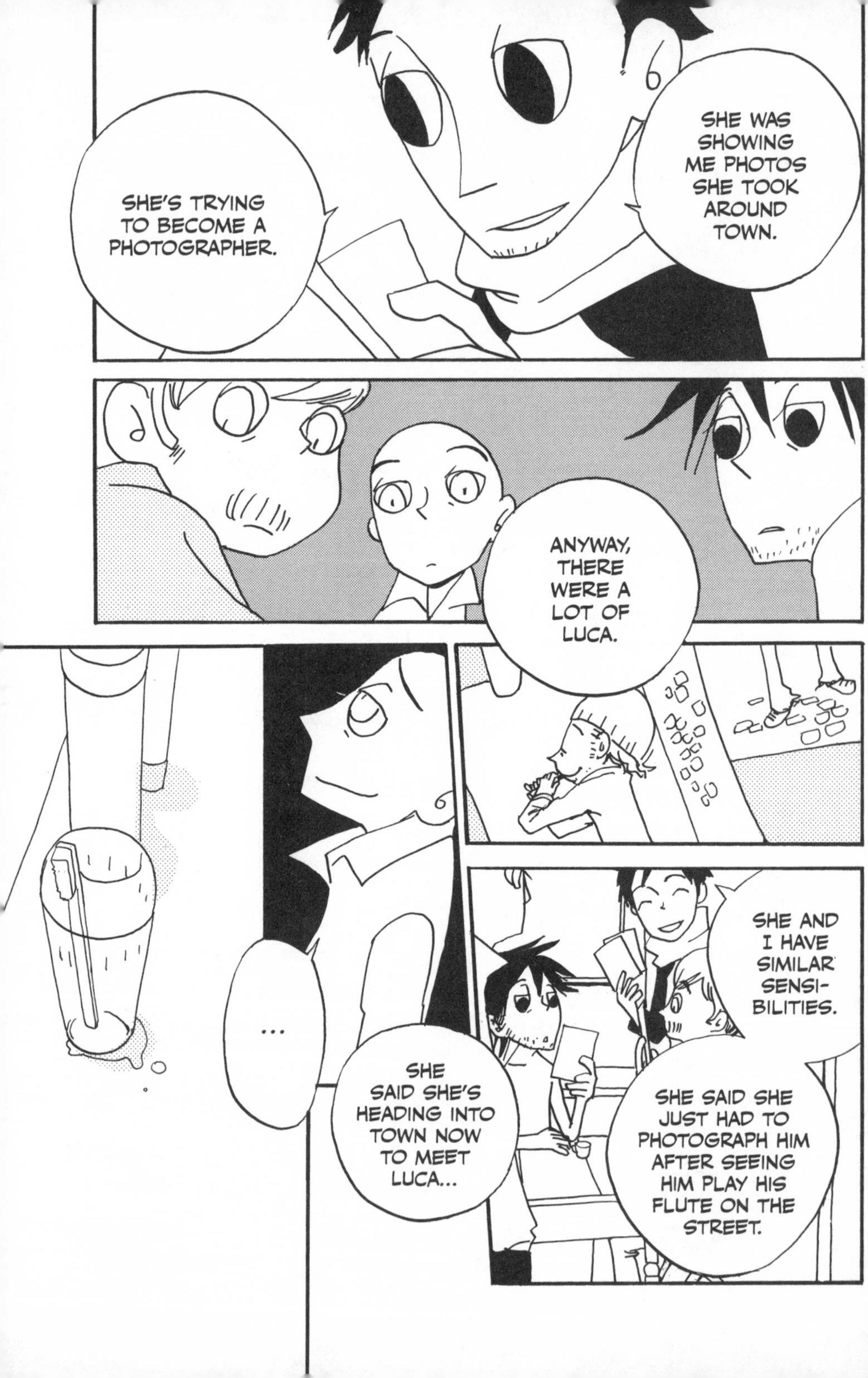
SHE WAS SHOWING ME PHOTOS SHE TOOK AROUND TOWN.
SHE'S TRYING TO BECOME A PHOTOGRAPHER.
ANYWAY, THERE WERE A LOT OF LUCA.
SHE AND I HAVE SIMILAR SENSI-BILITIES.
SHE SAID SHE JUST HAD TO PHOTOGRAPH HIM AFTER SEEING HIM PLAY HIS FLUTE ON THE STREET.
SHE SAID SHE'S HEADING INTO TOWN NOW TO MEET LUCA...
...

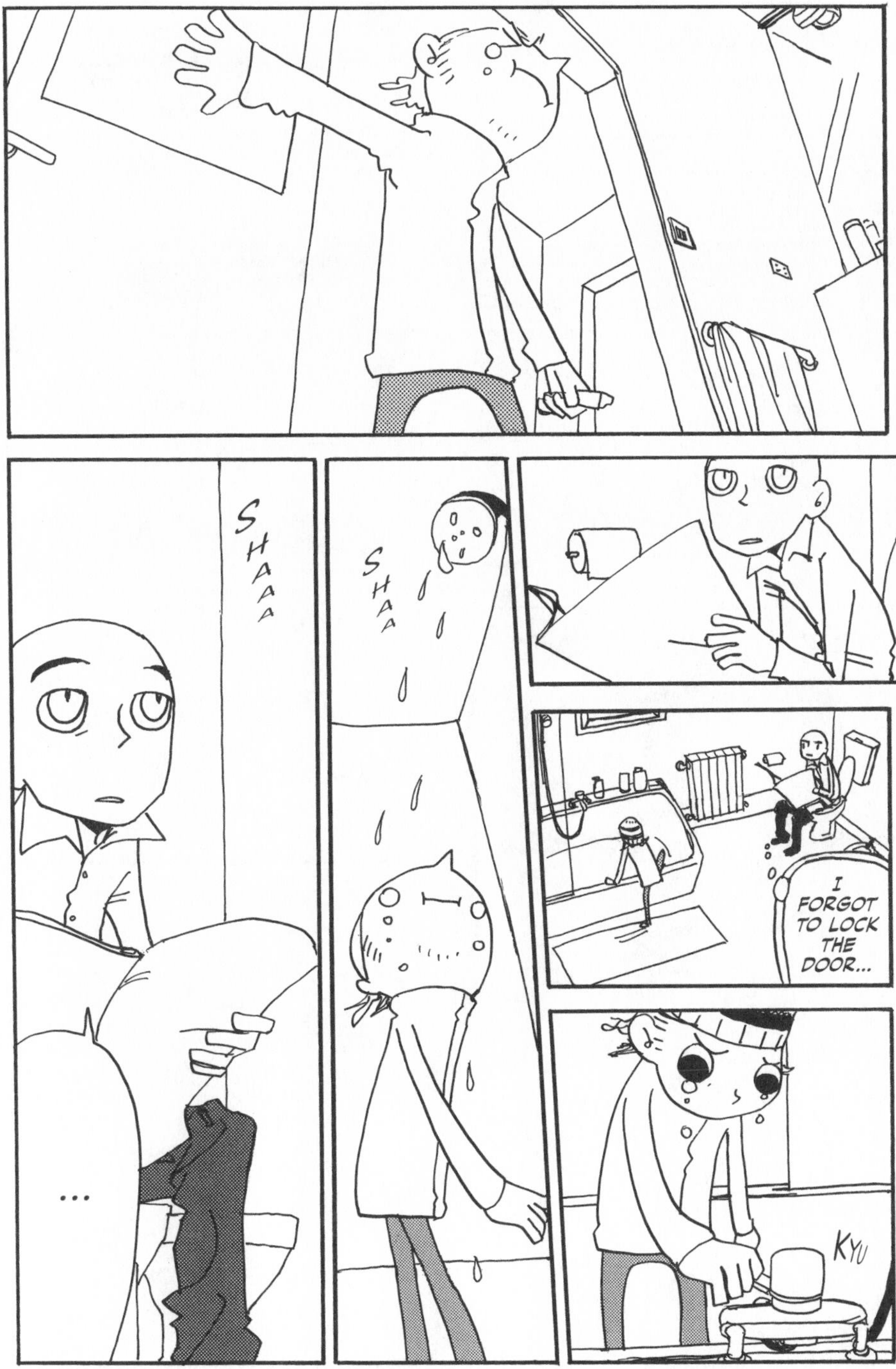
I FORGOT TO LOCK THE DOOR...
KYU
SHAAA
SHAAA
...

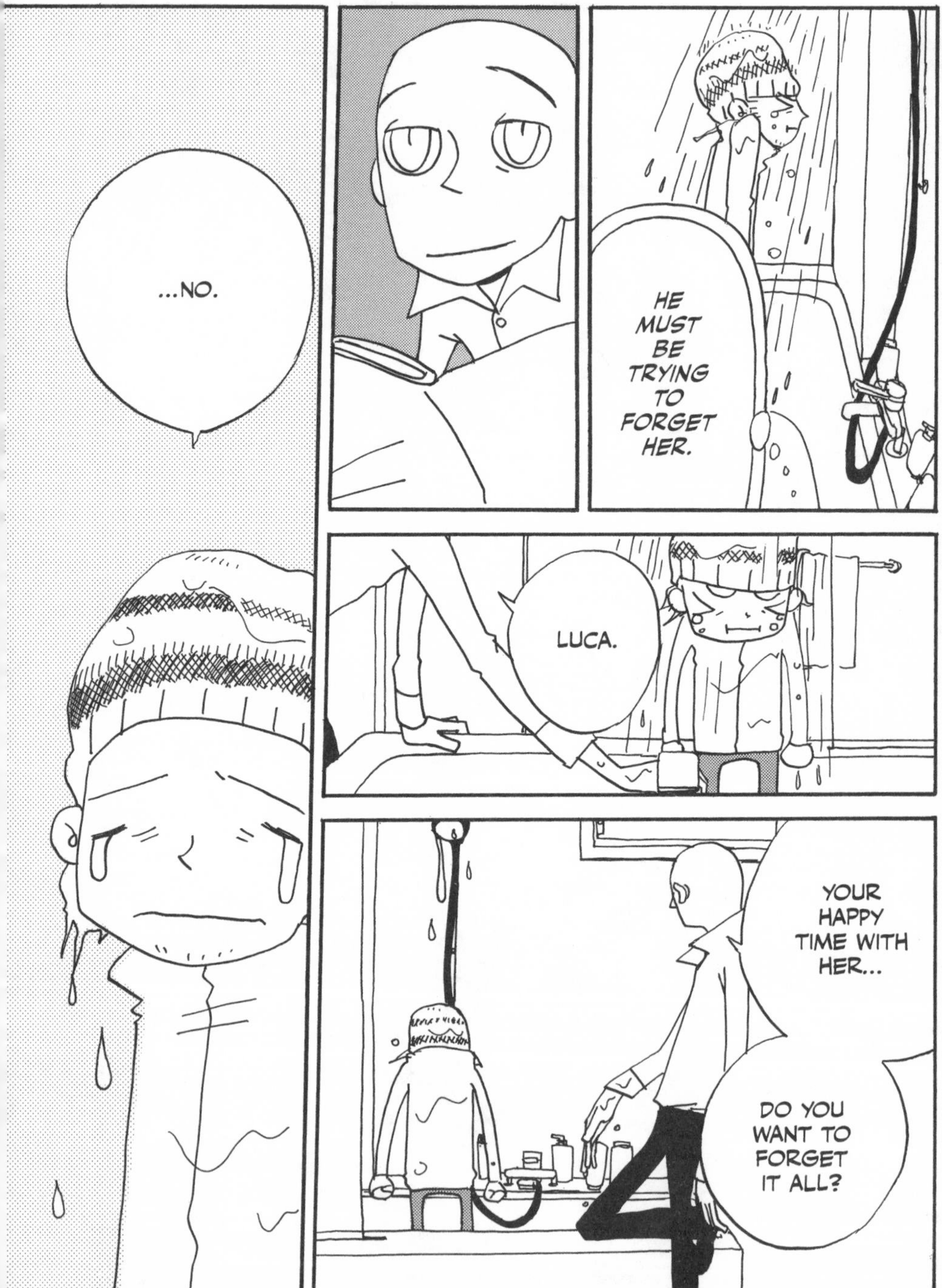
HE MUST BE TRYING TO FORGET HER.
LUCA.
YOUR HAPPY TIME WITH HER...
DO YOU WANT TO FORGET IT ALL?
...NO.

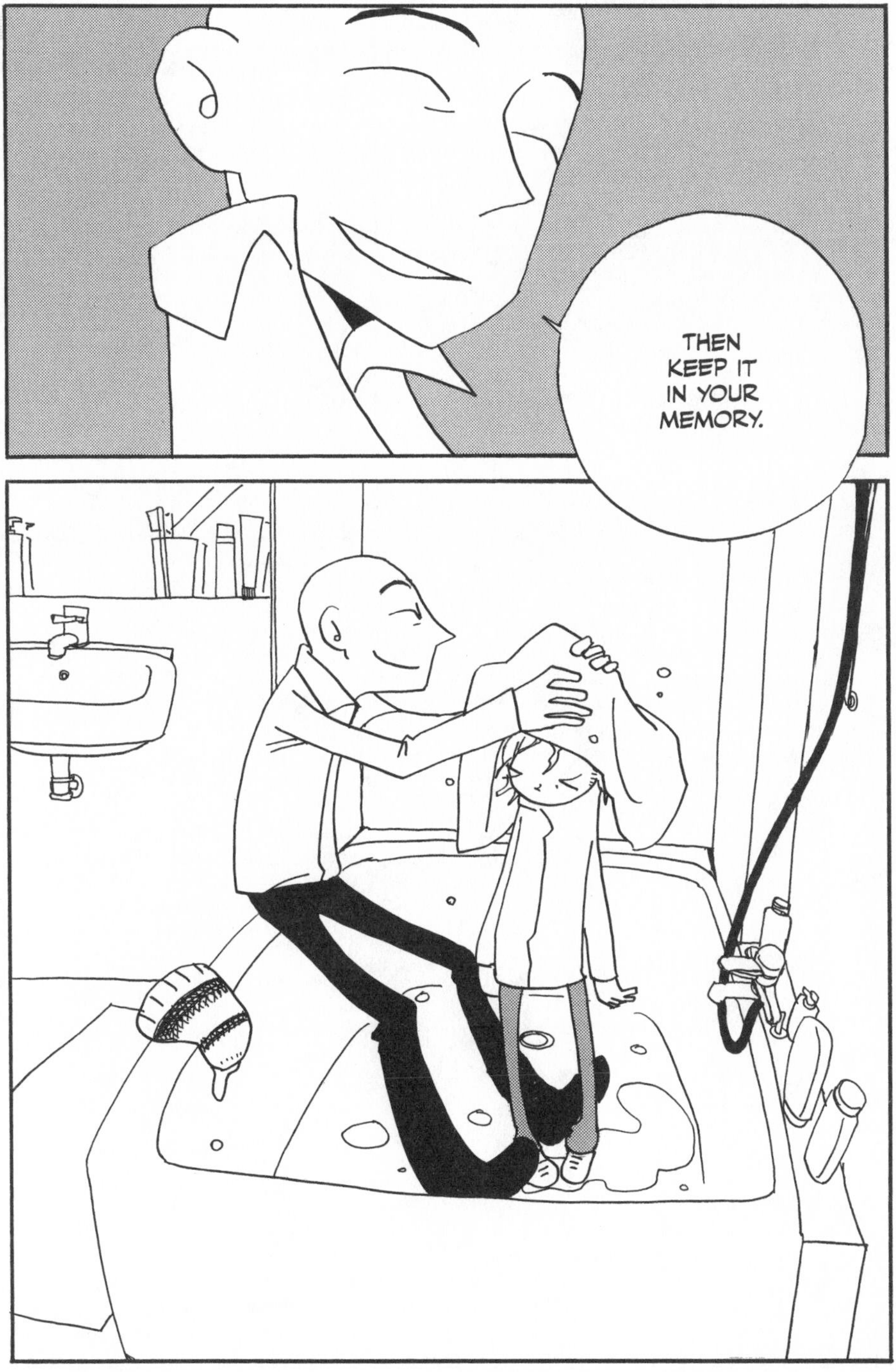
THEN KEEP IT IN YOUR MEMORY.

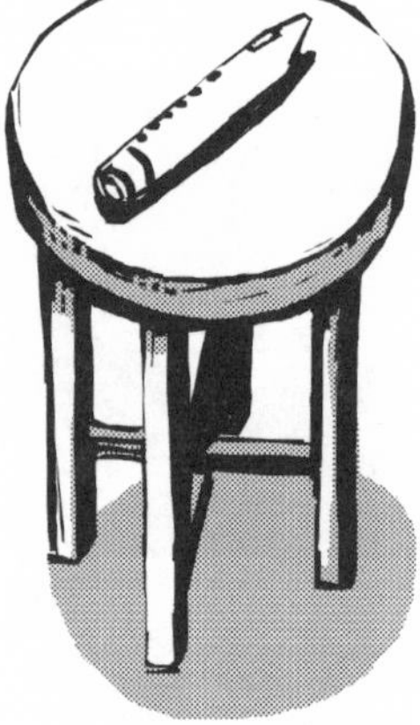

LA QUINTA CAMERA
Capitolo 2

LA QUINTA CAMERA
Capitolo 3

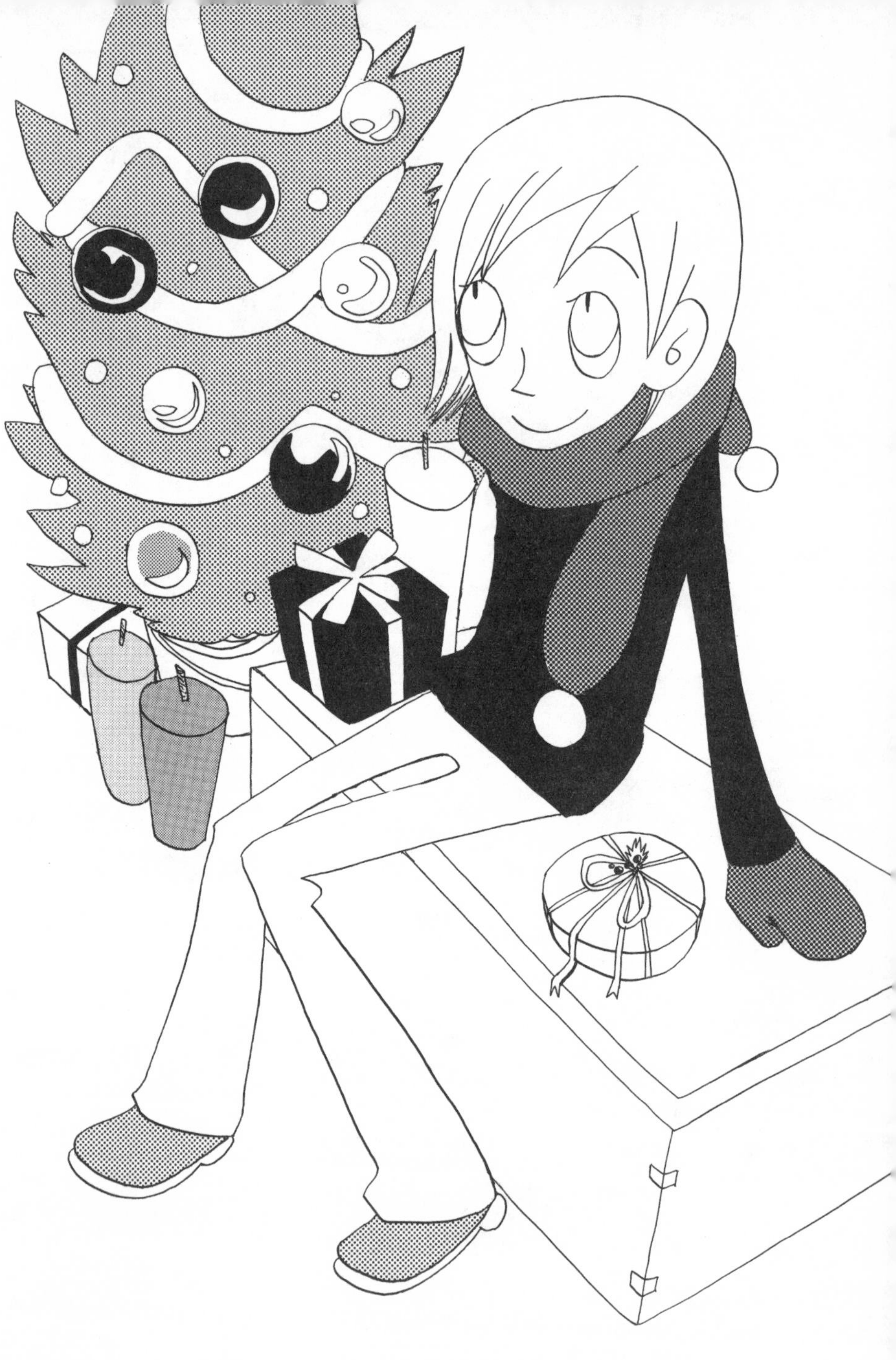

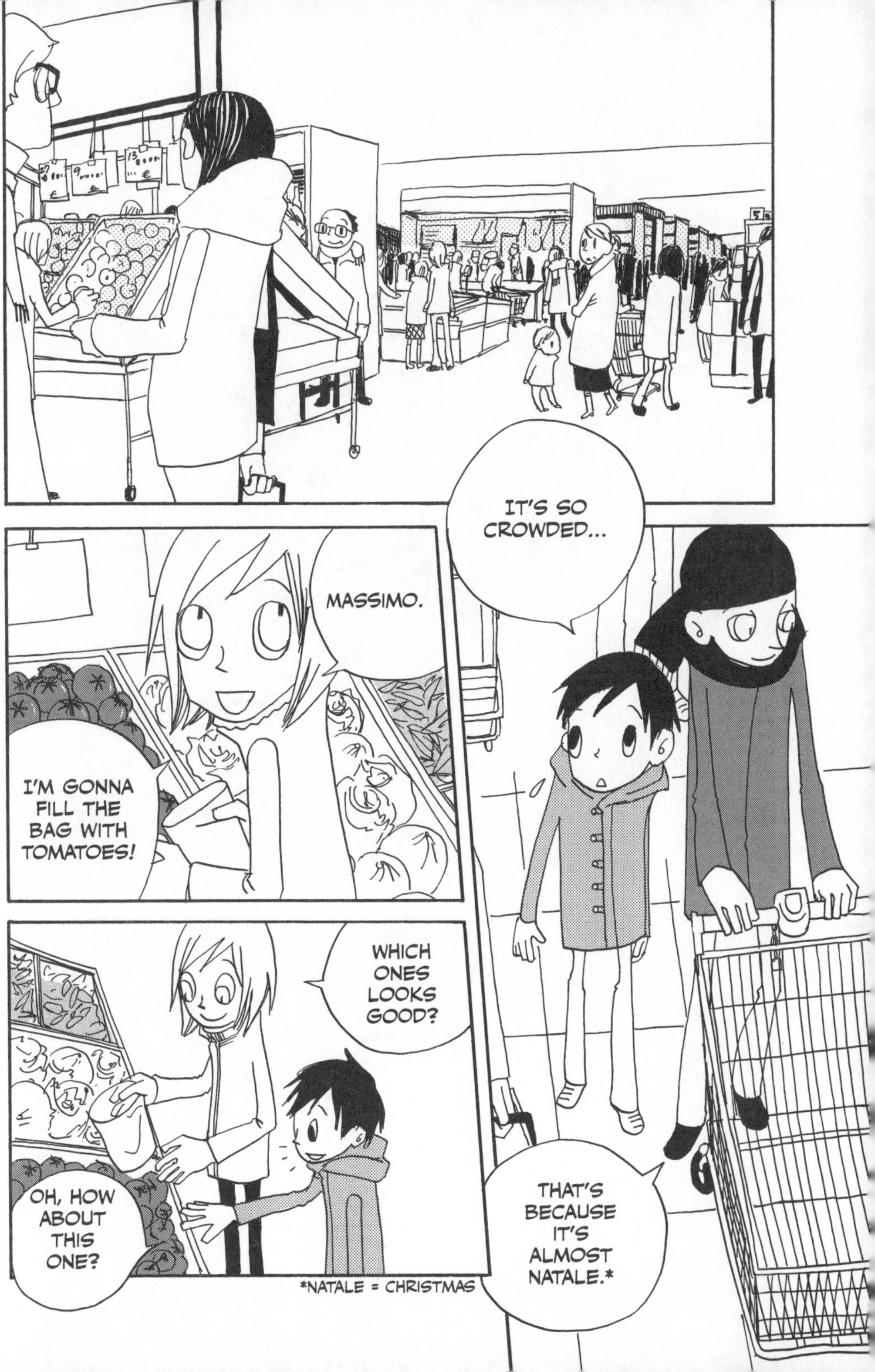
IT'S SO CROWDED...
THAT'S BECAUSE IT'S ALMOST NATALE.*
MASSIMO.
I'M GONNA FILL THE BAG WITH TOMATOES!
WHICH ONES LOOKS GOOD?
OH, HOW ABOUT THIS ONE?
*NATALE = CHRISTMAS

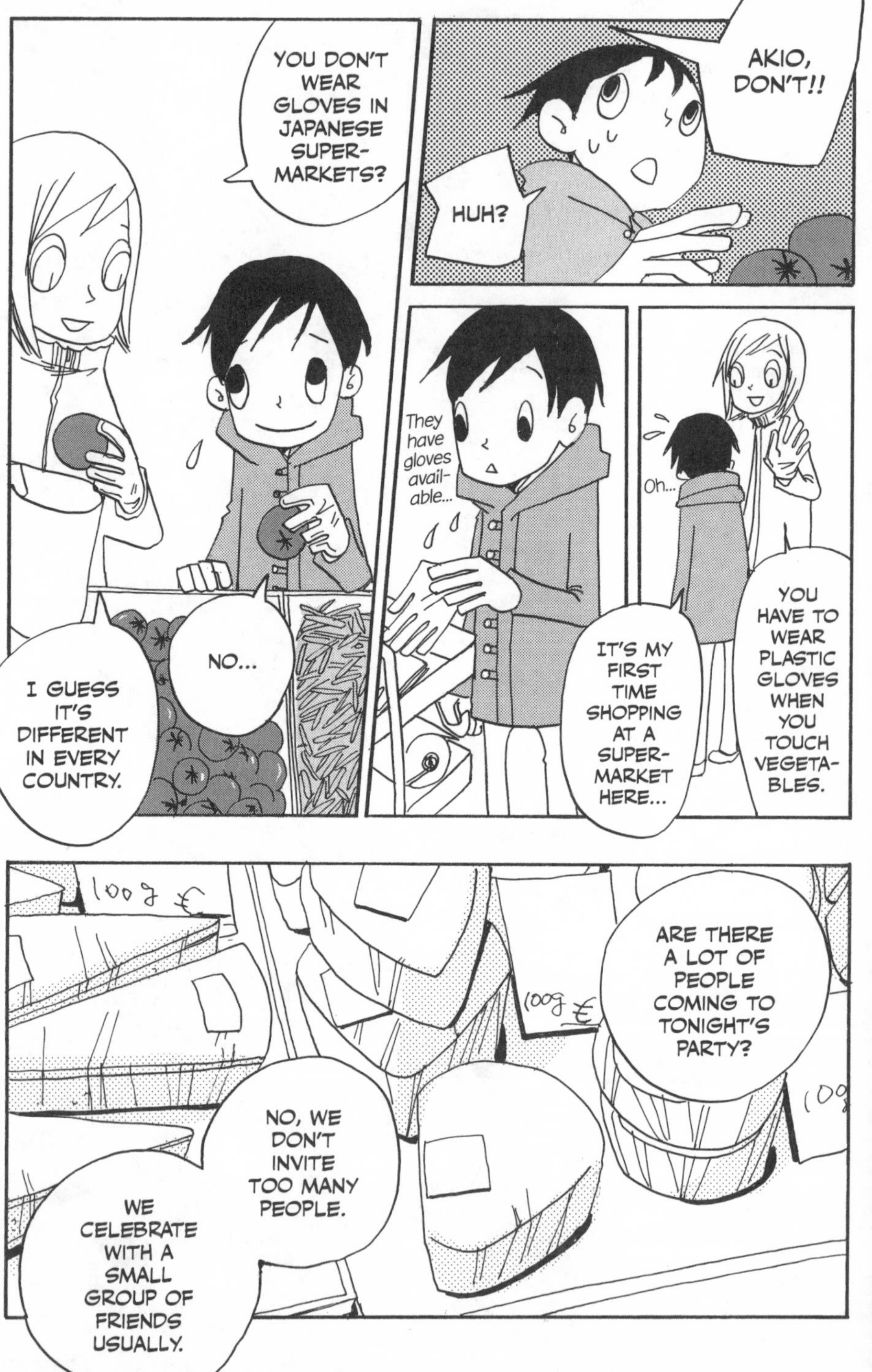
AKIO, DON'T!!
HUH?
YOU HAVE TO WEAR PLASTIC GLOVES WHEN YOU TOUCH VEGETA-BLES.
Oh...
IT'S MY FIRST TIME SHOPPING AT A SUPER-MARKET HERE...
They have gloves avail-able...
YOU DON'T WEAR GLOVES IN JAPANESE SUPER-MARKETS?
NO...
I GUESS IT'S DIFFERENT IN EVERY COUNTRY.
ARE THERE A LOT OF PEOPLE COMING TO TONIGHT'S PARTY?
100g €
NO, WE DON'T INVITE TOO MANY PEOPLE.
WE CELEBRATE WITH A SMALL GROUP OF FRIENDS USUALLY.

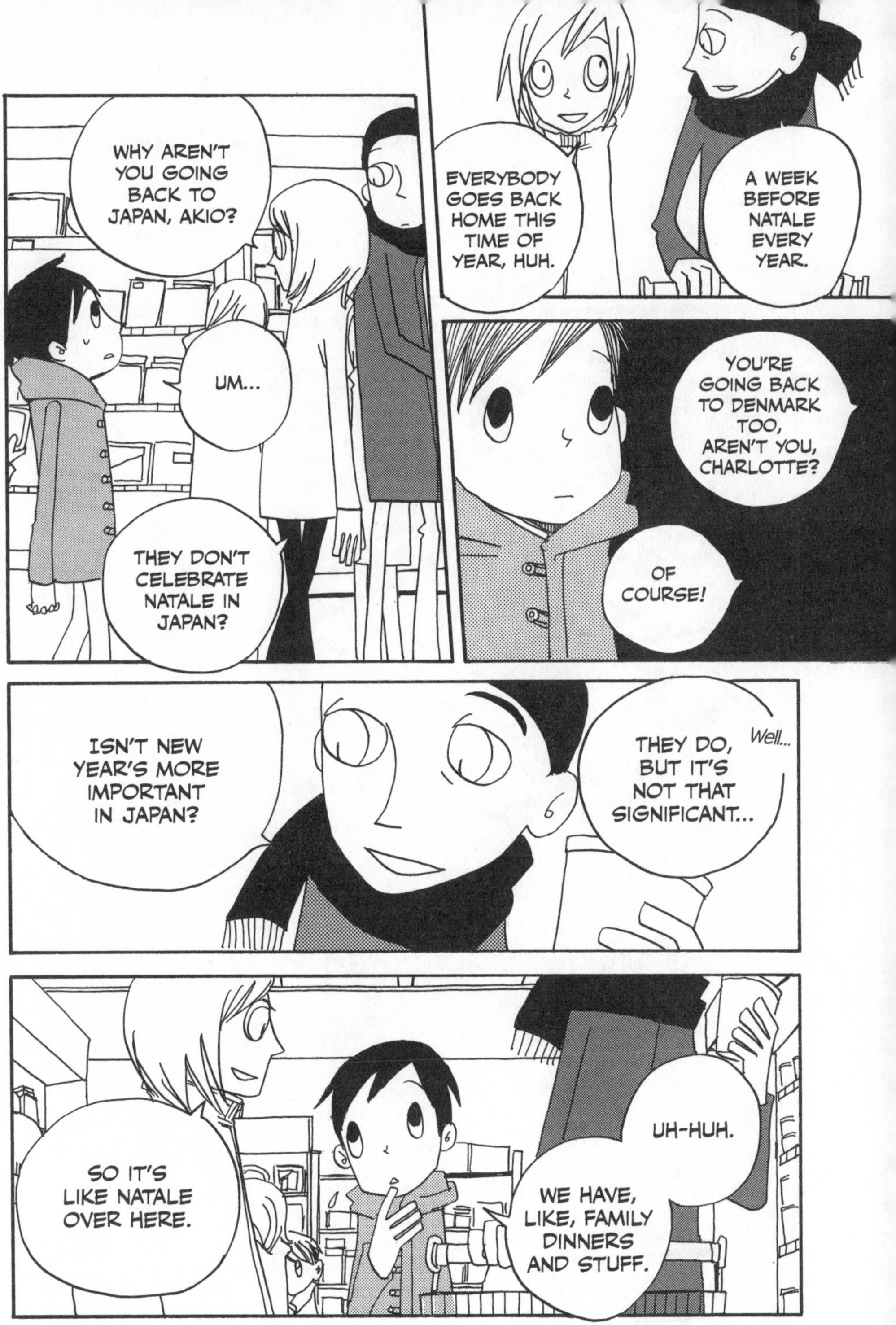
EVERYBODY GOES BACK HOME THIS TIME OF YEAR, HUH.
A WEEK BEFORE NATALE EVERY YEAR.
YOU'RE GOING BACK TO DENMARK TOO, AREN'T YOU, CHARLOTTE?
OF COURSE!
WHY AREN'T YOU GOING BACK TO JAPAN, AKIO?
UM...
THEY DON'T CELEBRATE NATALE IN JAPAN?
Well...
THEY DO, BUT IT'S NOT THAT SIGNIFICANT...
ISN'T NEW YEAR'S MORE IMPORTANT IN JAPAN?
UH-HUH.
WE HAVE, LIKE, FAMILY DINNERS AND STUFF.
SO IT'S LIKE NATALE OVER HERE.

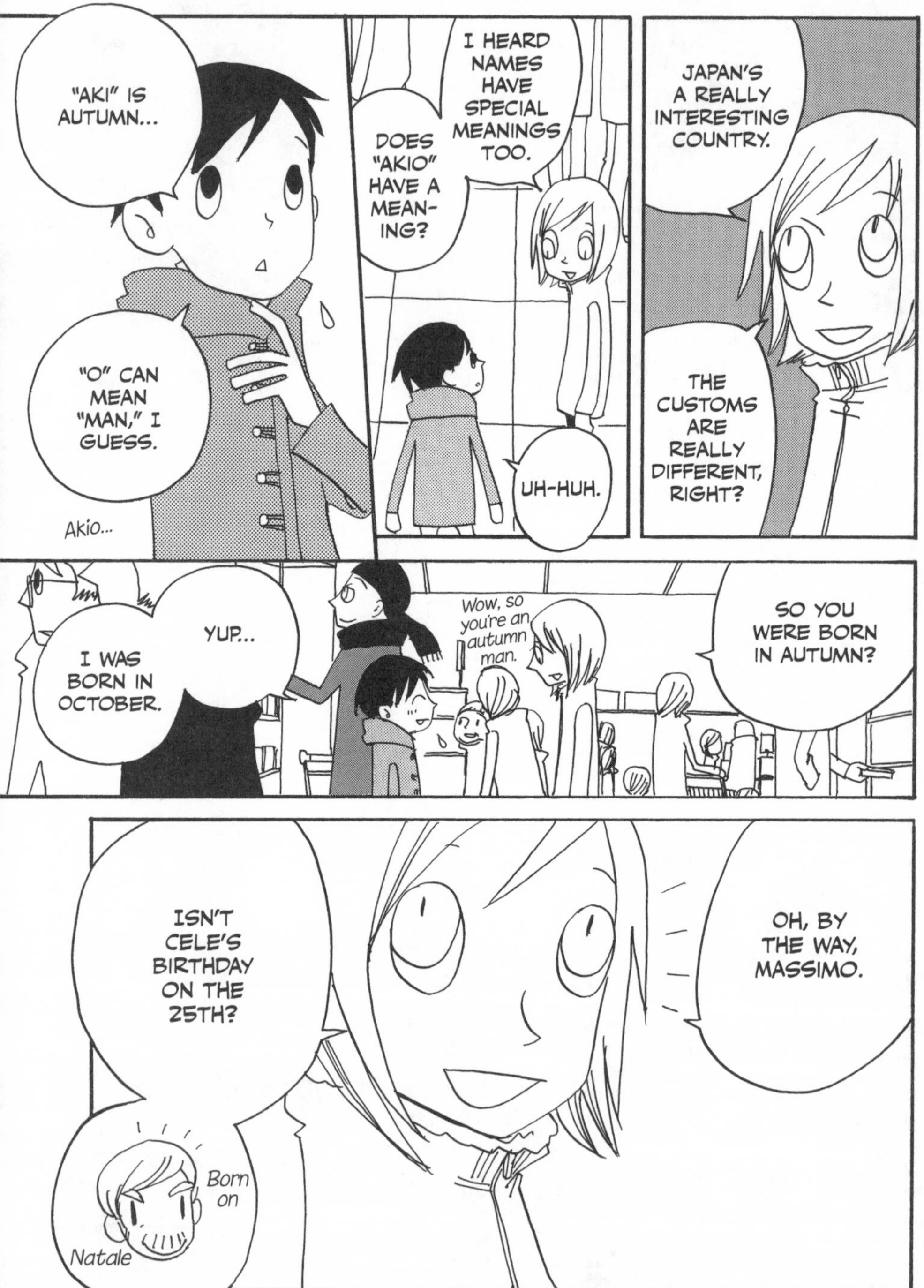
JAPAN'S A REALLY INTERESTING COUNTRY.
THE CUSTOMS ARE REALLY DIFFERENT, RIGHT?
I HEARD NAMES HAVE SPECIAL MEANINGS TOO.
DOES "AKIO" HAVE A MEAN-ING?
UH-HUH.
"AKI" IS AUTUMN...
"O" CAN MEAN "MAN," I GUESS.
Akio...
SO YOU WERE BORN IN AUTUMN?
Wow, so you're an autumn man.
YUP...
I WAS BORN IN OCTOBER.
OH, BY THE WAY, MASSIMO.
ISN'T CELE'S BIRTHDAY ON THE 25TH?
Born on Natale

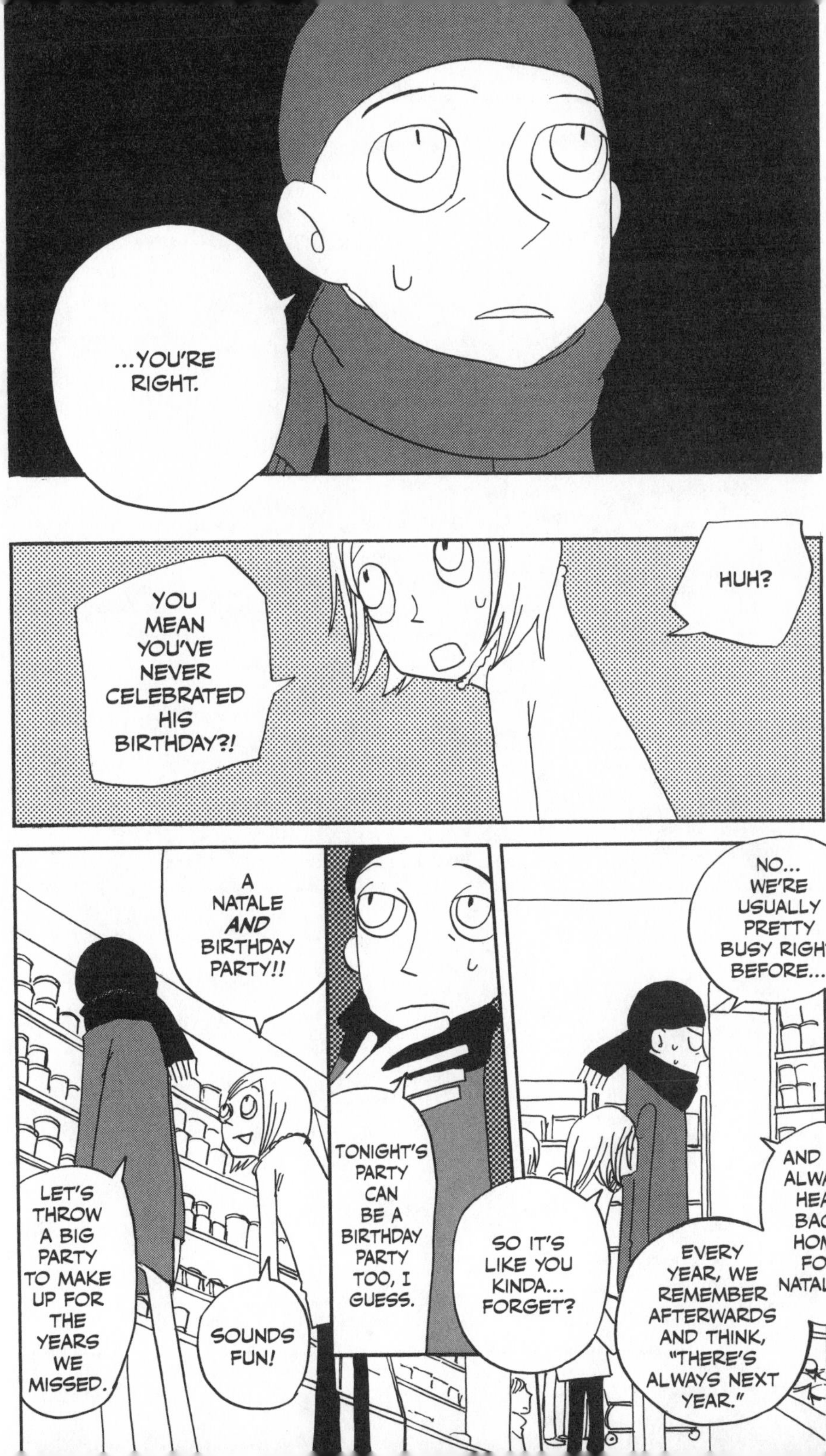
...YOU'RE RIGHT.
HUH?
YOU MEAN YOU'VE NEVER CELEBRATED HIS BIRTHDAY?!
NO... WE'RE USUALLY PRETTY BUSY RIGHT BEFORE...
AND WE ALWAYS HEAD BACK HOME FOR NATALE...
EVERY YEAR, WE REMEMBER AFTERWARDS AND THINK, "THERE'S ALWAYS NEXT YEAR."
SO IT'S LIKE YOU KINDA... FORGET?
TONIGHT'S PARTY CAN BE A BIRTHDAY PARTY TOO, I GUESS.
A NATALE *AND* BIRTHDAY PARTY!!
LET'S THROW A BIG PARTY TO MAKE UP FOR THE YEARS WE MISSED.
SOUNDS FUN!

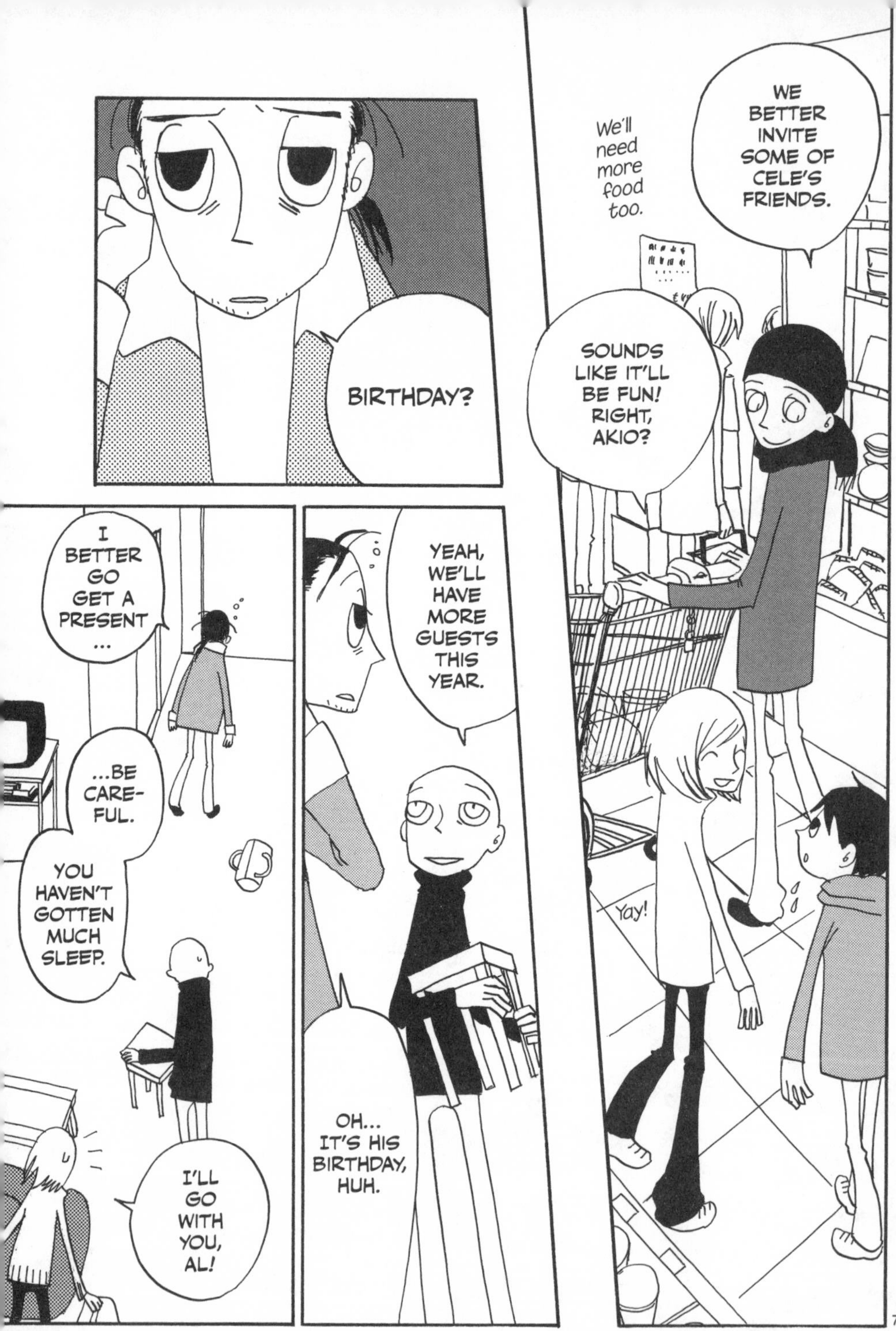
WE BETTER INVITE SOME OF CELE'S FRIENDS.
We'll need more food too.
SOUNDS LIKE IT'LL BE FUN! RIGHT, AKIO?
Yay!
BIRTHDAY?
YEAH, WE'LL HAVE MORE GUESTS THIS YEAR.
OH... IT'S HIS BIRTHDAY, HUH.
I BETTER GO GET A PRESENT ...
...BE CARE-FUL.
YOU HAVEN'T GOTTEN MUCH SLEEP.
I'LL GO WITH YOU, AL!

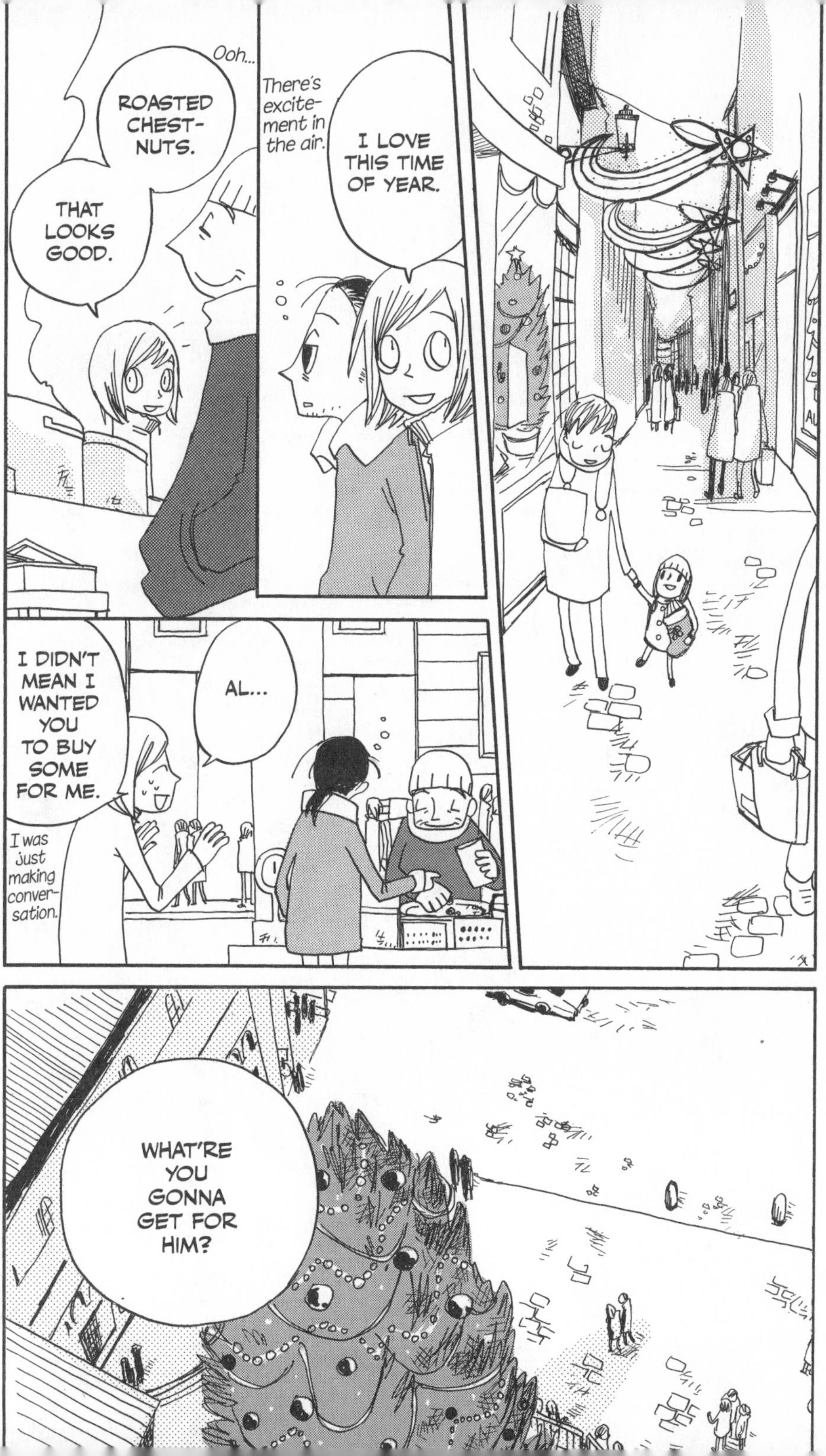
I LOVE THIS TIME OF YEAR.
There's excitement in the air.
Ooh...
ROASTED CHEST-NUTS.
THAT LOOKS GOOD.
AL...
I DIDN'T MEAN I WANTED YOU TO BUY SOME FOR ME.
I was just making conversation.
WHAT'RE YOU GONNA GET FOR HIM?

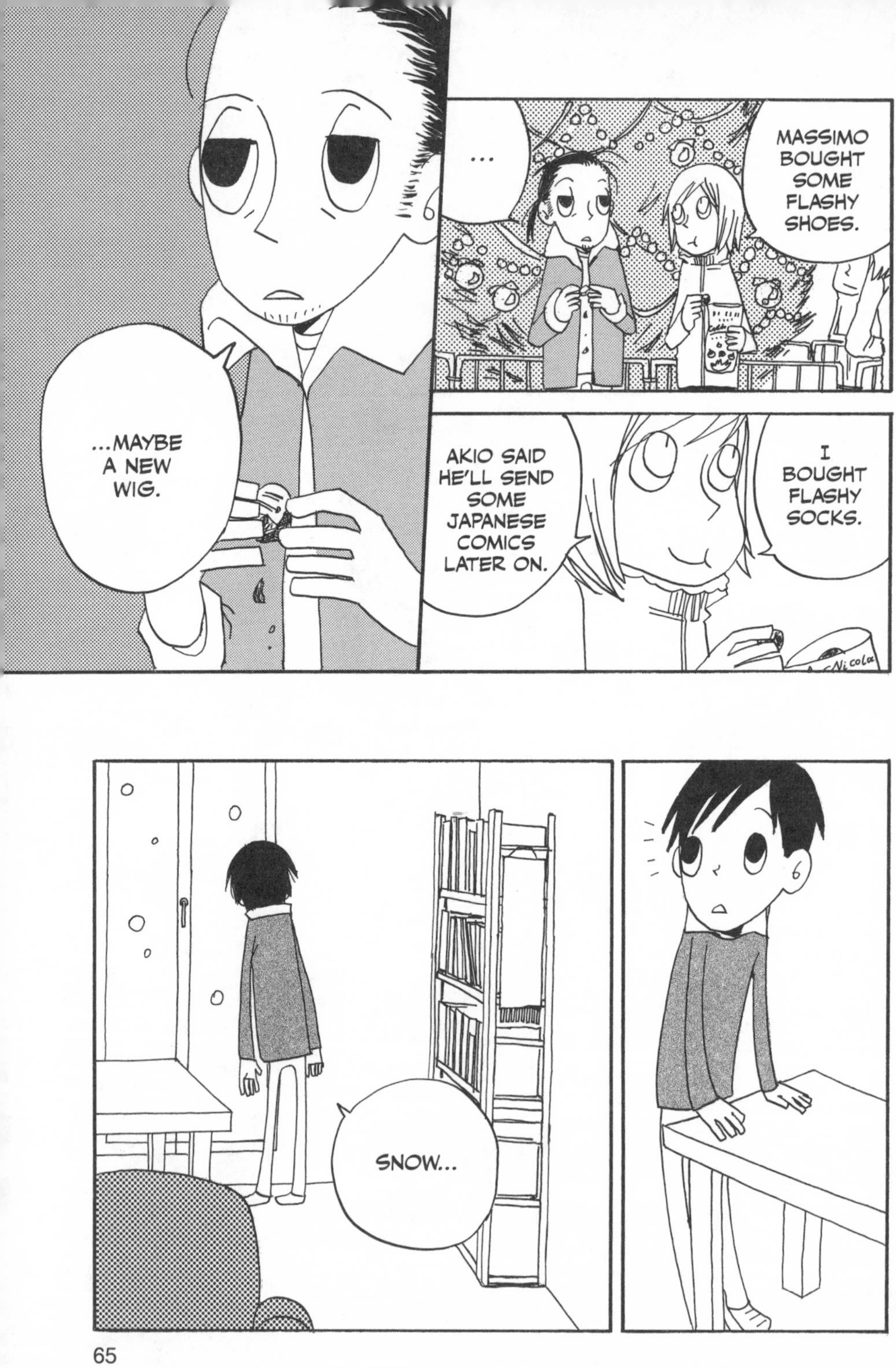
MASSIMO BOUGHT SOME FLASHY SHOES.
...
I BOUGHT FLASHY SOCKS.
AKIO SAID HE'LL SEND SOME JAPANESE COMICS LATER ON.
...MAYBE A NEW WIG.
SNOW...

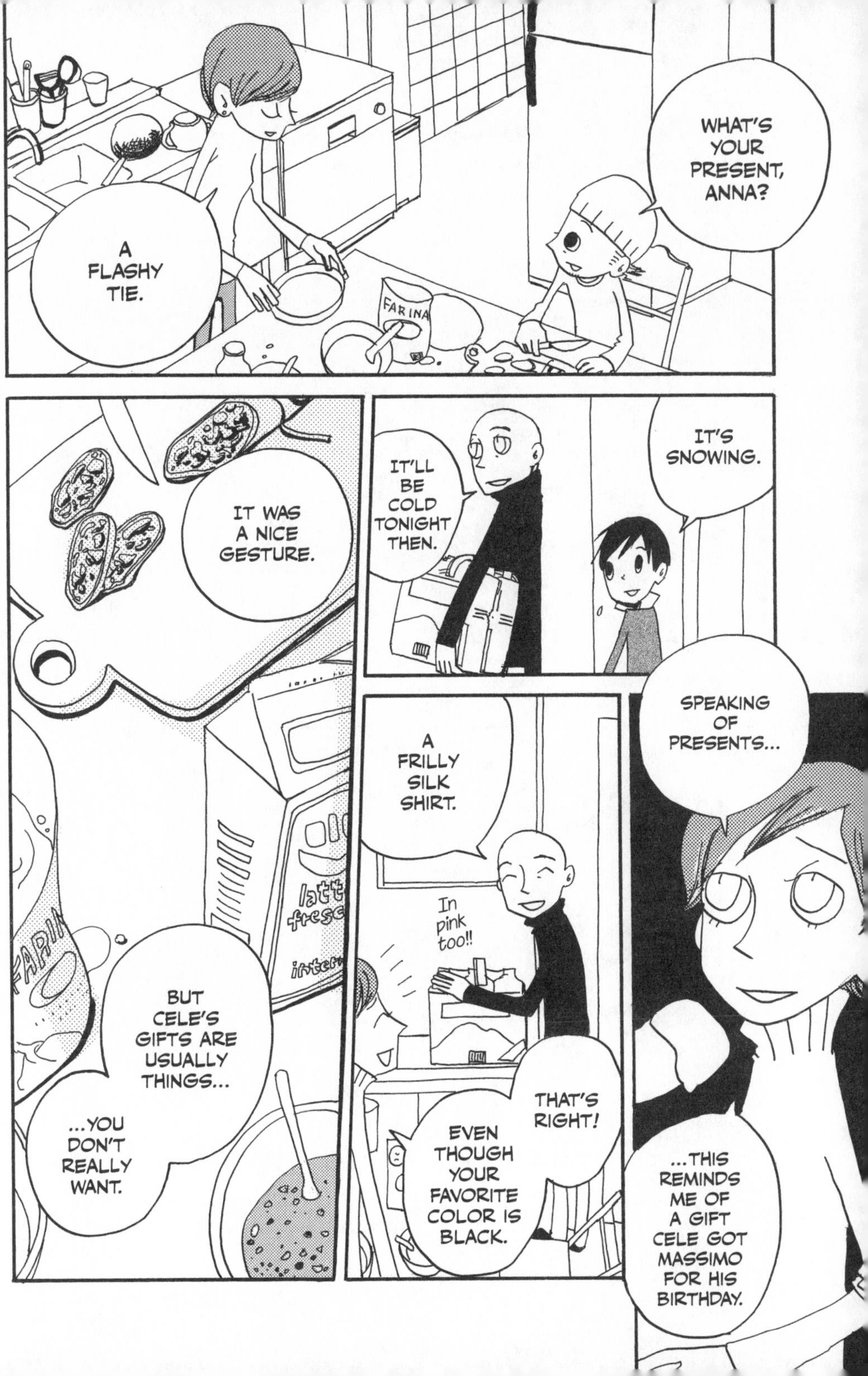
WHAT'S YOUR PRESENT, ANNA?
A FLASHY TIE.
IT'S SNOWING.
IT'LL BE COLD TONIGHT THEN.
SPEAKING OF PRESENTS...
...THIS REMINDS ME OF A GIFT CELE GOT MASSIMO FOR HIS BIRTHDAY.
A FRILLY SILK SHIRT.
In pink too!!
THAT'S RIGHT!
EVEN THOUGH YOUR FAVORITE COLOR IS BLACK.
IT WAS A NICE GESTURE.
BUT CELE'S GIFTS ARE USUALLY THINGS...
...YOU DON'T REALLY WANT.

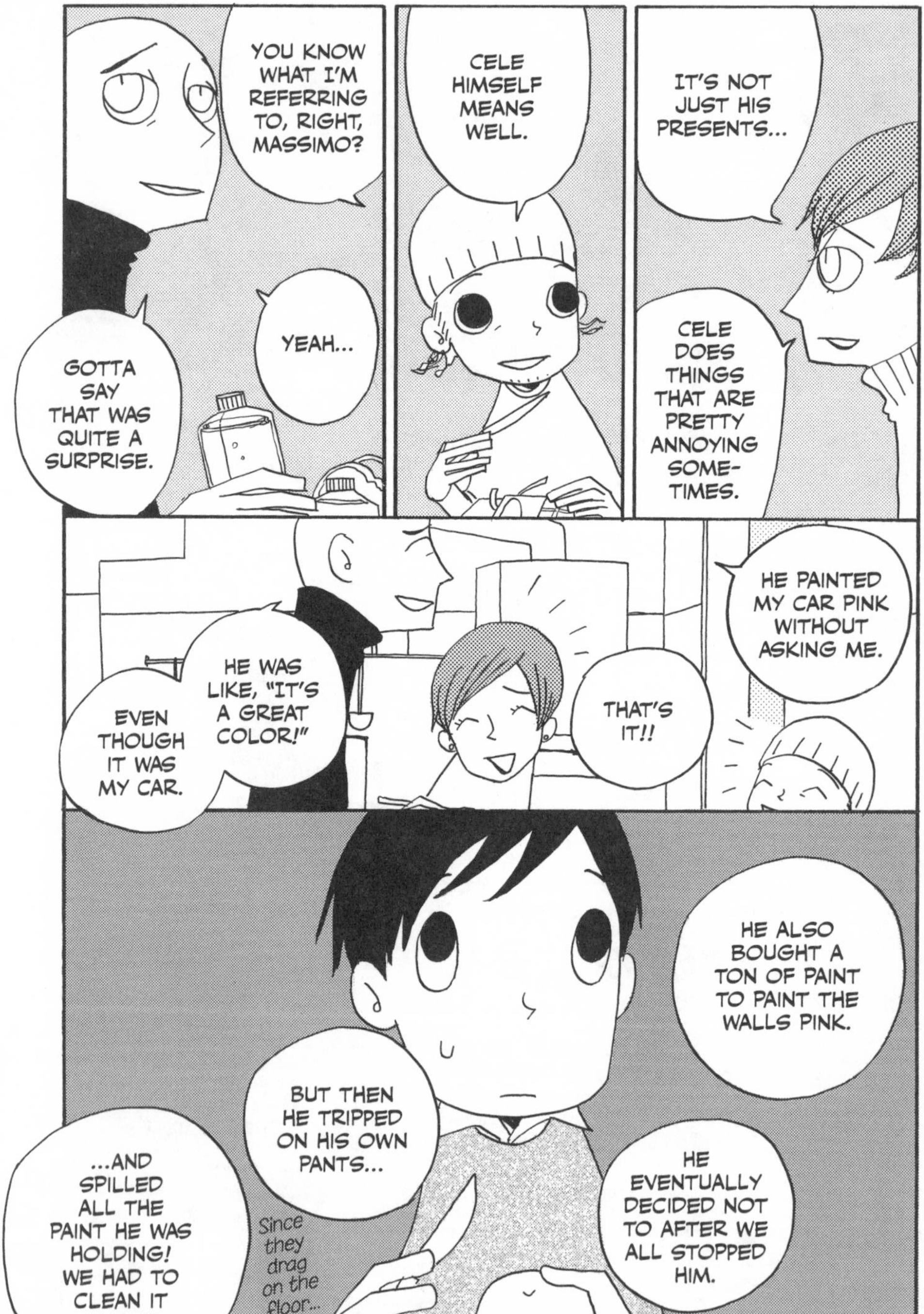
IT'S NOT JUST HIS PRESENTS...
CELE DOES THINGS THAT ARE PRETTY ANNOYING SOME-TIMES.
CELE HIMSELF MEANS WELL.
YOU KNOW WHAT I'M REFERRING TO, RIGHT, MASSIMO?
YEAH...
GOTTA SAY THAT WAS QUITE A SURPRISE.
HE PAINTED MY CAR PINK WITHOUT ASKING ME.
THAT'S IT!!
HE WAS LIKE, "IT'S A GREAT COLOR!"
EVEN THOUGH IT WAS MY CAR.
HE ALSO BOUGHT A TON OF PAINT TO PAINT THE WALLS PINK.
HE EVENTUALLY DECIDED NOT TO AFTER WE ALL STOPPED HIM.
BUT THEN HE TRIPPED ON HIS OWN PANTS...
Since they drag on the floor...
...AND SPILLED ALL THE PAINT HE WAS HOLDING! WE HAD TO CLEAN IT ALL UP.

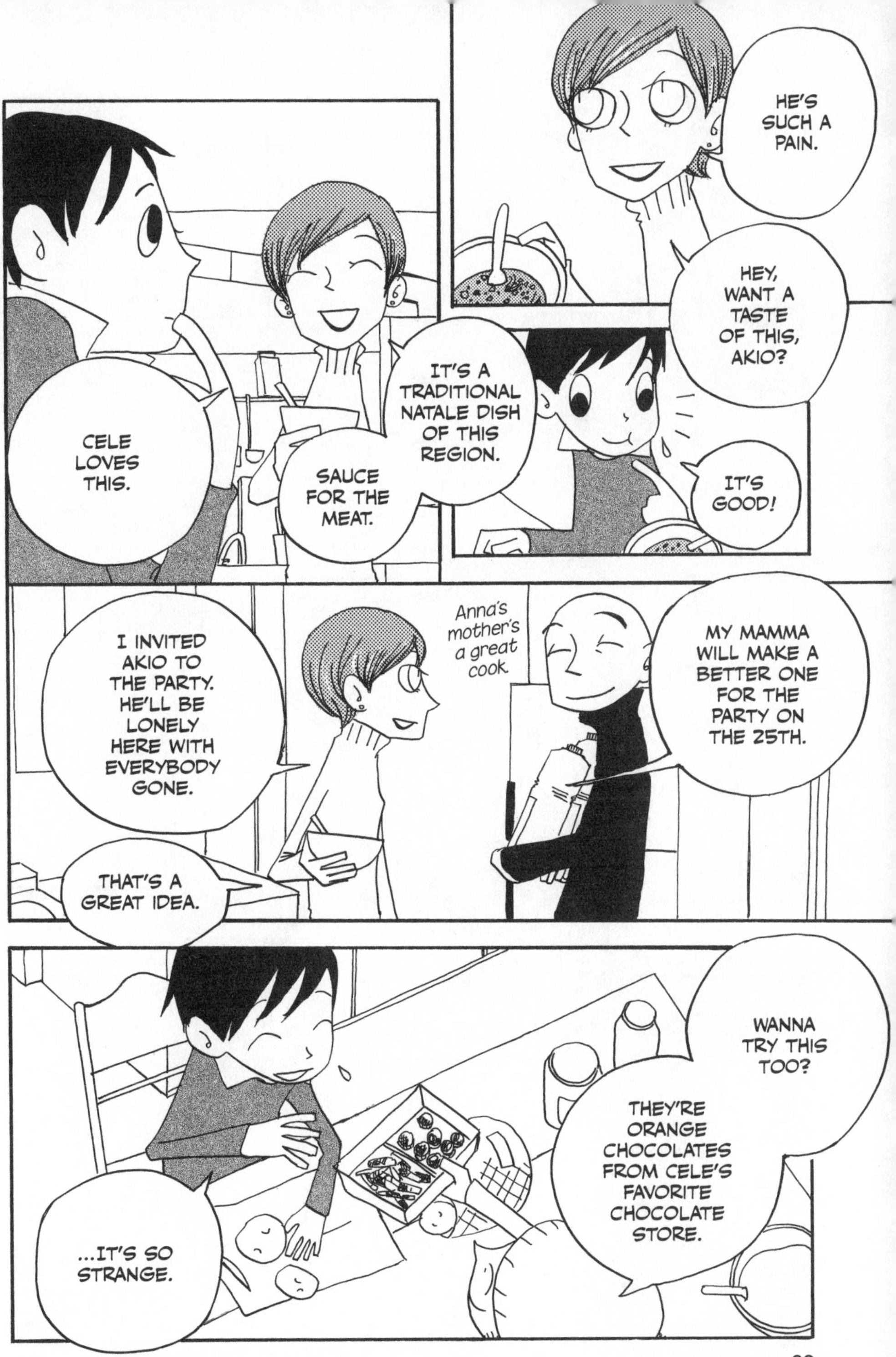
HE'S SUCH A PAIN.
HEY, WANT A TASTE OF THIS, AKIO?
IT'S GOOD!
IT'S A TRADITIONAL NATALE DISH OF THIS REGION.
SAUCE FOR THE MEAT.
CELE LOVES THIS.
MY MAMMA WILL MAKE A BETTER ONE FOR THE PARTY ON THE 25TH.
Anna's mother's a great cook.
I INVITED AKIO TO THE PARTY. HE'LL BE LONELY HERE WITH EVERYBODY GONE.
THAT'S A GREAT IDEA.
WANNA TRY THIS TOO?
THEY'RE ORANGE CHOCOLATES FROM CELE'S FAVORITE CHOCOLATE STORE.
...IT'S SO STRANGE.

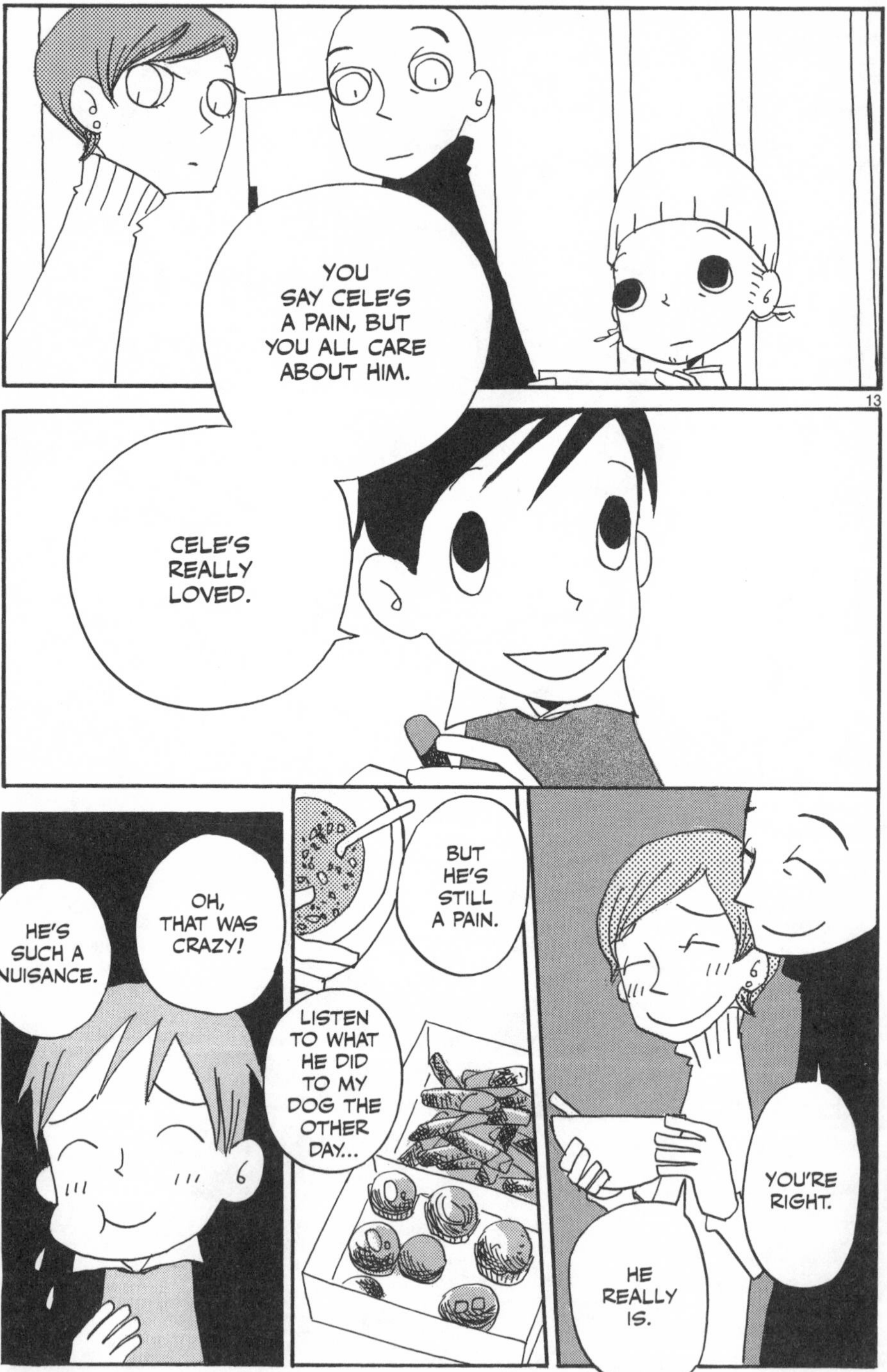
YOU SAY CELE'S A PAIN, BUT YOU ALL CARE ABOUT HIM.
CELE'S REALLY LOVED.
YOU'RE RIGHT.
HE REALLY IS.
BUT HE'S STILL A PAIN.
LISTEN TO WHAT HE DID TO MY DOG THE OTHER DAY...
OH, THAT WAS CRAZY!
HE'S SUCH A NUISANCE.

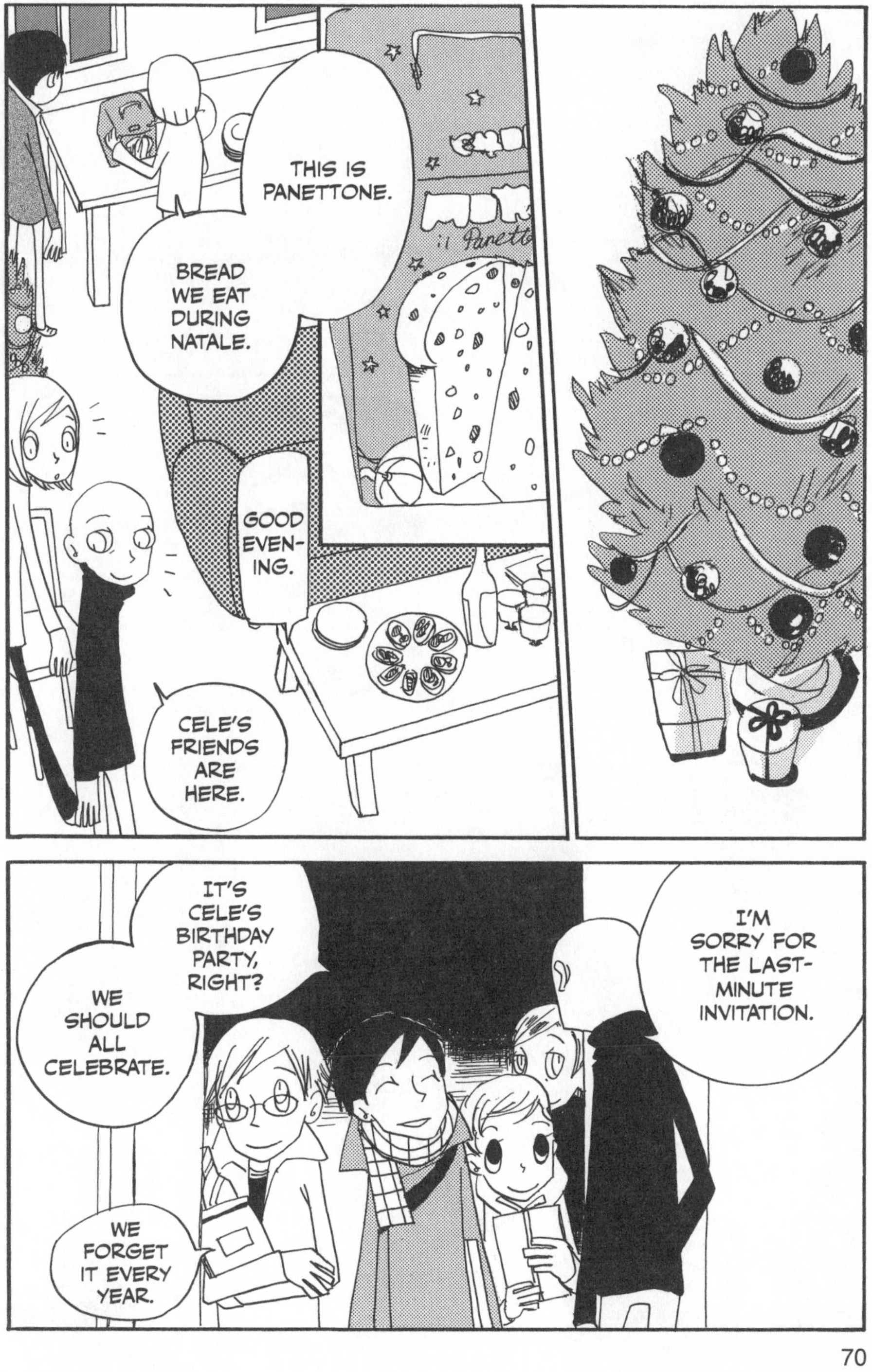
THIS IS PANETTONE.
BREAD WE EAT DURING NATALE.
GOOD EVENING.
CELE'S FRIENDS ARE HERE.
I'M SORRY FOR THE LAST-MINUTE INVITATION.
IT'S CELE'S BIRTHDAY PARTY, RIGHT?
WE SHOULD ALL CELEBRATE.
WE FORGET IT EVERY YEAR.

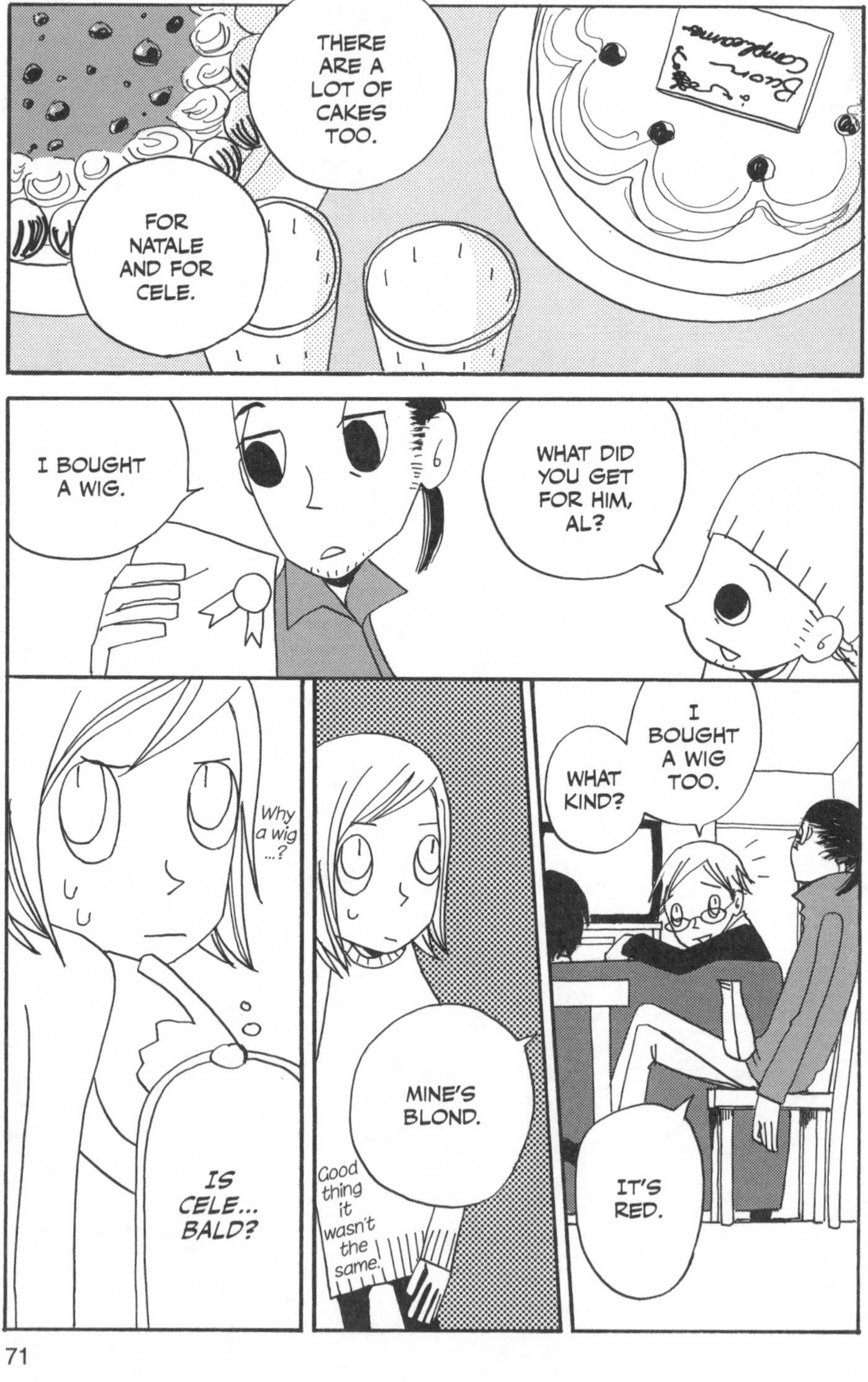
THERE ARE A LOT OF CAKES TOO.
FOR NATALE AND FOR CELE.
WHAT DID YOU GET FOR HIM, AL?
I BOUGHT A WIG.
I BOUGHT A WIG TOO.
WHAT KIND?
IT'S RED.
MINE'S BLOND.
Good thing it wasn't the same.
Why a wig ...?
IS CELE... BALD?

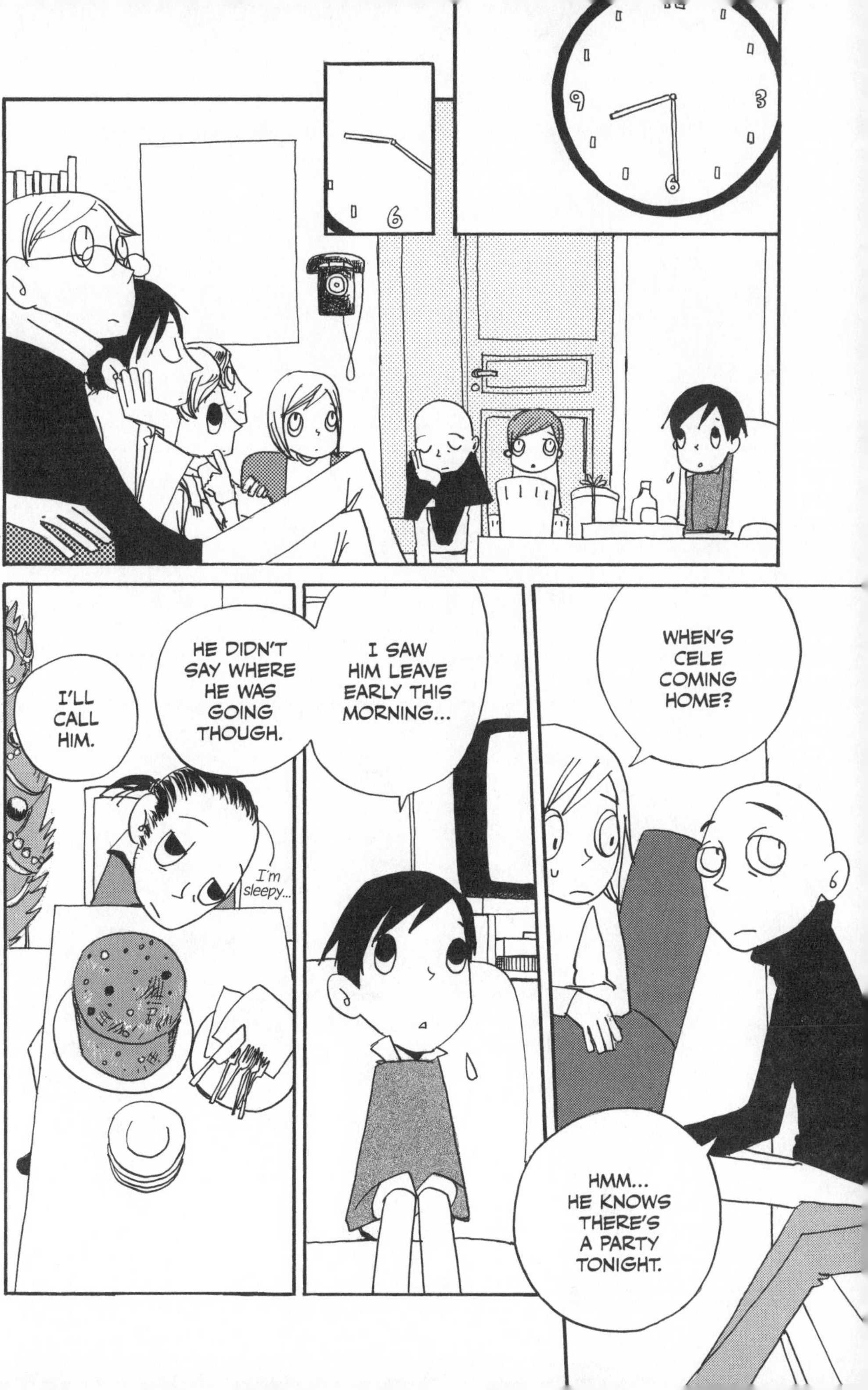
WHEN'S CELE COMING HOME?
HMM... HE KNOWS THERE'S A PARTY TONIGHT.
I SAW HIM LEAVE EARLY THIS MORNING...
HE DIDN'T SAY WHERE HE WAS GOING THOUGH.
I'LL CALL HIM.
I'm sleepy...

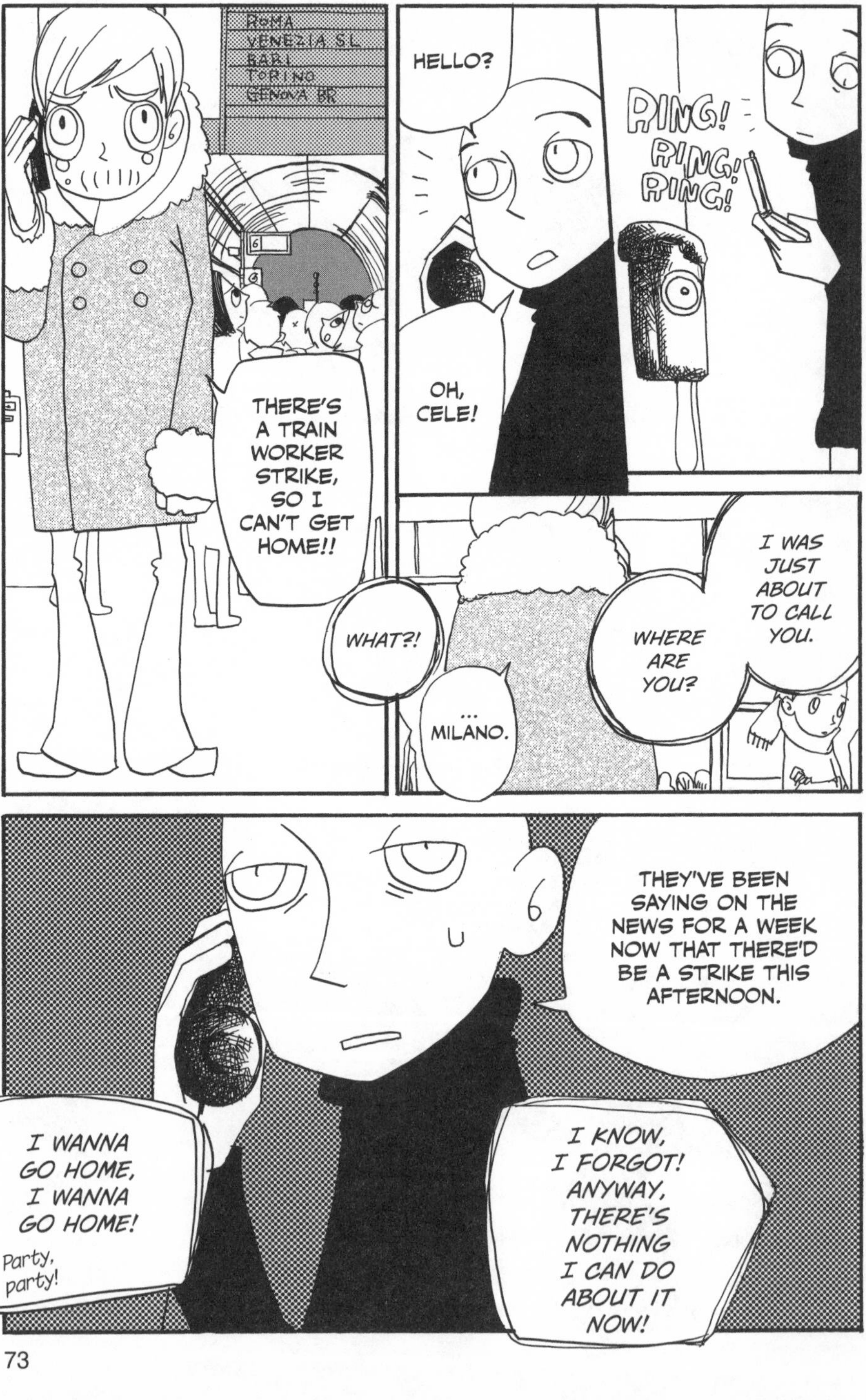
RING! RING! RING!
HELLO?
OH, CELE!
I WAS JUST ABOUT TO CALL YOU.
WHERE ARE YOU?
WHAT?!
... MILANO.
ROMA
VENEZIA SL
BARI
TORINO
GENOVA BR
THERE'S A TRAIN WORKER STRIKE, SO I CAN'T GET HOME!!
THEY'VE BEEN SAYING ON THE NEWS FOR A WEEK NOW THAT THERE'D BE A STRIKE THIS AFTERNOON.
I KNOW, I FORGOT! ANYWAY, THERE'S NOTHING I CAN DO ABOUT IT NOW!
I WANNA GO HOME, I WANNA GO HOME!
Party, party!

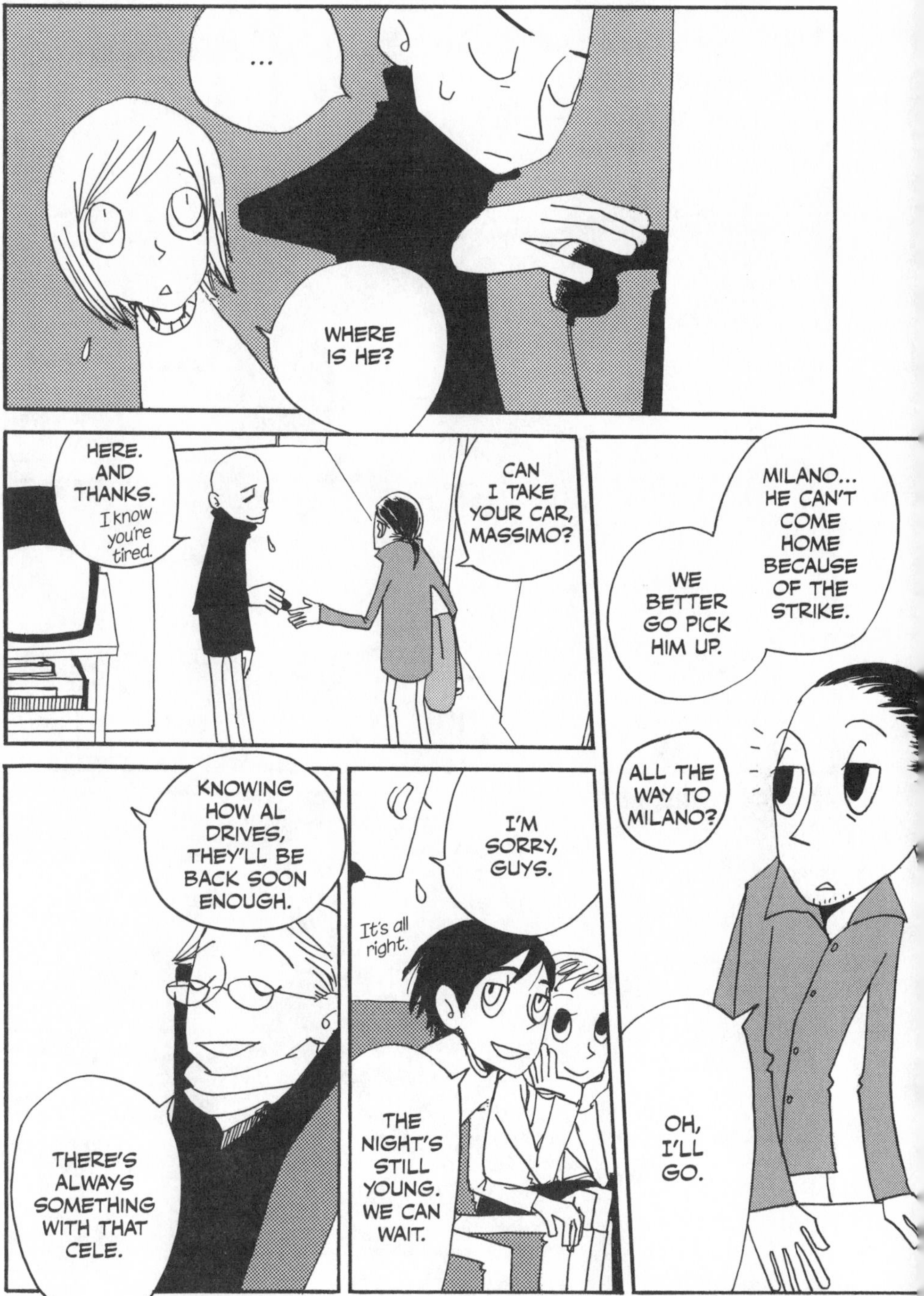
...
WHERE IS HE?
MILANO... HE CAN'T COME HOME BECAUSE OF THE STRIKE.
WE BETTER GO PICK HIM UP.
ALL THE WAY TO MILANO?
OH, I'LL GO.
CAN I TAKE YOUR CAR, MASSIMO?
HERE. AND THANKS.
I know you're tired.
I'M SORRY, GUYS.
It's all right.
THE NIGHT'S STILL YOUNG. WE CAN WAIT.
KNOWING HOW AL DRIVES, THEY'LL BE BACK SOON ENOUGH.
THERE'S ALWAYS SOMETHING WITH THAT CELE.

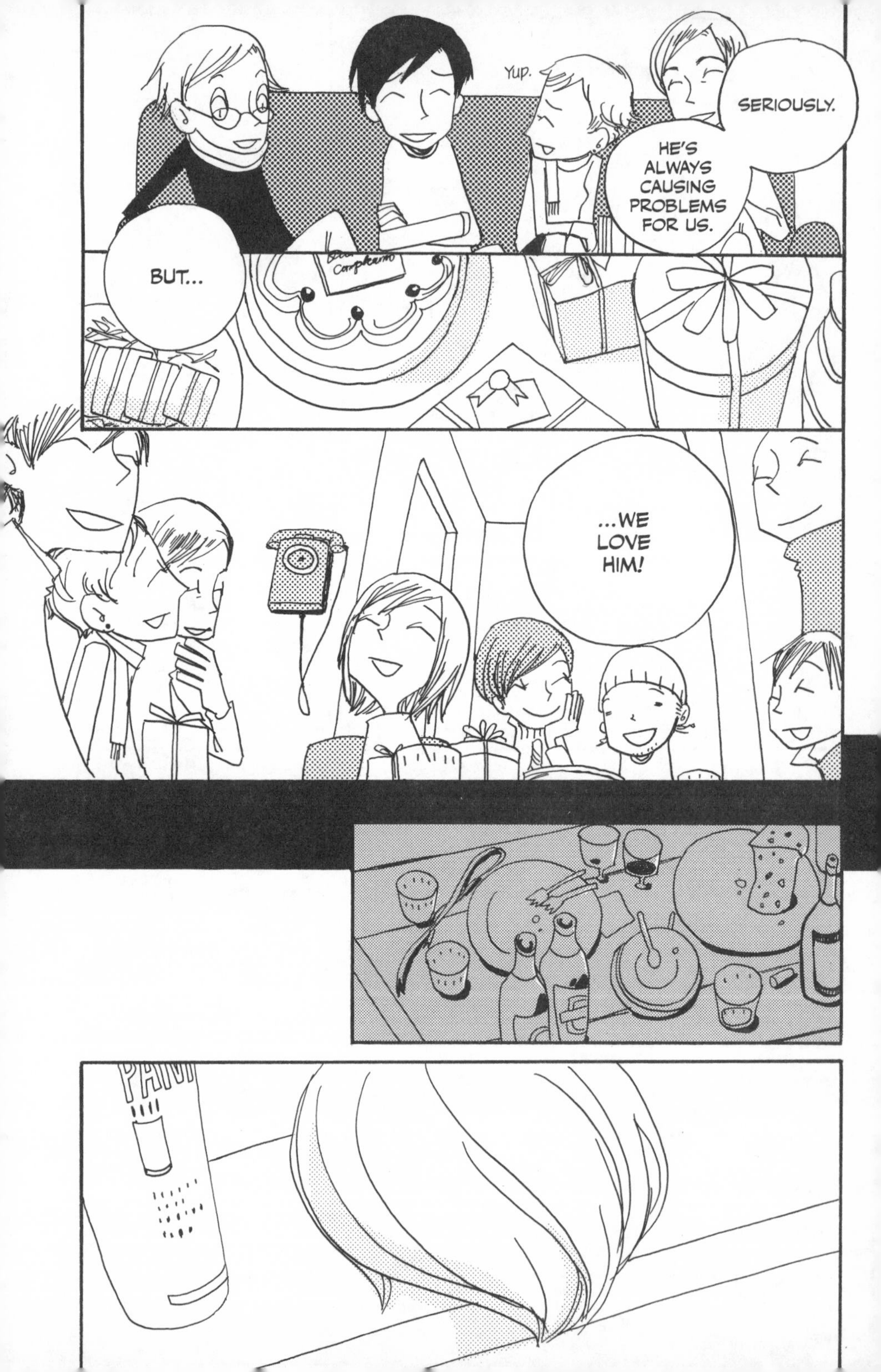
HE'S ALWAYS CAUSING PROBLEMS FOR US.
SERIOUSLY.
Yup.
BUT...
...WE LOVE HIM!

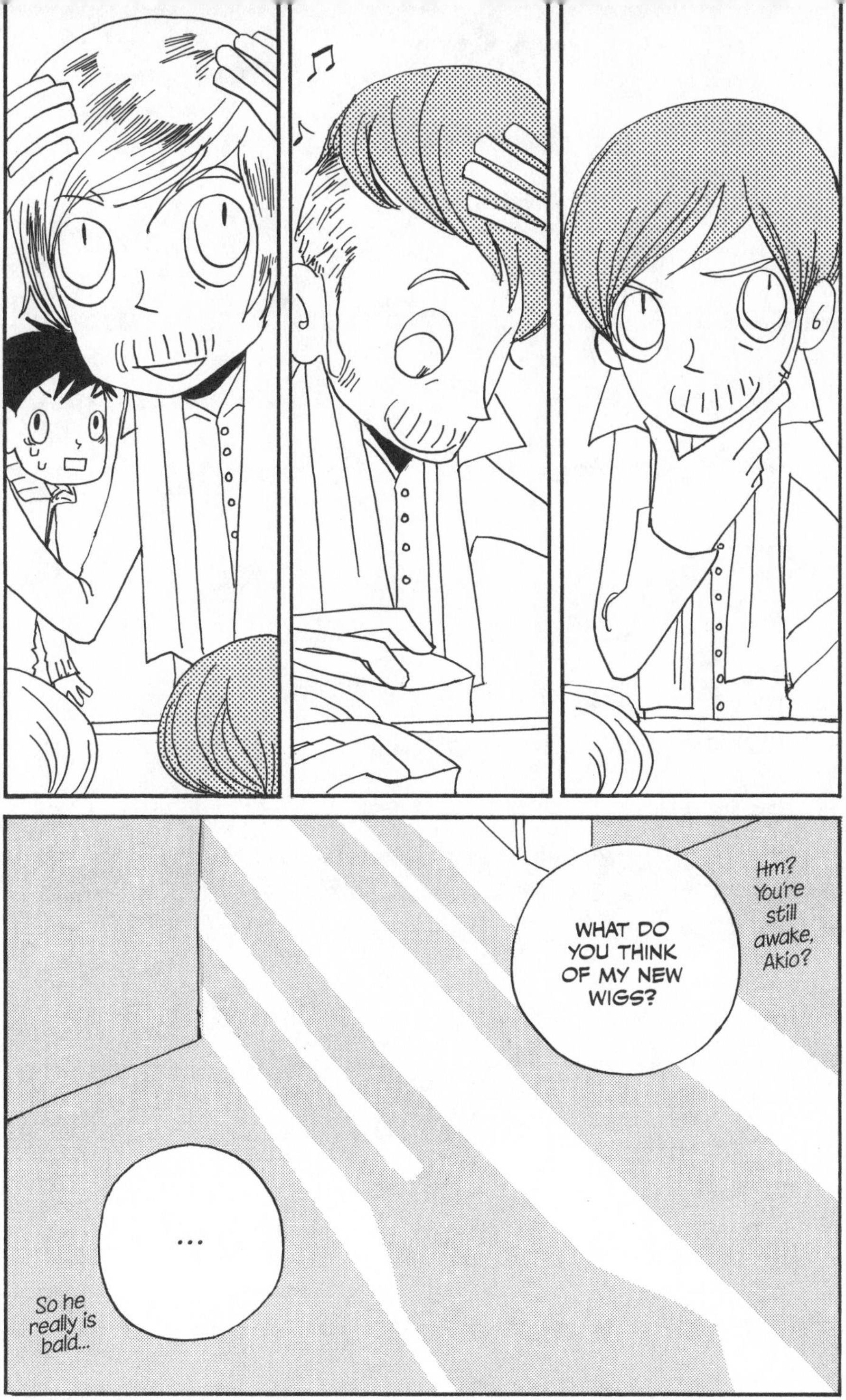
Hm? You're still awake, Akio?
WHAT DO YOU THINK OF MY NEW WIGS?
...
So he really is bald...

LA QUINTA CAMERA
Capitolo 3

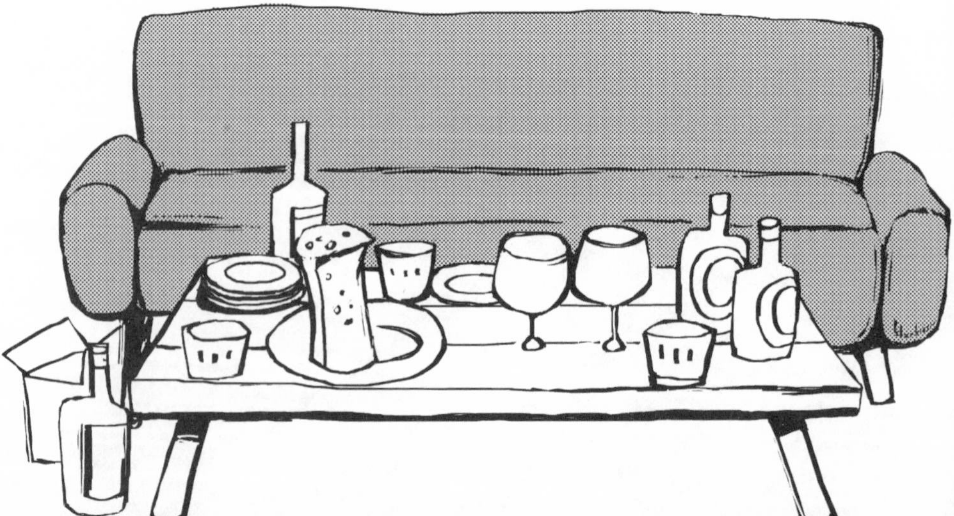

La Quinta Camera
Capitolo 4

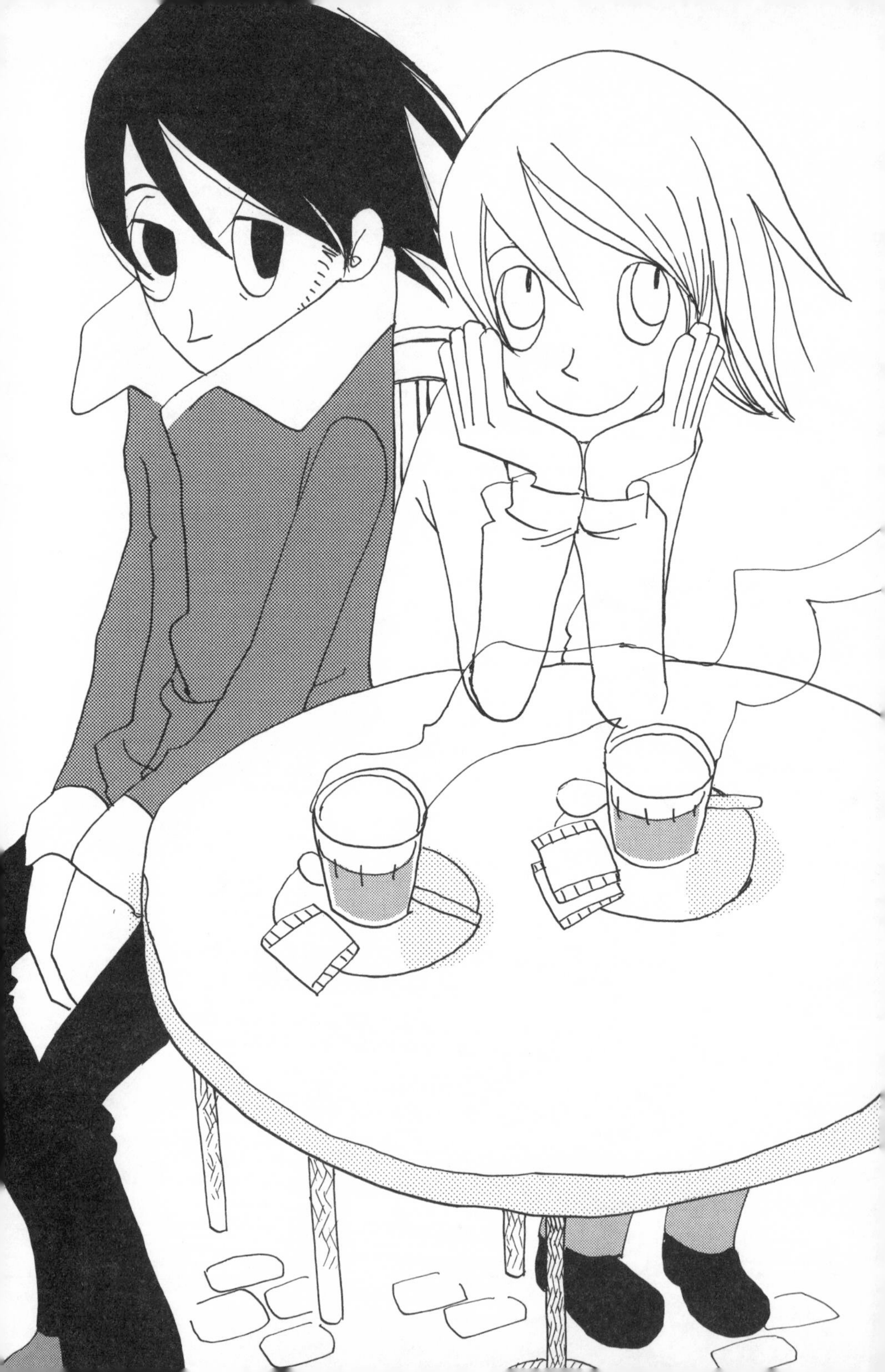

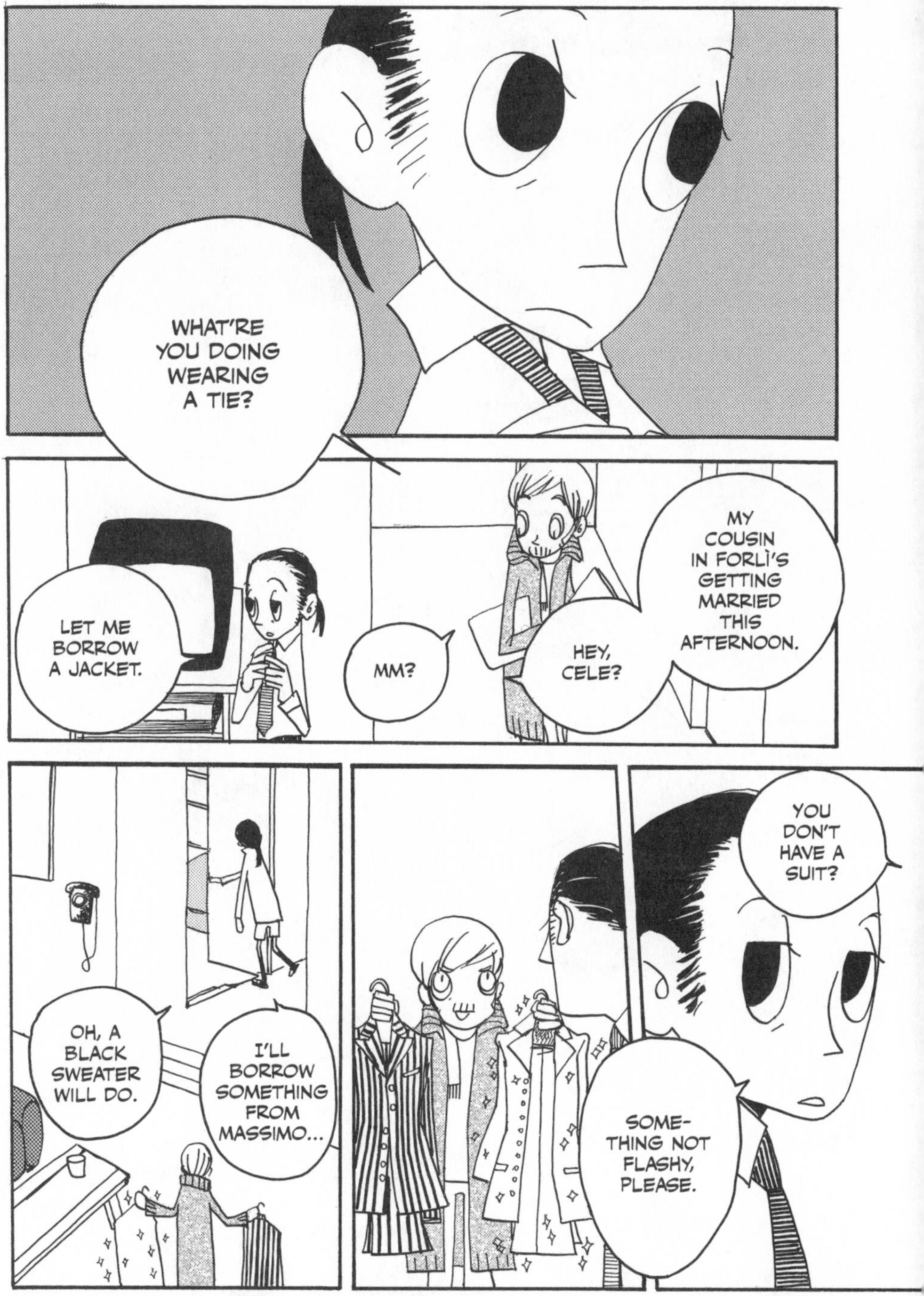
WHAT'RE YOU DOING WEARING A TIE?
HEY, CELE?
MM?
MY COUSIN IN FORLÌ'S GETTING MARRIED THIS AFTERNOON.
LET ME BORROW A JACKET.
YOU DON'T HAVE A SUIT?
SOME-THING NOT FLASHY, PLEASE.
I'LL BORROW SOMETHING FROM MASSIMO...
OH, A BLACK SWEATER WILL DO.

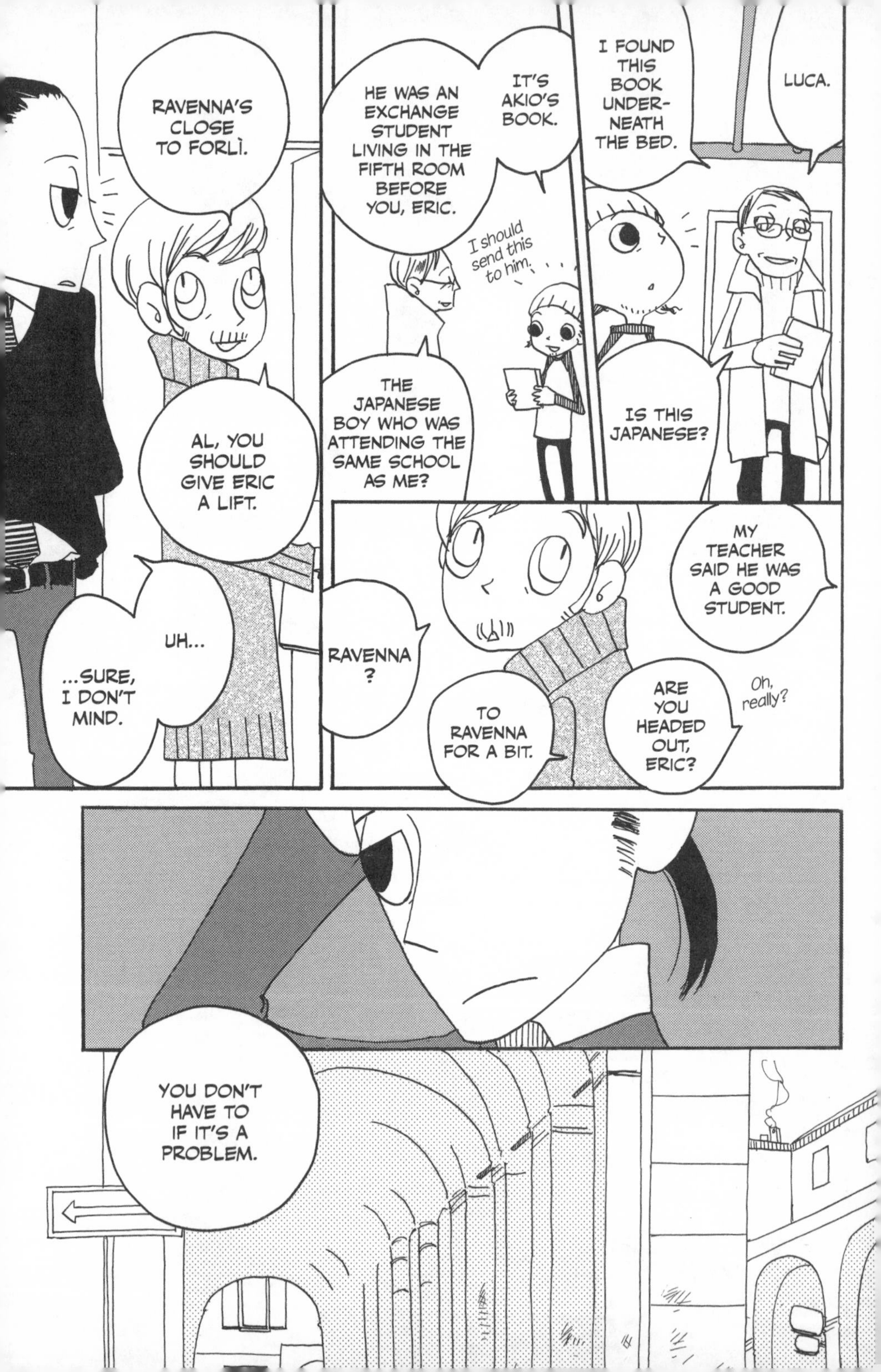
LUCA.
I FOUND THIS BOOK UNDERNEATH THE BED.
IS THIS JAPANESE?
IT'S AKIO'S BOOK.
HE WAS AN EXCHANGE STUDENT LIVING IN THE FIFTH ROOM BEFORE YOU, ERIC.
I should send this to him.
THE JAPANESE BOY WHO WAS ATTENDING THE SAME SCHOOL AS ME?
MY TEACHER SAID HE WAS A GOOD STUDENT.
Oh, really?
ARE YOU HEADED OUT, ERIC?
TO RAVENNA FOR A BIT.
RAVENNA?
RAVENNA'S CLOSE TO FORLÌ.
AL, YOU SHOULD GIVE ERIC A LIFT.
UH...
...SURE, I DON'T MIND.
YOU DON'T HAVE TO IF IT'S A PROBLEM.

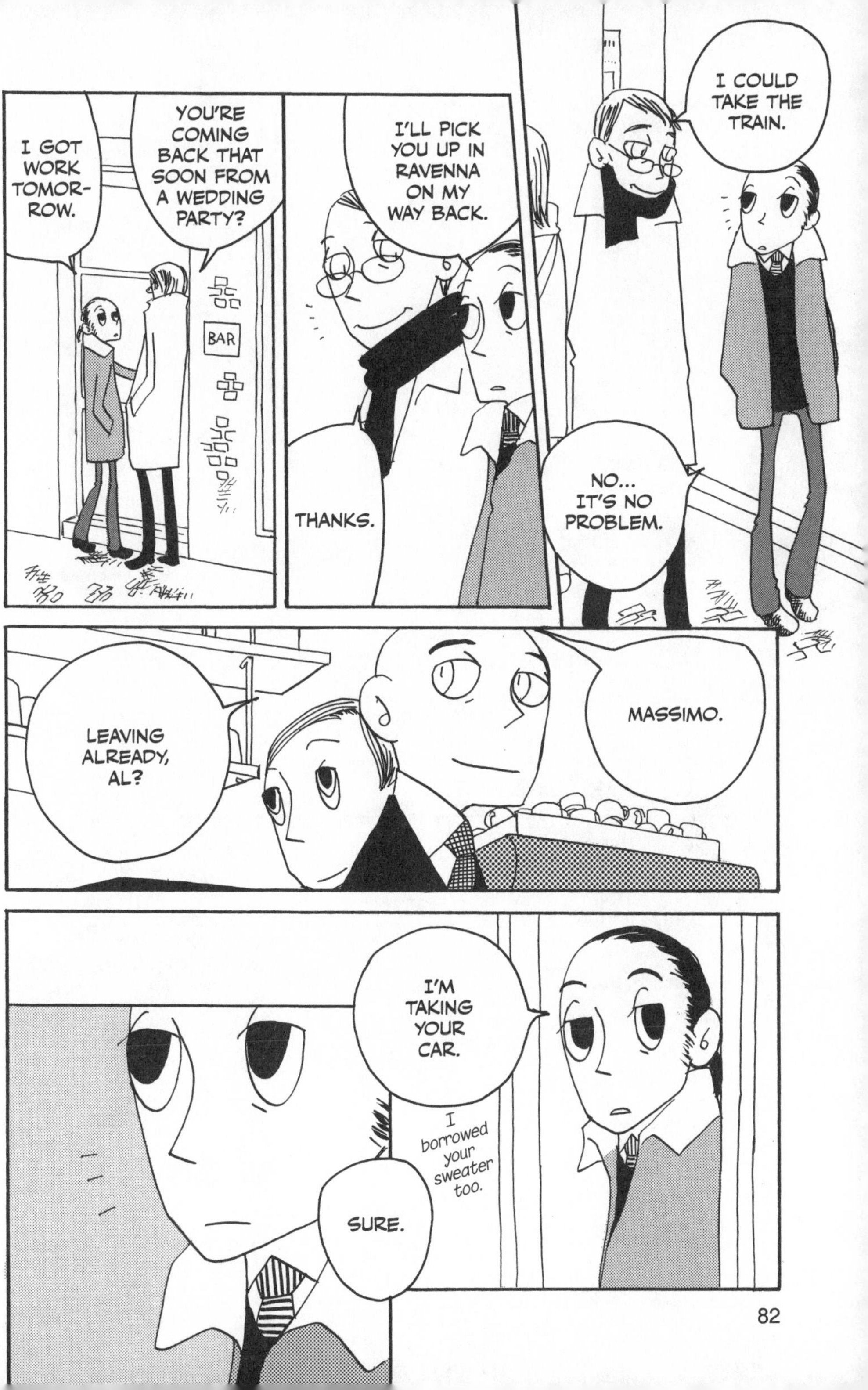
I COULD TAKE THE TRAIN.
NO... IT'S NO PROBLEM.
I'LL PICK YOU UP IN RAVENNA ON MY WAY BACK.
THANKS.
YOU'RE COMING BACK THAT SOON FROM A WEDDING PARTY?
I GOT WORK TOMOR-ROW.
BAR
MASSIMO.
LEAVING ALREADY, AL?
I'M TAKING YOUR CAR.
I borrowed your sweater too.
SURE.

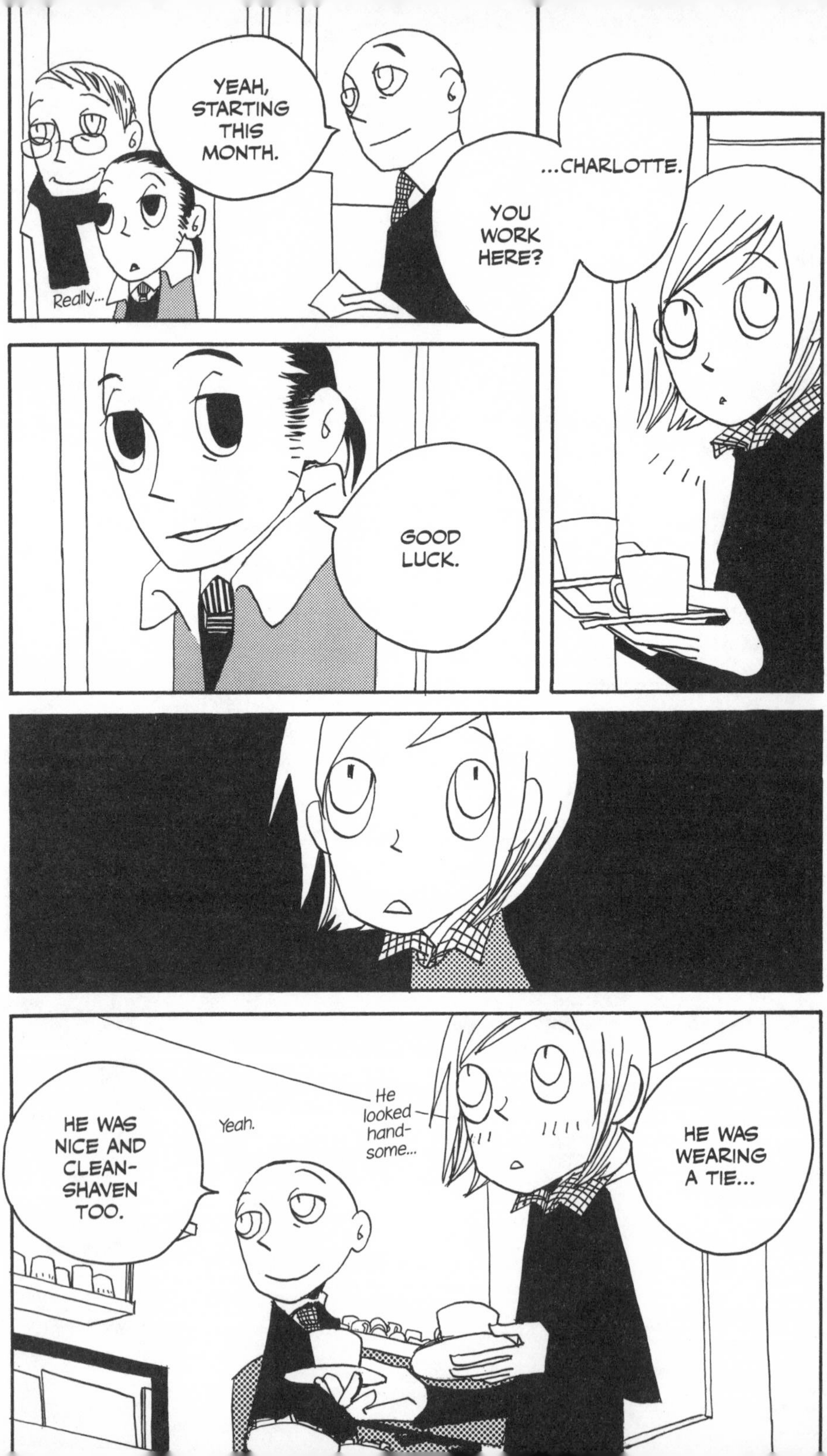
...CHARLOTTE.
YOU WORK HERE?
YEAH, STARTING THIS MONTH.
Really...
GOOD LUCK.
HE WAS WEARING A TIE...
He looked hand-some...
Yeah.
HE WAS NICE AND CLEAN-SHAVEN TOO.

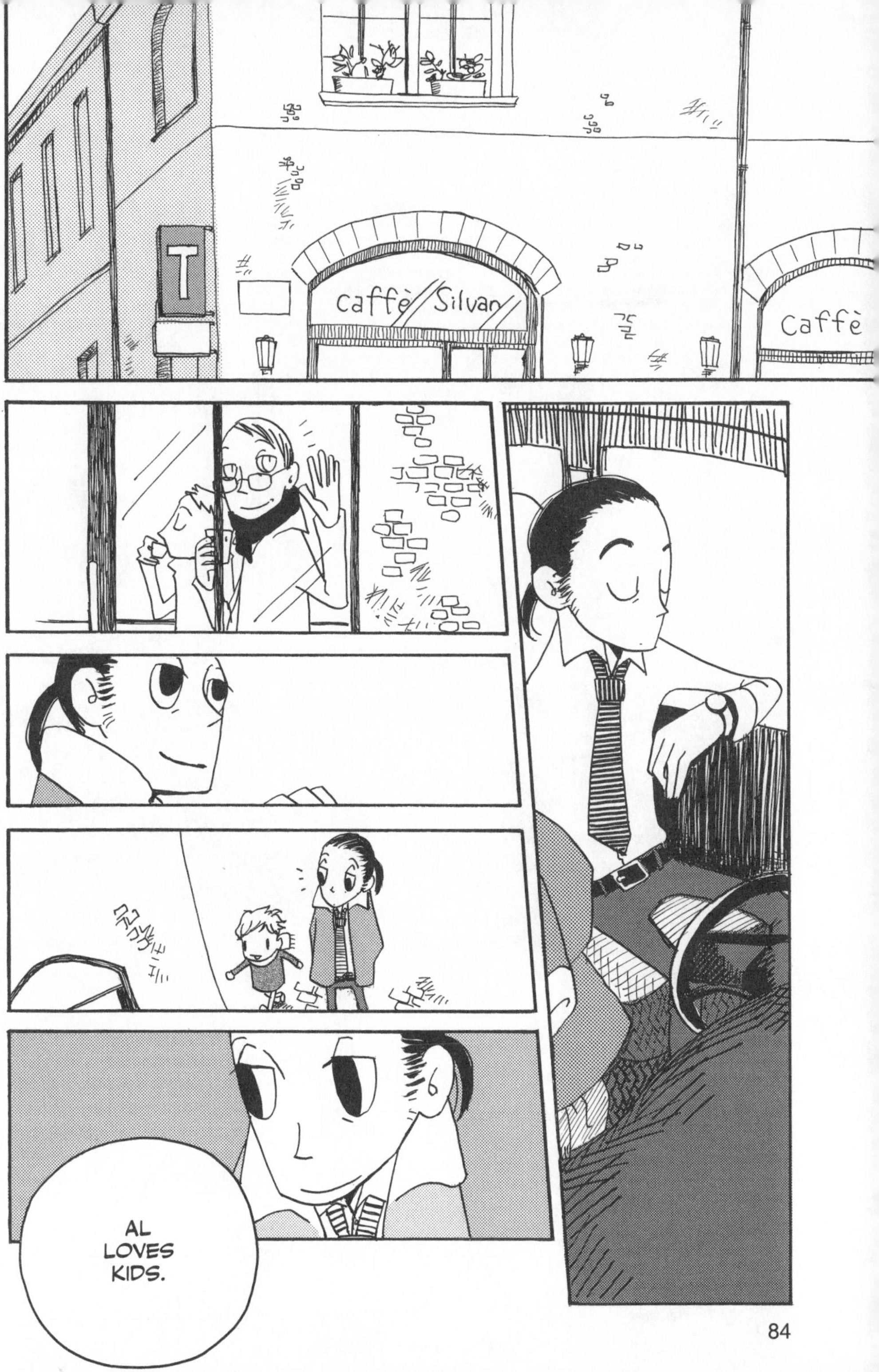
T
caffè Silvan
caffè
AL LOVES KIDS.

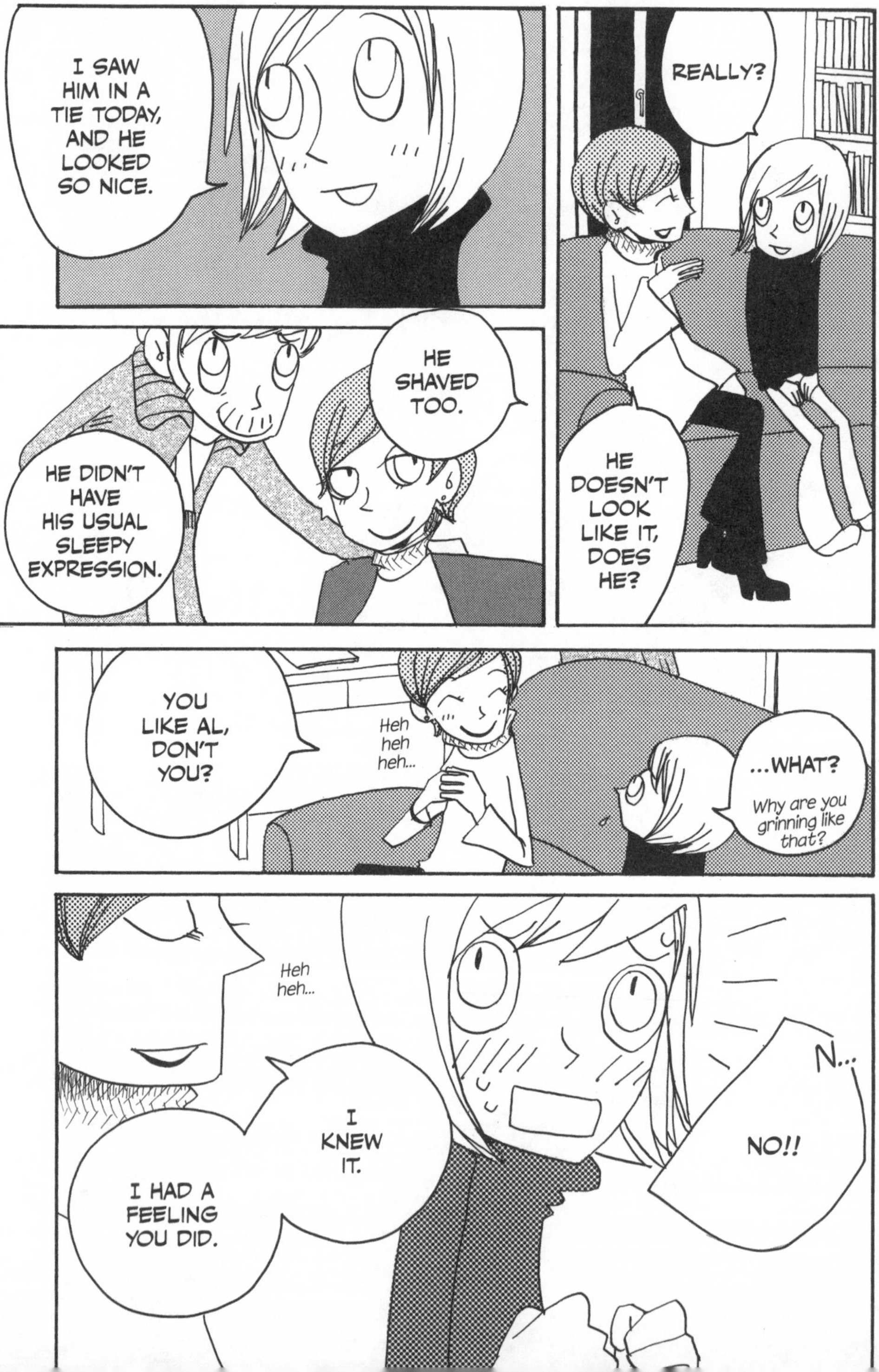
REALLY?
HE DOESN'T LOOK LIKE IT, DOES HE?
I SAW HIM IN A TIE TODAY, AND HE LOOKED SO NICE.
HE SHAVED TOO.
HE DIDN'T HAVE HIS USUAL SLEEPY EXPRESSION.
...WHAT?
Why are you grinning like that?
Heh heh heh...
YOU LIKE AL, DON'T YOU?
N...
NO!!
Heh heh...
I KNEW IT.
I HAD A FEELING YOU DID.

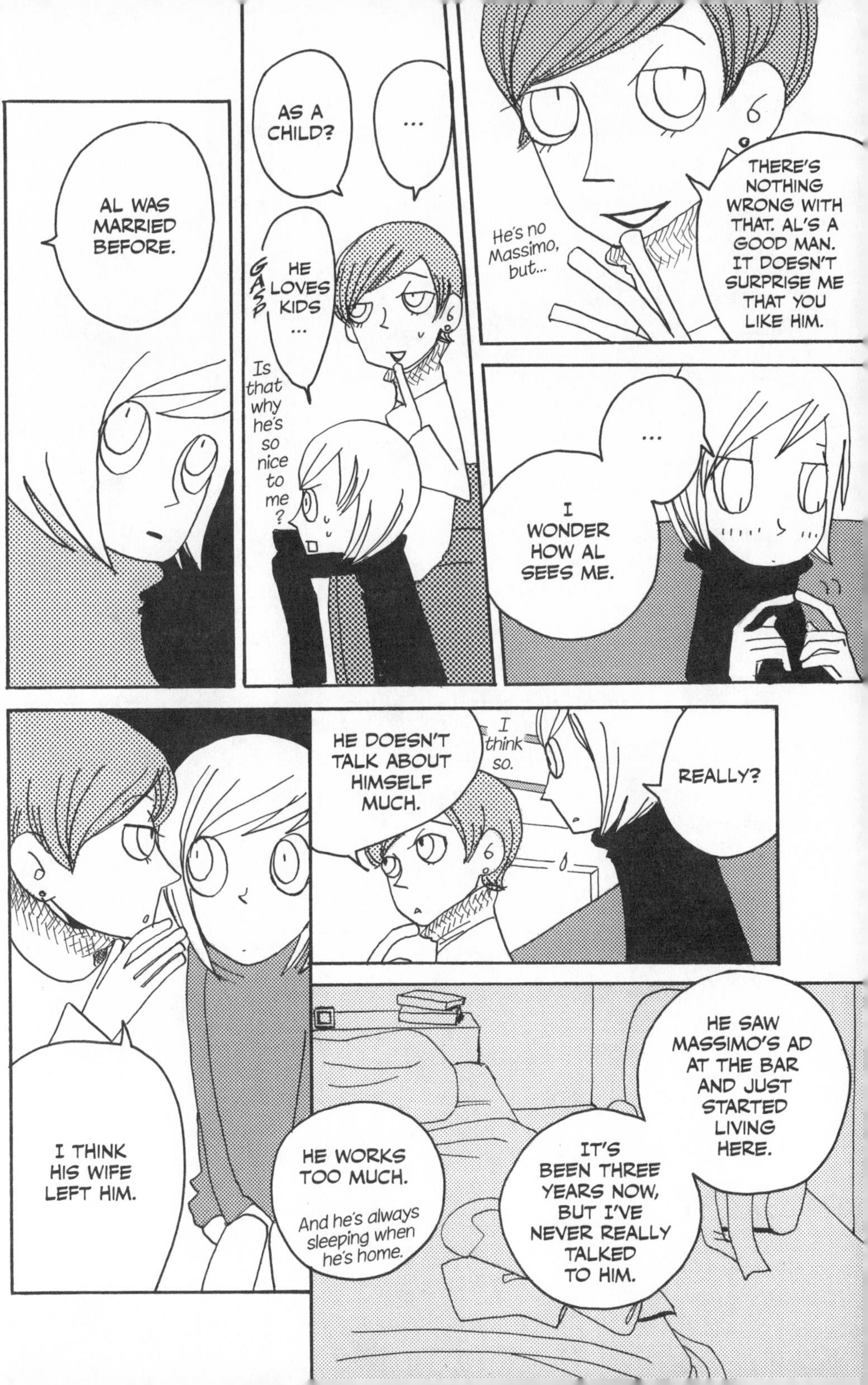
THERE'S NOTHING WRONG WITH THAT. AL'S A GOOD MAN. IT DOESN'T SURPRISE ME THAT YOU LIKE HIM.
He's no Massimo, but...
...
I WONDER HOW AL SEES ME.
...
AS A CHILD?
HE LOVES KIDS ...
GASP
Is that why he's so nice to me?
AL WAS MARRIED BEFORE.
REALLY?
I think so.
HE DOESN'T TALK ABOUT HIMSELF MUCH.
HE SAW MASSIMO'S AD AT THE BAR AND JUST STARTED LIVING HERE.
IT'S BEEN THREE YEARS NOW, BUT I'VE NEVER REALLY TALKED TO HIM.
HE WORKS TOO MUCH.
And he's always sleeping when he's home.
I THINK HIS WIFE LEFT HIM.

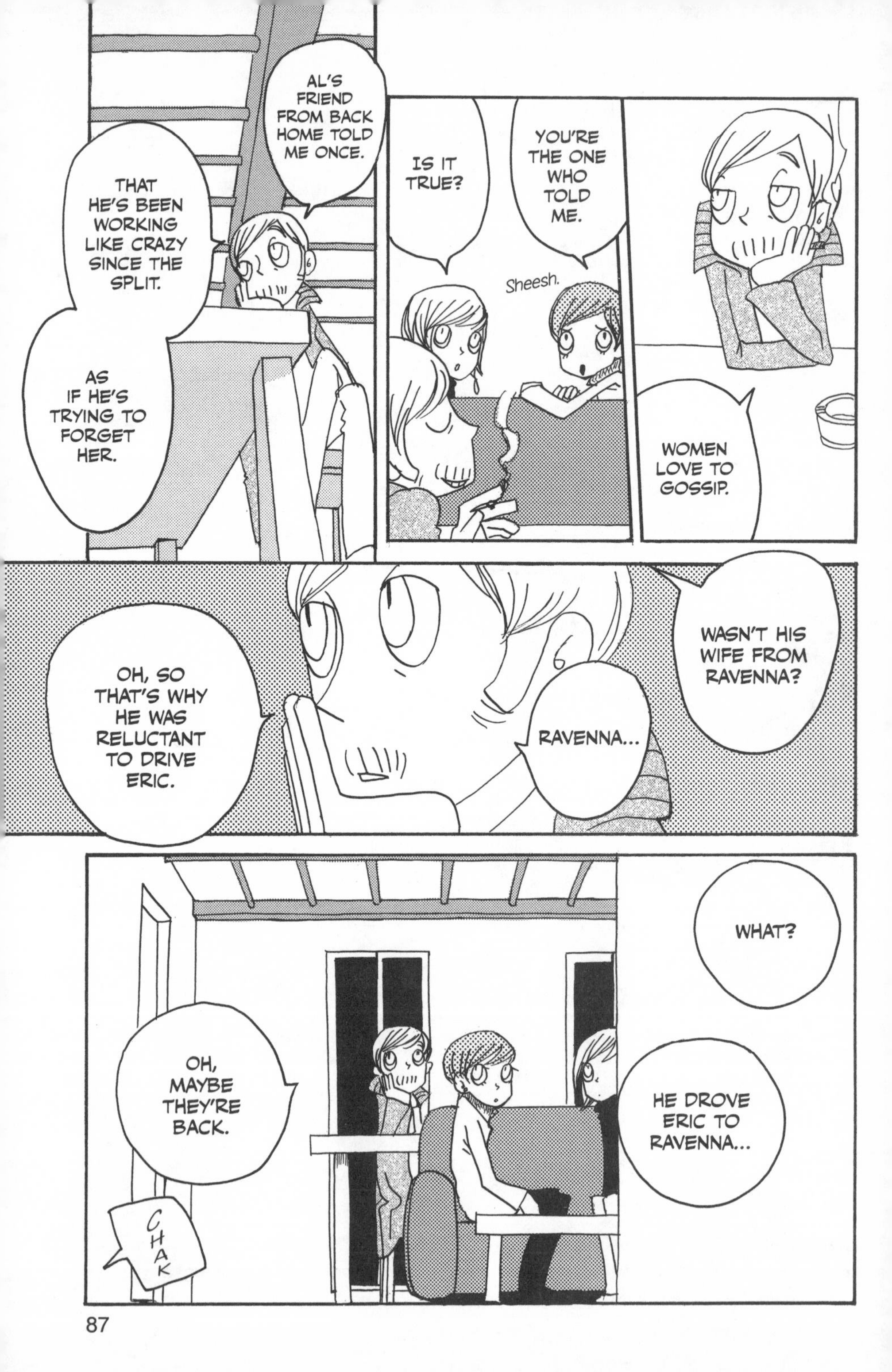
WOMEN LOVE TO GOSSIP.
YOU'RE THE ONE WHO TOLD ME.
IS IT TRUE?
Sheesh.
AL'S FRIEND FROM BACK HOME TOLD ME ONCE.
THAT HE'S BEEN WORKING LIKE CRAZY SINCE THE SPLIT.
AS IF HE'S TRYING TO FORGET HER.
WASN'T HIS WIFE FROM RAVENNA?
RAVENNA...
OH, SO THAT'S WHY HE WAS RELUCTANT TO DRIVE ERIC.
WHAT?
HE DROVE ERIC TO RAVENNA...
OH, MAYBE THEY'RE BACK.
CHAK

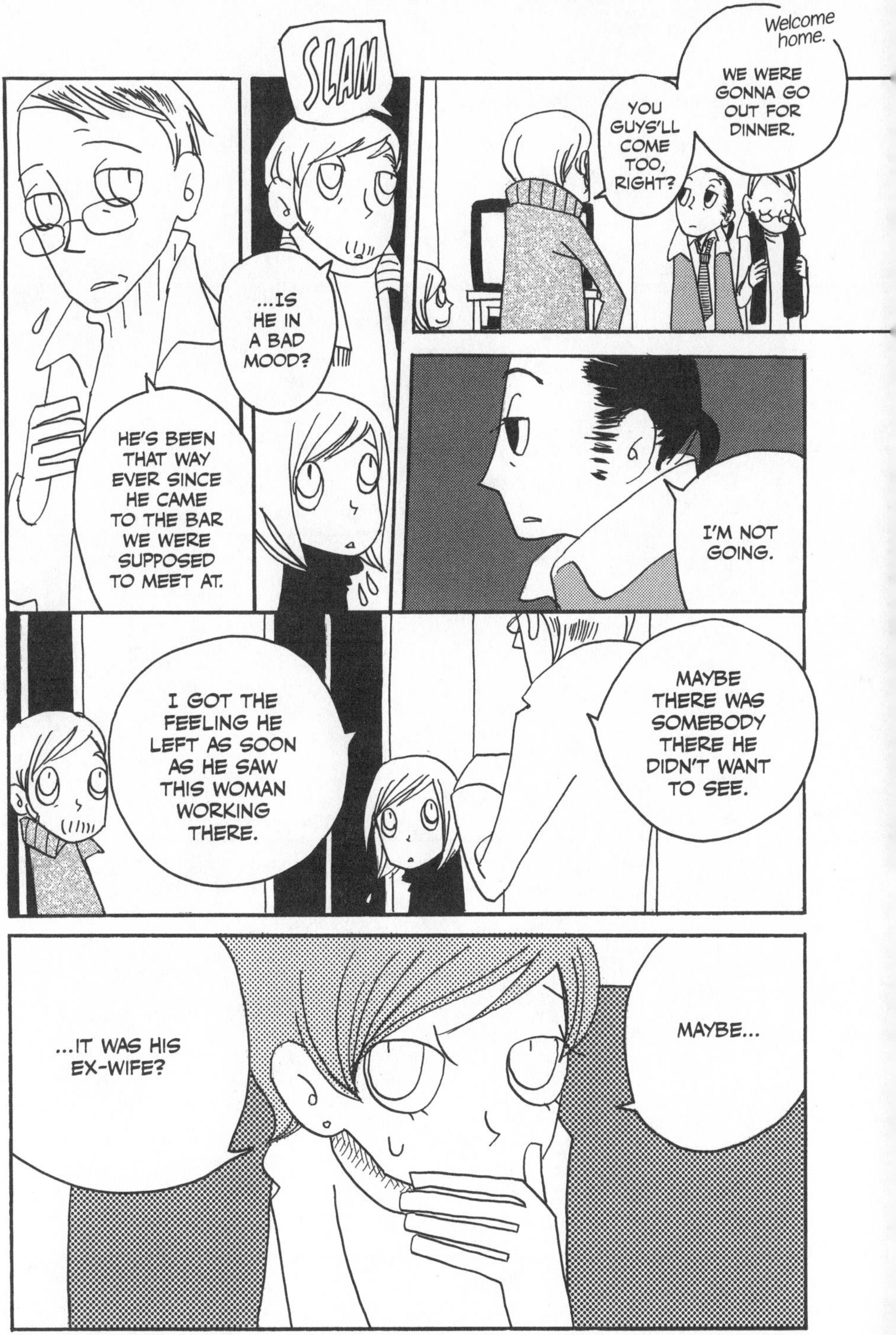
Welcome home.
WE WERE GONNA GO OUT FOR DINNER.
YOU GUYS'LL COME TOO, RIGHT?
I'M NOT GOING.
SLAM
...IS HE IN A BAD MOOD?
HE'S BEEN THAT WAY EVER SINCE HE CAME TO THE BAR WE WERE SUPPOSED TO MEET AT.
MAYBE THERE WAS SOMEBODY THERE HE DIDN'T WANT TO SEE.
I GOT THE FEELING HE LEFT AS SOON AS HE SAW THIS WOMAN WORKING THERE.
MAYBE...
...IT WAS HIS EX-WIFE?

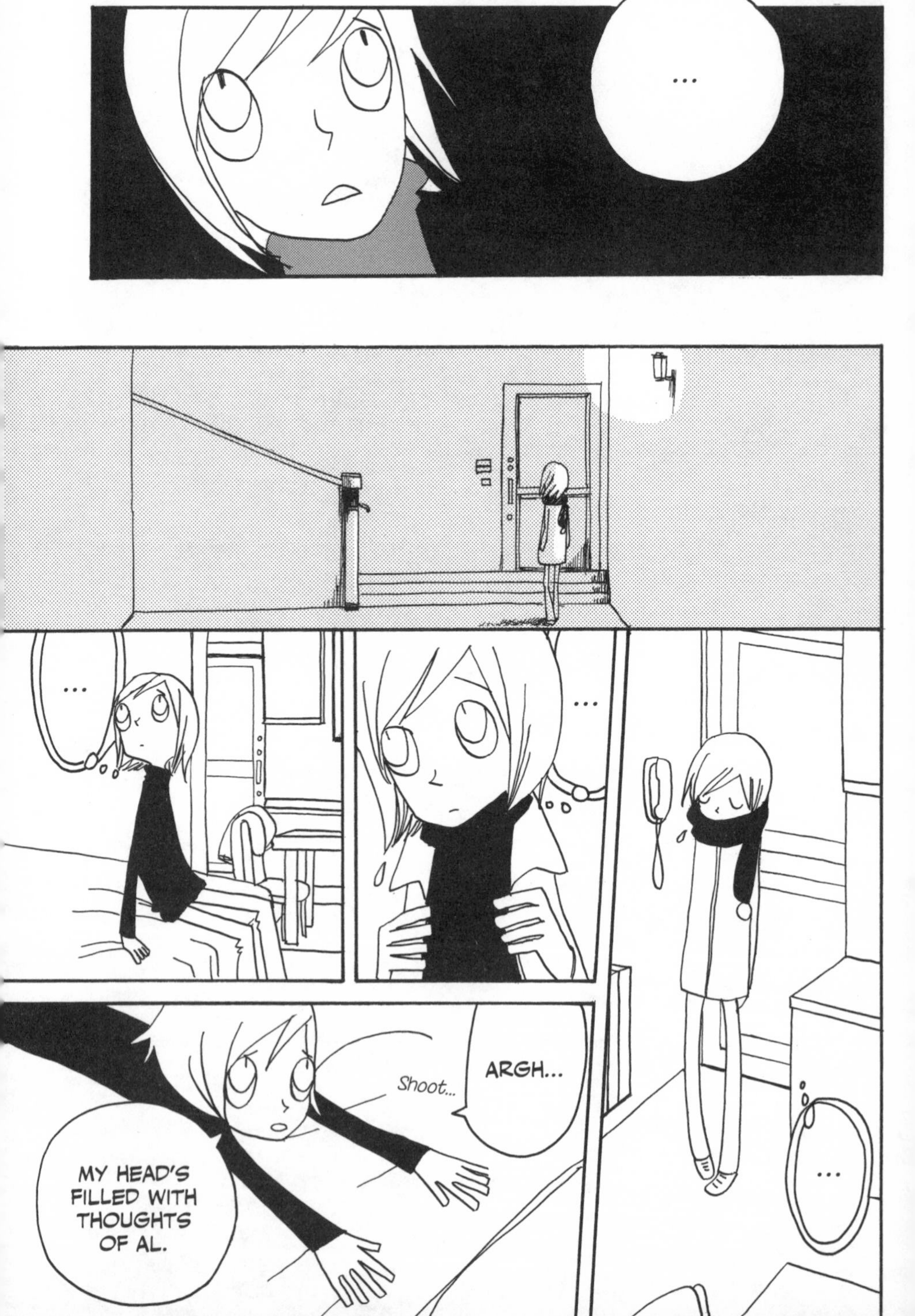
...
...
...
...
ARGH...
Shoot...
MY HEAD'S FILLED WITH THOUGHTS OF AL.

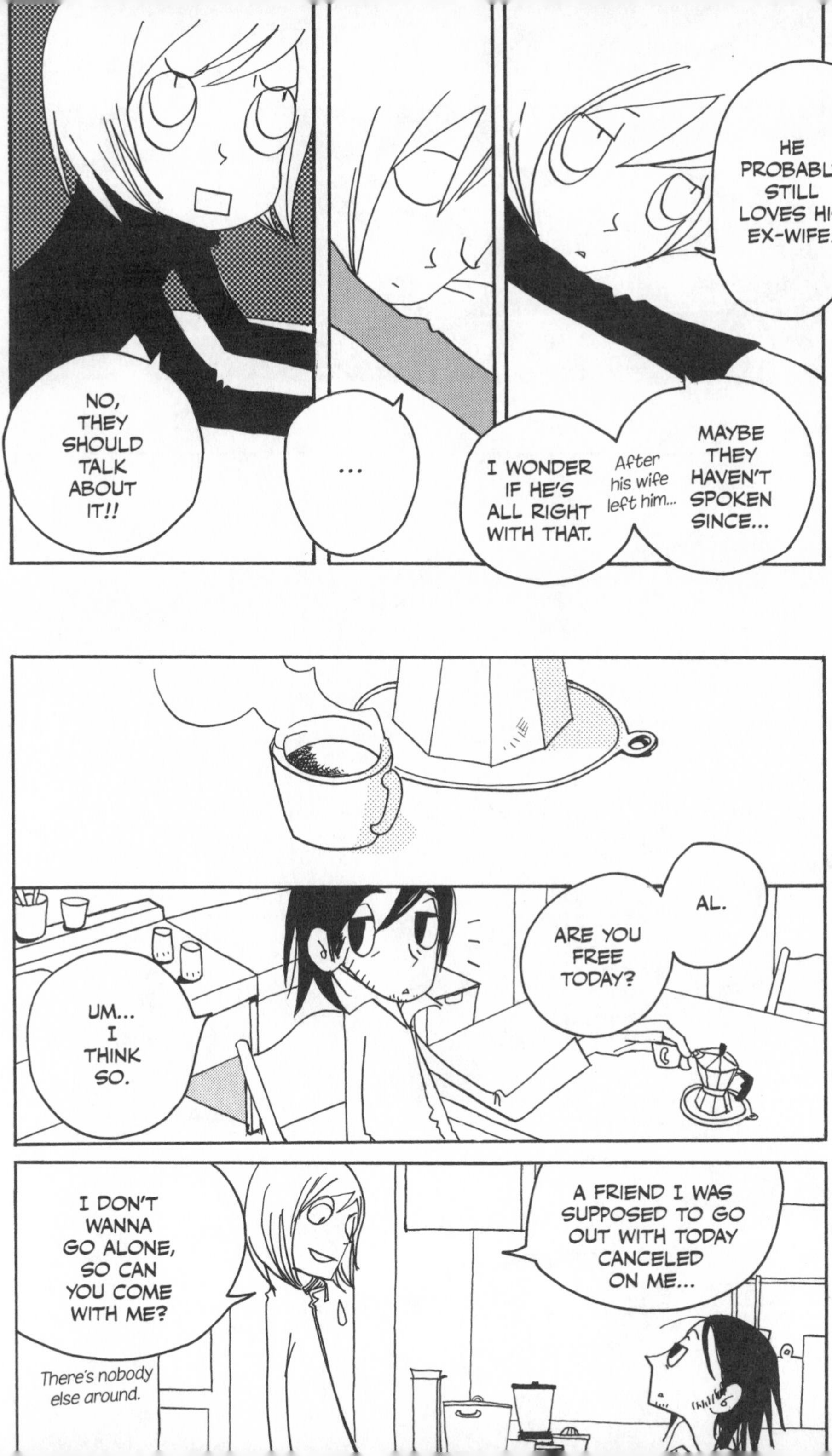
HE PROBABLY STILL LOVES HIS EX-WIFE.
MAYBE THEY HAVEN'T SPOKEN SINCE...
After his wife left him...
I WONDER IF HE'S ALL RIGHT WITH THAT.
...
NO, THEY SHOULD TALK ABOUT IT!!
AL.
ARE YOU FREE TODAY?
UM... I THINK SO.
A FRIEND I WAS SUPPOSED TO GO OUT WITH TODAY CANCELED ON ME...
I DON'T WANNA GO ALONE, SO CAN YOU COME WITH ME?
There's nobody else around.

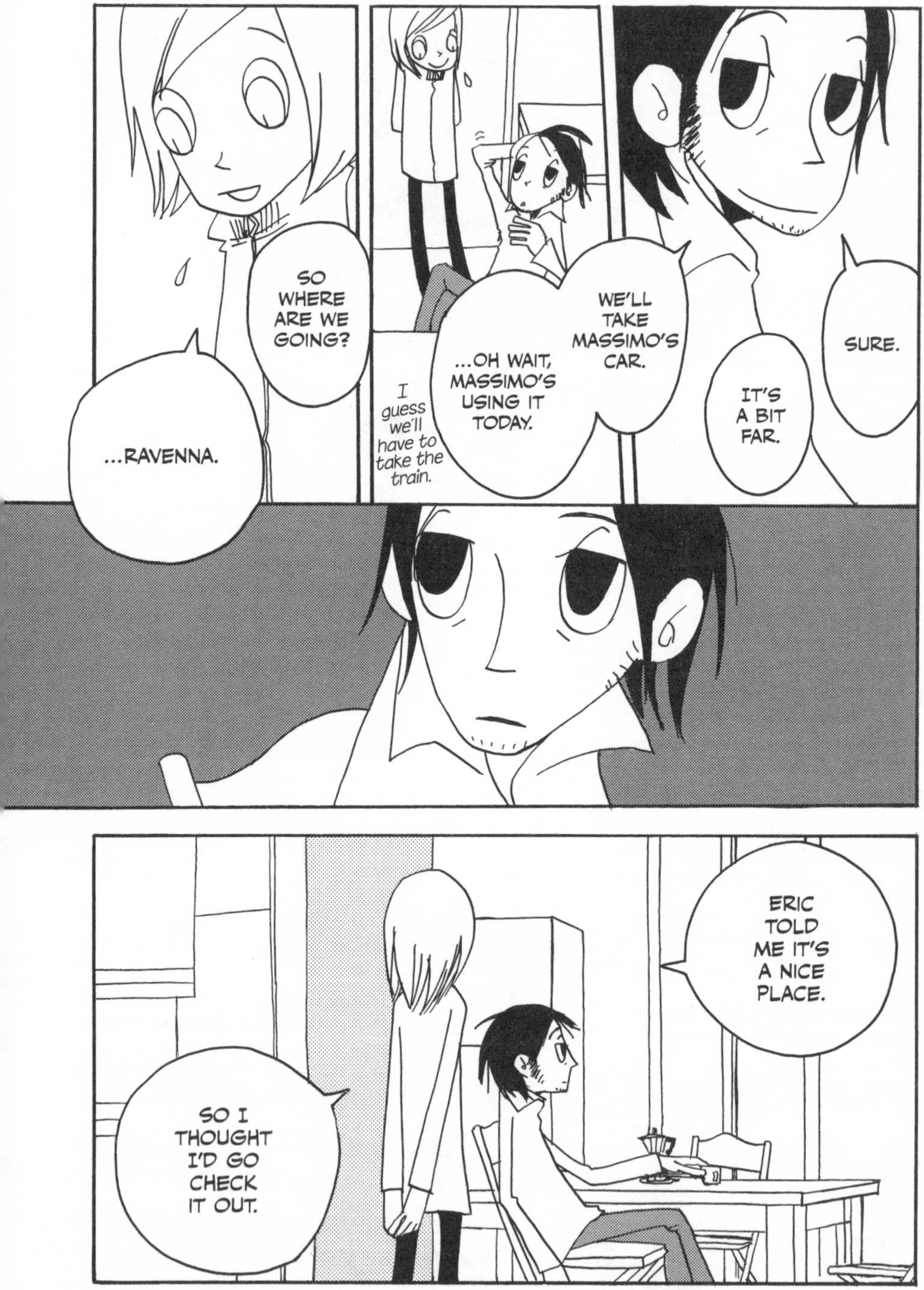
SURE.
IT'S A BIT FAR.
WE'LL TAKE MASSIMO'S CAR.
...OH WAIT, MASSIMO'S USING IT TODAY.
I guess we'll have to take the train.
SO WHERE ARE WE GOING?
...RAVENNA.
ERIC TOLD ME IT'S A NICE PLACE.
SO I THOUGHT I'D GO CHECK IT OUT.

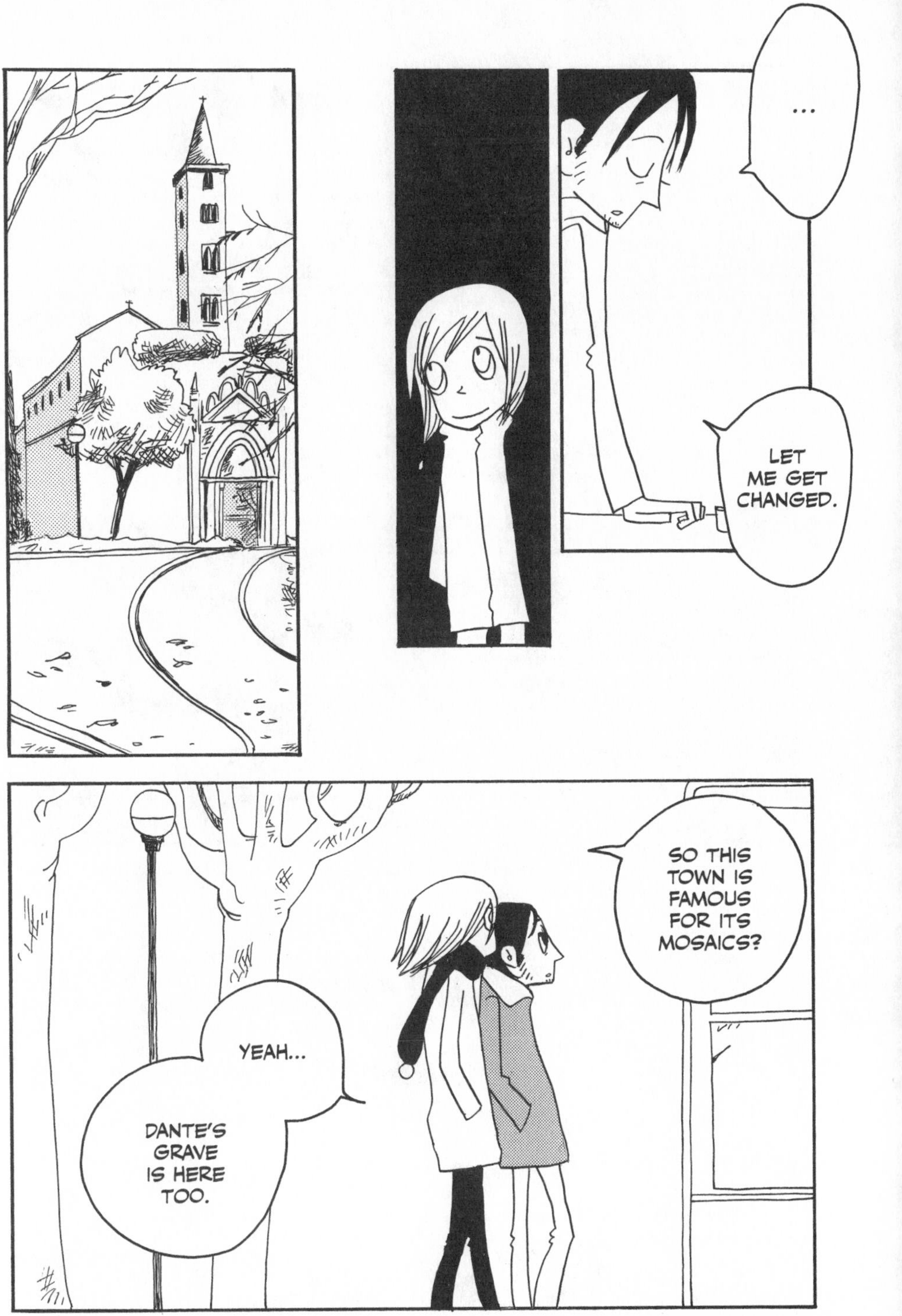
...
LET ME GET CHANGED.
SO THIS TOWN IS FAMOUS FOR ITS MOSAICS?
YEAH...
DANTE'S GRAVE IS HERE TOO.

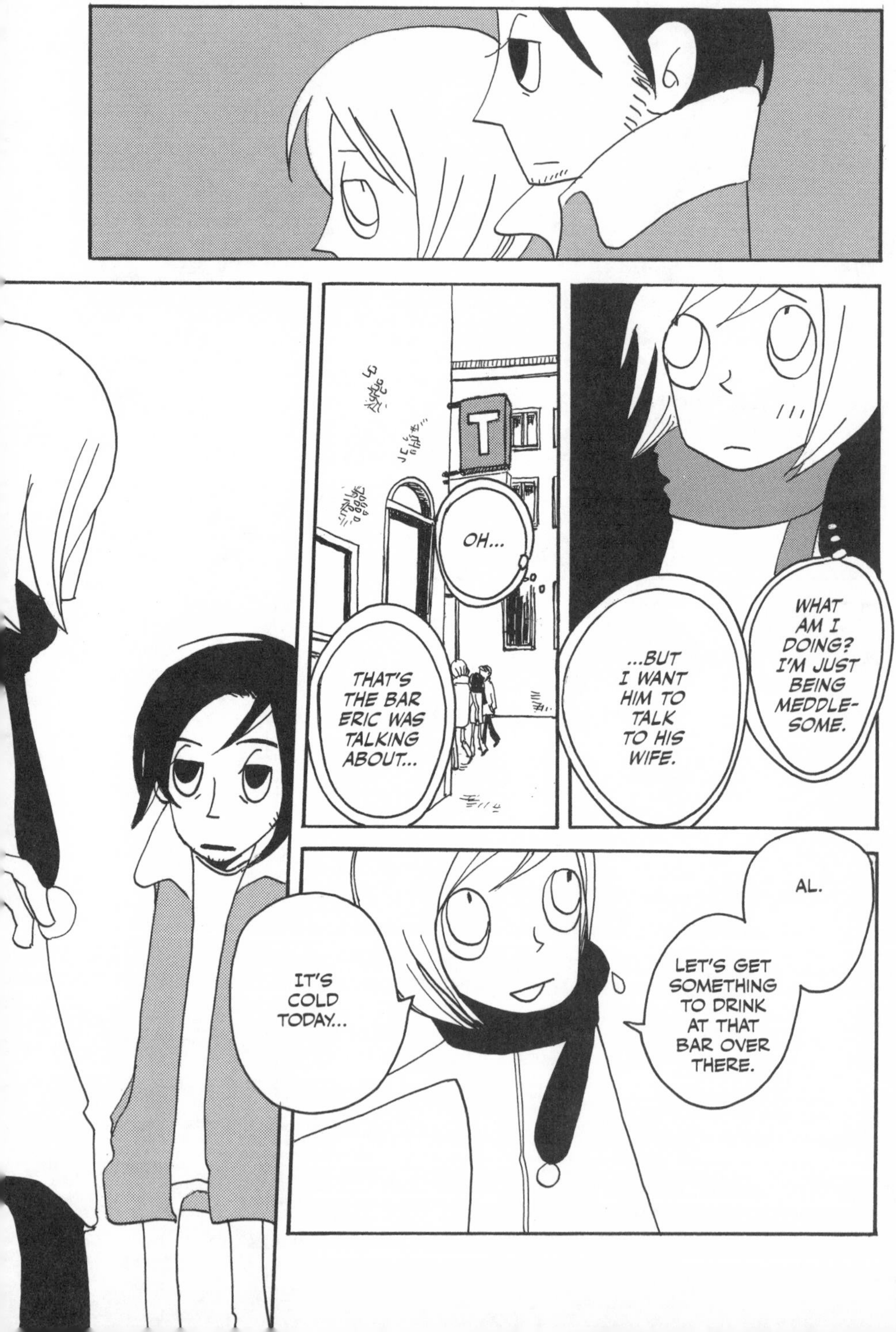
WHAT AM I DOING? I'M JUST BEING MEDDLE-SOME.
...BUT I WANT HIM TO TALK TO HIS WIFE.
OH...
THAT'S THE BAR ERIC WAS TALKING ABOUT...
AL.
LET'S GET SOMETHING TO DRINK AT THAT BAR OVER THERE.
IT'S COLD TODAY...

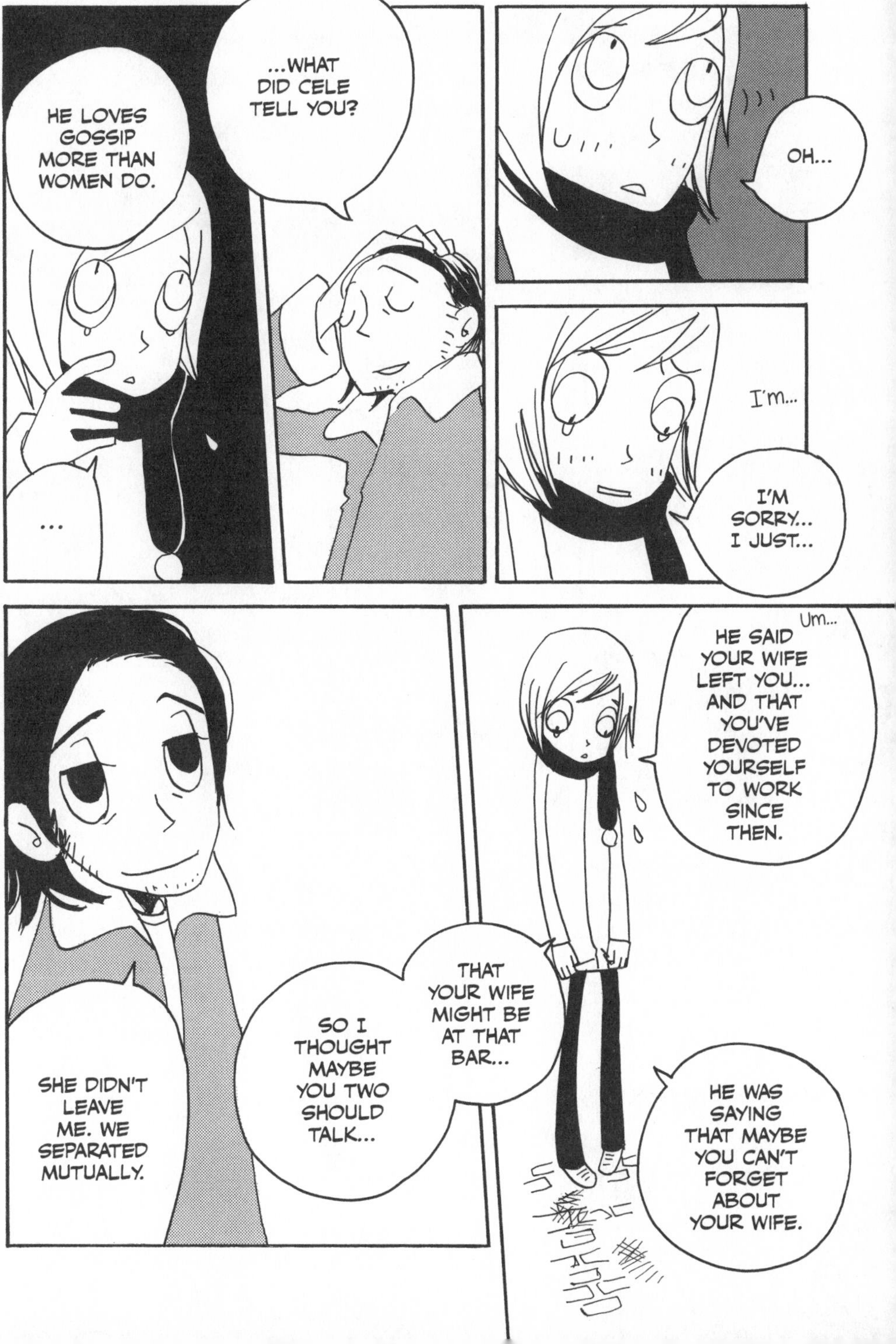
OH...
I'M...
I'M SORRY... I JUST...
...WHAT DID CELE TELL YOU?
HE LOVES GOSSIP MORE THAN WOMEN DO.
...
UM...
HE SAID YOUR WIFE LEFT YOU... AND THAT YOU'VE DEVOTED YOURSELF TO WORK SINCE THEN.
HE WAS SAYING THAT MAYBE YOU CAN'T FORGET ABOUT YOUR WIFE.
THAT YOUR WIFE MIGHT BE AT THAT BAR...
SO I THOUGHT MAYBE YOU TWO SHOULD TALK...
SHE DIDN'T LEAVE ME. WE SEPARATED MUTUALLY.

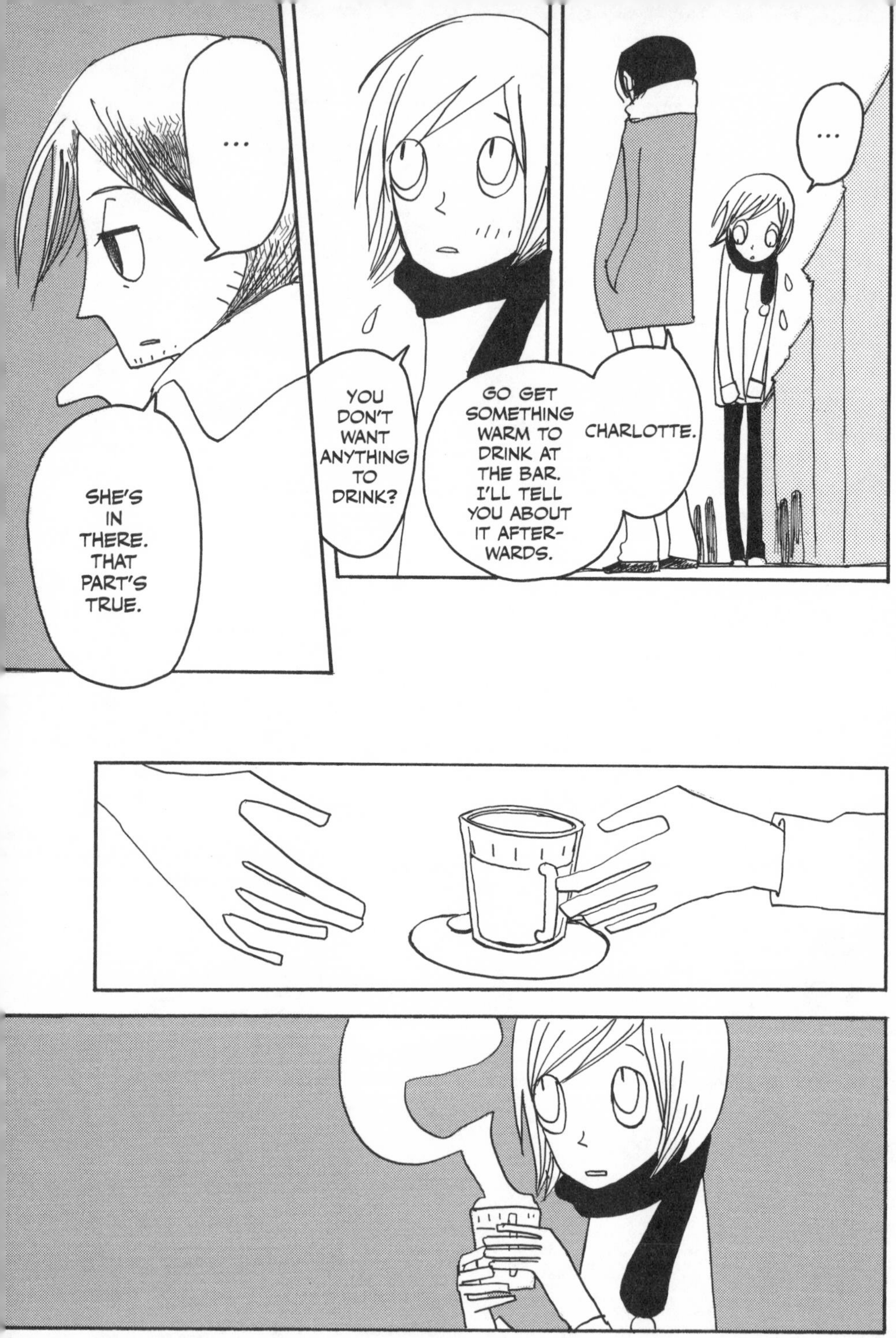
...
CHARLOTTE.
GO GET SOMETHING WARM TO DRINK AT THE BAR. I'LL TELL YOU ABOUT IT AFTER-WARDS.
YOU DON'T WANT ANYTHING TO DRINK?
...
SHE'S IN THERE. THAT PART'S TRUE.

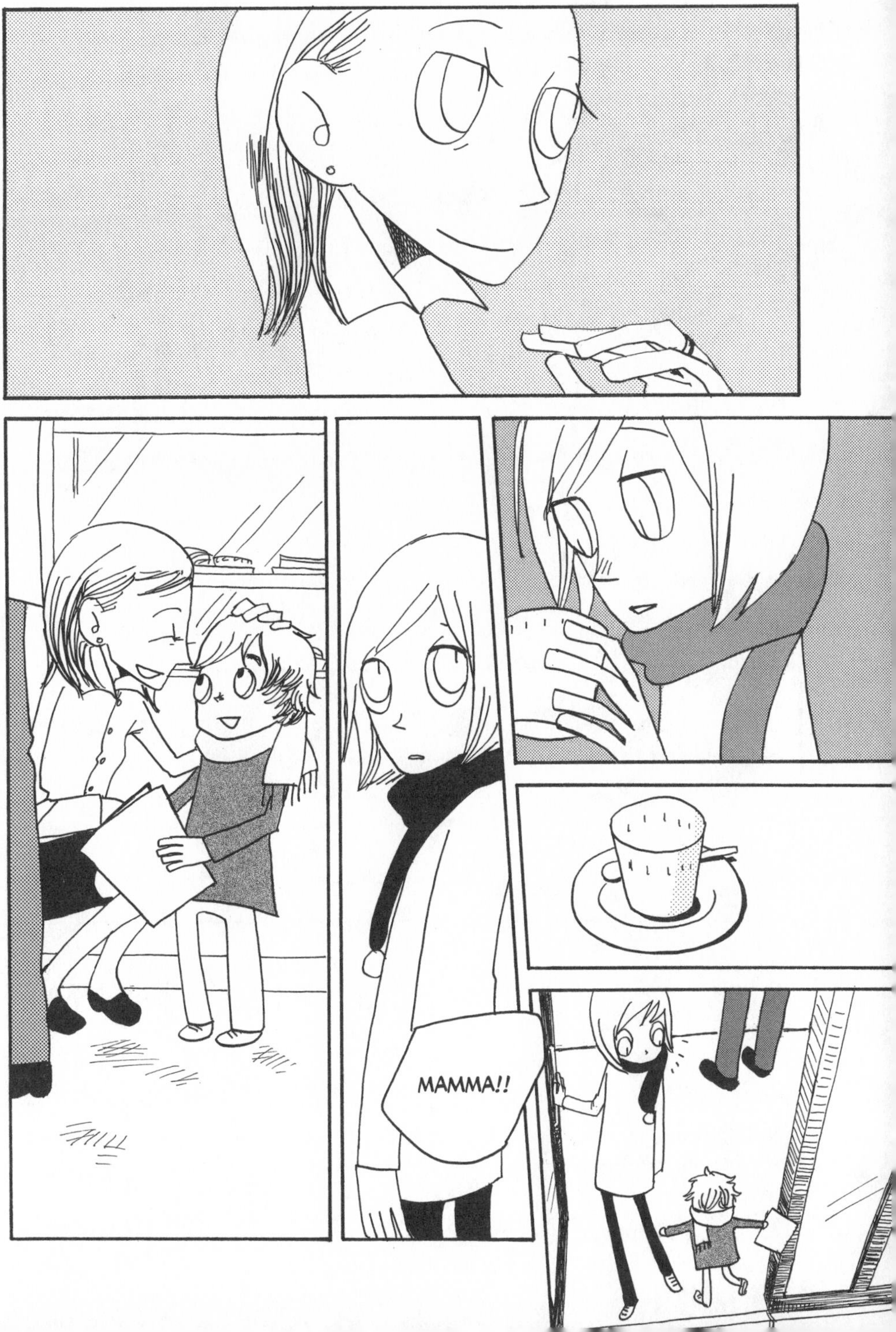
MAMMA!!

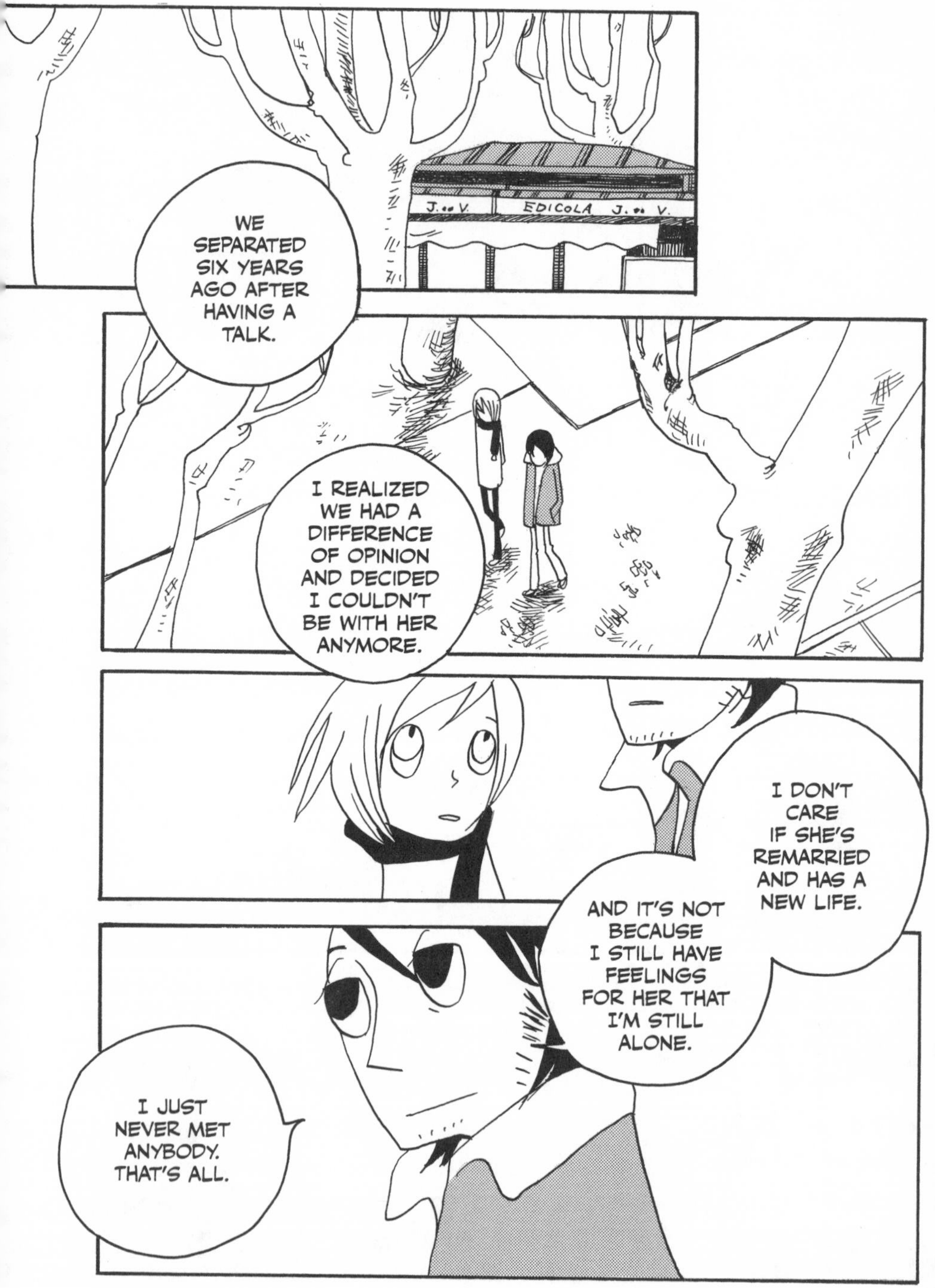
J. V.
EDICOLA J. V.
WE SEPARATED SIX YEARS AGO AFTER HAVING A TALK.
I REALIZED WE HAD A DIFFERENCE OF OPINION AND DECIDED I COULDN'T BE WITH HER ANYMORE.
I DON'T CARE IF SHE'S REMARRIED AND HAS A NEW LIFE.
AND IT'S NOT BECAUSE I STILL HAVE FEELINGS FOR HER THAT I'M STILL ALONE.
I JUST NEVER MET ANYBODY. THAT'S ALL.

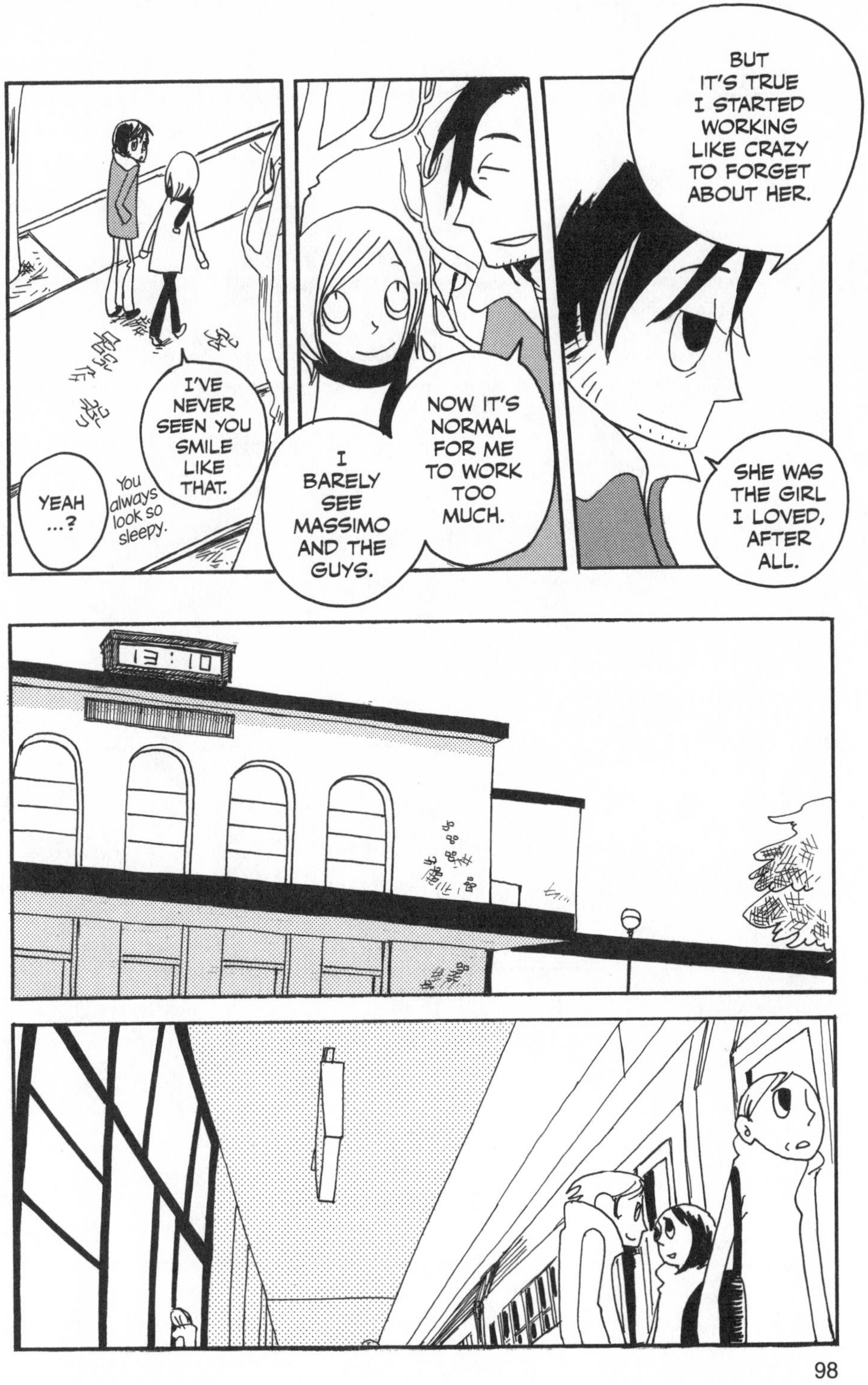
BUT IT'S TRUE I STARTED WORKING LIKE CRAZY TO FORGET ABOUT HER.
SHE WAS THE GIRL I LOVED, AFTER ALL.
NOW IT'S NORMAL FOR ME TO WORK TOO MUCH.
I BARELY SEE MASSIMO AND THE GUYS.
I'VE NEVER SEEN YOU SMILE LIKE THAT.
You always look so sleepy.
YEAH ...?

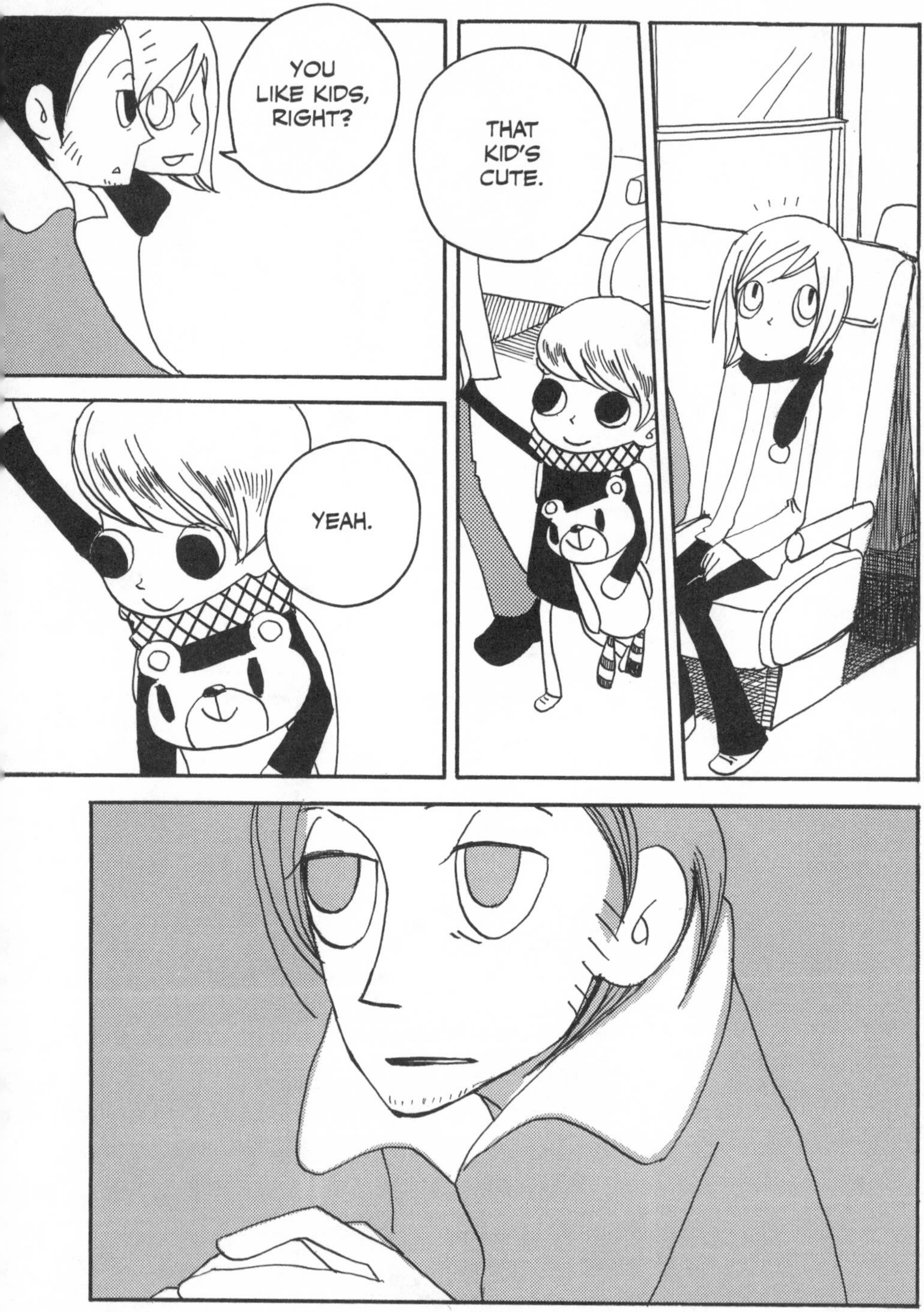
THAT KID'S CUTE.
YOU LIKE KIDS, RIGHT?
YEAH.

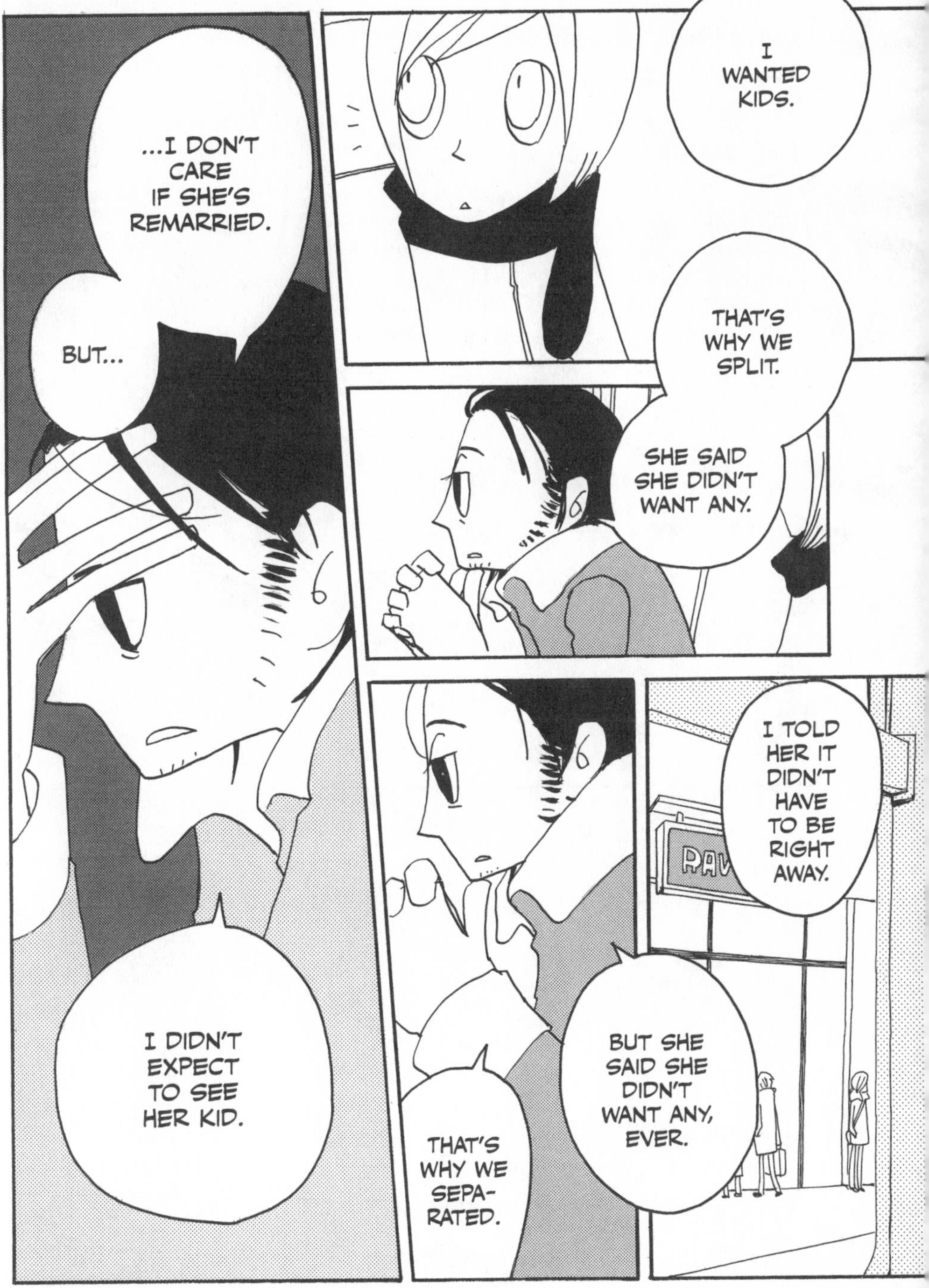
I WANTED KIDS.
THAT'S WHY WE SPLIT.
SHE SAID SHE DIDN'T WANT ANY.
I TOLD HER IT DIDN'T HAVE TO BE RIGHT AWAY.
BUT SHE SAID SHE DIDN'T WANT ANY, EVER.
THAT'S WHY WE SEPA-RATED.
...I DON'T CARE IF SHE'S REMARRIED.
BUT...
I DIDN'T EXPECT TO SEE HER KID.

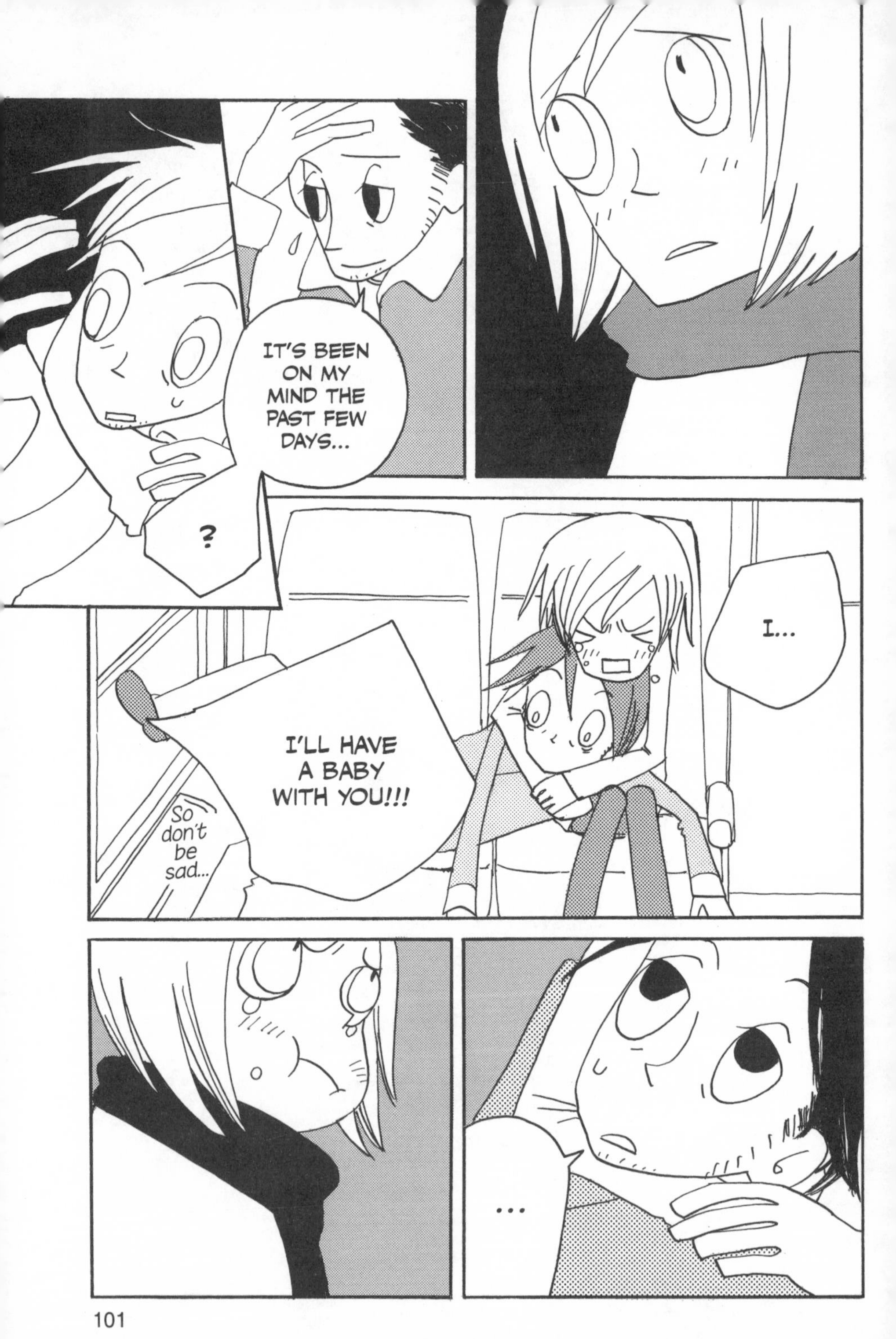
IT'S BEEN ON MY MIND THE PAST FEW DAYS...
?
I...
I'LL HAVE A BABY WITH YOU!!!
So don't be sad...
...

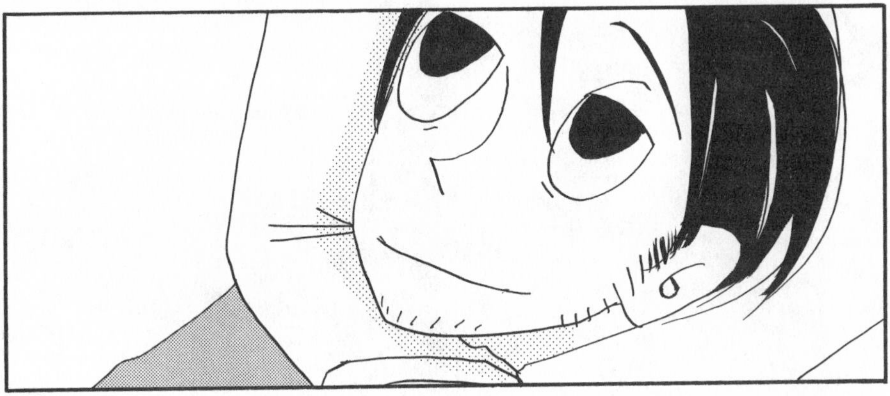

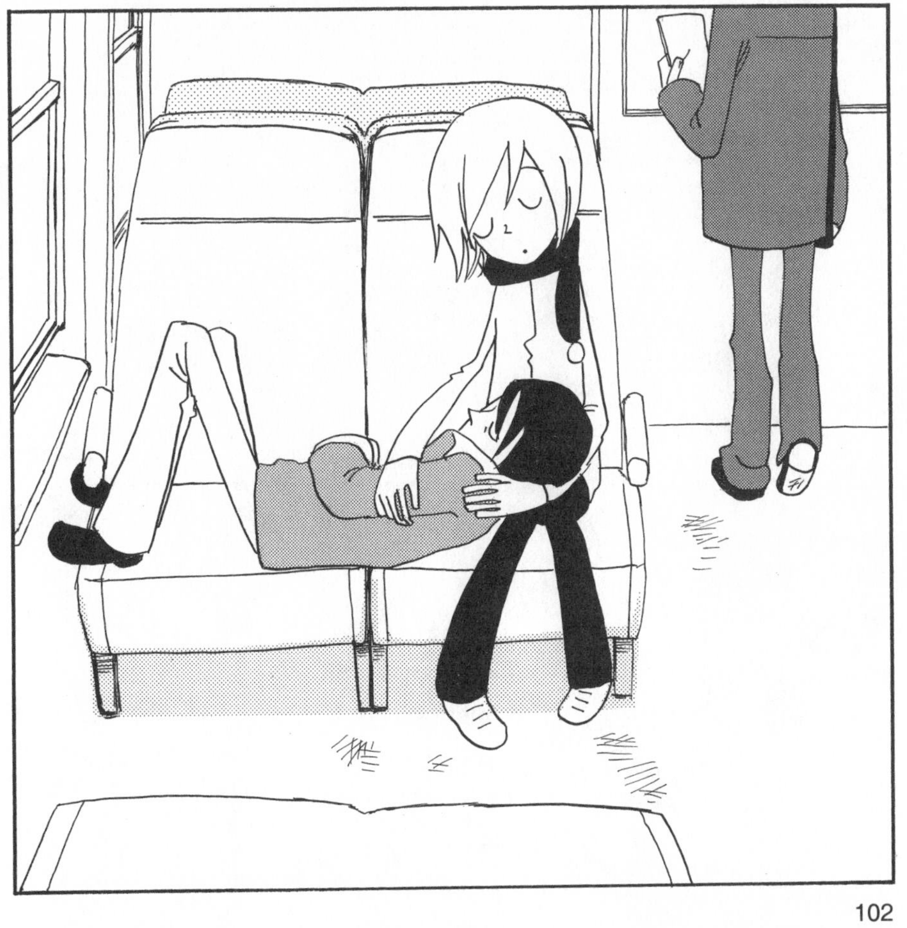

La Quinta Camera
Capitolo 4

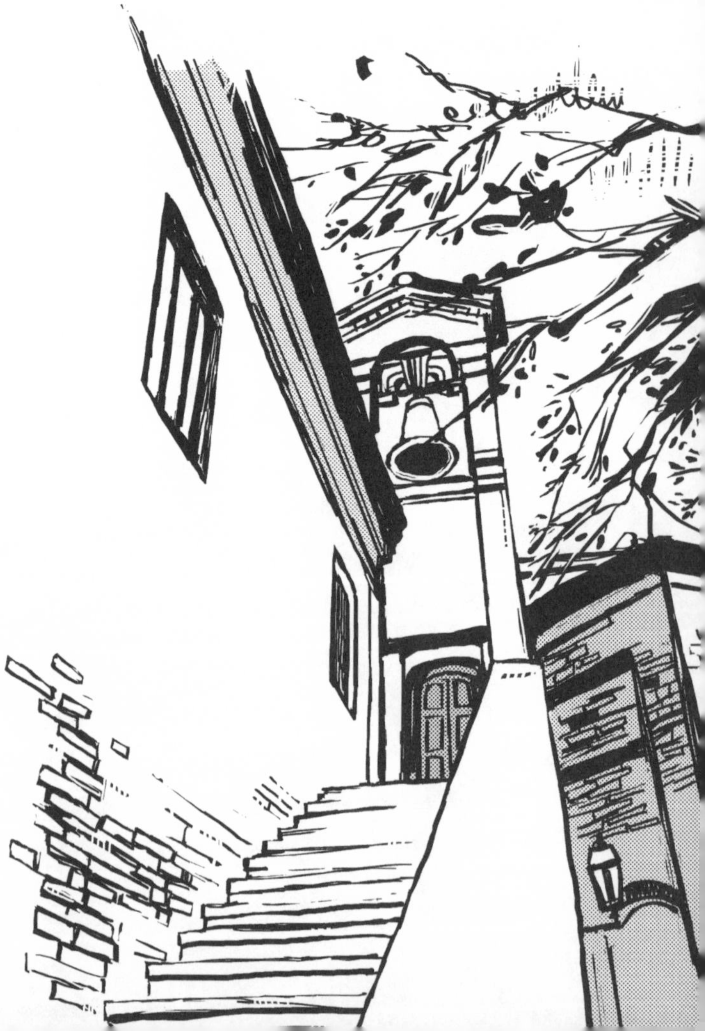

LA QUINTA CAMERA
Capitolo 5

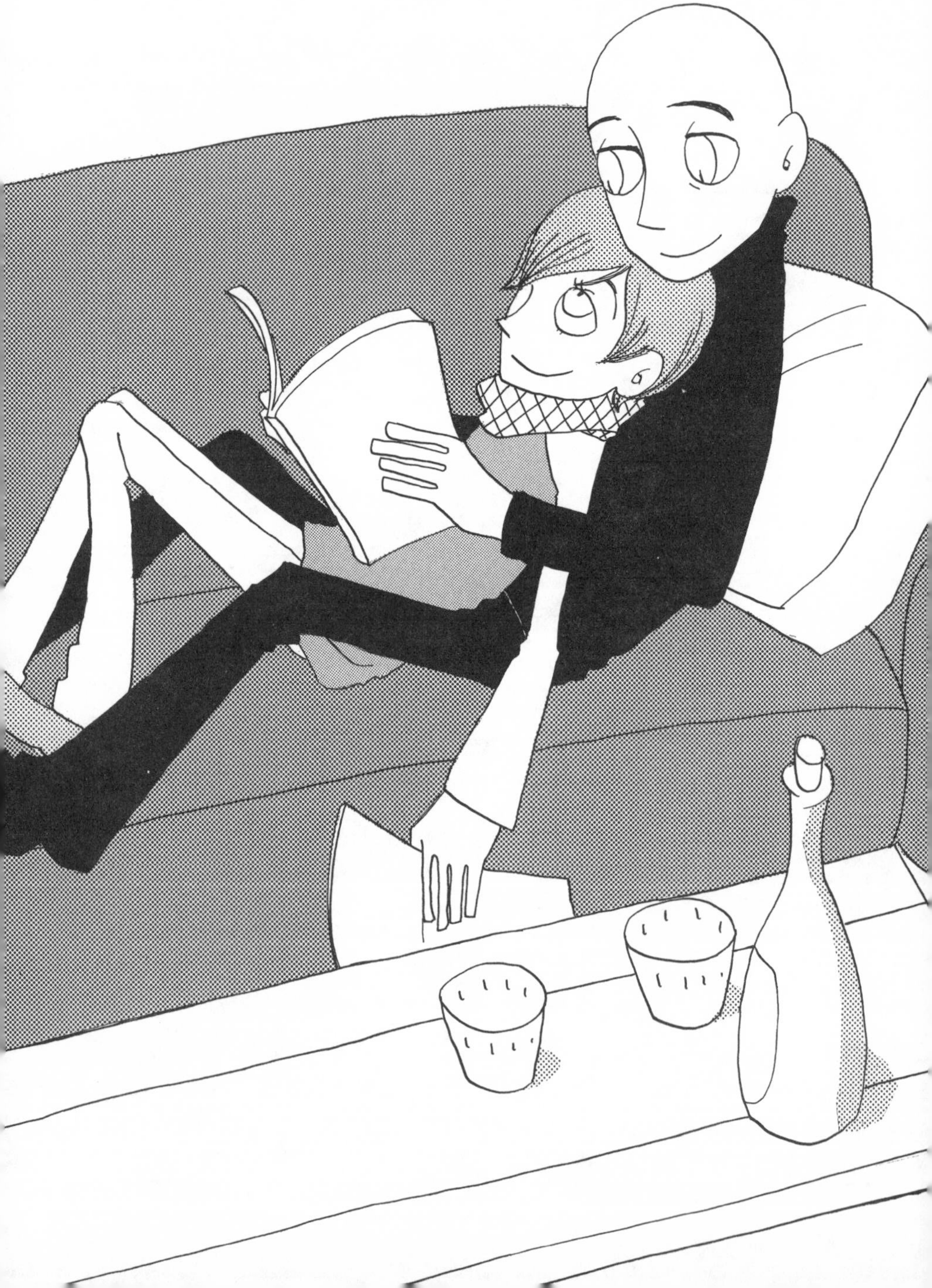

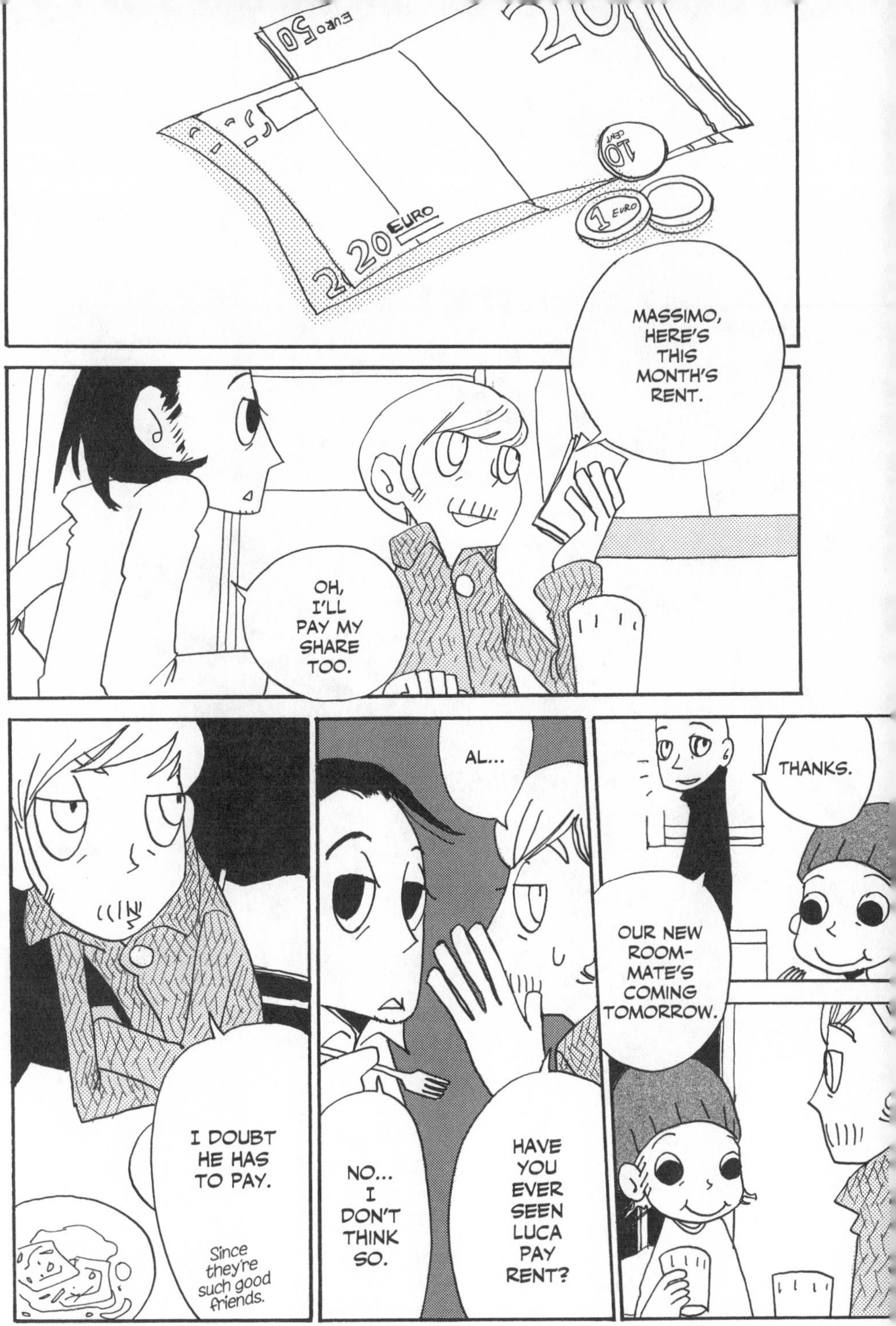
20 EURO
10 CENT
1 EURO
MASSIMO, HERE'S THIS MONTH'S RENT.
OH, I'LL PAY MY SHARE TOO.
THANKS.
OUR NEW ROOM-MATE'S COMING TOMORROW.
AL...
HAVE YOU EVER SEEN LUCA PAY RENT?
NO... I DON'T THINK SO.
I DOUBT HE HAS TO PAY.
Since they're such good friends.

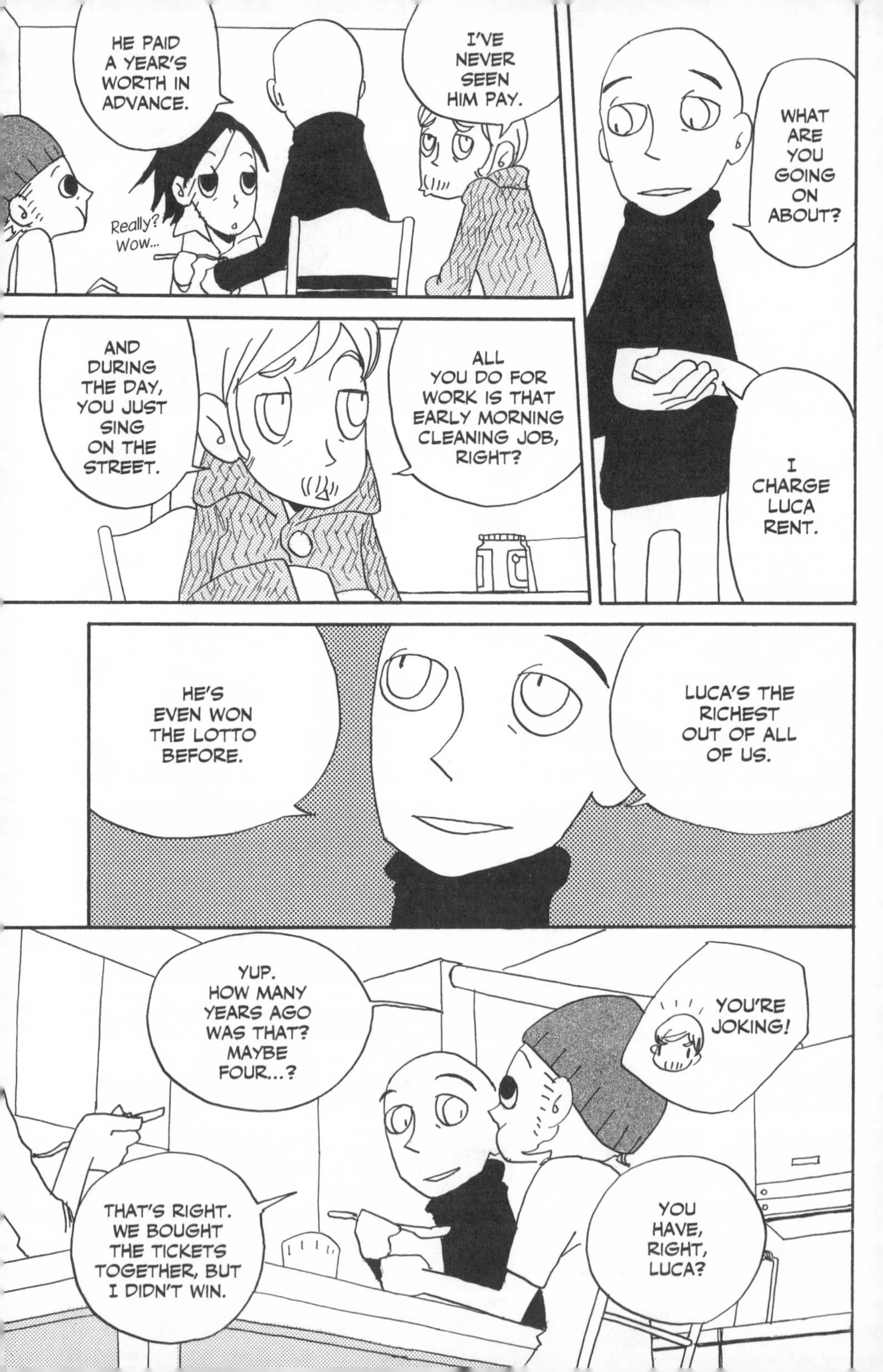
WHAT ARE YOU GOING ON ABOUT?
I CHARGE LUCA RENT.
I'VE NEVER SEEN HIM PAY.
HE PAID A YEAR'S WORTH IN ADVANCE.
Really? Wow...
ALL YOU DO FOR WORK IS THAT EARLY MORNING CLEANING JOB, RIGHT?
AND DURING THE DAY, YOU JUST SING ON THE STREET.
LUCA'S THE RICHEST OUT OF ALL OF US.
HE'S EVEN WON THE LOTTO BEFORE.
YOU'RE JOKING!
YOU HAVE, RIGHT, LUCA?
YUP. HOW MANY YEARS AGO WAS THAT? MAYBE FOUR...?
THAT'S RIGHT. WE BOUGHT THE TICKETS TOGETHER, BUT I DIDN'T WIN.

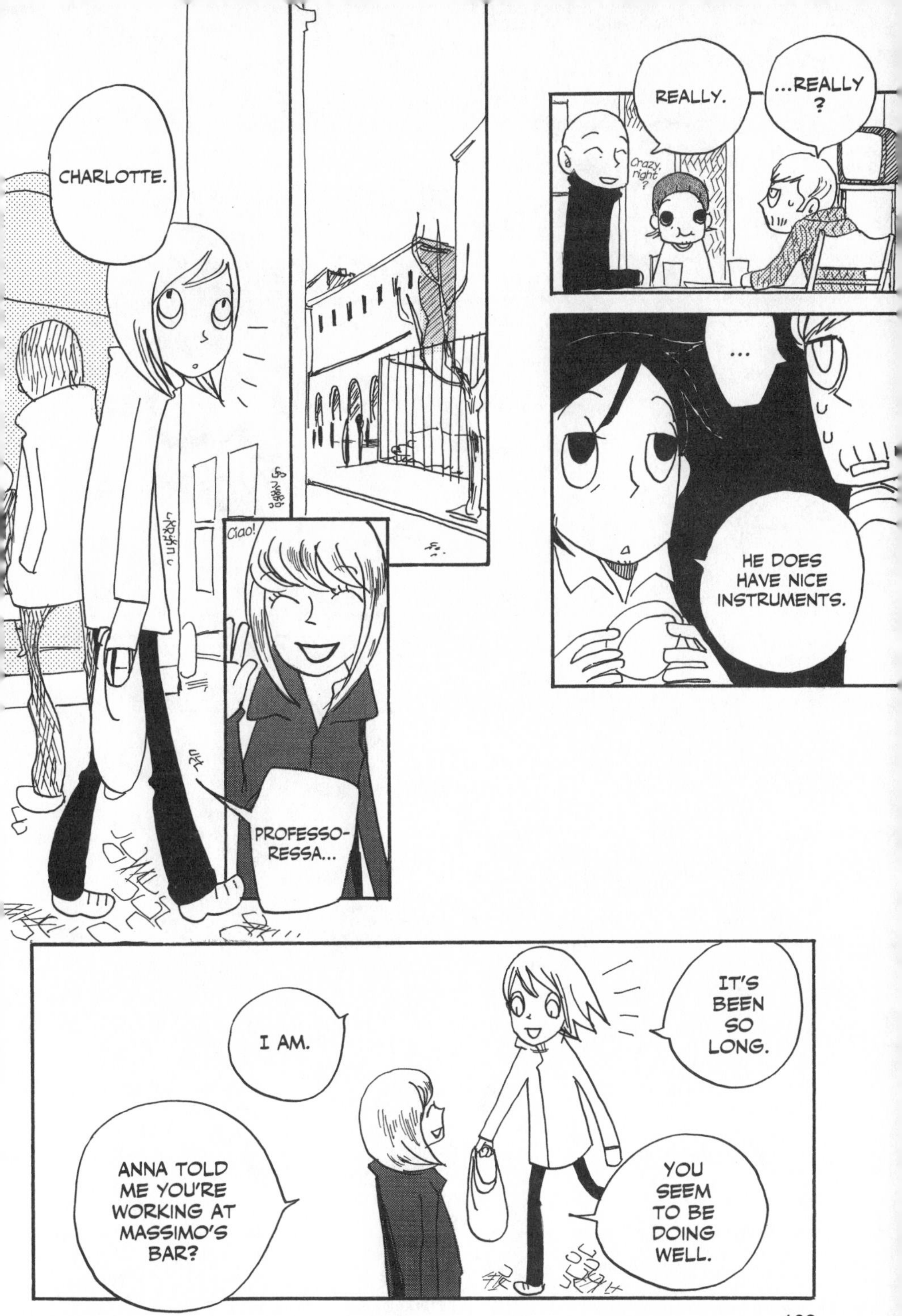
...REALLY ?
REALLY.
Crazy, right?
...
HE DOES HAVE NICE INSTRUMENTS.
Ciao!
PROFESSO-RESSA...
CHARLOTTE.
IT'S BEEN SO LONG.
YOU SEEM TO BE DOING WELL.
ANNA TOLD ME YOU'RE WORKING AT MASSIMO'S BAR?
I AM.

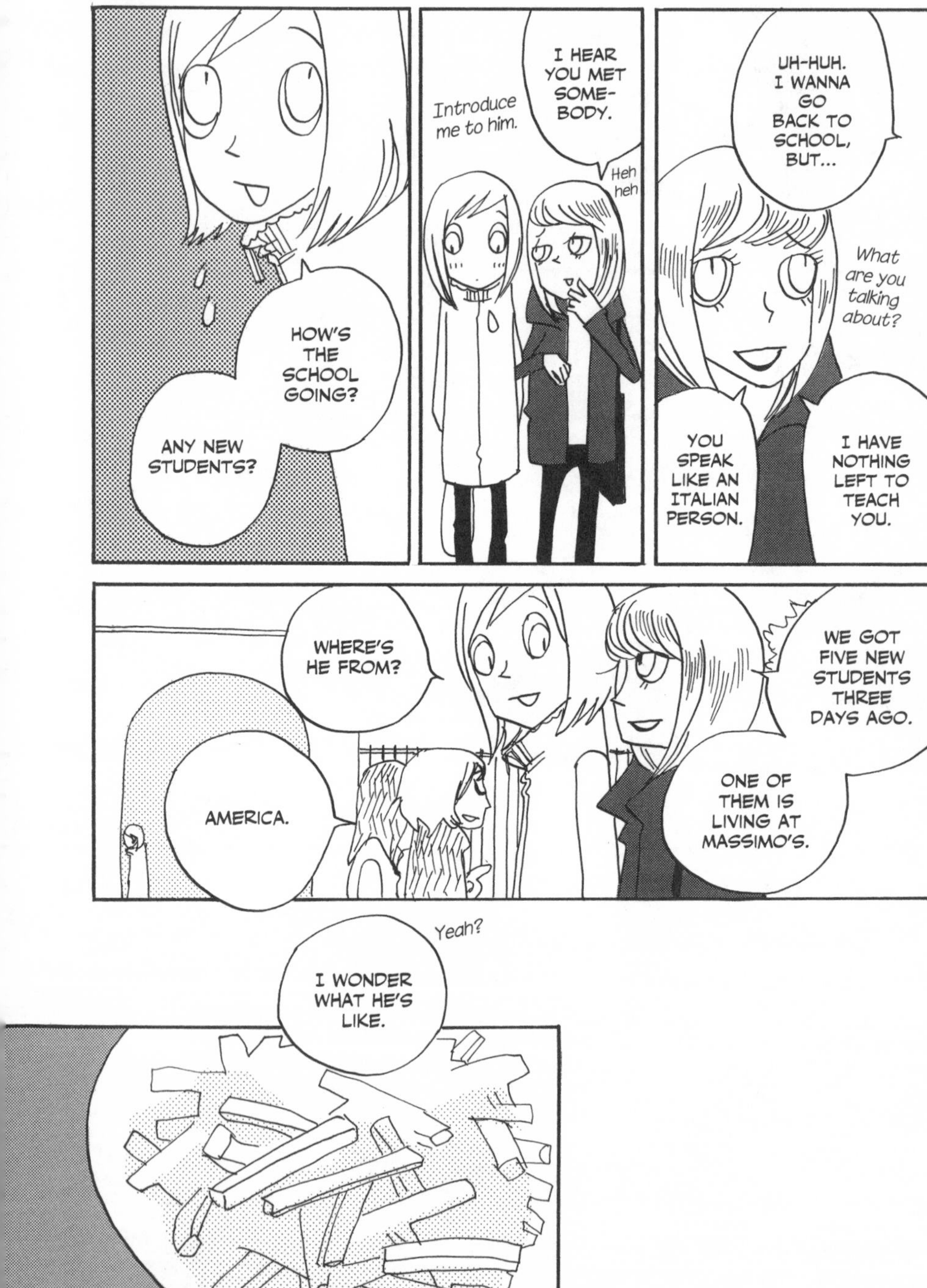
UH-HUH. I WANNA GO BACK TO SCHOOL, BUT...
What are you talking about?
I HAVE NOTHING LEFT TO TEACH YOU.
YOU SPEAK LIKE AN ITALIAN PERSON.
I HEAR YOU MET SOME-BODY.
Heh heh
Introduce me to him.
HOW'S THE SCHOOL GOING?
ANY NEW STUDENTS?
WE GOT FIVE NEW STUDENTS THREE DAYS AGO.
ONE OF THEM IS LIVING AT MASSIMO'S.
WHERE'S HE FROM?
AMERICA.
Yeah?
I WONDER WHAT HE'S LIKE.

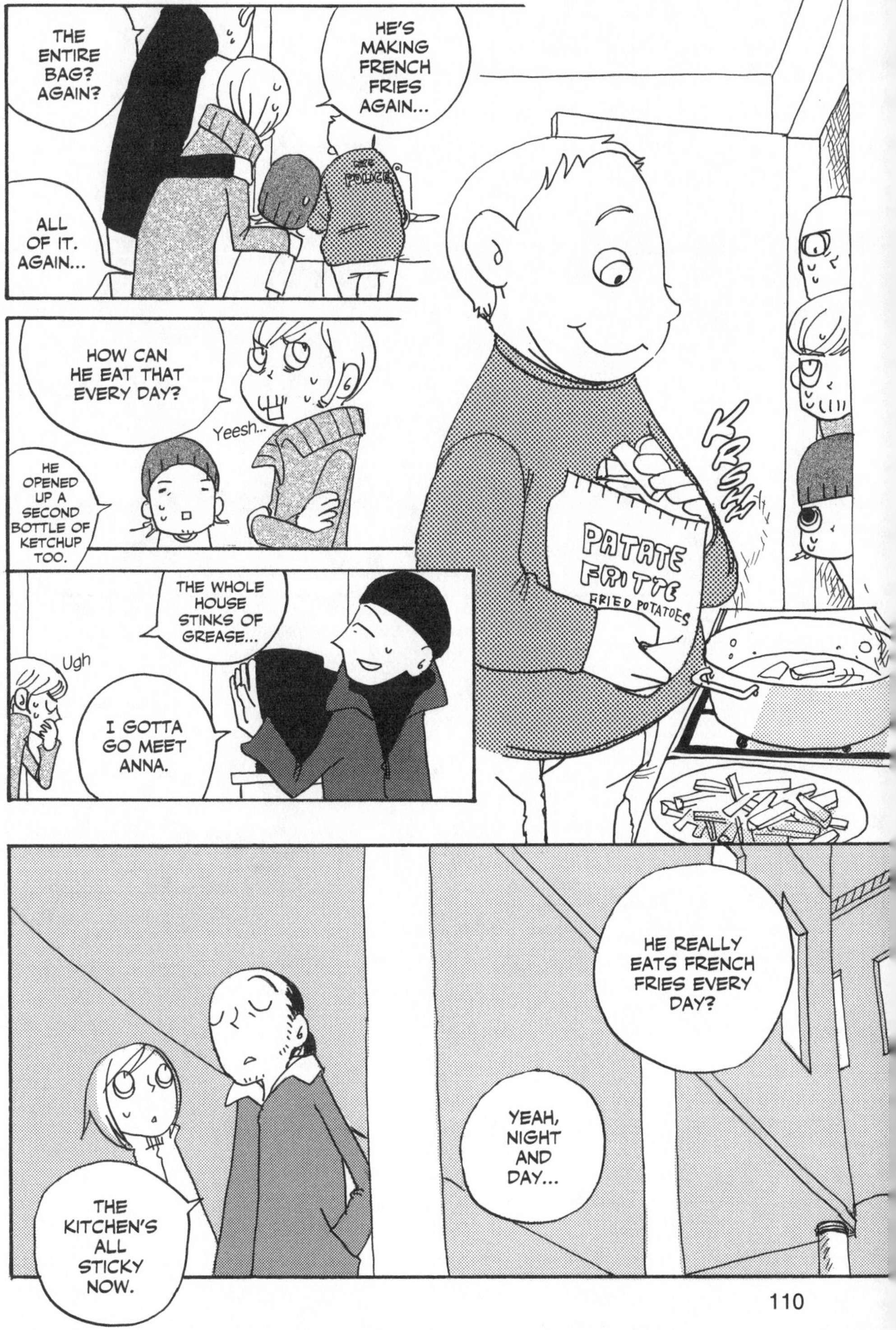
PATATE FRITTE FRIED POTATOES
HE'S MAKING FRENCH FRIES AGAIN...
THE ENTIRE BAG? AGAIN?
ALL OF IT. AGAIN...
HOW CAN HE EAT THAT EVERY DAY?
Yeesh...
HE OPENED UP A SECOND BOTTLE OF KETCHUP TOO.
THE WHOLE HOUSE STINKS OF GREASE...
I GOTTA GO MEET ANNA.
Ugh
HE REALLY EATS FRENCH FRIES EVERY DAY?
YEAH, NIGHT AND DAY...
THE KITCHEN'S ALL STICKY NOW.

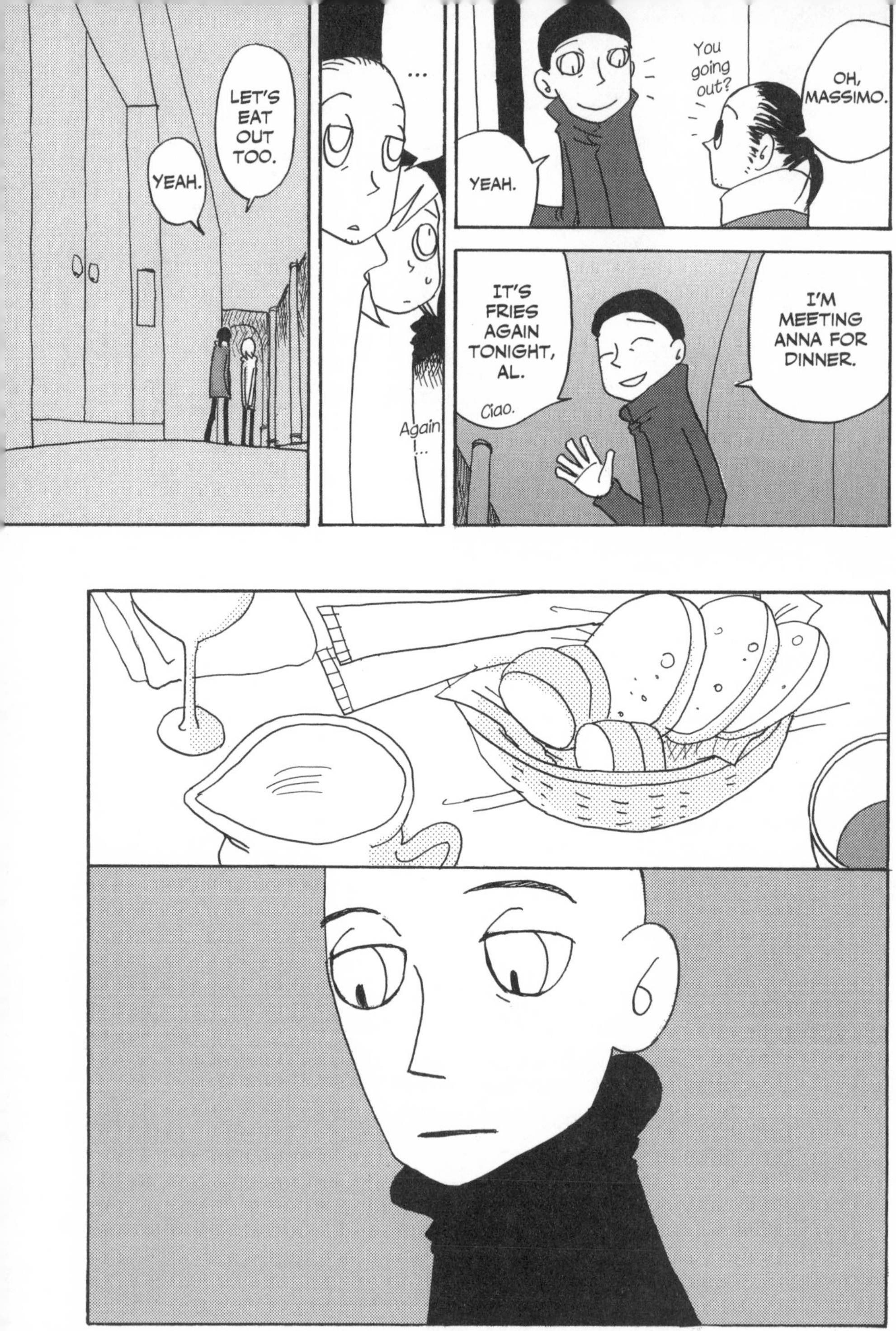
OH, MASSIMO.
You going out?
YEAH.
I'M MEETING ANNA FOR DINNER.
IT'S FRIES AGAIN TONIGHT, AL.
Ciao.
...
Again...
LET'S EAT OUT TOO.
YEAH.

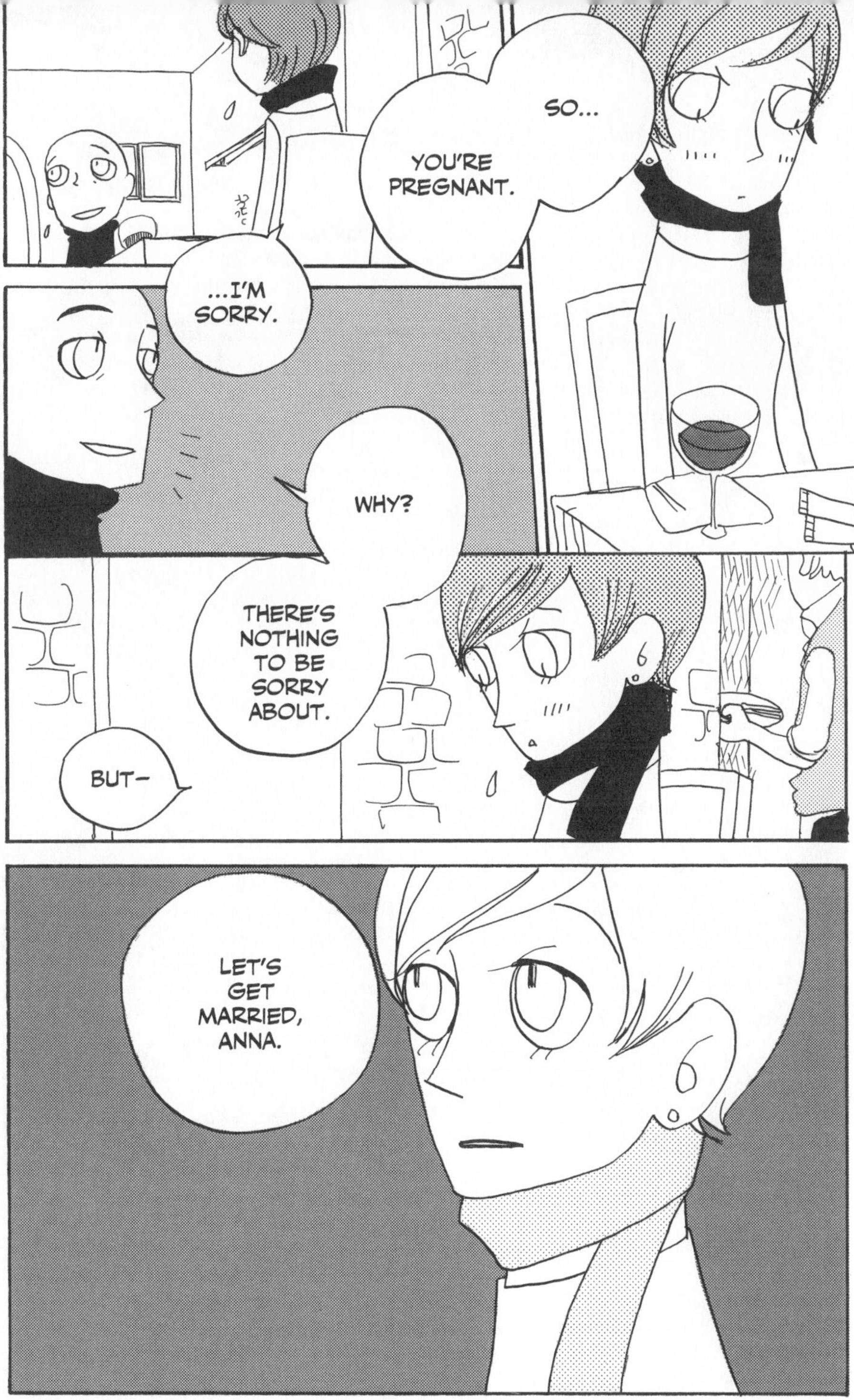
SO... YOU'RE PREGNANT.
...I'M SORRY.
WHY?
THERE'S NOTHING TO BE SORRY ABOUT.
BUT-
LET'S GET MARRIED, ANNA.

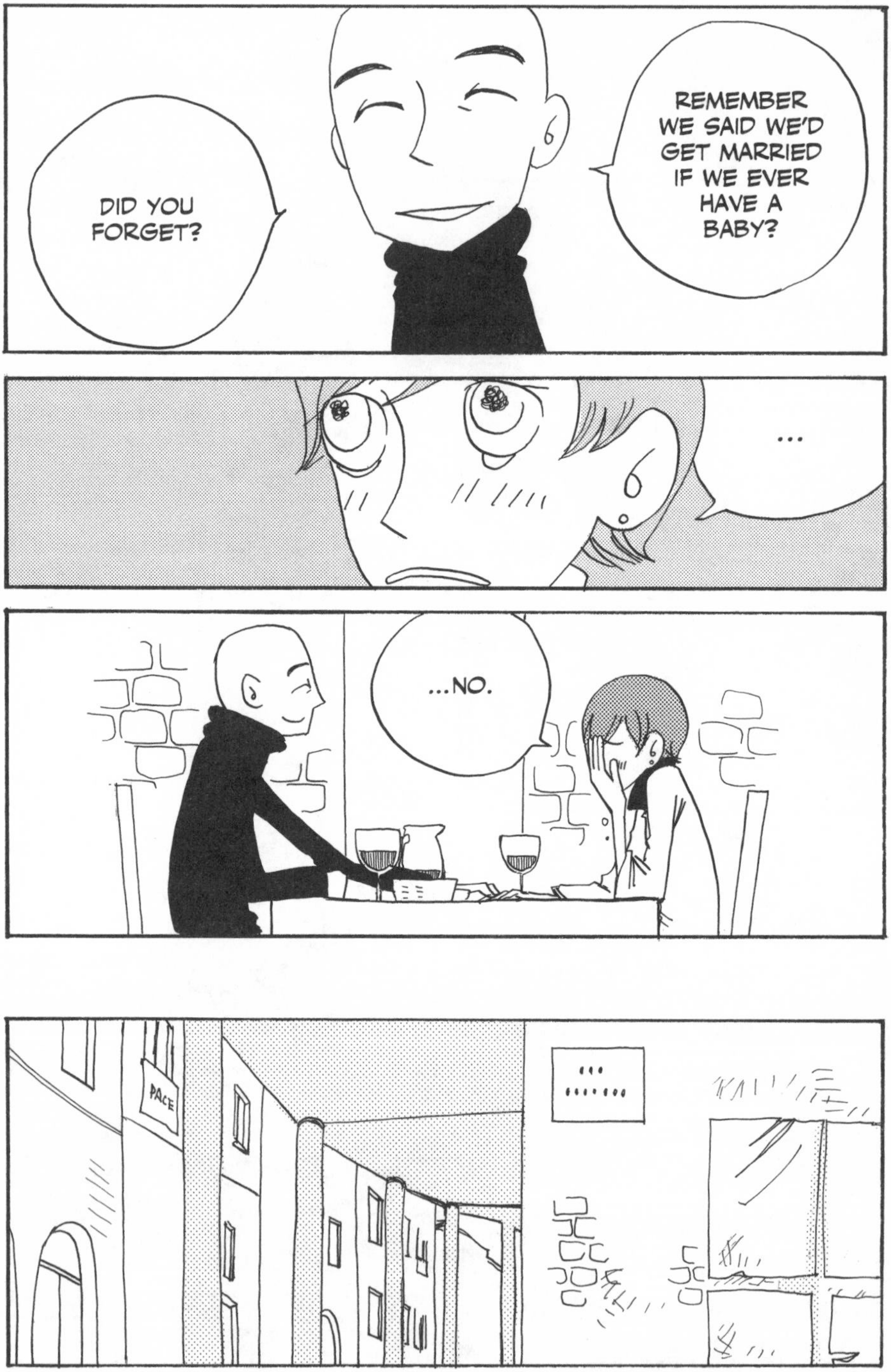
REMEMBER WE SAID WE'D GET MARRIED IF WE EVER HAVE A BABY?
DID YOU FORGET?
...
...NO.
PACE

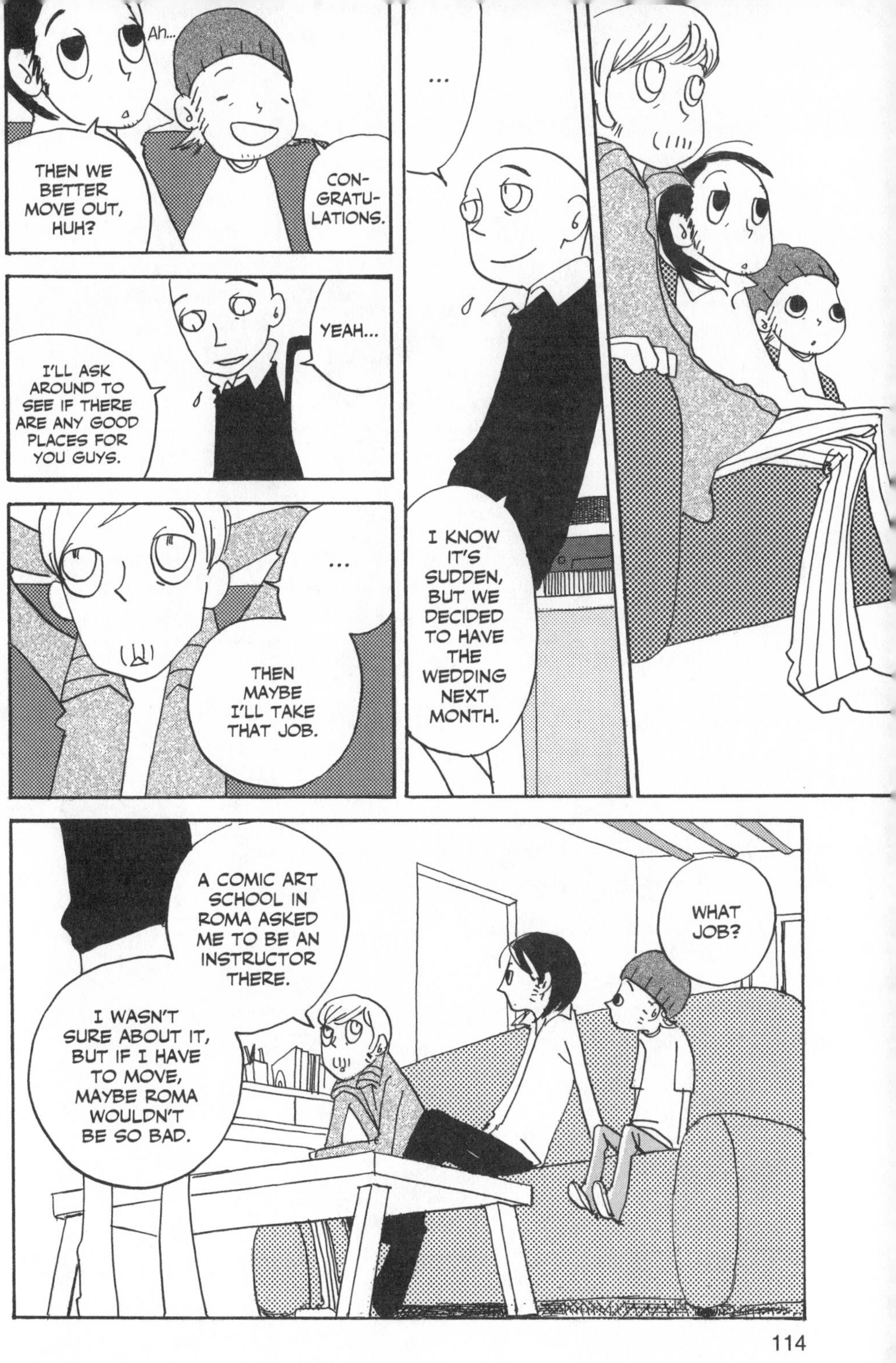
...
I KNOW IT'S SUDDEN, BUT WE DECIDED TO HAVE THE WEDDING NEXT MONTH.
CON-GRATU-LATIONS.
Ah...
THEN WE BETTER MOVE OUT, HUH?
YEAH...
I'LL ASK AROUND TO SEE IF THERE ARE ANY GOOD PLACES FOR YOU GUYS.
...
THEN MAYBE I'LL TAKE THAT JOB.
WHAT JOB?
A COMIC ART SCHOOL IN ROMA ASKED ME TO BE AN INSTRUCTOR THERE.
I WASN'T SURE ABOUT IT, BUT IF I HAVE TO MOVE, MAYBE ROMA WOULDN'T BE SO BAD.

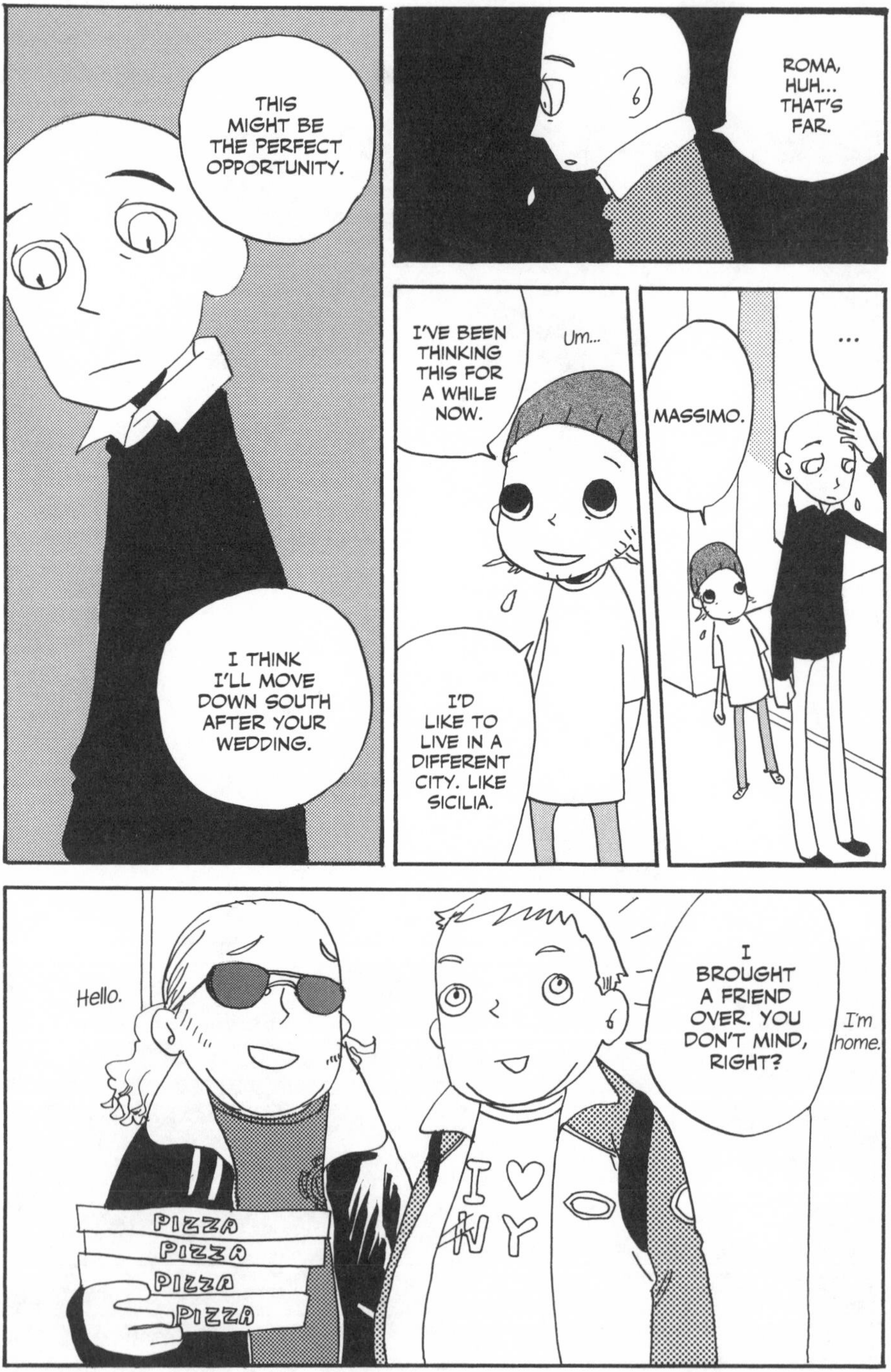
ROMA, HUH... THAT'S FAR.
...
MASSIMO.
Um...
I'VE BEEN THINKING THIS FOR A WHILE NOW.
I'D LIKE TO LIVE IN A DIFFERENT CITY. LIKE SICILIA.
THIS MIGHT BE THE PERFECT OPPORTUNITY.
I THINK I'LL MOVE DOWN SOUTH AFTER YOUR WEDDING.
I'm home.
I BROUGHT A FRIEND OVER. YOU DON'T MIND, RIGHT?
I ♥ NY
Hello.
PIZZA
PIZZA
PIZZA
PIZZA

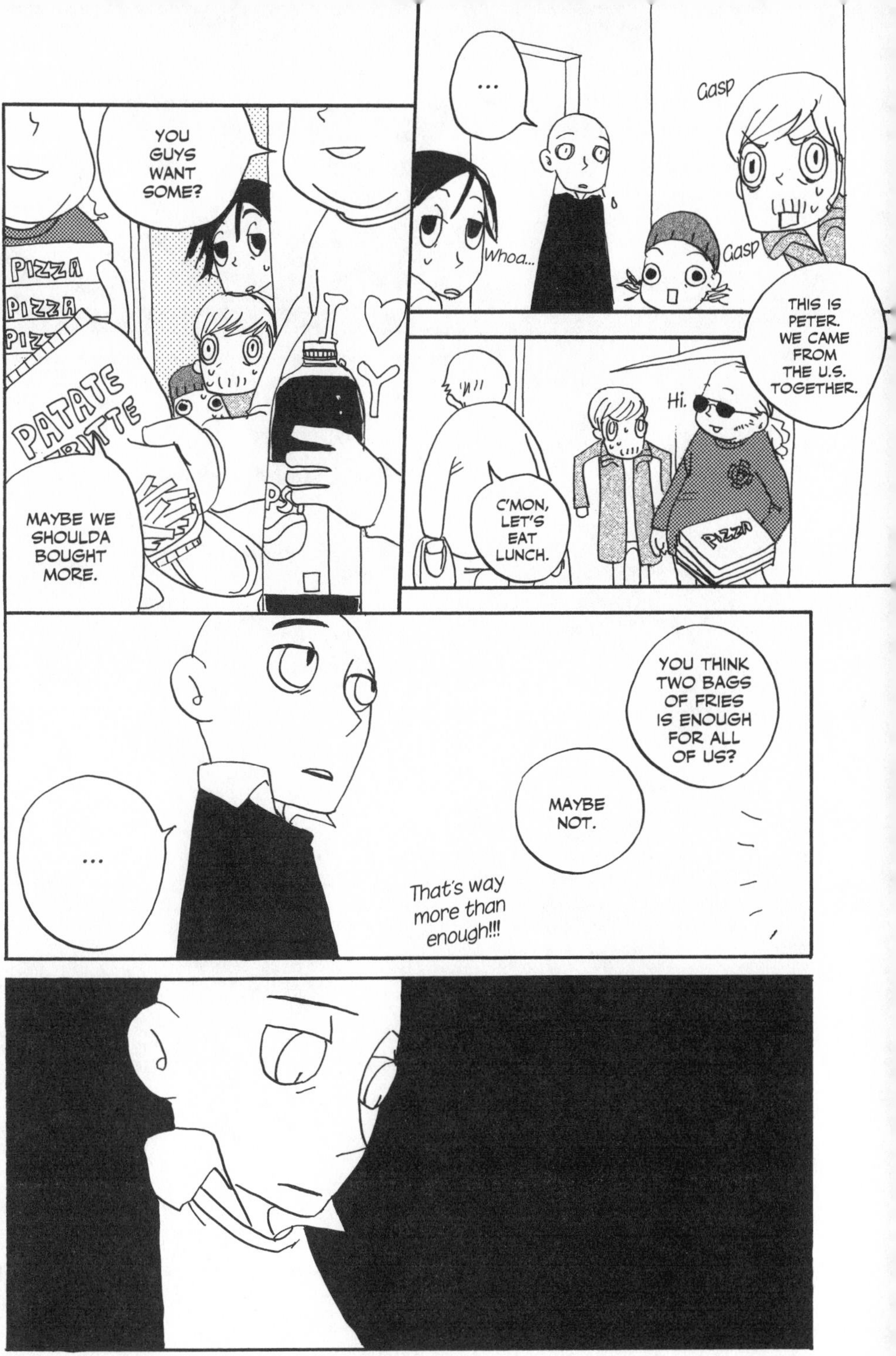

Gasp
...
Gasp
Whoa...
THIS IS PETER. WE CAME FROM THE U.S. TOGETHER.
Hi.
C'MON, LET'S EAT LUNCH.
YOU GUYS WANT SOME?
PIZZA
PIZZA
PATATE FRITTE
MAYBE WE SHOULDA BOUGHT MORE.
YOU THINK TWO BAGS OF FRIES IS ENOUGH FOR ALL OF US?
MAYBE NOT.
That's way more than enough!!!
...

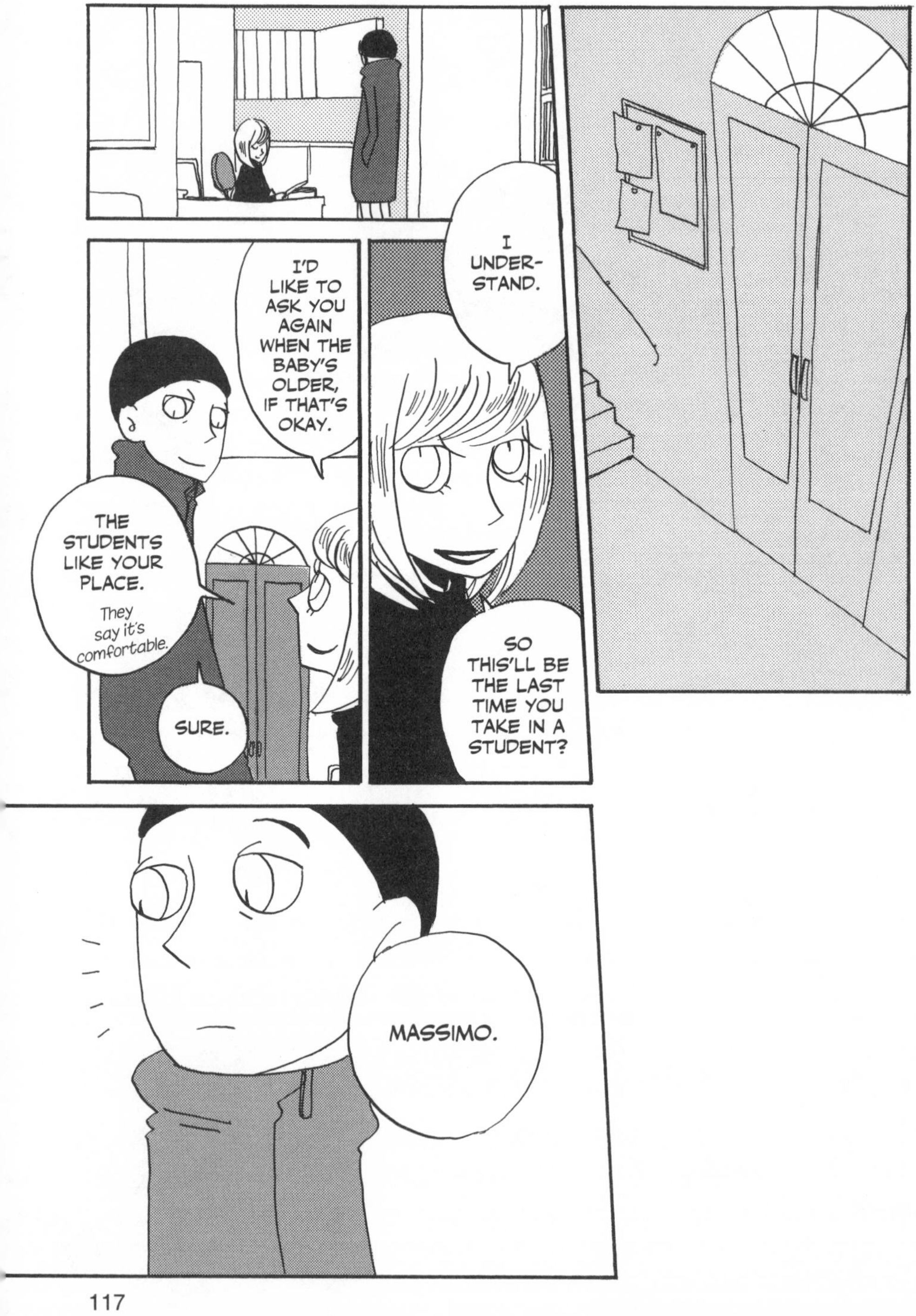

I UNDER-STAND.
SO THIS'LL BE THE LAST TIME YOU TAKE IN A STUDENT?
I'D LIKE TO ASK YOU AGAIN WHEN THE BABY'S OLDER, IF THAT'S OKAY.
SURE.
THE STUDENTS LIKE YOUR PLACE. They say it's comfortable.
MASSIMO.

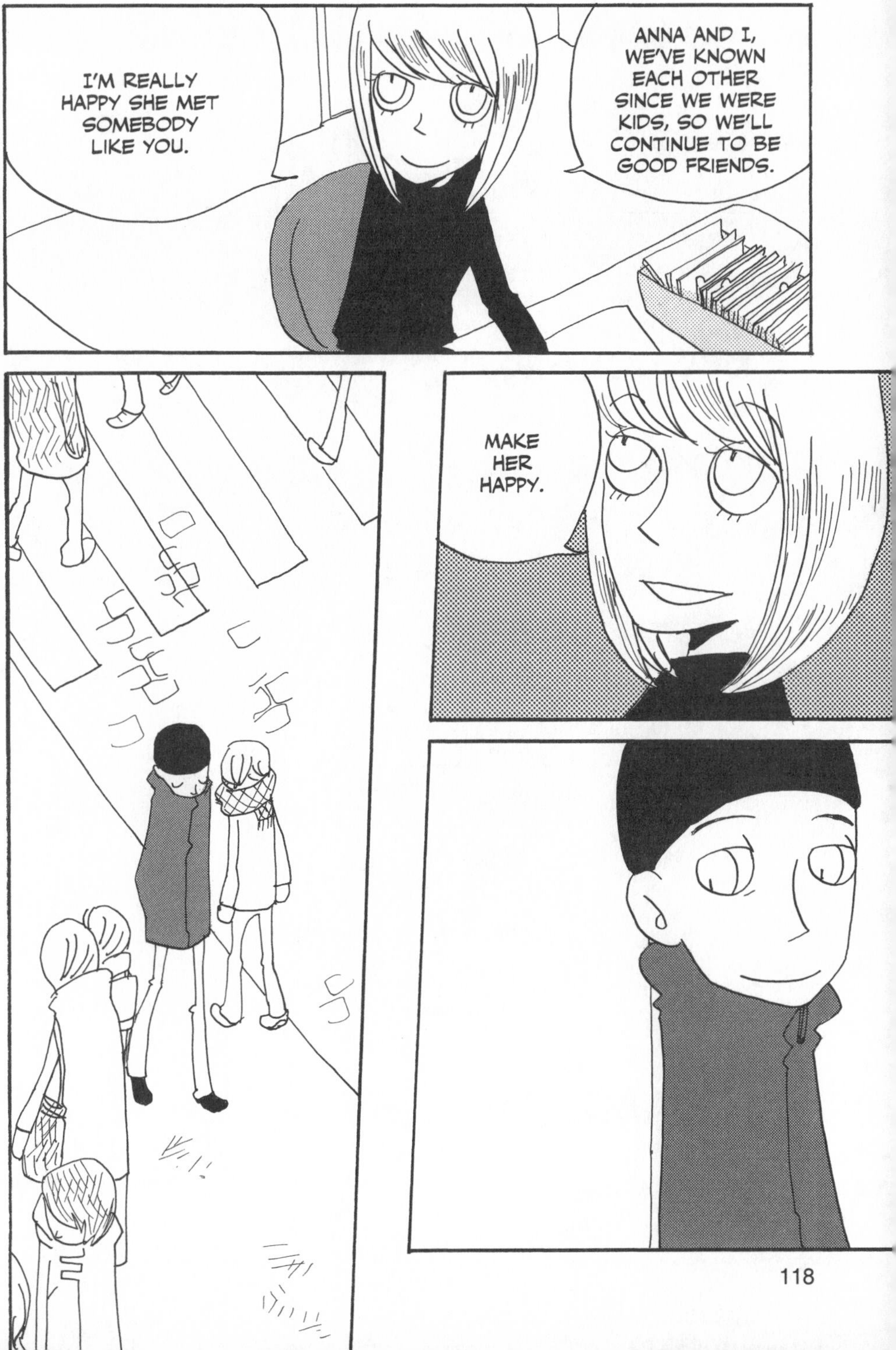
ANNA AND I, WE'VE KNOWN EACH OTHER SINCE WE WERE KIDS, SO WE'LL CONTINUE TO BE GOOD FRIENDS.
I'M REALLY HAPPY SHE MET SOMEBODY LIKE YOU.
MAKE HER HAPPY.

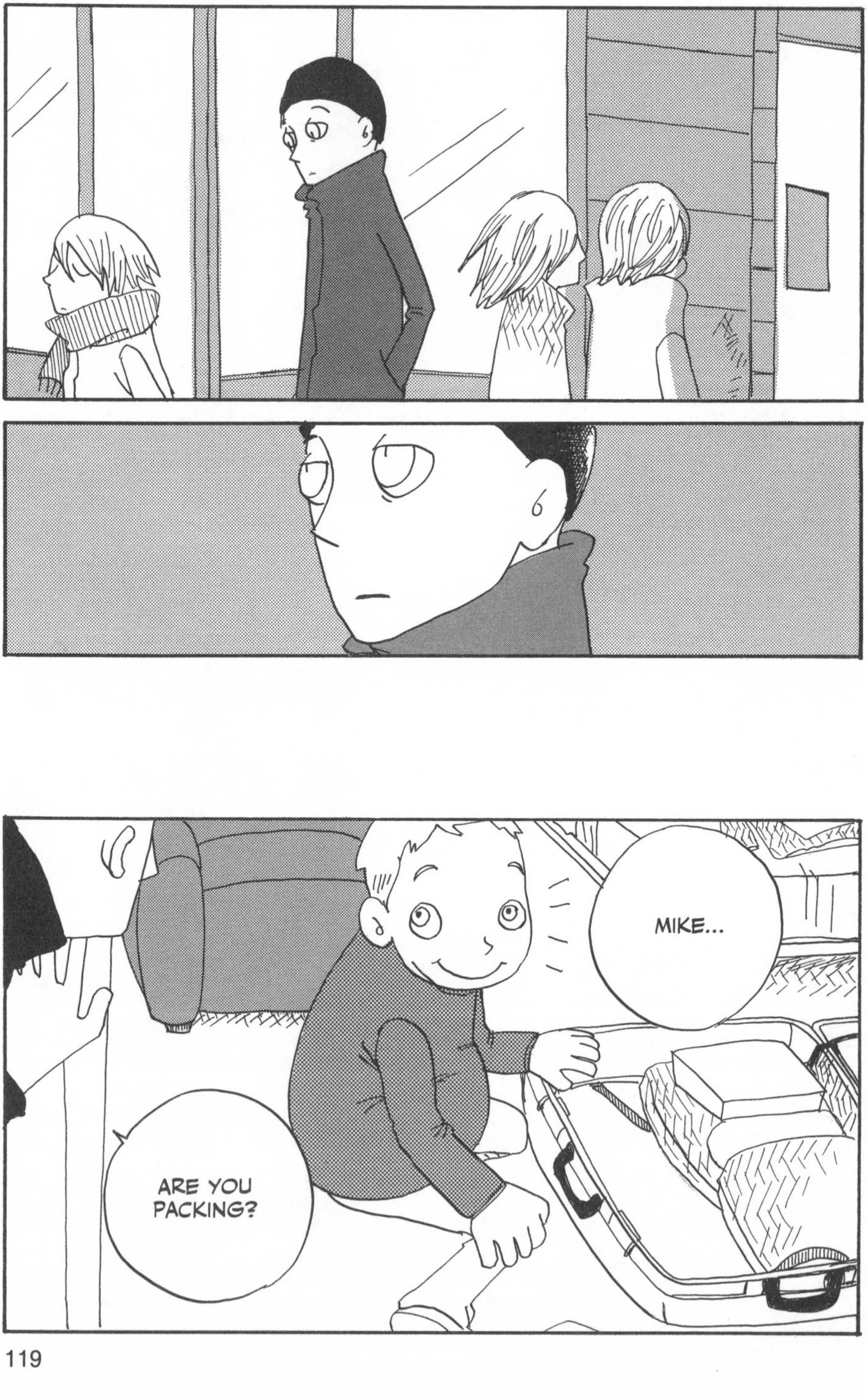
MIKE...
ARE YOU PACKING?

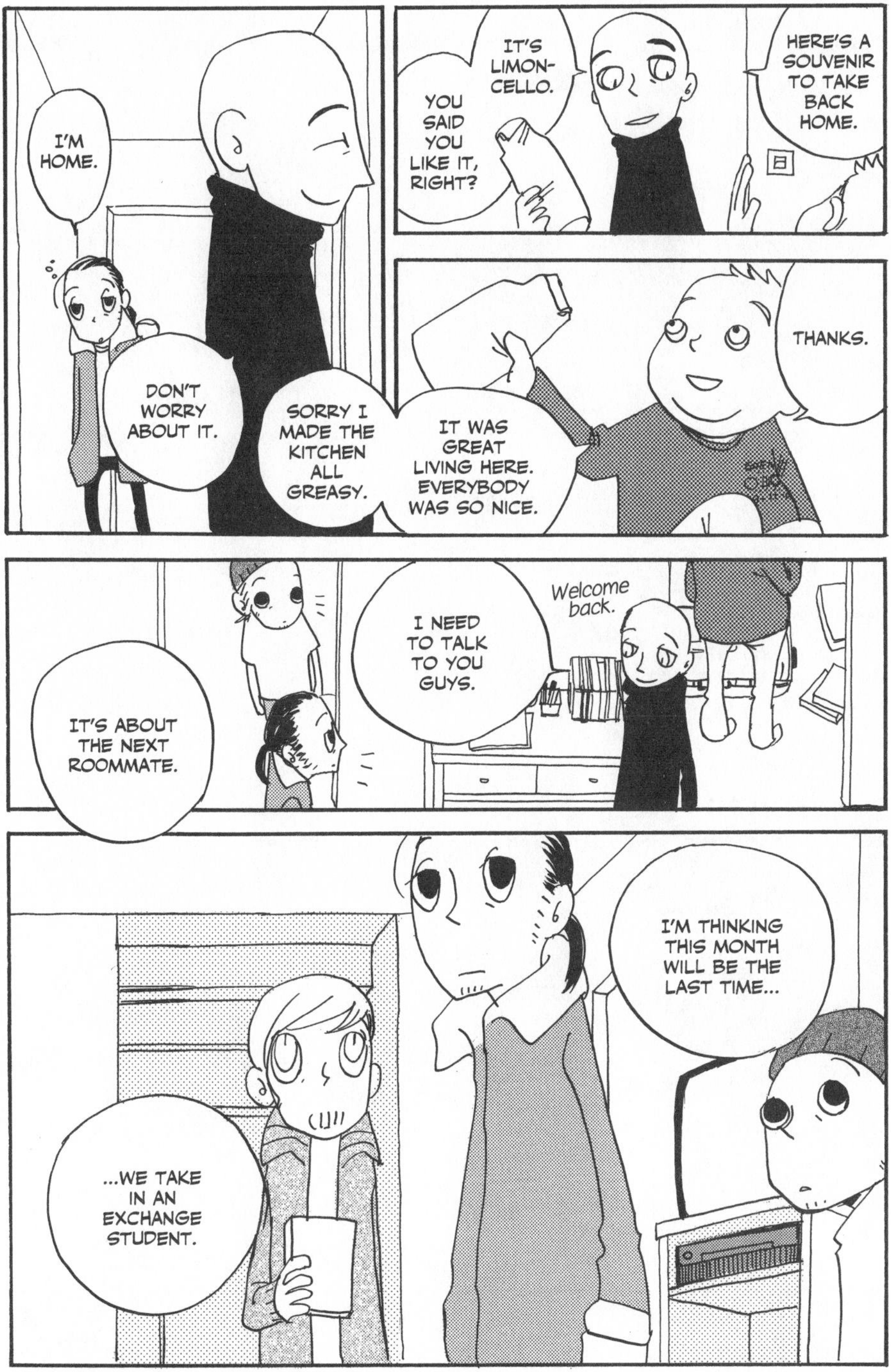
HERE'S A SOUVENIR TO TAKE BACK HOME.
IT'S LIMONCELLO.
YOU SAID YOU LIKE IT, RIGHT?
THANKS.
IT WAS GREAT LIVING HERE. EVERYBODY WAS SO NICE.
I'M HOME.
SORRY I MADE THE KITCHEN ALL GREASY.
DON'T WORRY ABOUT IT.
Welcome back.
I NEED TO TALK TO YOU GUYS.
IT'S ABOUT THE NEXT ROOMMATE.
I'M THINKING THIS MONTH WILL BE THE LAST TIME...
...WE TAKE IN AN EXCHANGE STUDENT.

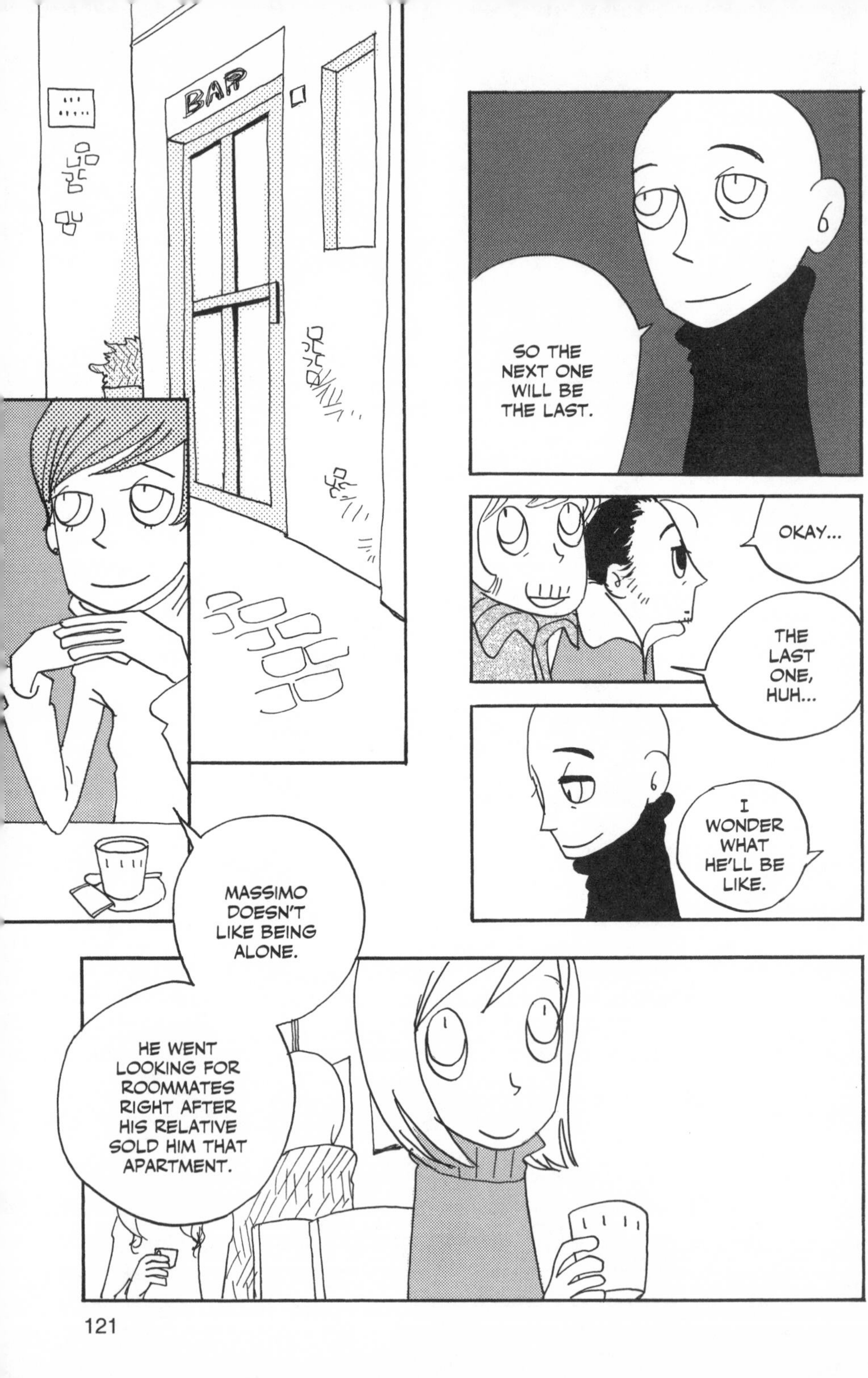
SO THE NEXT ONE WILL BE THE LAST.
OKAY...
THE LAST ONE, HUH...
I WONDER WHAT HE'LL BE LIKE.
BAR
MASSIMO DOESN'T LIKE BEING ALONE.
HE WENT LOOKING FOR ROOMMATES RIGHT AFTER HIS RELATIVE SOLD HIM THAT APARTMENT.

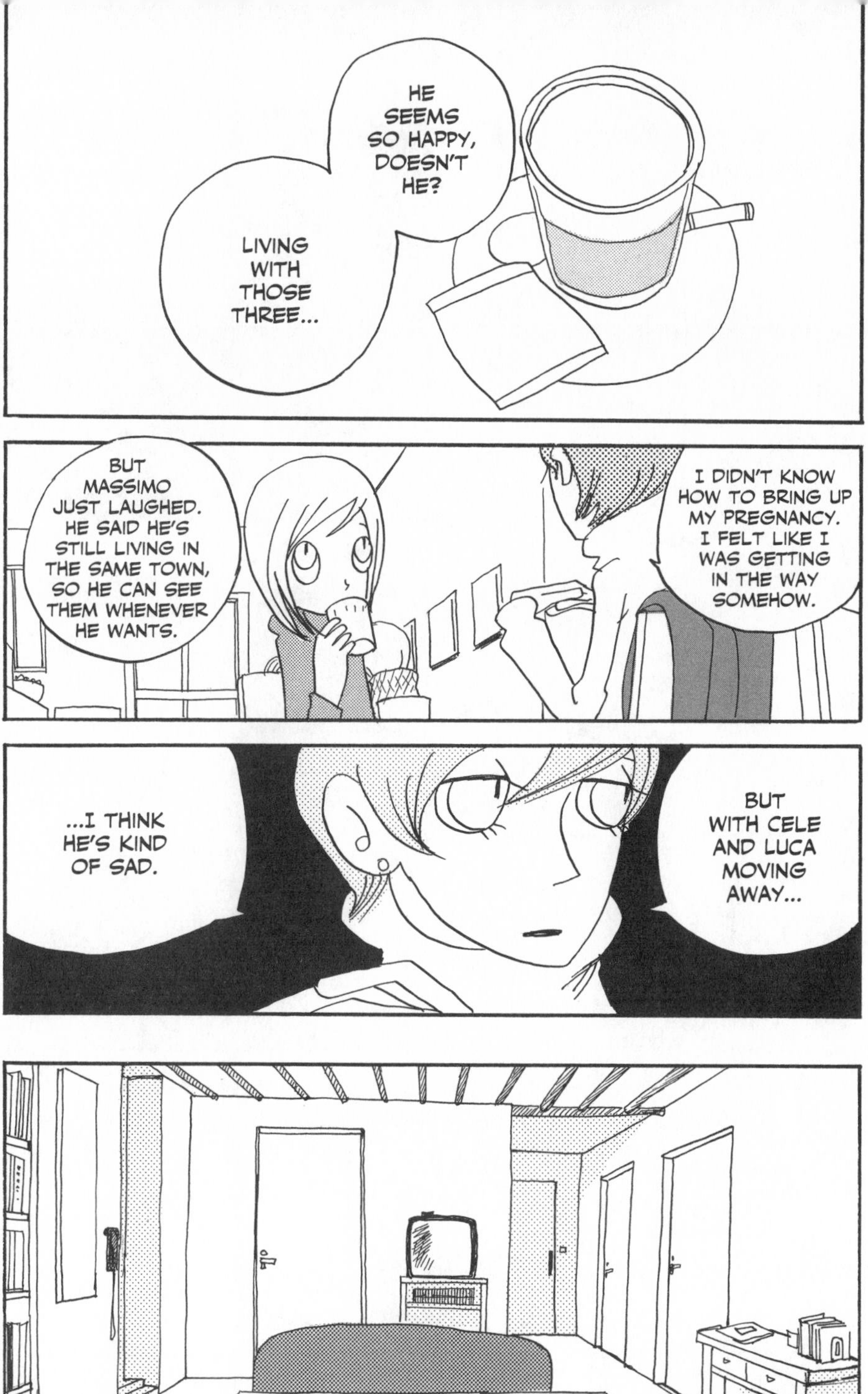
HE SEEMS SO HAPPY, DOESN'T HE?
LIVING WITH THOSE THREE...
I DIDN'T KNOW HOW TO BRING UP MY PREGNANCY. I FELT LIKE I WAS GETTING IN THE WAY SOMEHOW.
BUT MASSIMO JUST LAUGHED. HE SAID HE'S STILL LIVING IN THE SAME TOWN, SO HE CAN SEE THEM WHENEVER HE WANTS.
BUT WITH CELE AND LUCA MOVING AWAY...
...I THINK HE'S KIND OF SAD.

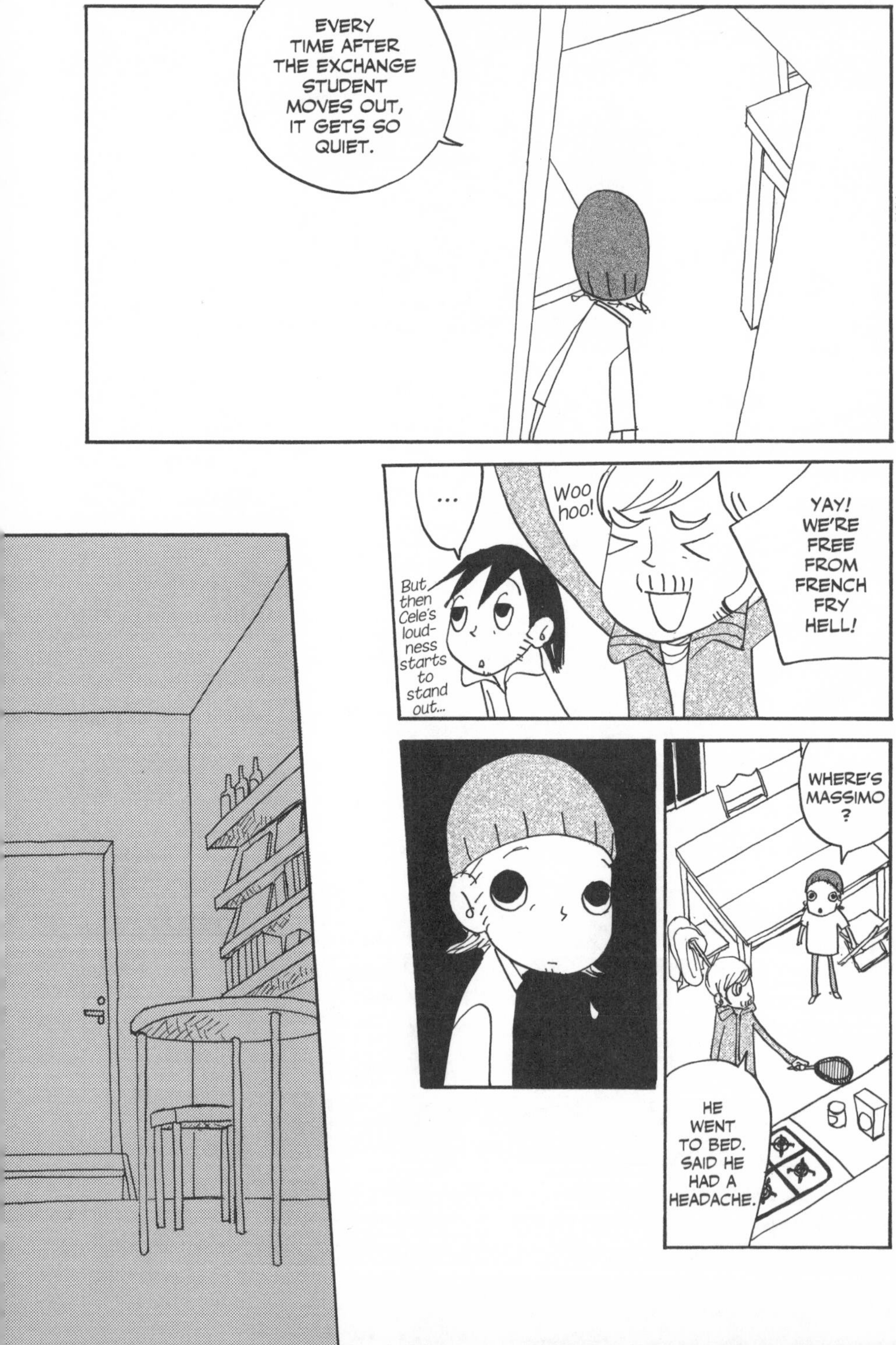
EVERY TIME AFTER THE EXCHANGE STUDENT MOVES OUT, IT GETS SO QUIET.
YAY! WE'RE FREE FROM FRENCH FRY HELL!
Woo hoo!
...
But then Cele's loud-ness starts to stand out...
WHERE'S MASSIMO?
HE WENT TO BED. SAID HE HAD A HEADACHE.

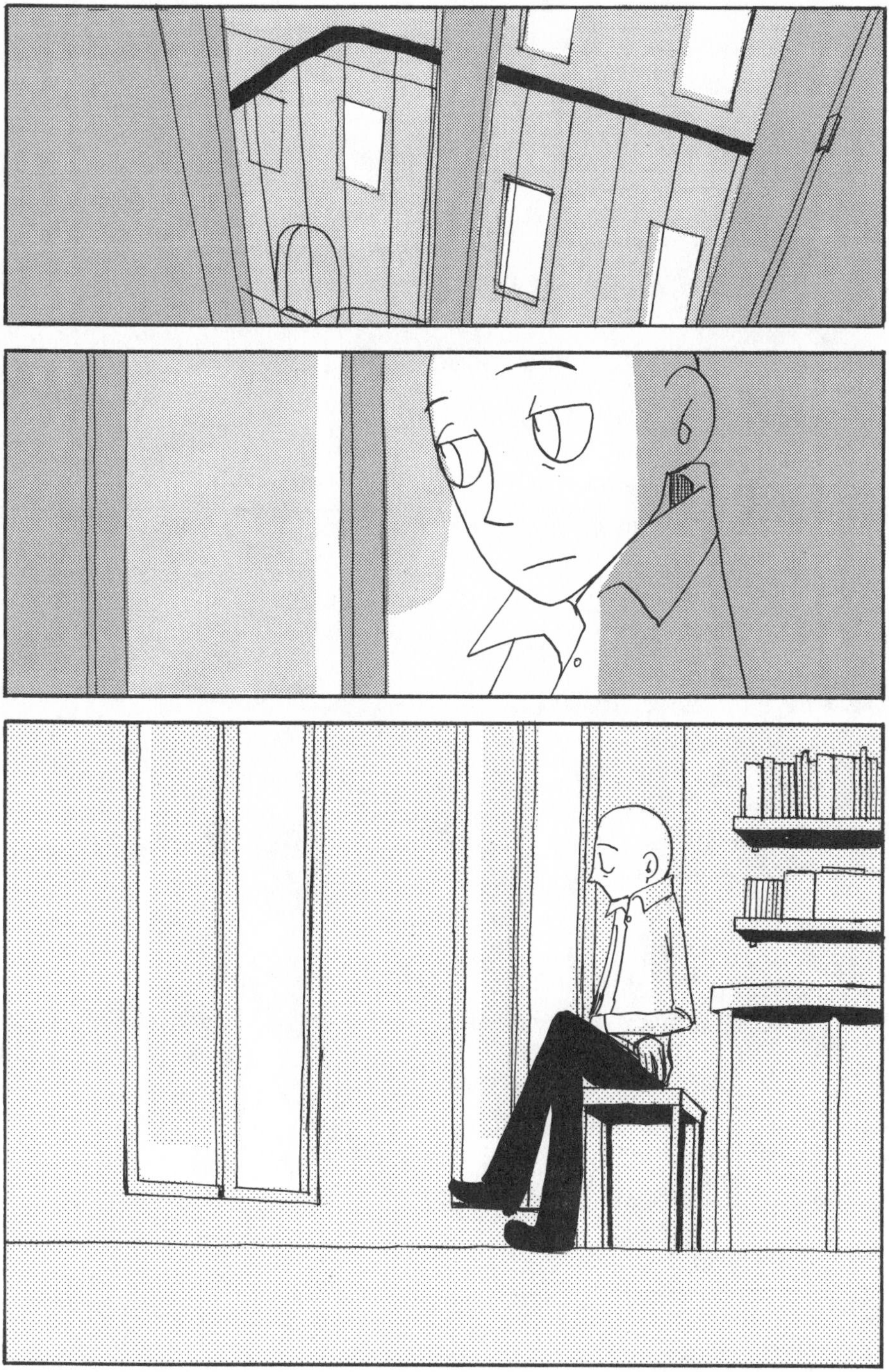

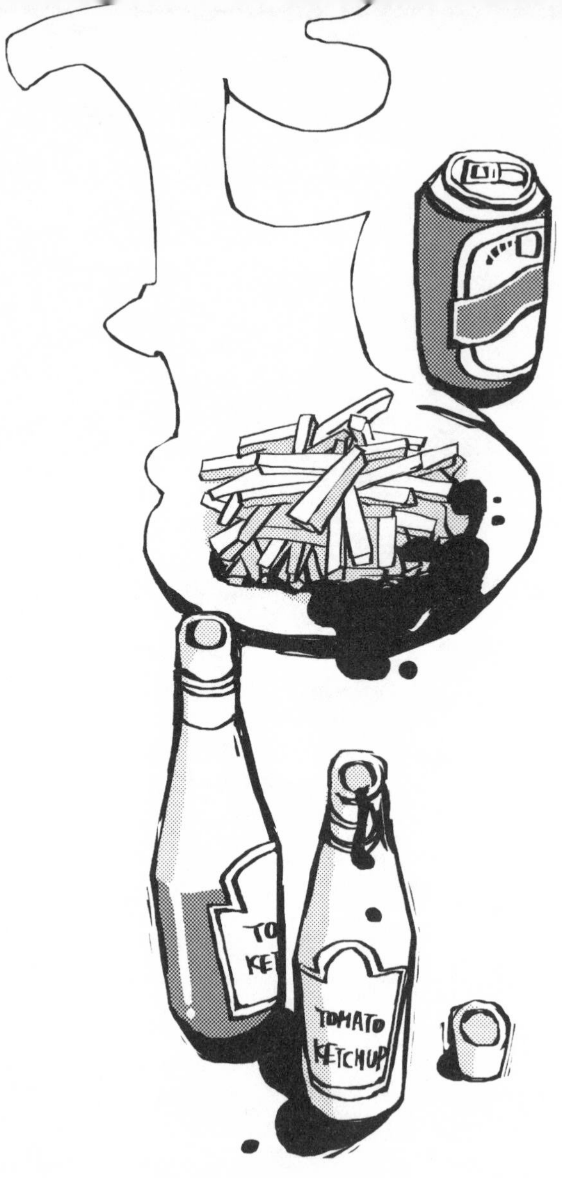
TO
KET
TOMATO
KETCHUP

LA QUINTA CAMERA
Capitolo 5

La Quinta Camera
Capitolo 6

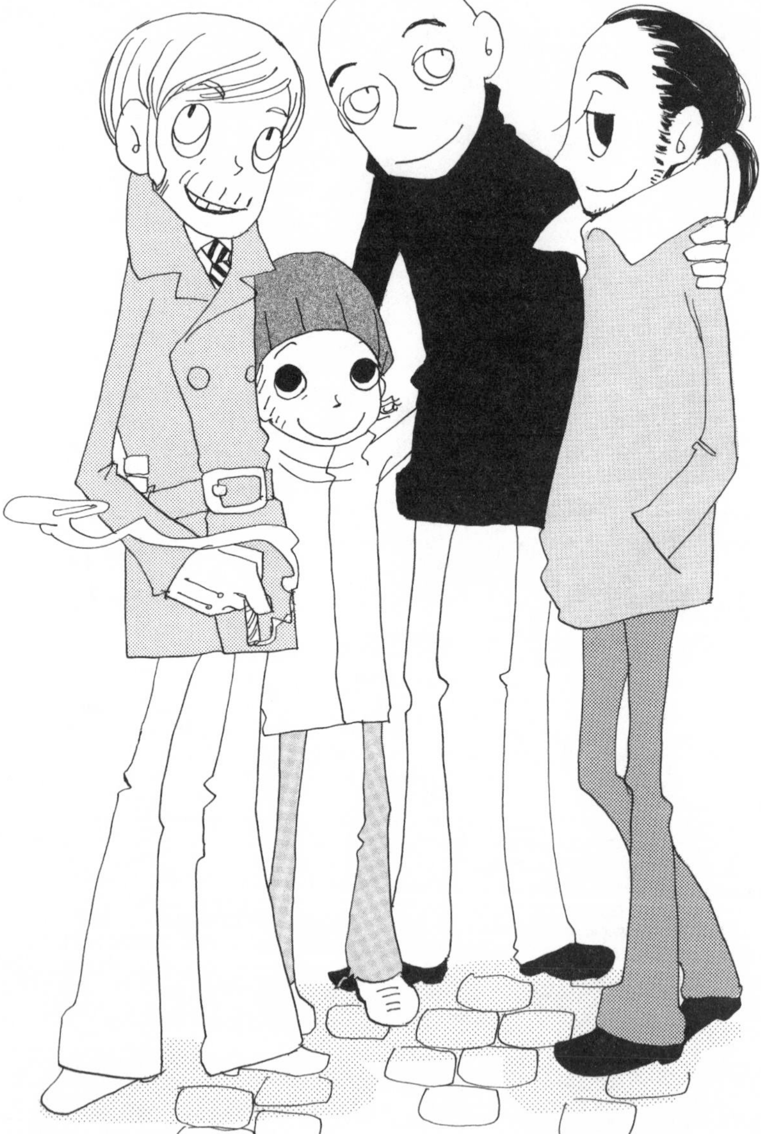

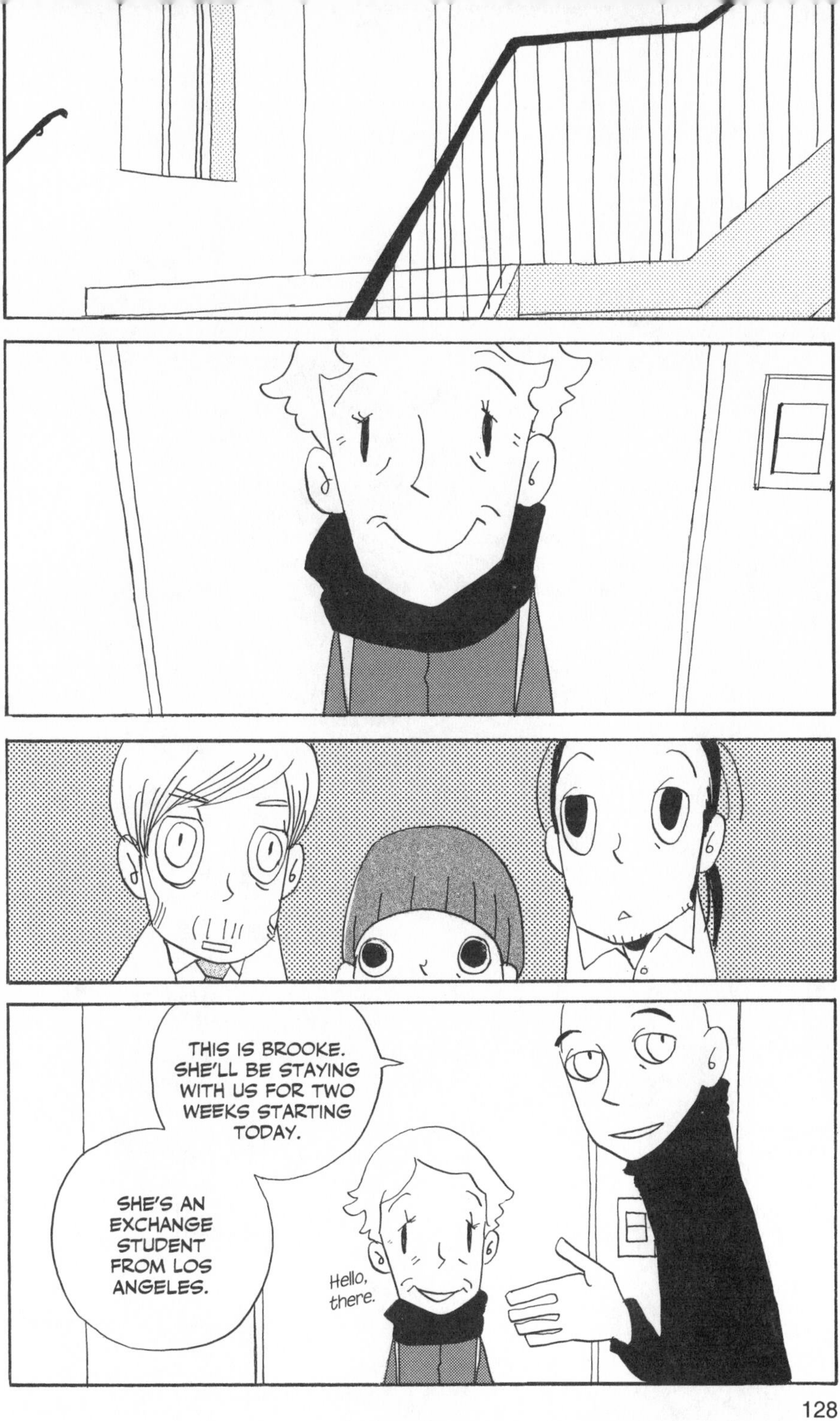
THIS IS BROOKE. SHE'LL BE STAYING WITH US FOR TWO WEEKS STARTING TODAY.
SHE'S AN EXCHANGE STUDENT FROM LOS ANGELES.
Hello, there.

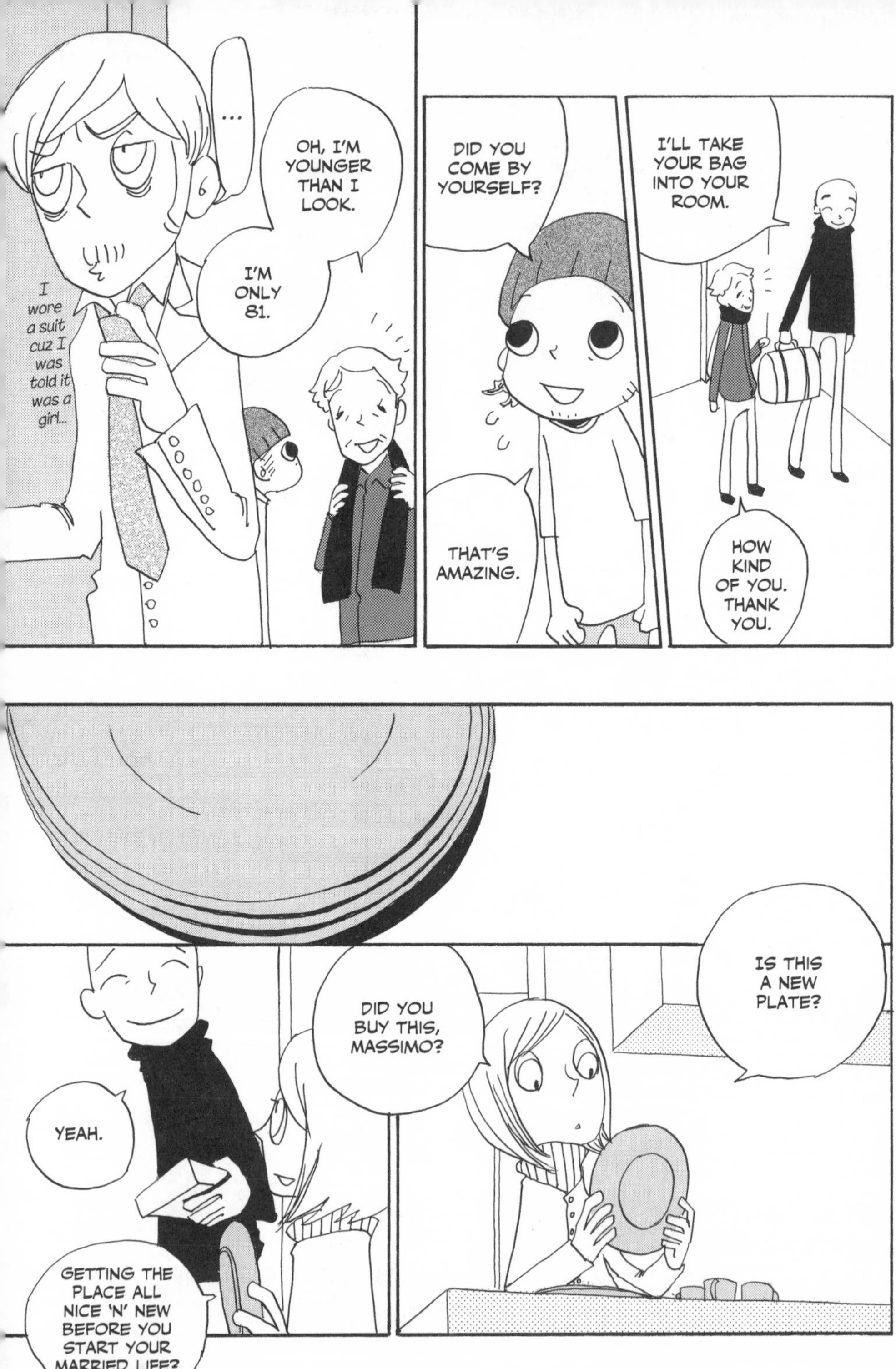
I'LL TAKE YOUR BAG INTO YOUR ROOM.
HOW KIND OF YOU. THANK YOU.
DID YOU COME BY YOURSELF?
THAT'S AMAZING.
...
OH, I'M YOUNGER THAN I LOOK.
I'M ONLY 81.
I wore a suit cuz I was told it was a girl...
IS THIS A NEW PLATE?
DID YOU BUY THIS, MASSIMO?
YEAH.
GETTING THE PLACE ALL NICE 'N' NEW BEFORE YOU START YOUR MARRIED LIFE?

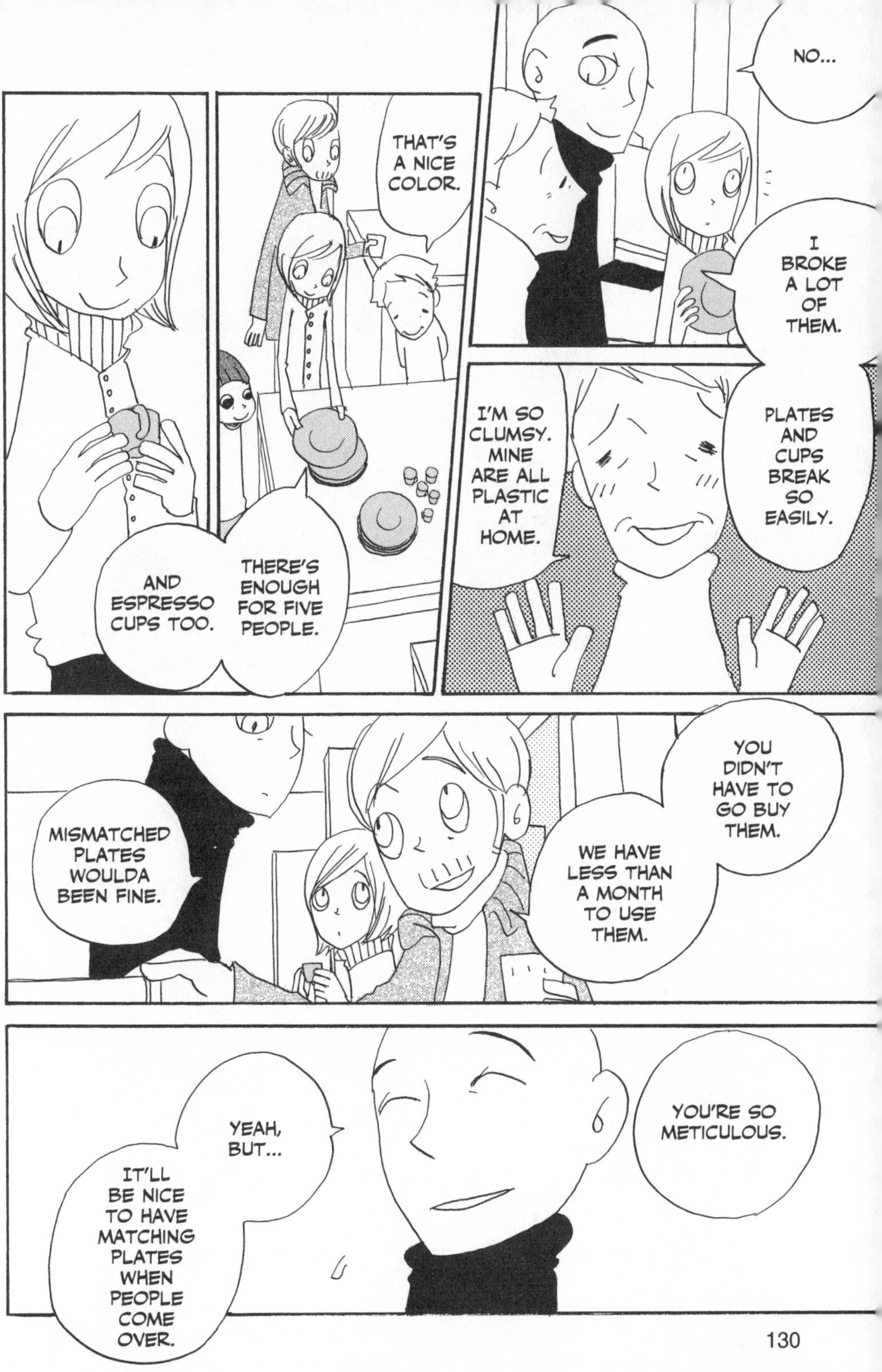
NO...
I BROKE A LOT OF THEM.
PLATES AND CUPS BREAK SO EASILY.
I'M SO CLUMSY. MINE ARE ALL PLASTIC AT HOME.
THAT'S A NICE COLOR.
THERE'S ENOUGH FOR FIVE PEOPLE.
AND ESPRESSO CUPS TOO.
YOU DIDN'T HAVE TO GO BUY THEM.
WE HAVE LESS THAN A MONTH TO USE THEM.
MISMATCHED PLATES WOULDA BEEN FINE.
YOU'RE SO METICULOUS.
YEAH, BUT...
IT'LL BE NICE TO HAVE MATCHING PLATES WHEN PEOPLE COME OVER.

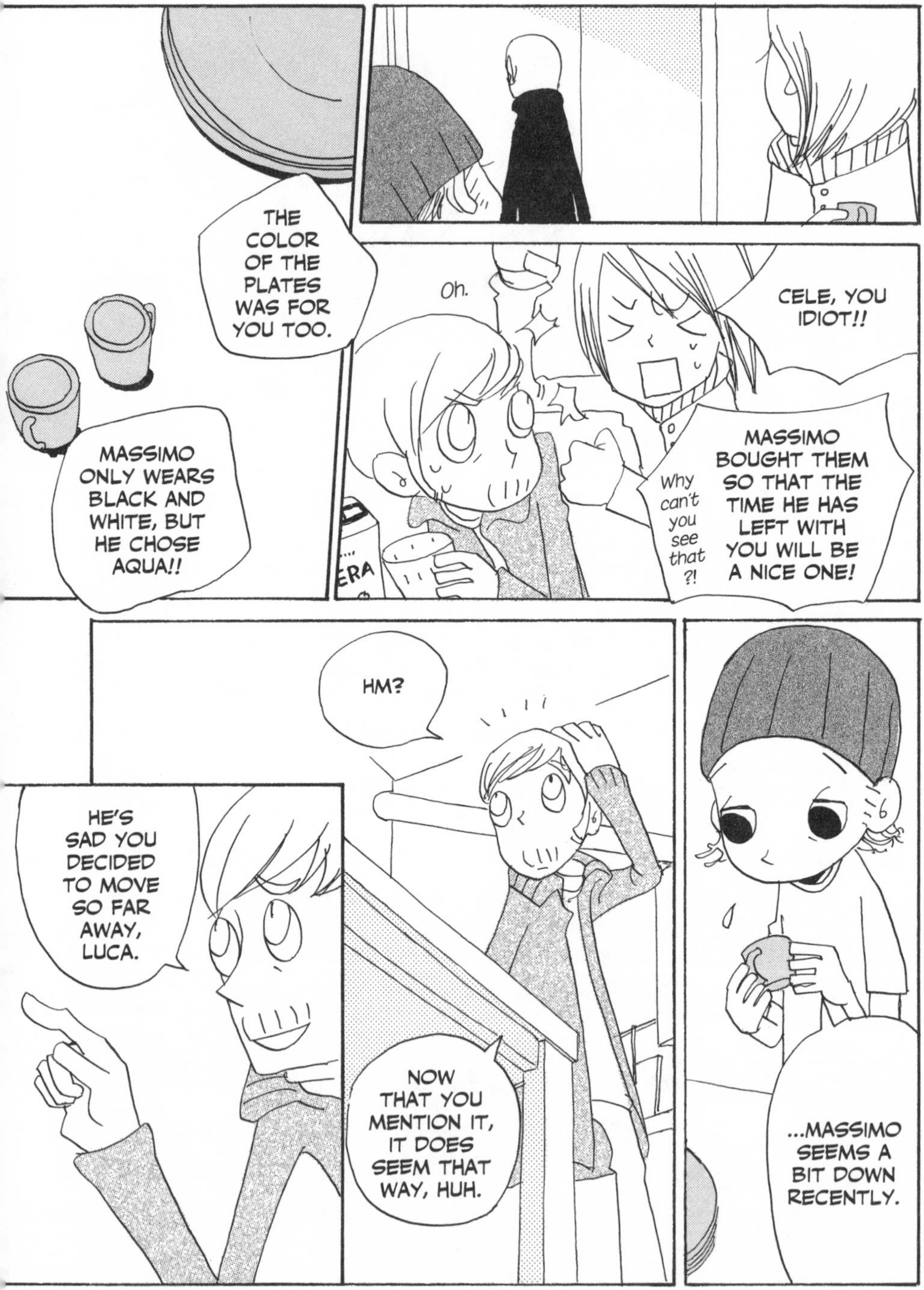
CELE, YOU IDIOT!!
MASSIMO BOUGHT THEM SO THAT THE TIME HE HAS LEFT WITH YOU WILL BE A NICE ONE!
Why can't you see that?!
Oh.
THE COLOR OF THE PLATES WAS FOR YOU TOO.
MASSIMO ONLY WEARS BLACK AND WHITE, BUT HE CHOSE AQUA!!
...MASSIMO SEEMS A BIT DOWN RECENTLY.
HM?
HE'S SAD YOU DECIDED TO MOVE SO FAR AWAY, LUCA.
NOW THAT YOU MENTION IT, IT DOES SEEM THAT WAY, HUH.

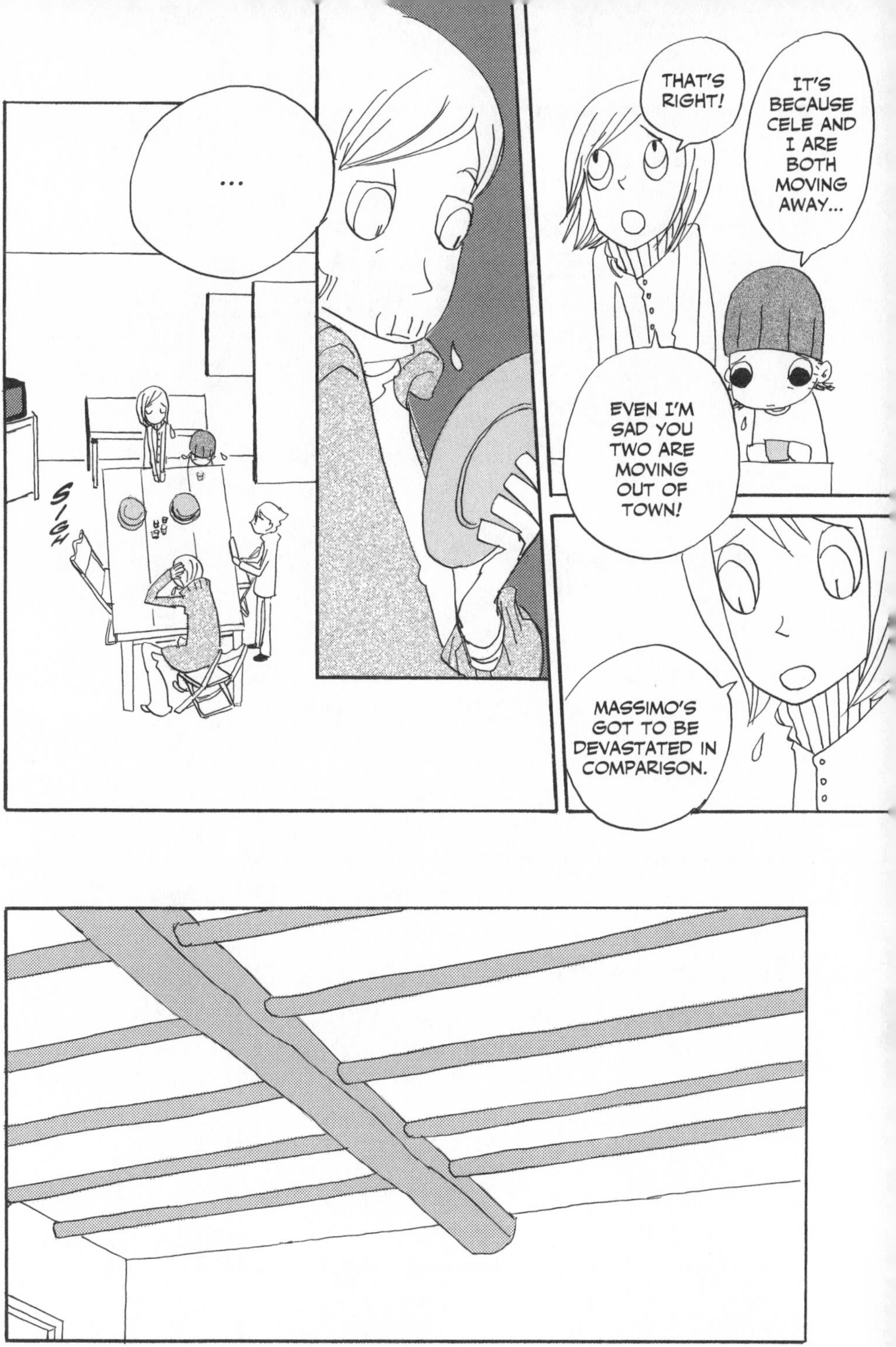
THAT'S RIGHT!
IT'S BECAUSE CELE AND I ARE BOTH MOVING AWAY...
EVEN I'M SAD YOU TWO ARE MOVING OUT OF TOWN!
MASSIMO'S GOT TO BE DEVASTATED IN COMPARISON.
...
SIGH

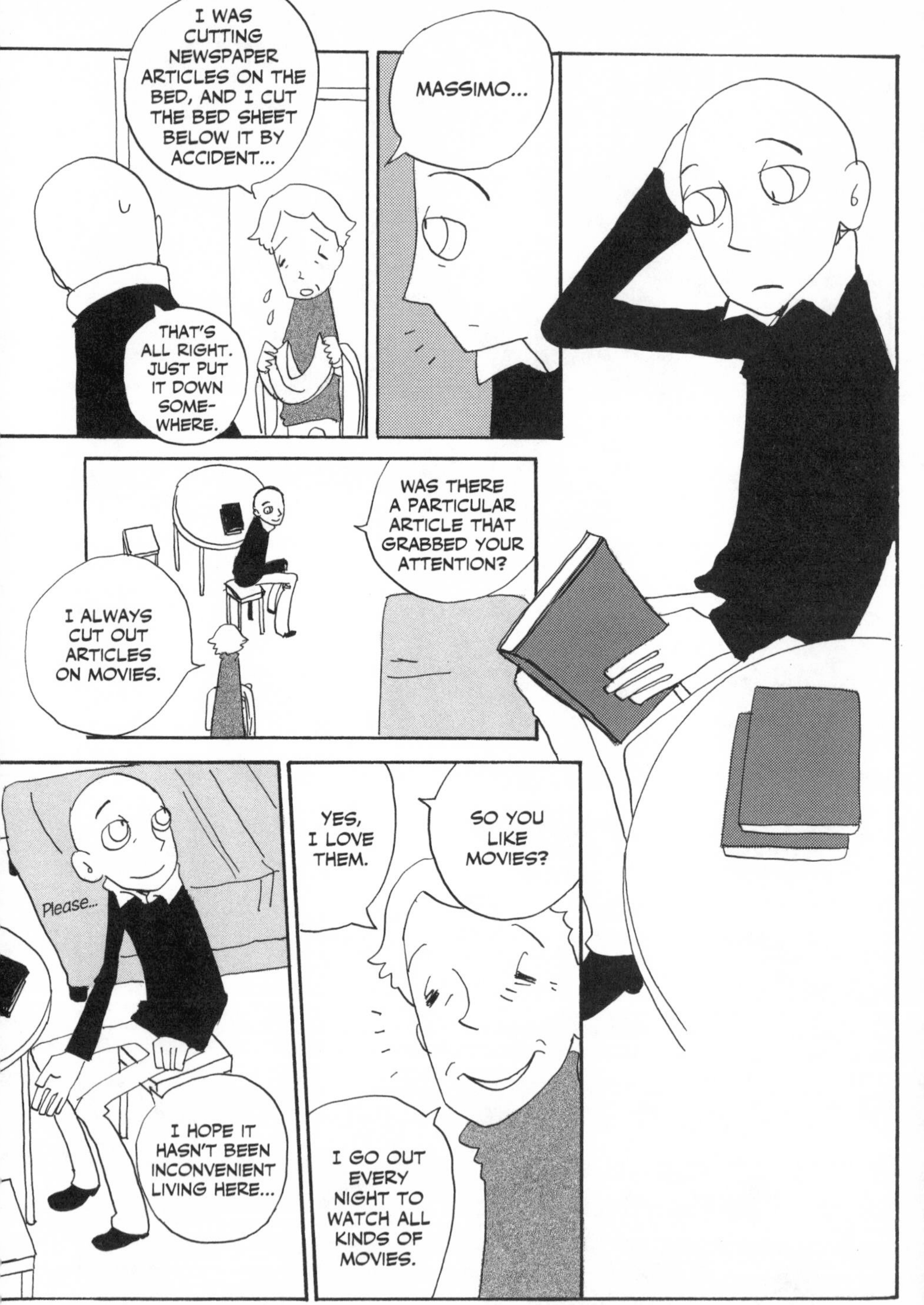
MASSIMO...
I WAS CUTTING NEWSPAPER ARTICLES ON THE BED, AND I CUT THE BED SHEET BELOW IT BY ACCIDENT...
THAT'S ALL RIGHT. JUST PUT IT DOWN SOME-WHERE.
WAS THERE A PARTICULAR ARTICLE THAT GRABBED YOUR ATTENTION?
I ALWAYS CUT OUT ARTICLES ON MOVIES.
SO YOU LIKE MOVIES?
YES, I LOVE THEM.
I GO OUT EVERY NIGHT TO WATCH ALL KINDS OF MOVIES.
Please...
I HOPE IT HASN'T BEEN INCONVENIENT LIVING HERE...

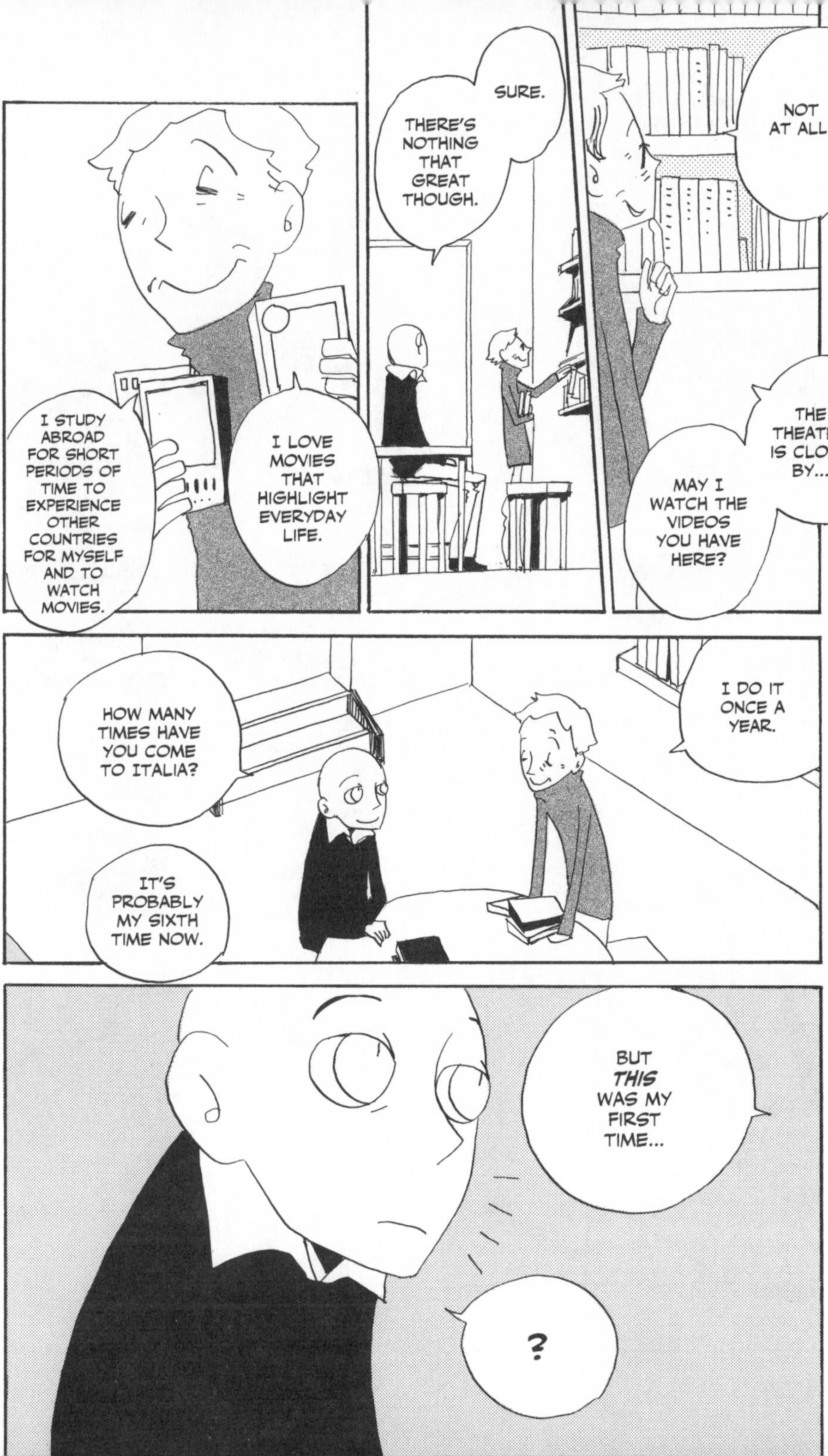
NOT AT ALL.
THE THEATER IS CLOSE BY...
MAY I WATCH THE VIDEOS YOU HAVE HERE?
SURE.
THERE'S NOTHING THAT GREAT THOUGH.
I LOVE MOVIES THAT HIGHLIGHT EVERYDAY LIFE.
I STUDY ABROAD FOR SHORT PERIODS OF TIME TO EXPERIENCE OTHER COUNTRIES FOR MYSELF AND TO WATCH MOVIES.
I DO IT ONCE A YEAR.
HOW MANY TIMES HAVE YOU COME TO ITALIA?
IT'S PROBABLY MY SIXTH TIME NOW.
BUT *THIS* WAS MY FIRST TIME...
?

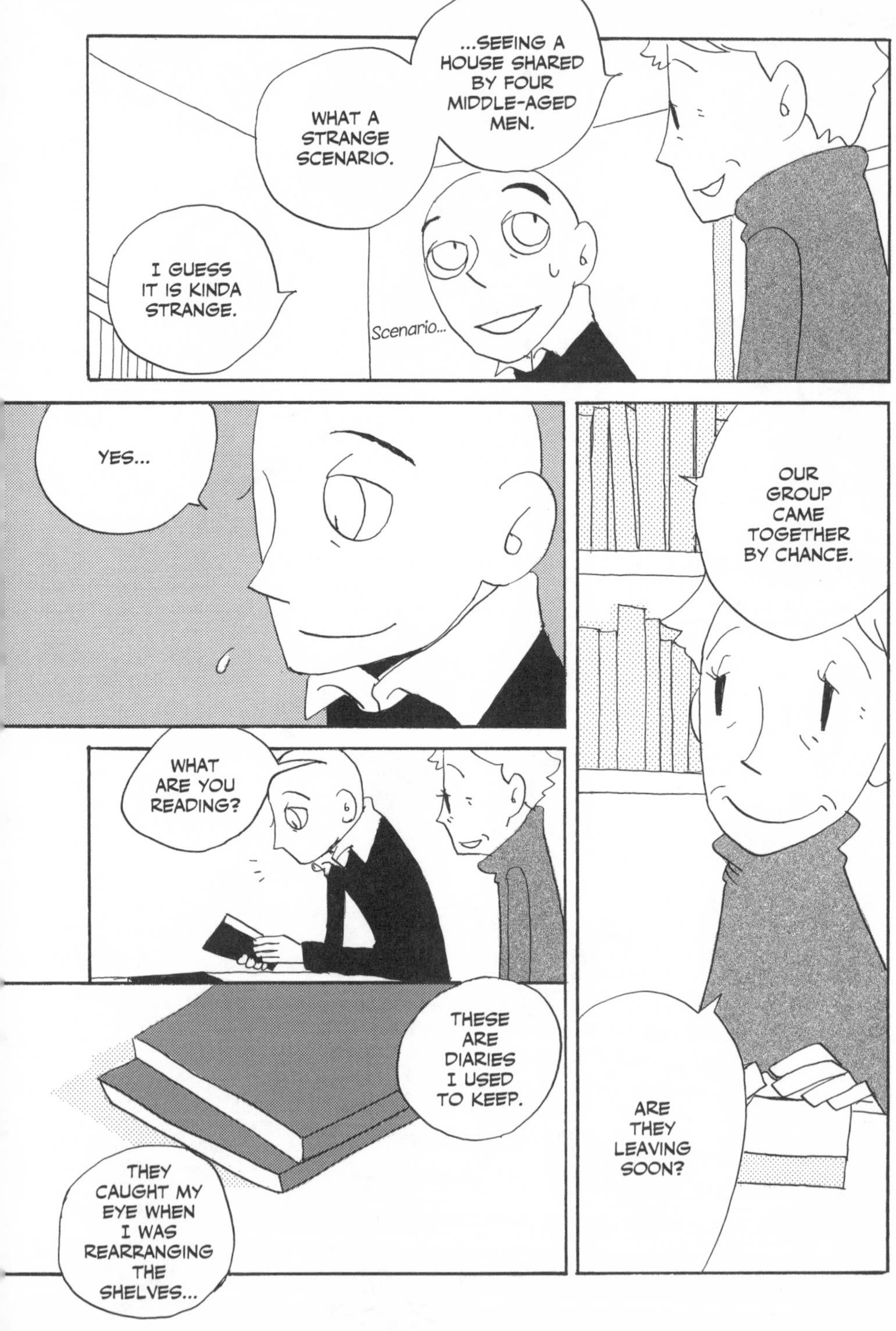
...SEEING A HOUSE SHARED BY FOUR MIDDLE-AGED MEN.
WHAT A STRANGE SCENARIO.
Scenario...
I GUESS IT IS KINDA STRANGE.
OUR GROUP CAME TOGETHER BY CHANCE.
ARE THEY LEAVING SOON?
YES...
WHAT ARE YOU READING?
THESE ARE DIARIES I USED TO KEEP.
THEY CAUGHT MY EYE WHEN I WAS REARRANGING THE SHELVES...

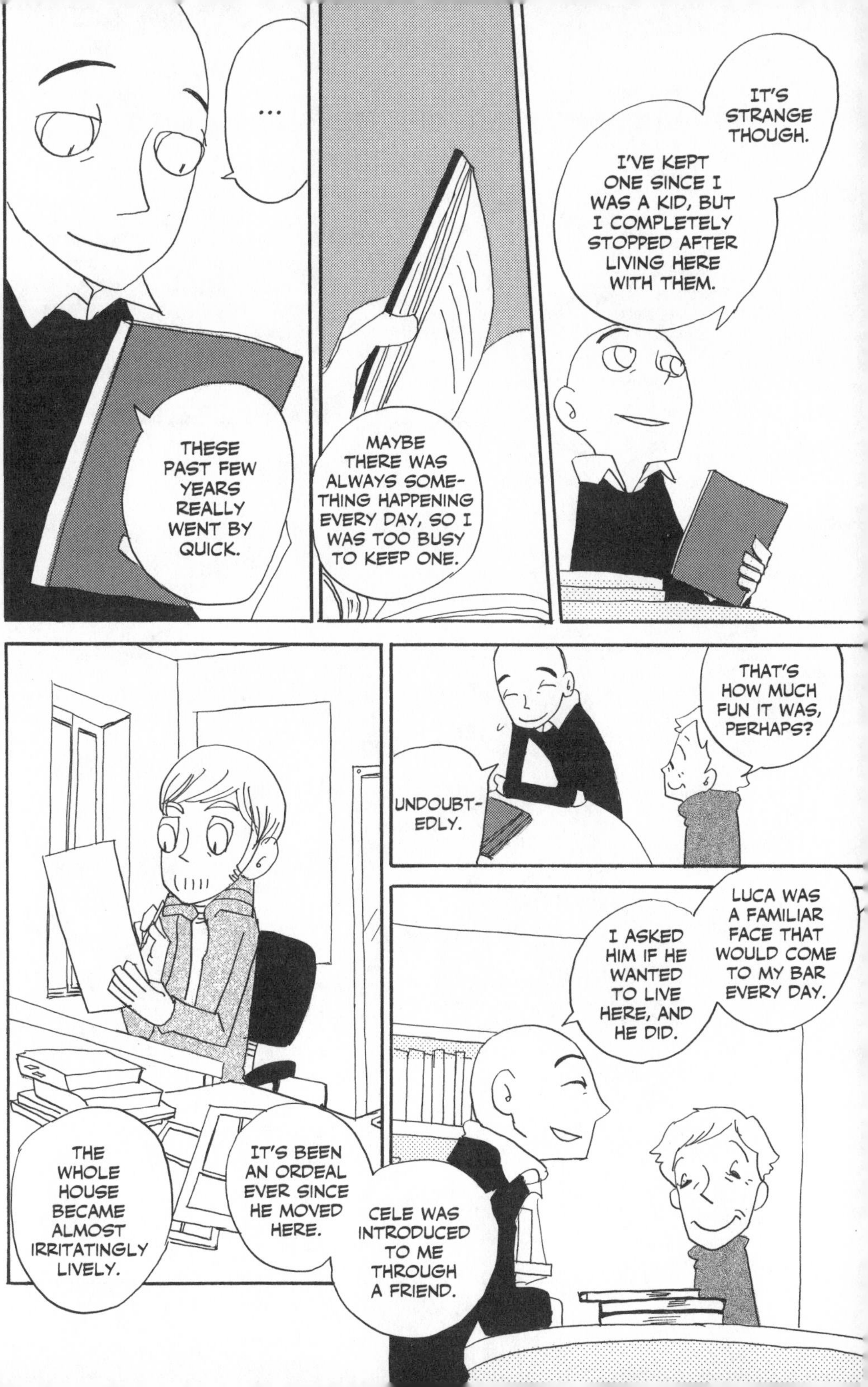
IT'S STRANGE THOUGH.
I'VE KEPT ONE SINCE I WAS A KID, BUT I COMPLETELY STOPPED AFTER LIVING HERE WITH THEM.
MAYBE THERE WAS ALWAYS SOME-THING HAPPENING EVERY DAY, SO I WAS TOO BUSY TO KEEP ONE.
...
THESE PAST FEW YEARS REALLY WENT BY QUICK.
THAT'S HOW MUCH FUN IT WAS, PERHAPS?
UNDOUBT-EDLY.
LUCA WAS A FAMILIAR FACE THAT WOULD COME TO MY BAR EVERY DAY.
I ASKED HIM IF HE WANTED TO LIVE HERE, AND HE DID.
CELE WAS INTRODUCED TO ME THROUGH A FRIEND.
IT'S BEEN AN ORDEAL EVER SINCE HE MOVED HERE.
THE WHOLE HOUSE BECAME ALMOST IRRITATINGLY LIVELY.

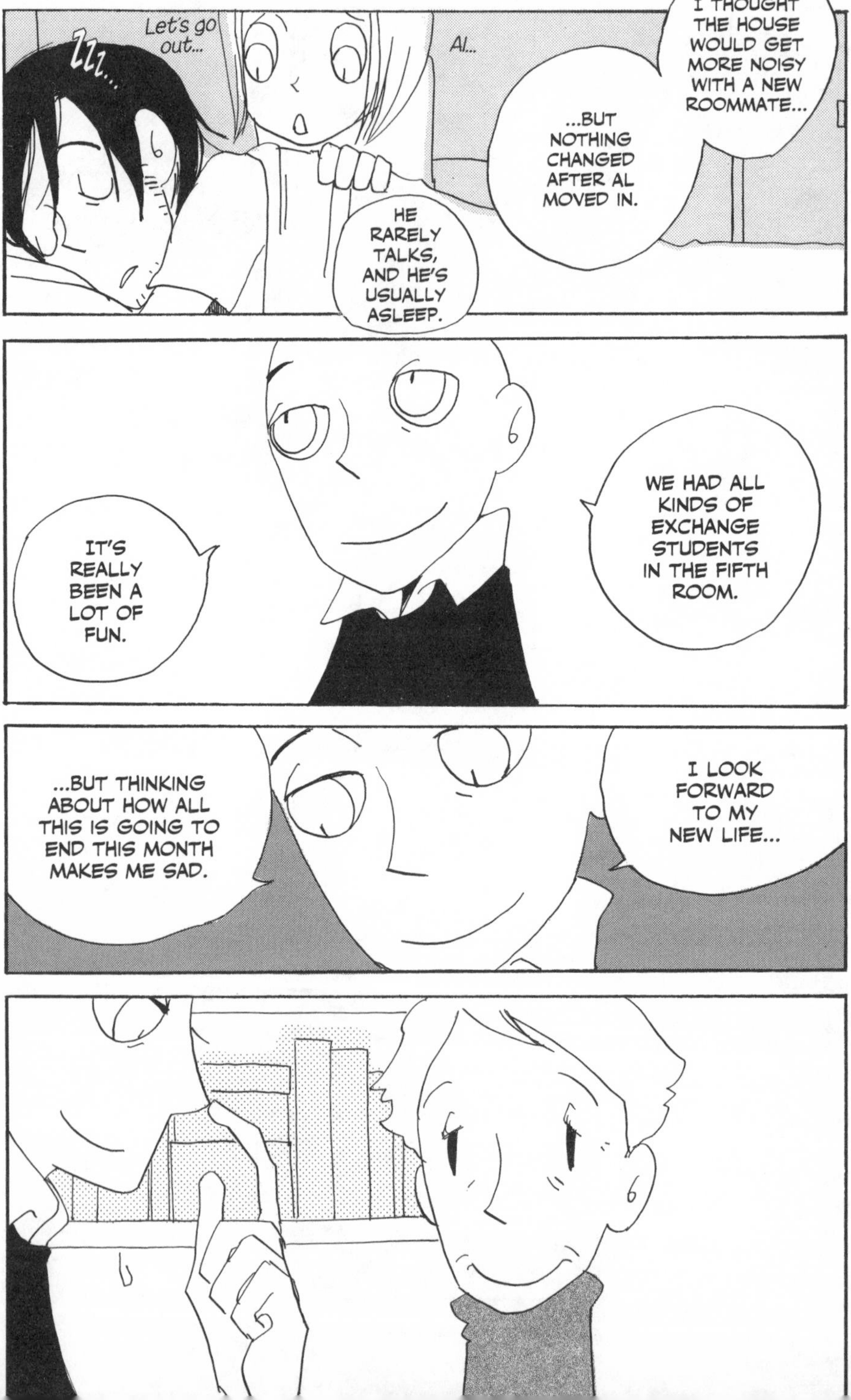
I THOUGHT THE HOUSE WOULD GET MORE NOISY WITH A NEW ROOMMATE...
...BUT NOTHING CHANGED AFTER AL MOVED IN.
Al...
Let's go out...
ZZZ...
HE RARELY TALKS, AND HE'S USUALLY ASLEEP.
WE HAD ALL KINDS OF EXCHANGE STUDENTS IN THE FIFTH ROOM.
IT'S REALLY BEEN A LOT OF FUN.
I LOOK FORWARD TO MY NEW LIFE...
...BUT THINKING ABOUT HOW ALL THIS IS GOING TO END THIS MONTH MAKES ME SAD.

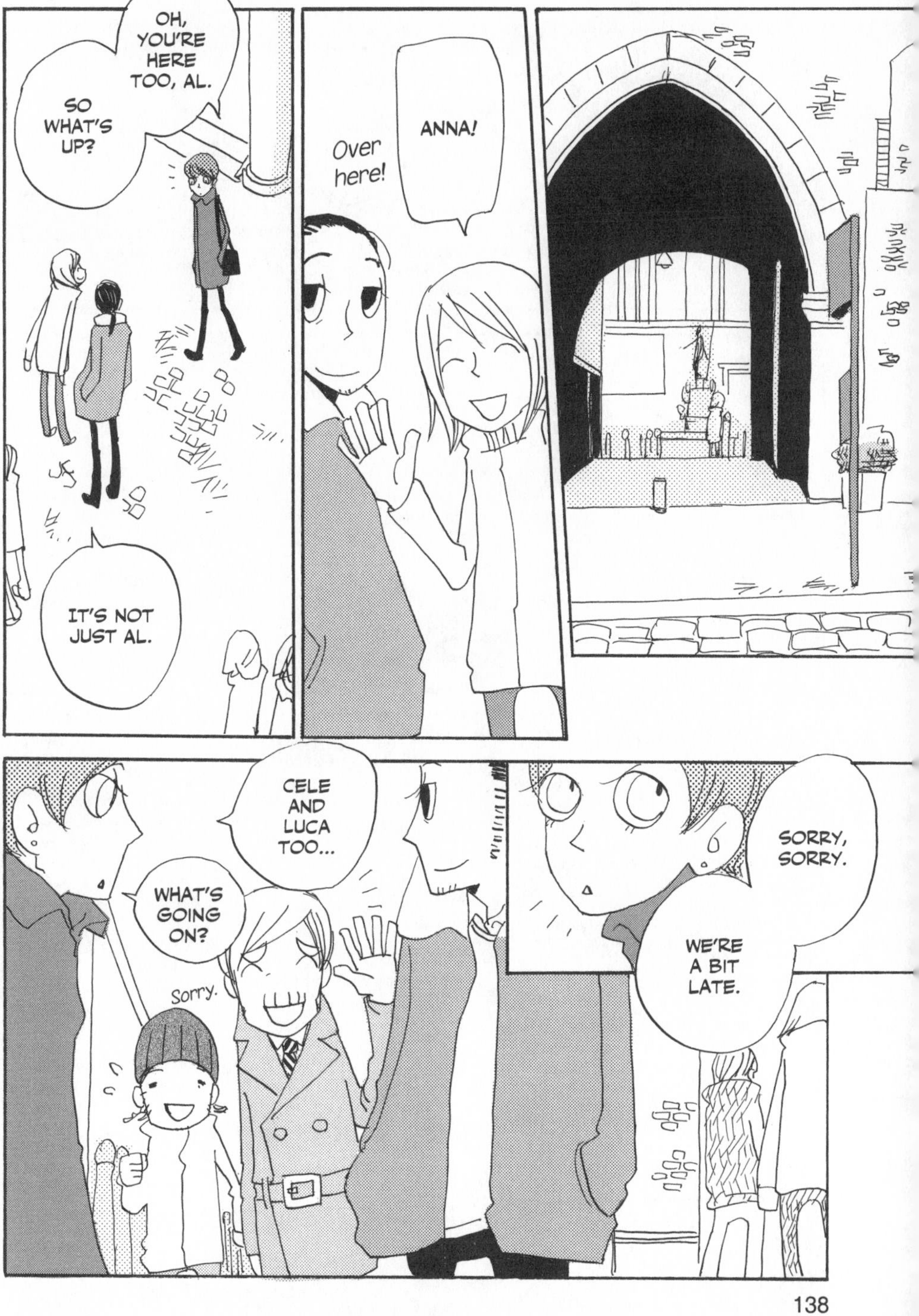
ANNA!
Over here!
OH, YOU'RE HERE TOO, AL.
SO WHAT'S UP?
IT'S NOT JUST AL.
SORRY, SORRY.
WE'RE A BIT LATE.
CELE AND LUCA TOO...
WHAT'S GOING ON?
Sorry.

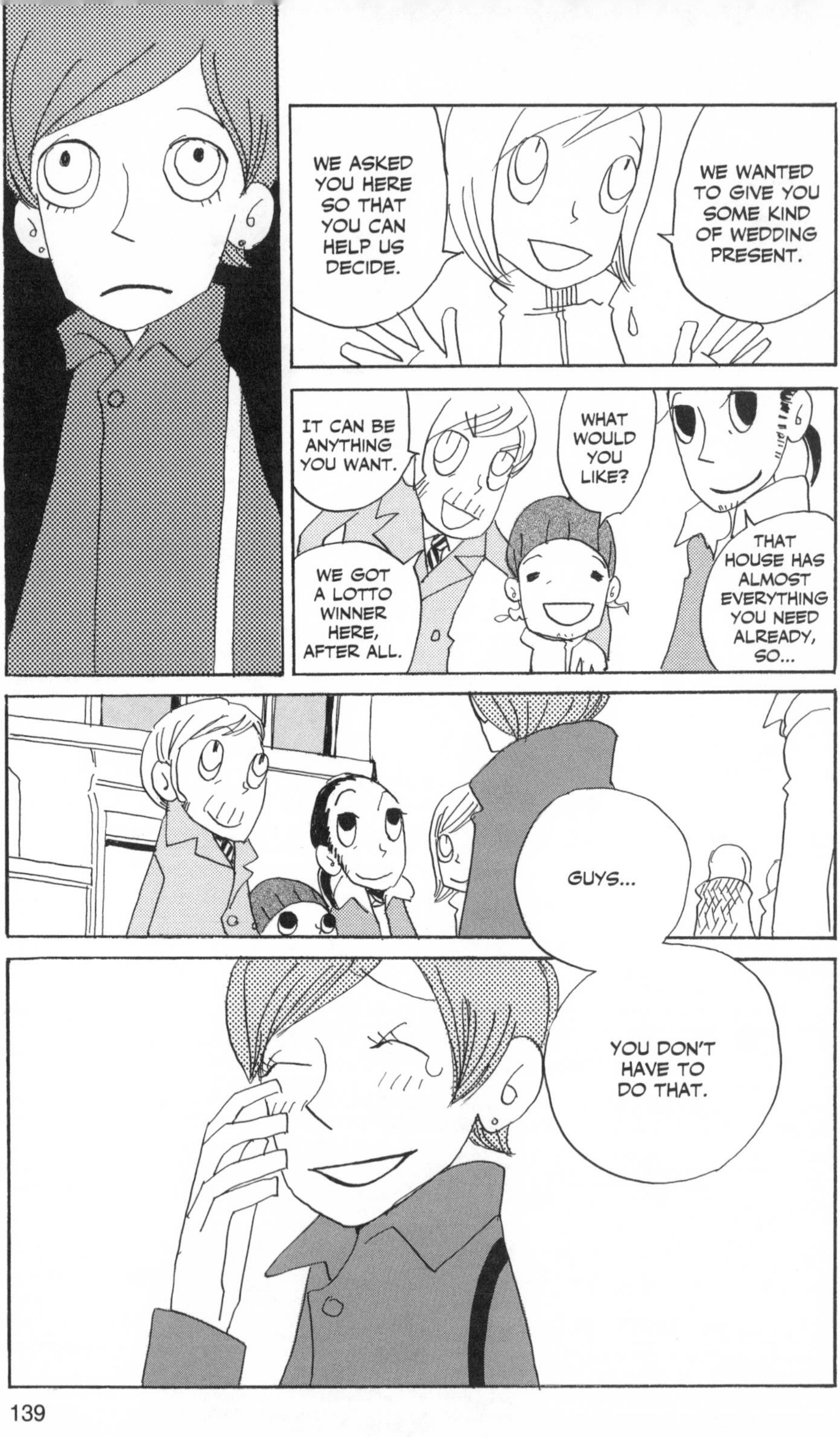
WE WANTED TO GIVE YOU SOME KIND OF WEDDING PRESENT.
WE ASKED YOU HERE SO THAT YOU CAN HELP US DECIDE.
WHAT WOULD YOU LIKE?
IT CAN BE ANYTHING YOU WANT.
THAT HOUSE HAS ALMOST EVERYTHING YOU NEED ALREADY, SO...
WE GOT A LOTTO WINNER HERE, AFTER ALL.
GUYS...
YOU DON'T HAVE TO DO THAT.

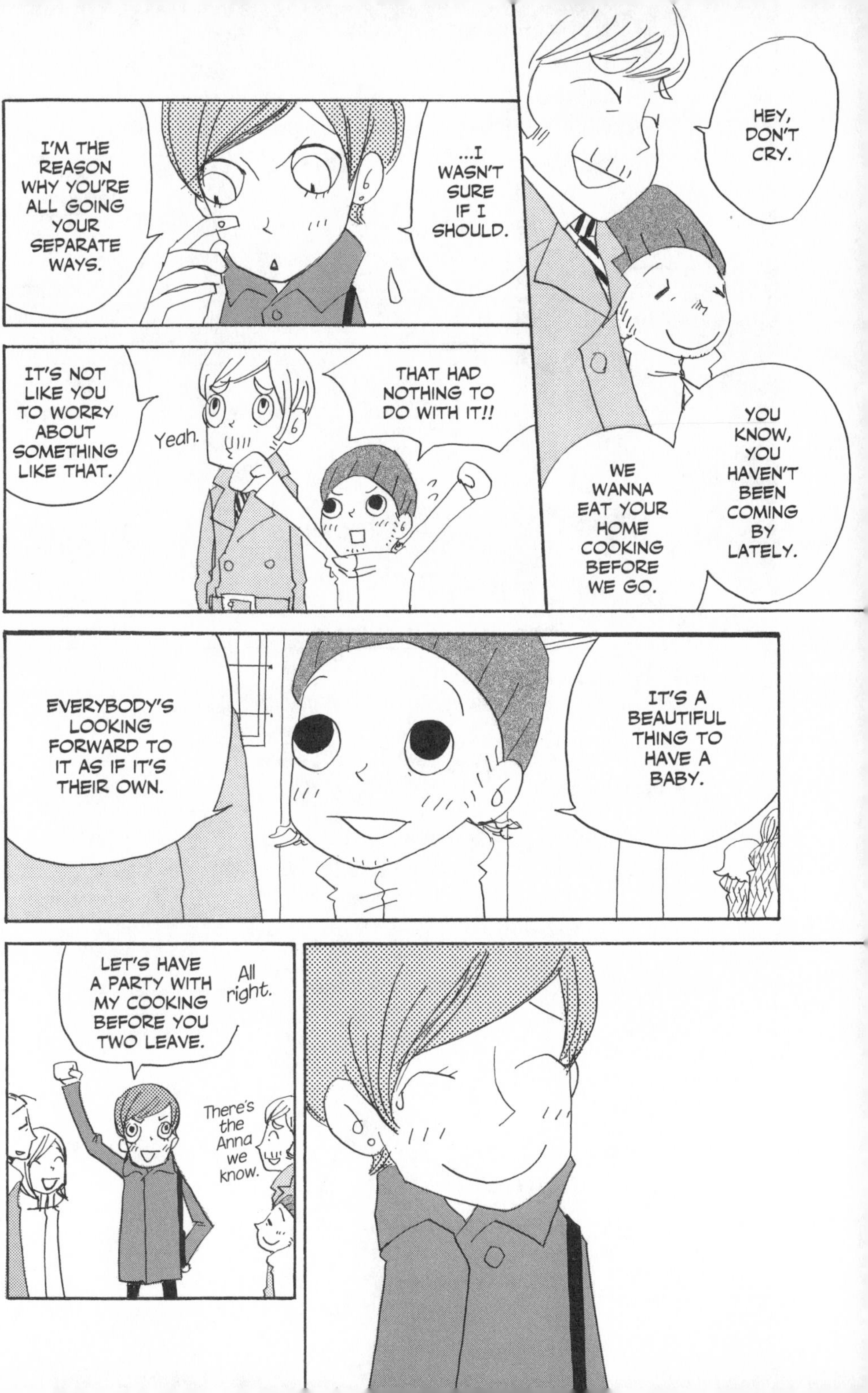
HEY, DON'T CRY.
YOU KNOW, YOU HAVEN'T BEEN COMING BY LATELY.
WE WANNA EAT YOUR HOME COOKING BEFORE WE GO.
...I WASN'T SURE IF I SHOULD.
I'M THE REASON WHY YOU'RE ALL GOING YOUR SEPARATE WAYS.
THAT HAD NOTHING TO DO WITH IT!!
Yeah.
IT'S NOT LIKE YOU TO WORRY ABOUT SOMETHING LIKE THAT.
IT'S A BEAUTIFUL THING TO HAVE A BABY.
EVERYBODY'S LOOKING FORWARD TO IT AS IF IT'S THEIR OWN.
LET'S HAVE A PARTY WITH MY COOKING BEFORE YOU TWO LEAVE.
All right.
There's the Anna we know.

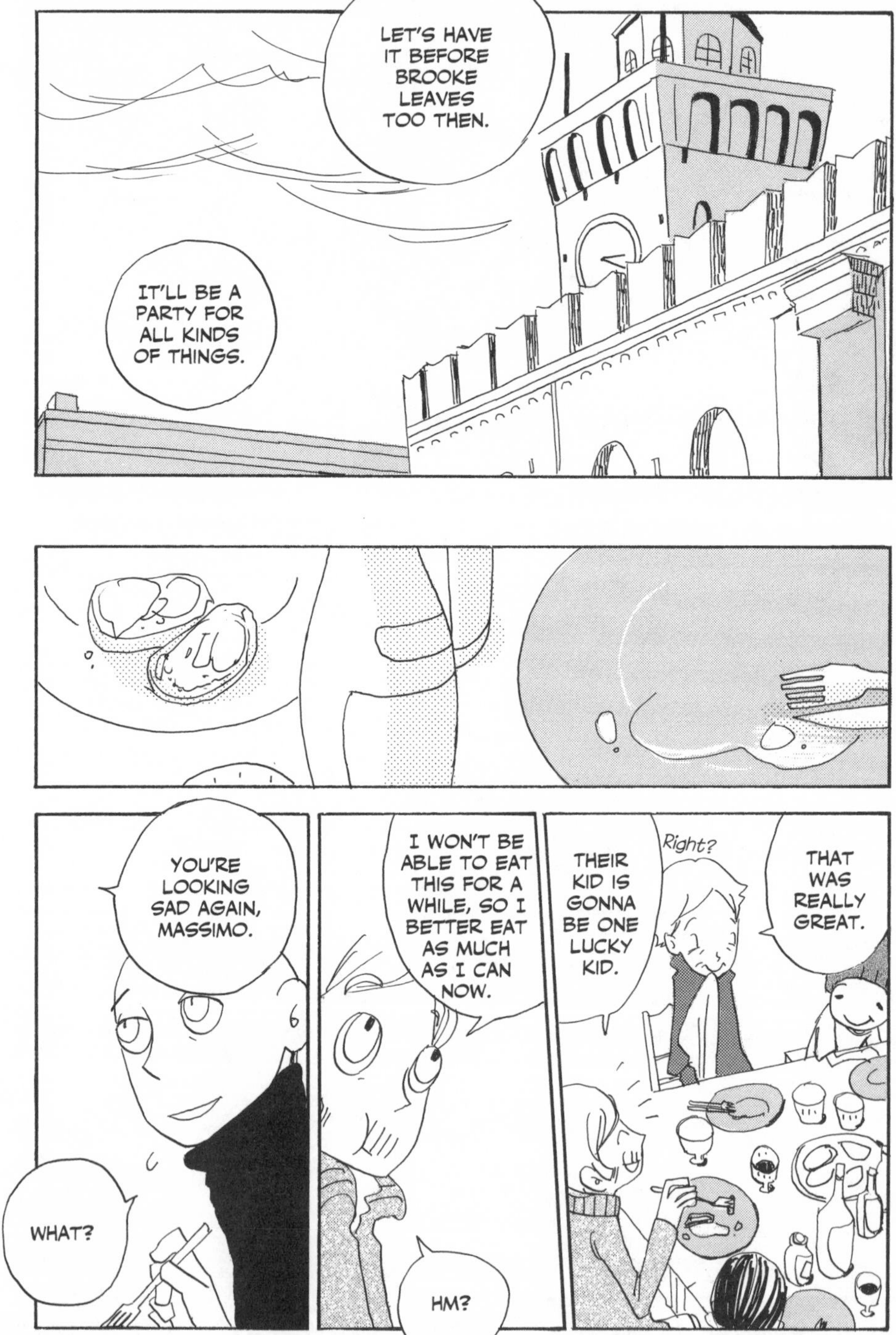
LET'S HAVE IT BEFORE BROOKE LEAVES TOO THEN.
IT'LL BE A PARTY FOR ALL KINDS OF THINGS.
THAT WAS REALLY GREAT.
Right?
THEIR KID IS GONNA BE ONE LUCKY KID.
I WON'T BE ABLE TO EAT THIS FOR A WHILE, SO I BETTER EAT AS MUCH AS I CAN NOW.
HM?
YOU'RE LOOKING SAD AGAIN, MASSIMO.
WHAT?

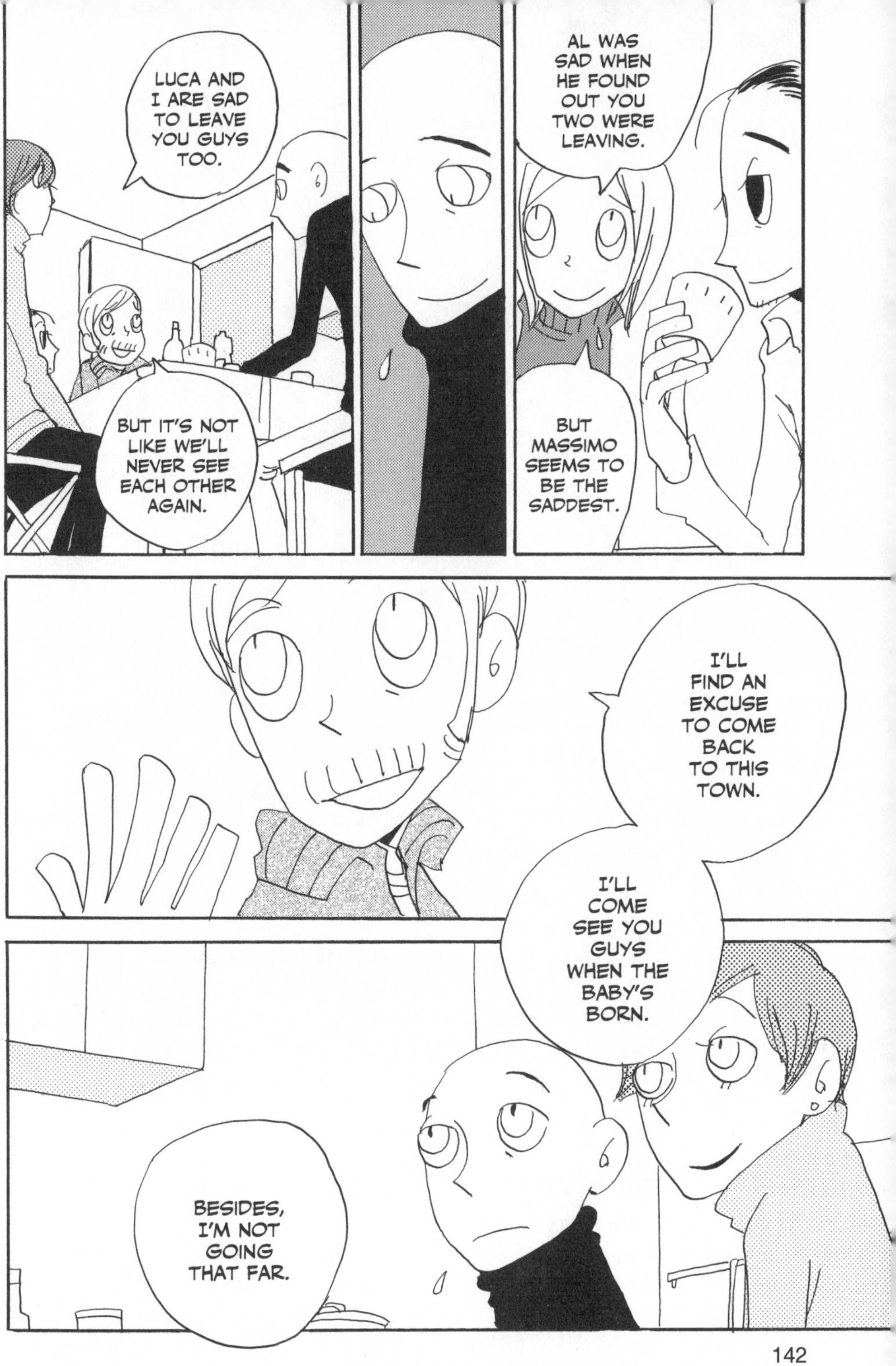
AL WAS SAD WHEN HE FOUND OUT YOU TWO WERE LEAVING.
BUT MASSIMO SEEMS TO BE THE SADDEST.
LUCA AND I ARE SAD TO LEAVE YOU GUYS TOO.
BUT IT'S NOT LIKE WE'LL NEVER SEE EACH OTHER AGAIN.
I'LL FIND AN EXCUSE TO COME BACK TO THIS TOWN.
I'LL COME SEE YOU GUYS WHEN THE BABY'S BORN.
BESIDES, I'M NOT GOING THAT FAR.

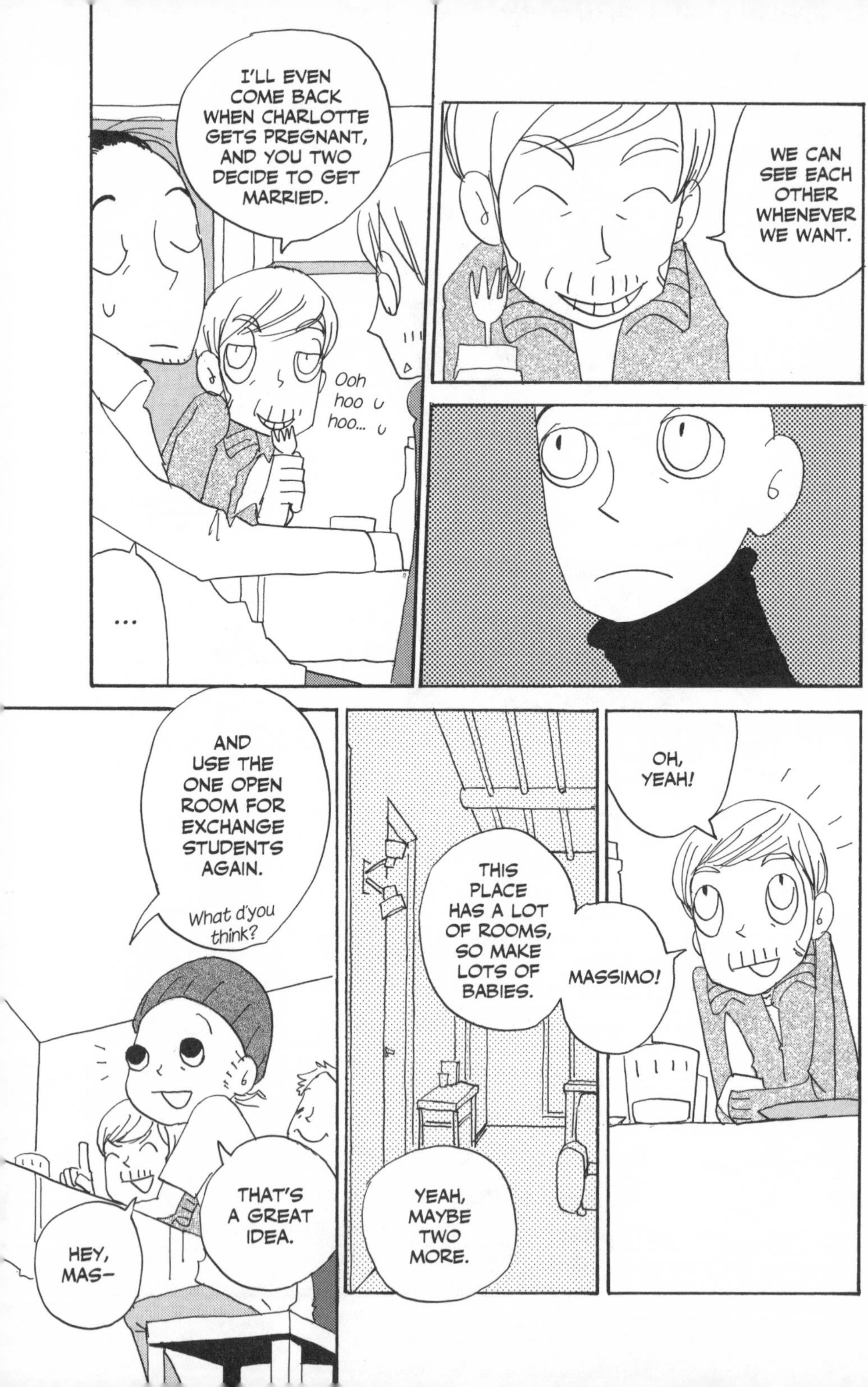
WE CAN SEE EACH OTHER WHENEVER WE WANT.
I'LL EVEN COME BACK WHEN CHARLOTTE GETS PREGNANT, AND YOU TWO DECIDE TO GET MARRIED.
Ooh hoo hoo...
...
OH, YEAH!
THIS PLACE HAS A LOT OF ROOMS, SO MAKE LOTS OF BABIES.
MASSIMO!
YEAH, MAYBE TWO MORE.
AND USE THE ONE OPEN ROOM FOR EXCHANGE STUDENTS AGAIN.
What d'you think?
THAT'S A GREAT IDEA.
HEY, MAS–

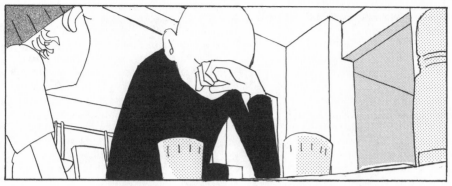

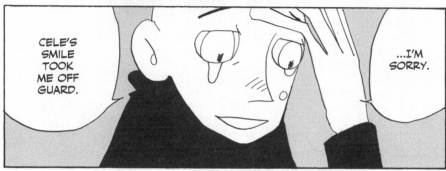

CELE'S SMILE TOOK ME OFF GUARD.

...I'M SORRY.

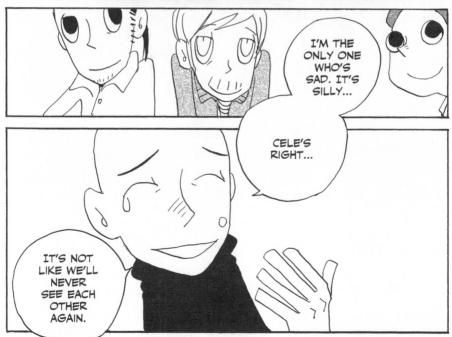

I'M THE ONLY ONE WHO'S SAD. IT'S SILLY...

CELE'S RIGHT...

IT'S NOT LIKE WE'LL NEVER SEE EACH OTHER AGAIN.

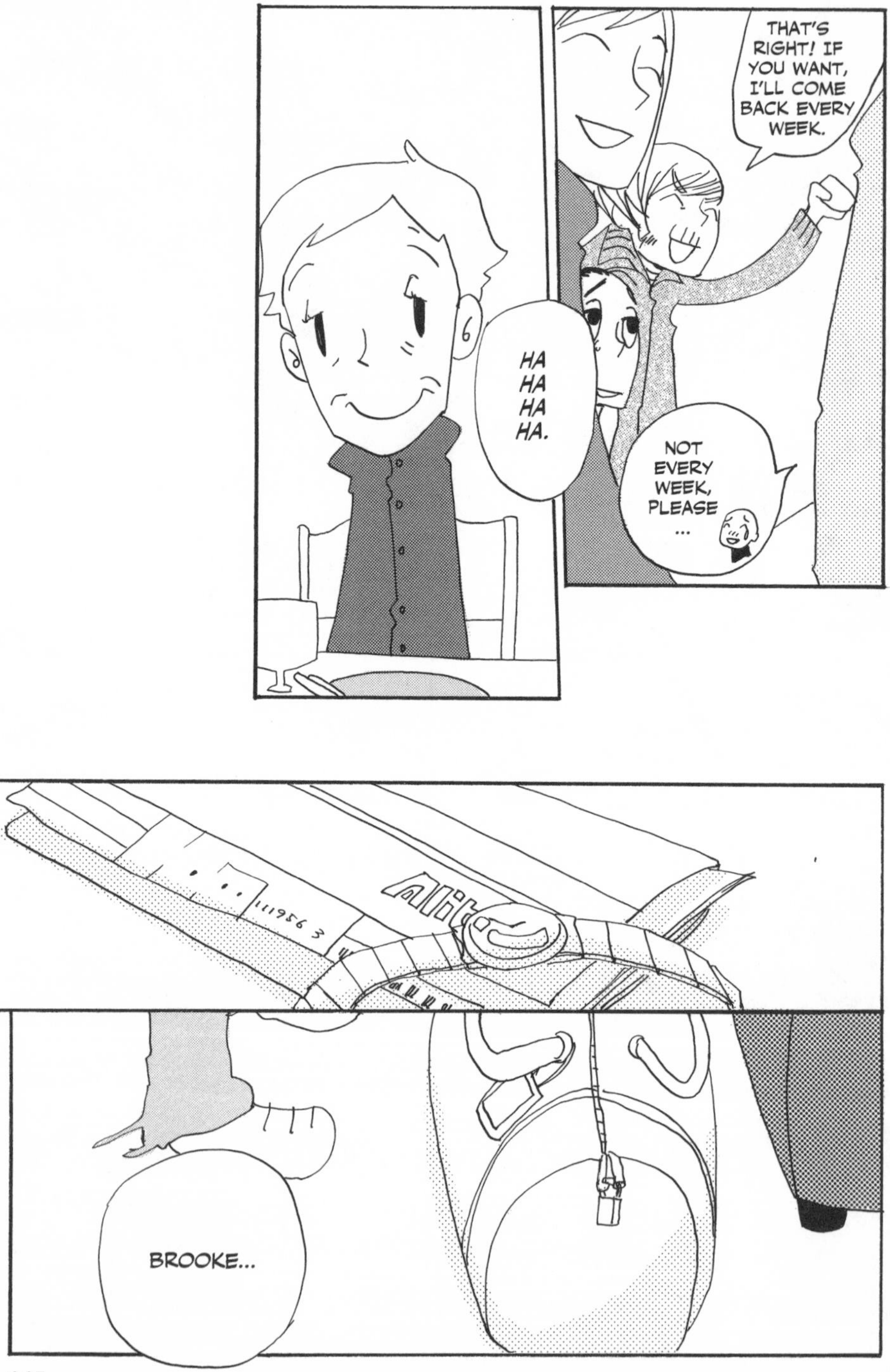
THAT'S RIGHT! IF YOU WANT, I'LL COME BACK EVERY WEEK.
NOT EVERY WEEK, PLEASE ...
HA HA HA HA.
BROOKE...

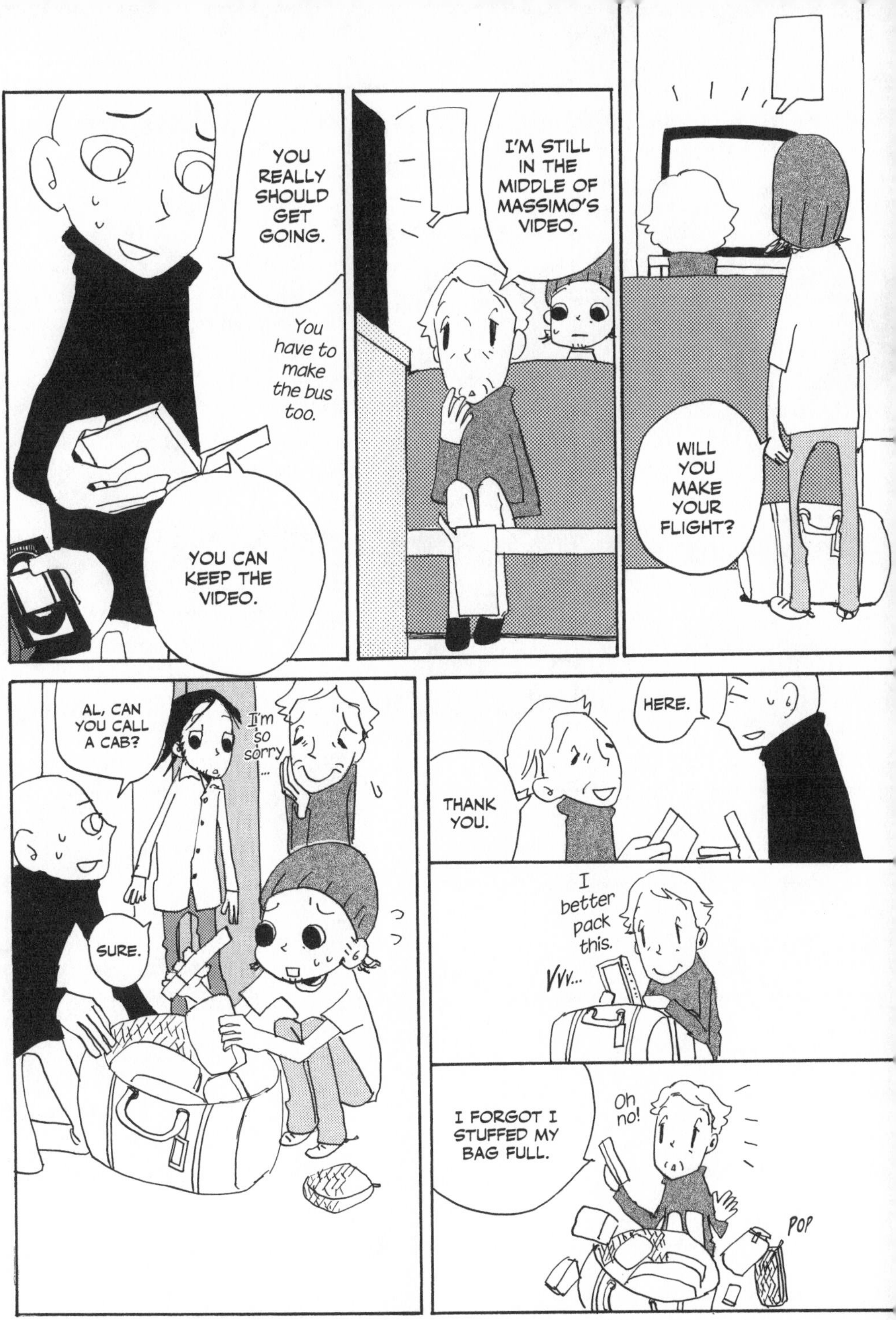
WILL YOU MAKE YOUR FLIGHT?
I'M STILL IN THE MIDDLE OF MASSIMO'S VIDEO.
YOU REALLY SHOULD GET GOING.
You have to make the bus too.
YOU CAN KEEP THE VIDEO.
HERE.
THANK YOU.
I better pack this.
Vvv...
Oh no!
I FORGOT I STUFFED MY BAG FULL.
POP
AL, CAN YOU CALL A CAB?
I'm so sorry ...
SURE.

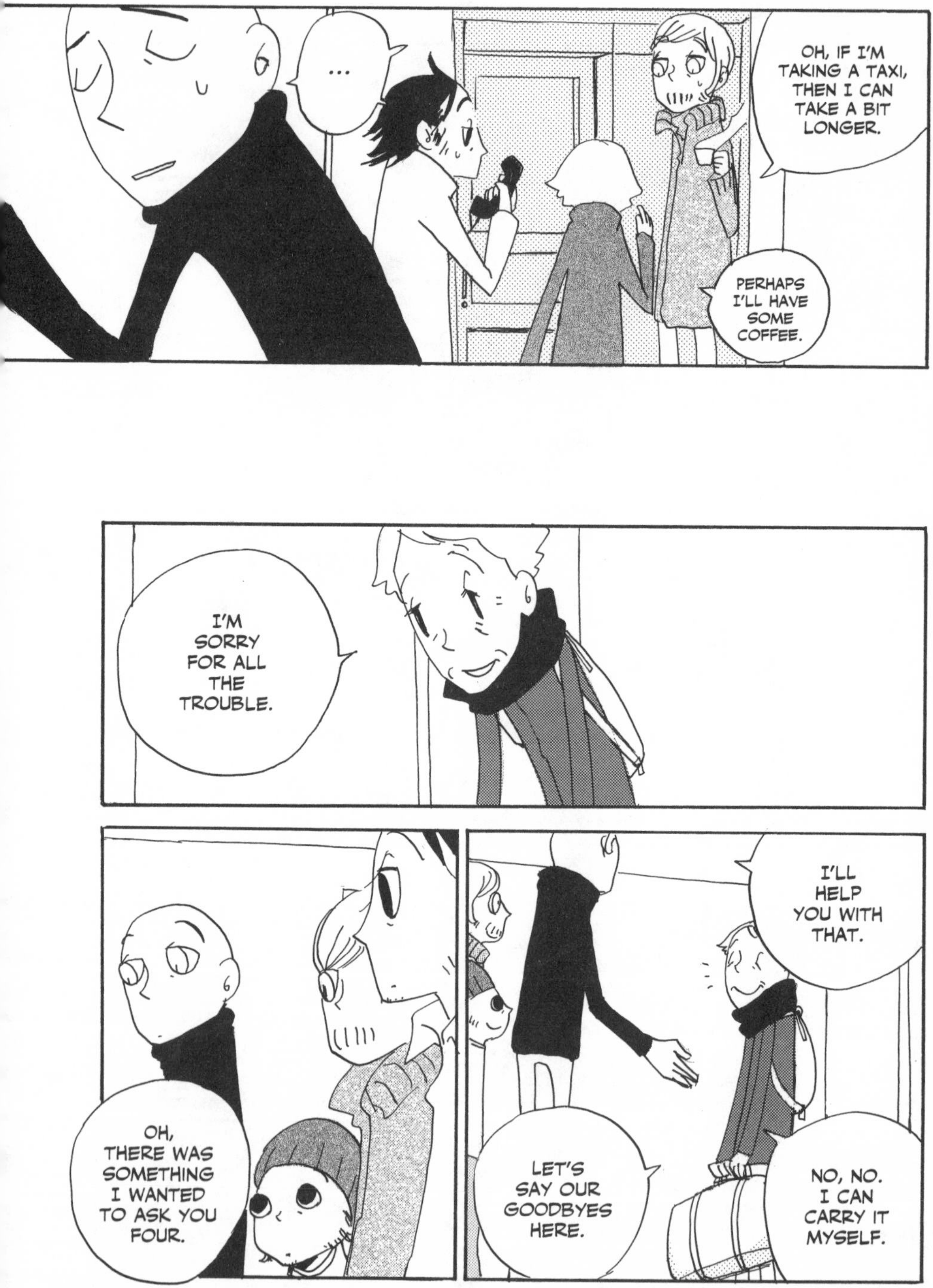
OH, IF I'M TAKING A TAXI, THEN I CAN TAKE A BIT LONGER.
PERHAPS I'LL HAVE SOME COFFEE.
...
I'M SORRY FOR ALL THE TROUBLE.
I'LL HELP YOU WITH THAT.
NO, NO. I CAN CARRY IT MYSELF.
LET'S SAY OUR GOODBYES HERE.
OH, THERE WAS SOMETHING I WANTED TO ASK YOU FOUR.

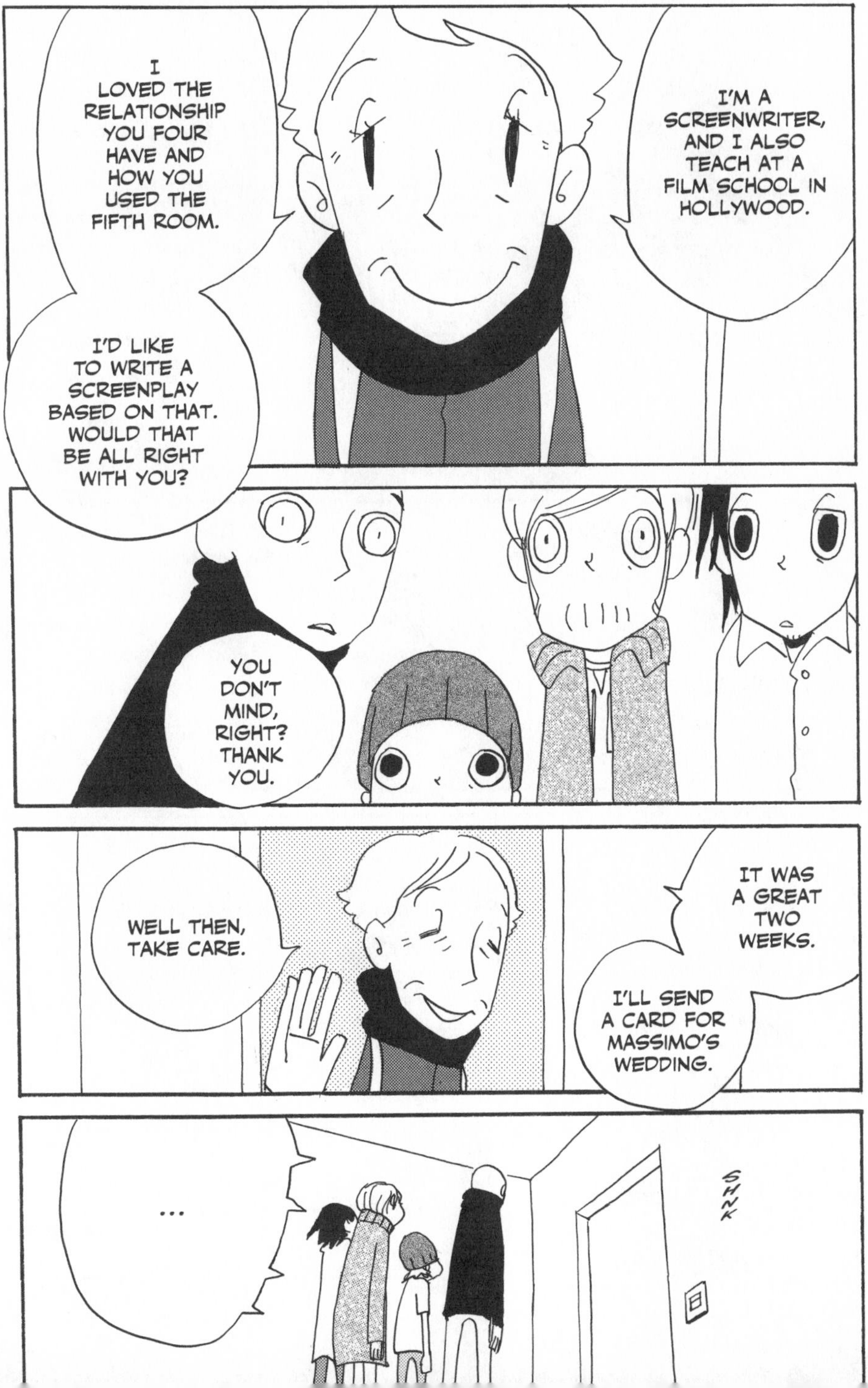
I'M A SCREENWRITER, AND I ALSO TEACH AT A FILM SCHOOL IN HOLLYWOOD.
I LOVED THE RELATIONSHIP YOU FOUR HAVE AND HOW YOU USED THE FIFTH ROOM.
I'D LIKE TO WRITE A SCREENPLAY BASED ON THAT. WOULD THAT BE ALL RIGHT WITH YOU?
YOU DON'T MIND, RIGHT? THANK YOU.
IT WAS A GREAT TWO WEEKS.
I'LL SEND A CARD FOR MASSIMO'S WEDDING.
WELL THEN, TAKE CARE.
SHNK
...

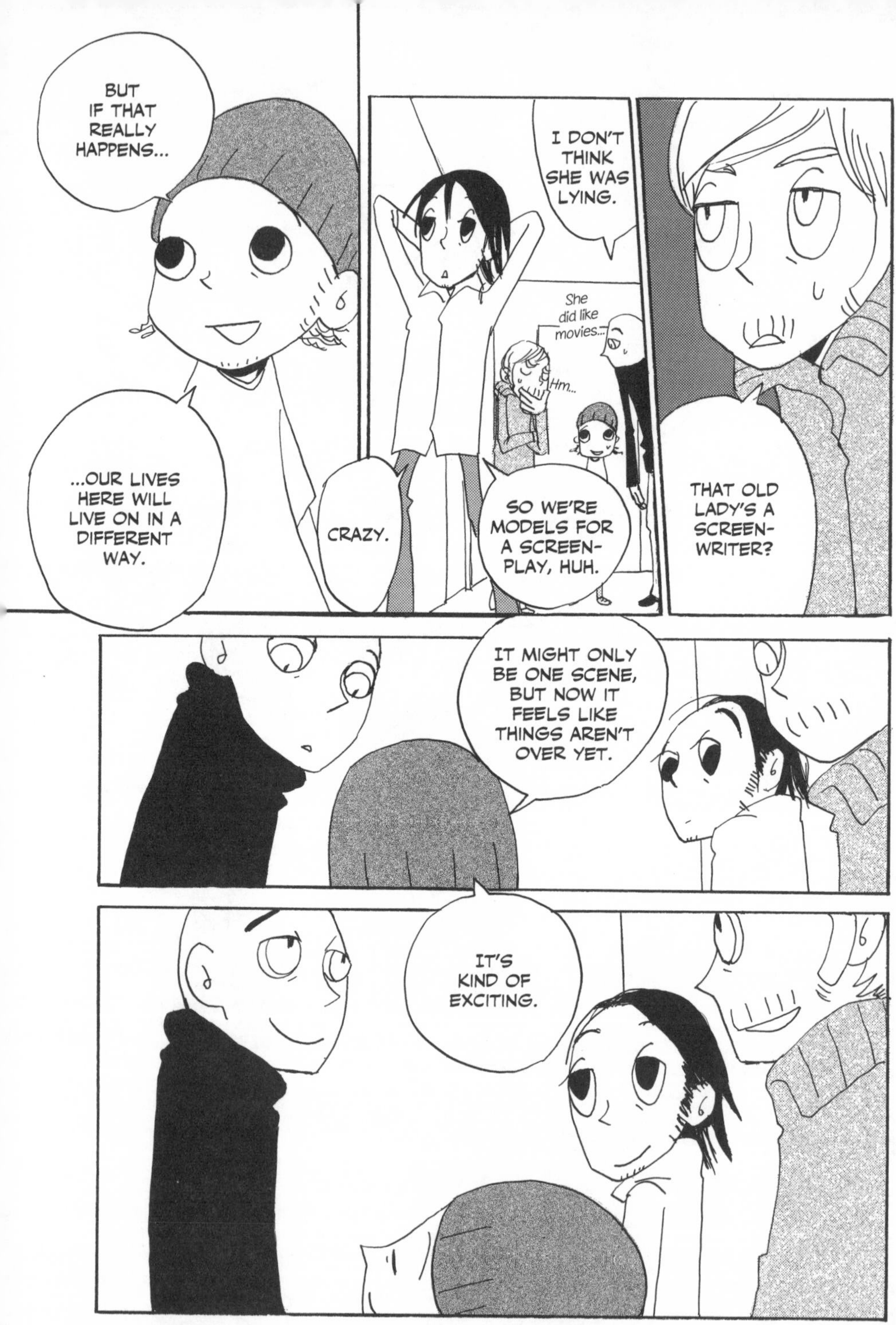
THAT OLD LADY'S A SCREEN-WRITER?
I DON'T THINK SHE WAS LYING.
She did like movies...
Hm...
SO WE'RE MODELS FOR A SCREEN-PLAY, HUH.
CRAZY.
BUT IF THAT REALLY HAPPENS...
...OUR LIVES HERE WILL LIVE ON IN A DIFFERENT WAY.
IT MIGHT ONLY BE ONE SCENE, BUT NOW IT FEELS LIKE THINGS AREN'T OVER YET.
IT'S KIND OF EXCITING.

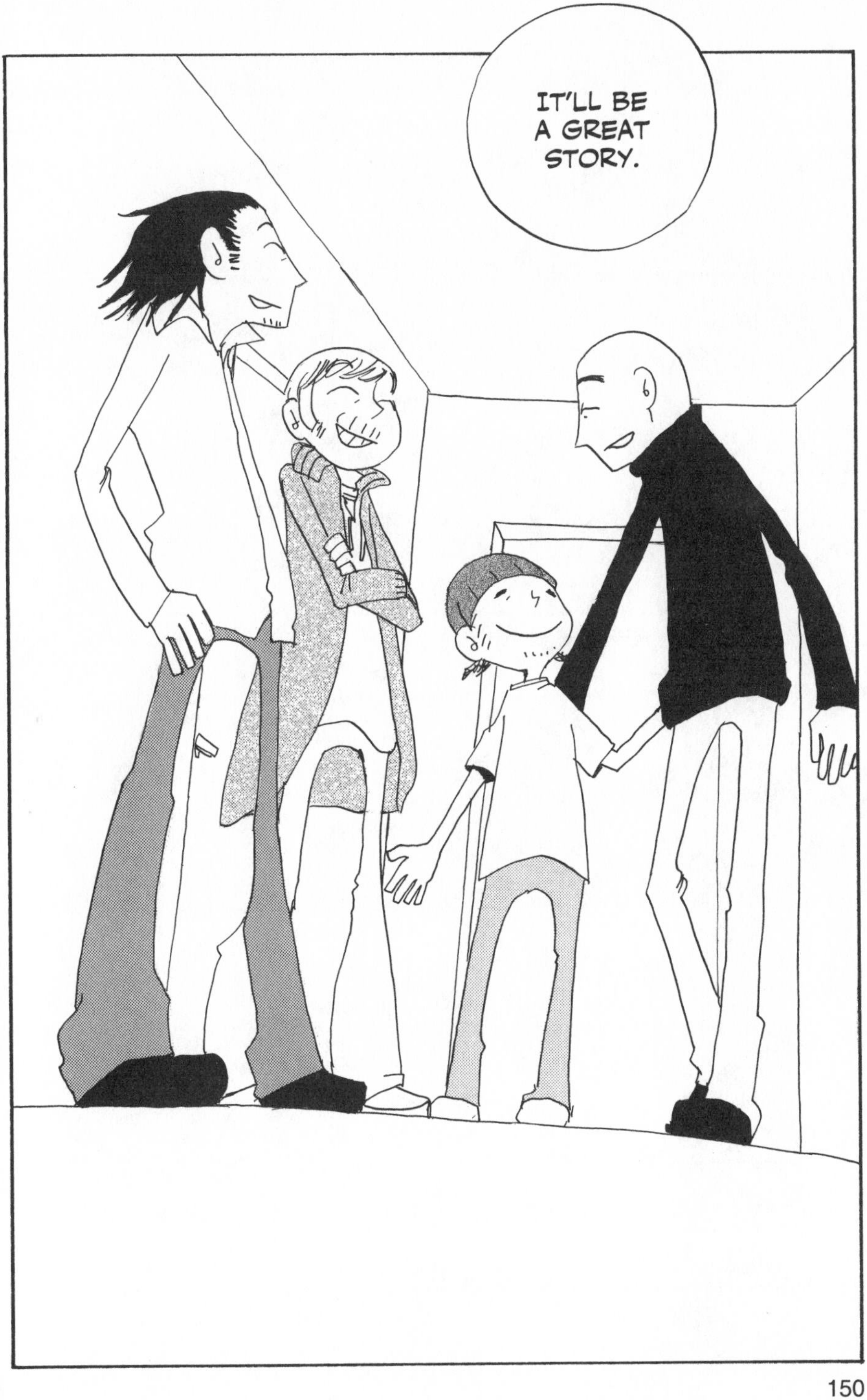
IT'LL BE
A GREAT
STORY.

La Quinta Camera
Capitolo 6

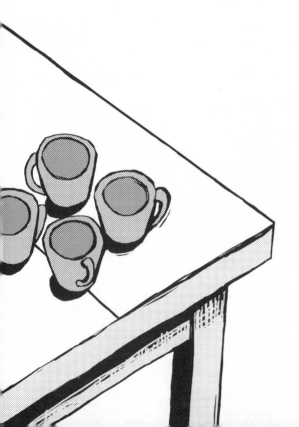

IL SUO POSTO
~HIS PLACE~

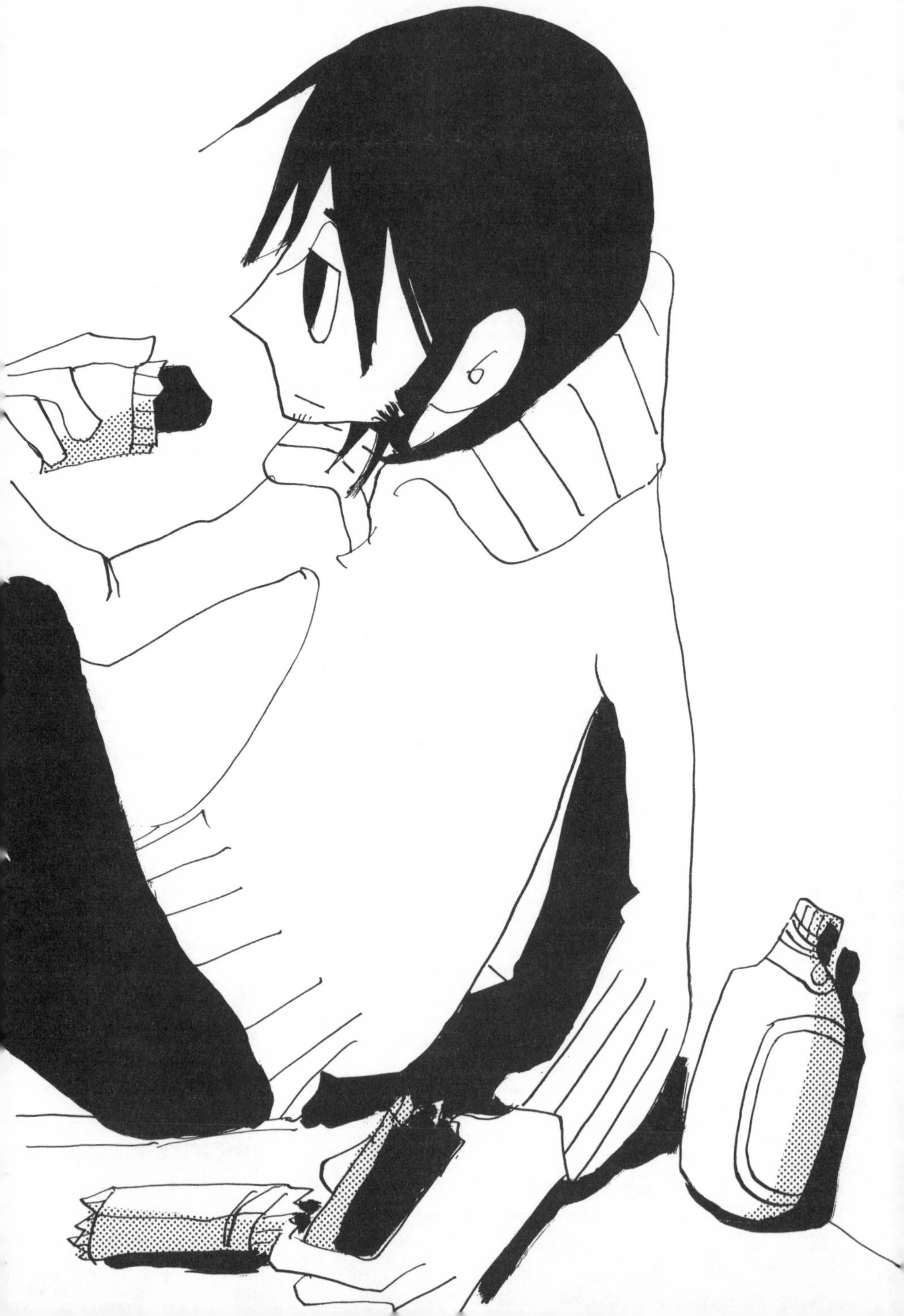

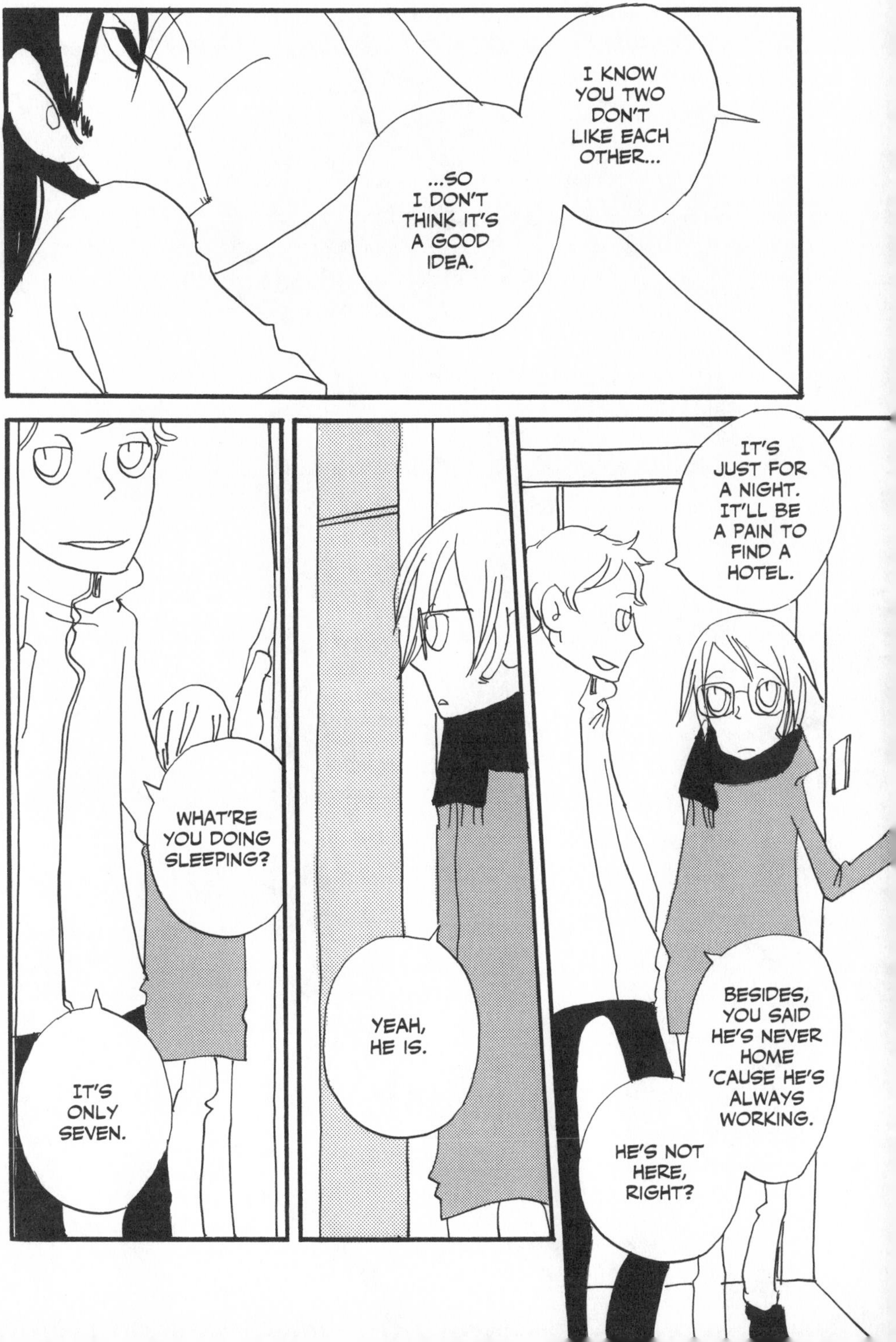
I KNOW YOU TWO DON'T LIKE EACH OTHER...
...SO I DON'T THINK IT'S A GOOD IDEA.
IT'S JUST FOR A NIGHT. IT'LL BE A PAIN TO FIND A HOTEL.
BESIDES, YOU SAID HE'S NEVER HOME 'CAUSE HE'S ALWAYS WORKING.
HE'S NOT HERE, RIGHT?
YEAH, HE IS.
WHAT'RE YOU DOING SLEEPING?
IT'S ONLY SEVEN.

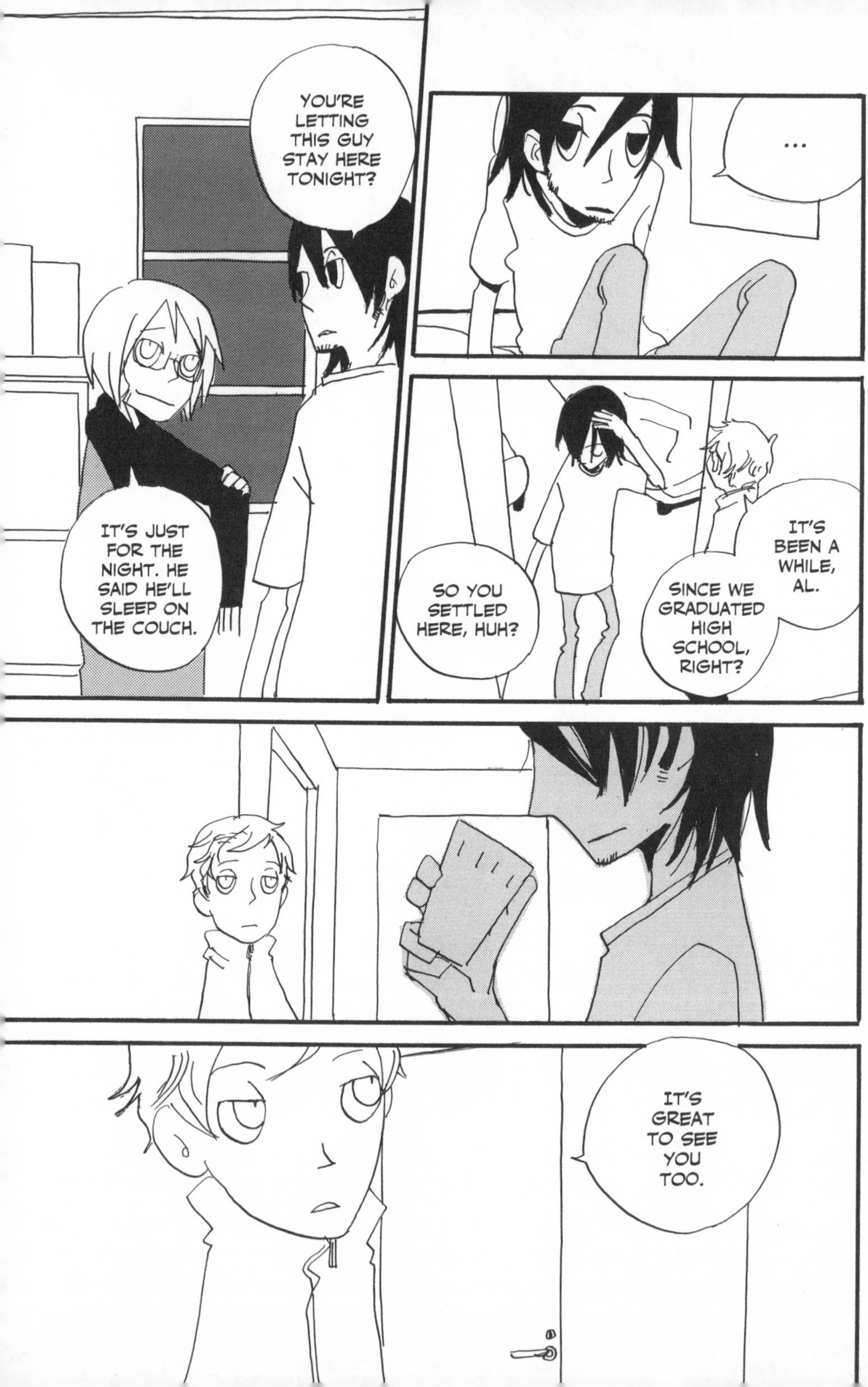
...
IT'S BEEN A WHILE, AL.
SINCE WE GRADUATED HIGH SCHOOL, RIGHT?
SO YOU SETTLED HERE, HUH?
YOU'RE LETTING THIS GUY STAY HERE TONIGHT?
IT'S JUST FOR THE NIGHT. HE SAID HE'LL SLEEP ON THE COUCH.
IT'S GREAT TO SEE YOU TOO.

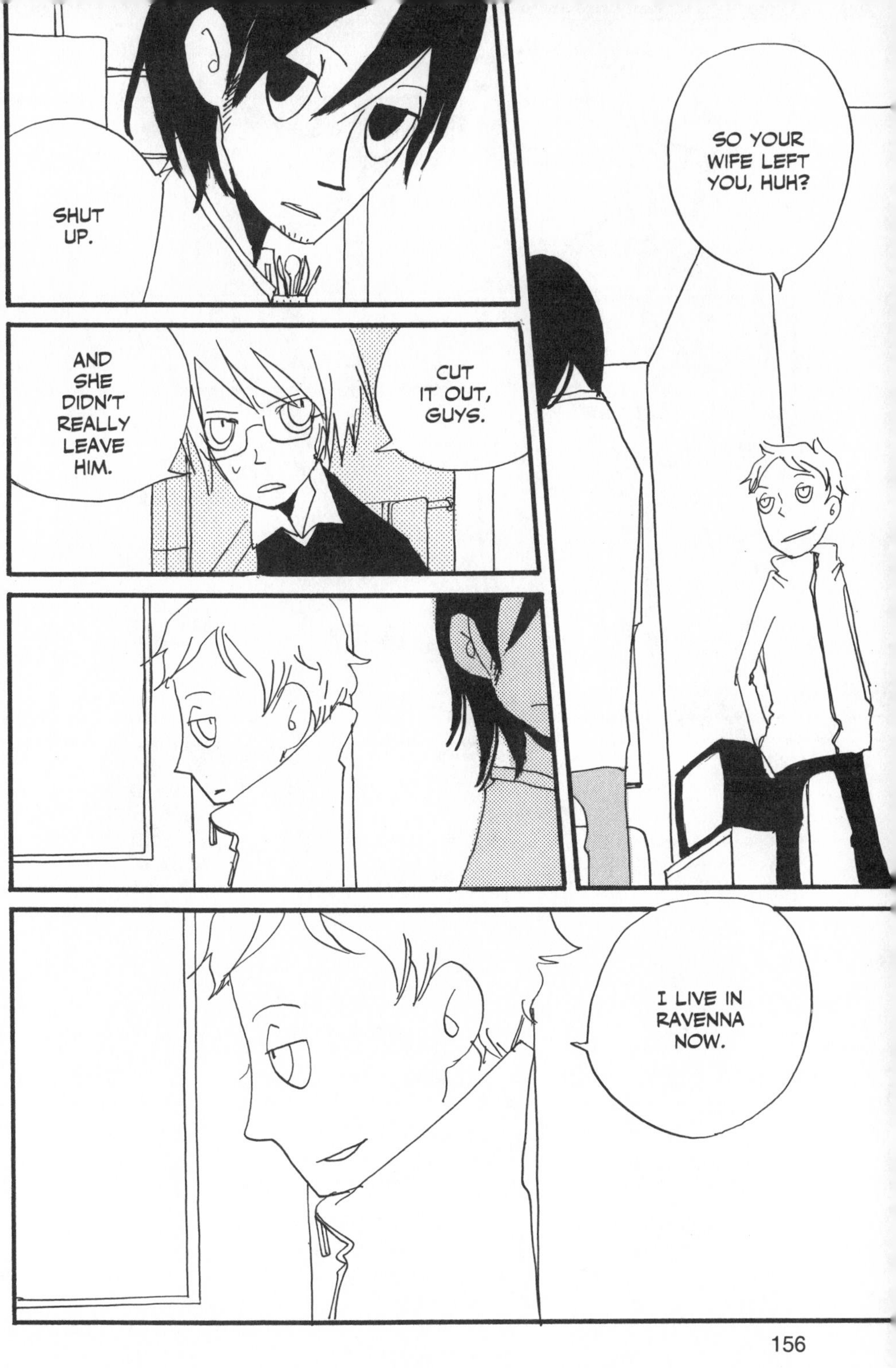
SO YOUR WIFE LEFT YOU, HUH?
SHUT UP.
CUT IT OUT, GUYS.
AND SHE DIDN'T REALLY LEAVE HIM.
I LIVE IN RAVENNA NOW.

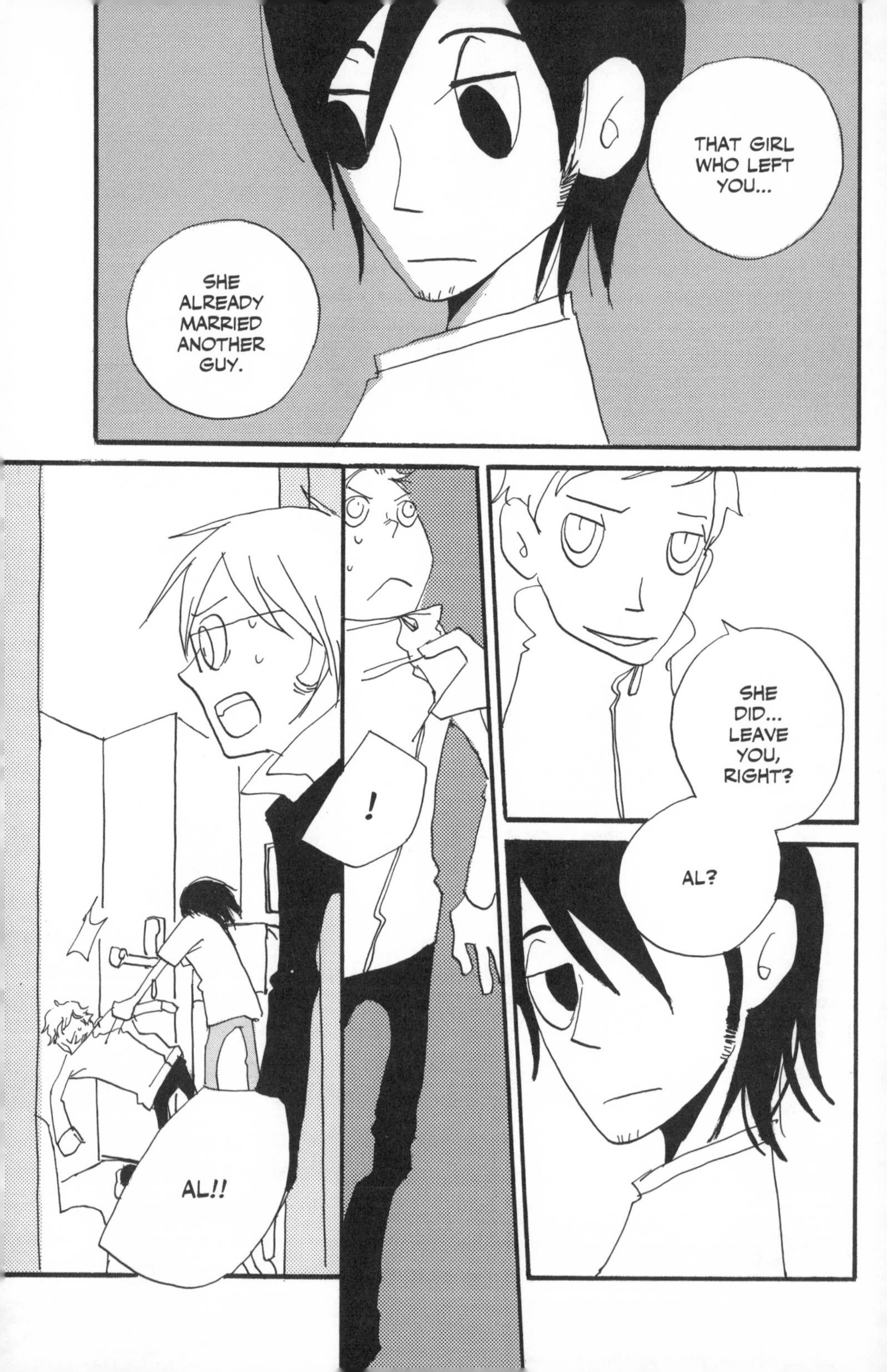
THAT GIRL WHO LEFT YOU...
SHE ALREADY MARRIED ANOTHER GUY.
SHE DID... LEAVE YOU, RIGHT?
AL?
!
AL!!

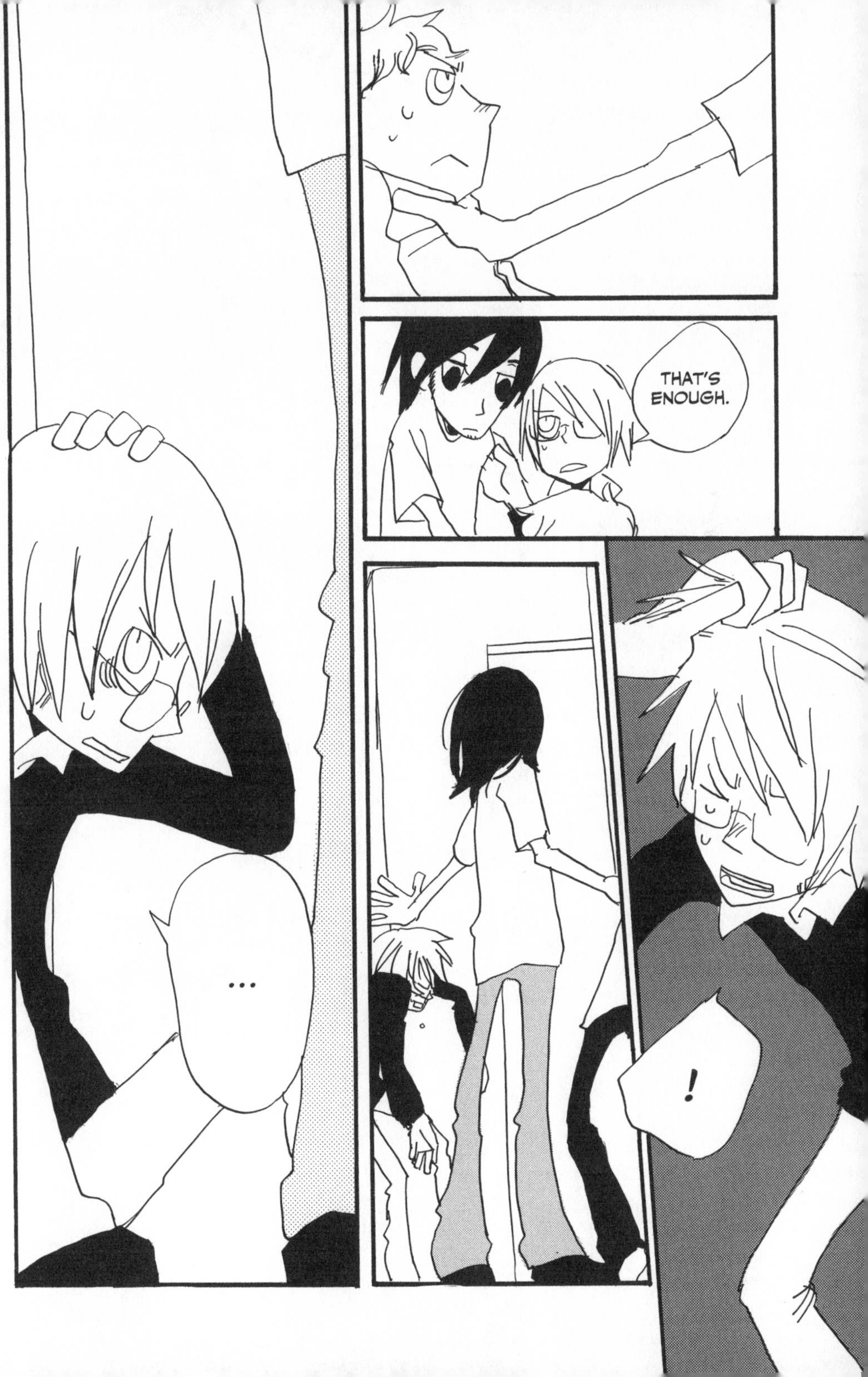
THAT'S ENOUGH.
!
...

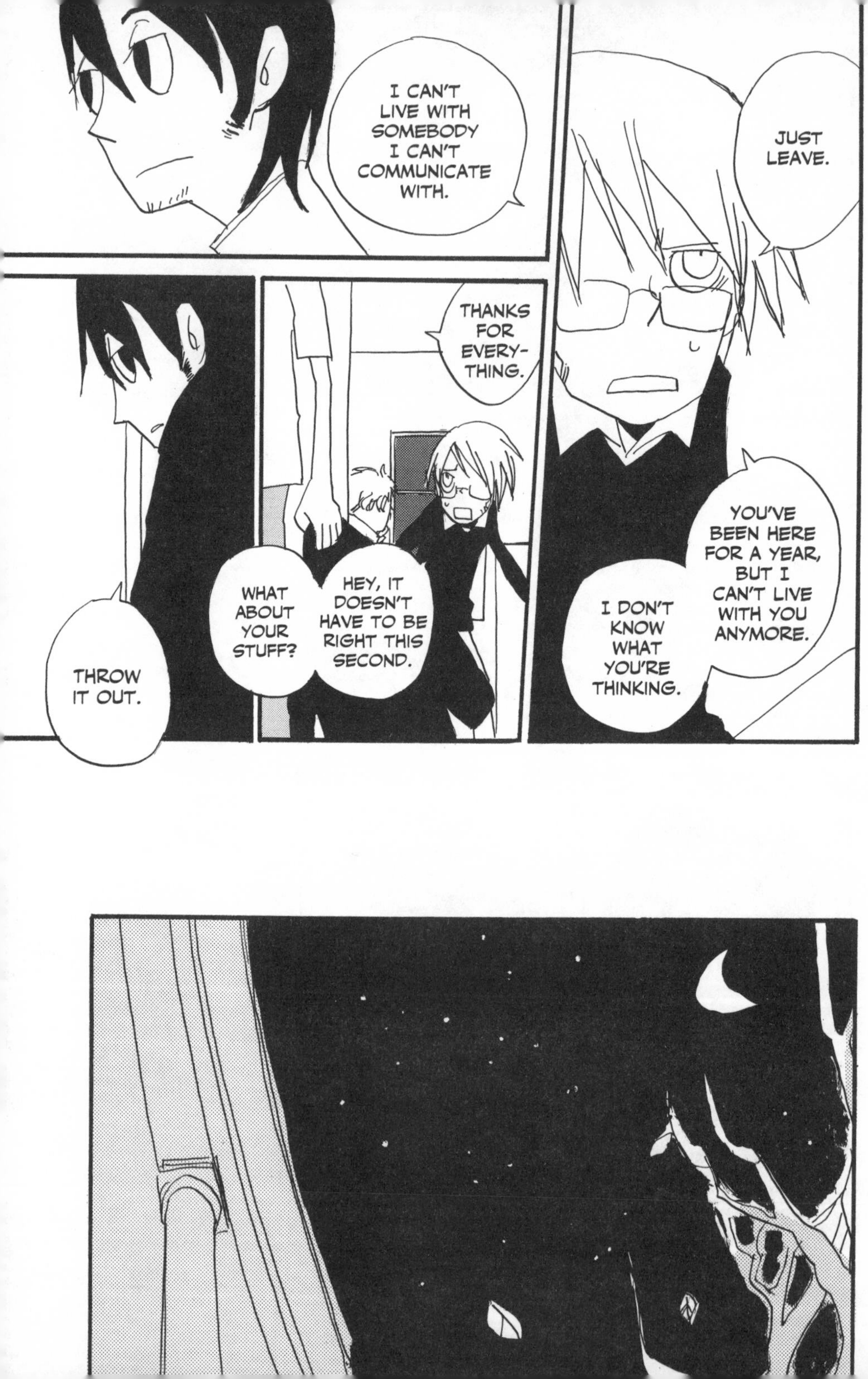
JUST LEAVE.
YOU'VE BEEN HERE FOR A YEAR, BUT I CAN'T LIVE WITH YOU ANYMORE.
I DON'T KNOW WHAT YOU'RE THINKING.
I CAN'T LIVE WITH SOMEBODY I CAN'T COMMUNICATE WITH.
THANKS FOR EVERY-THING.
HEY, IT DOESN'T HAVE TO BE RIGHT THIS SECOND.
WHAT ABOUT YOUR STUFF?
THROW IT OUT.

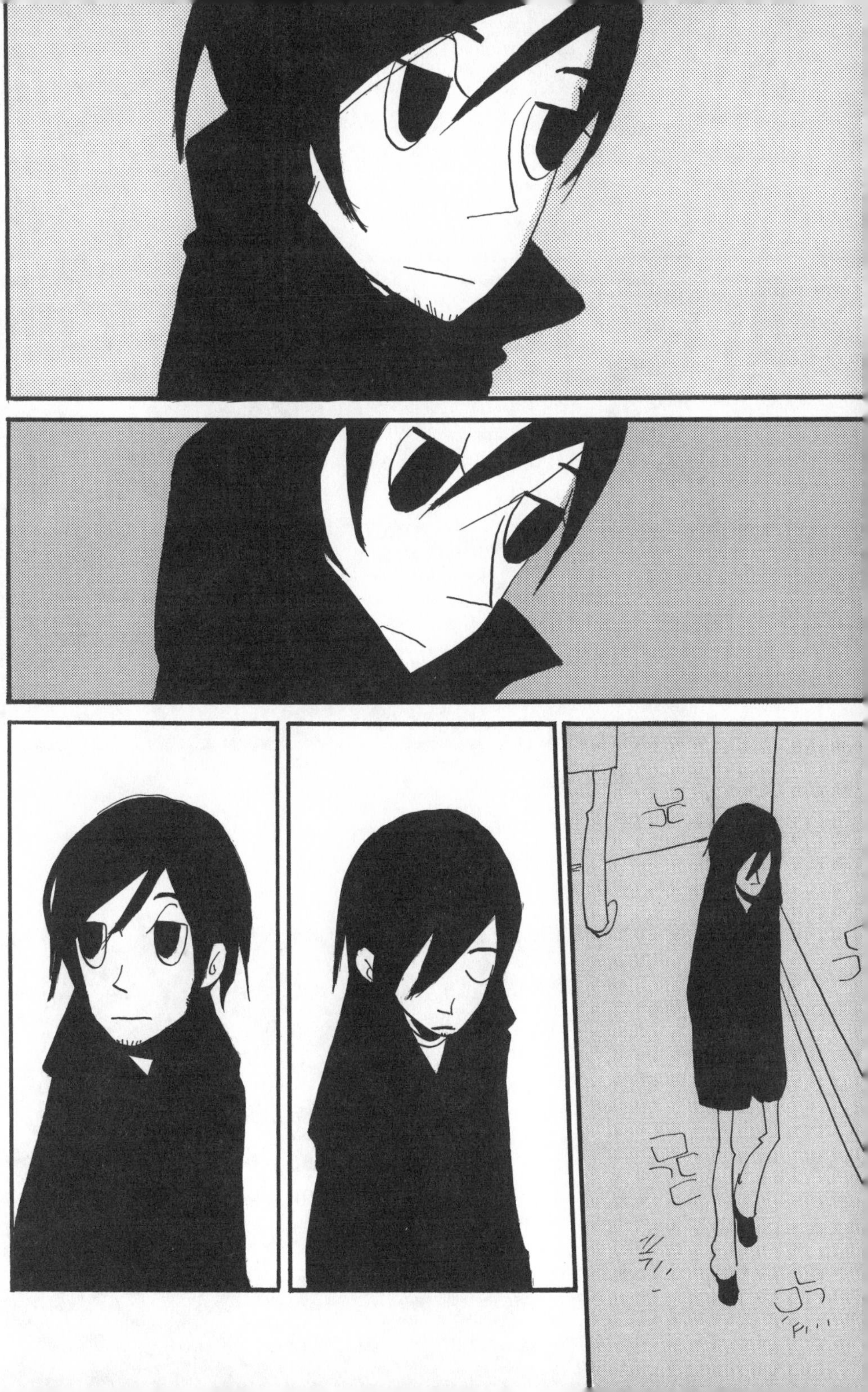

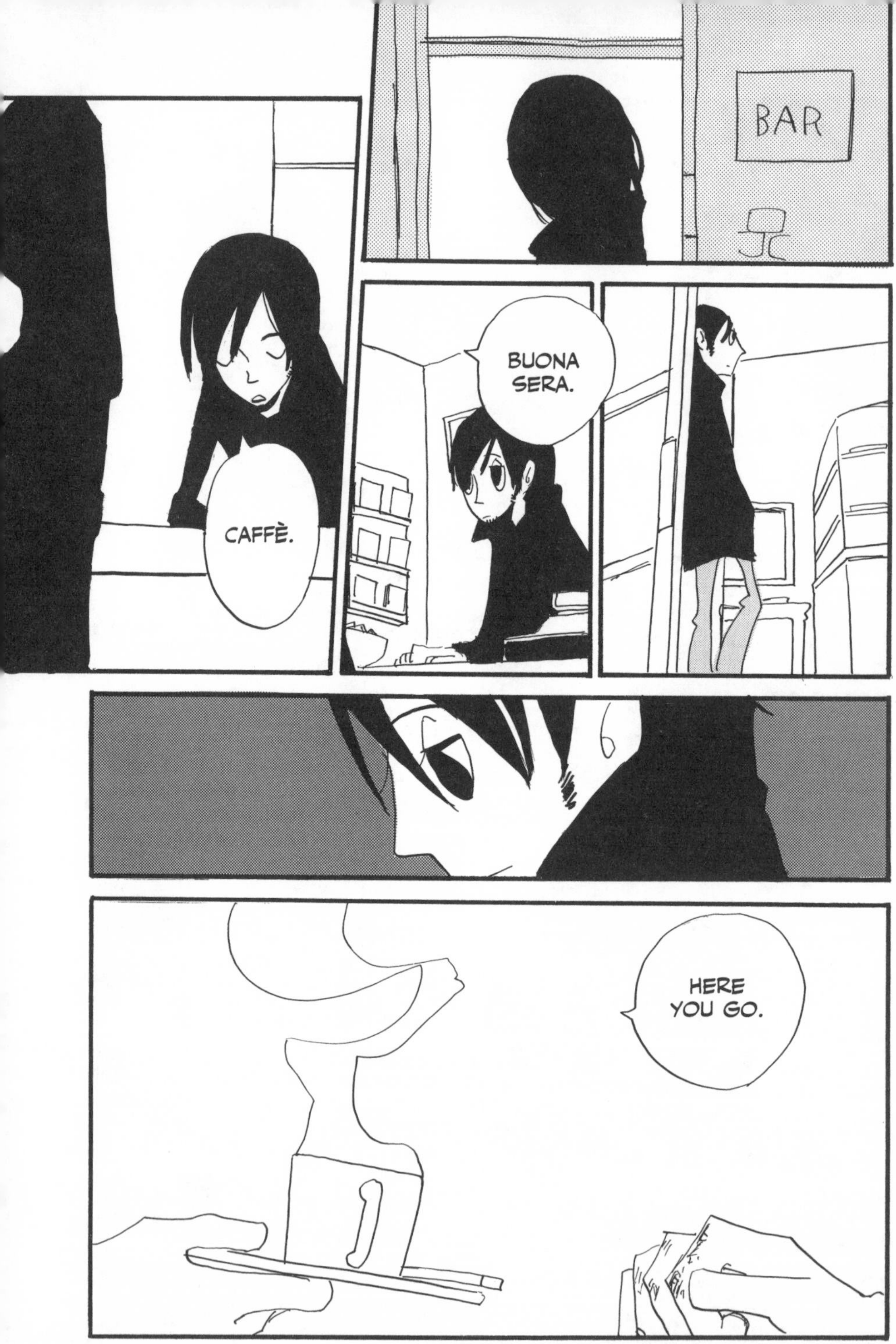
BAR
BUONA SERA.
CAFFÈ.
HERE YOU GO.

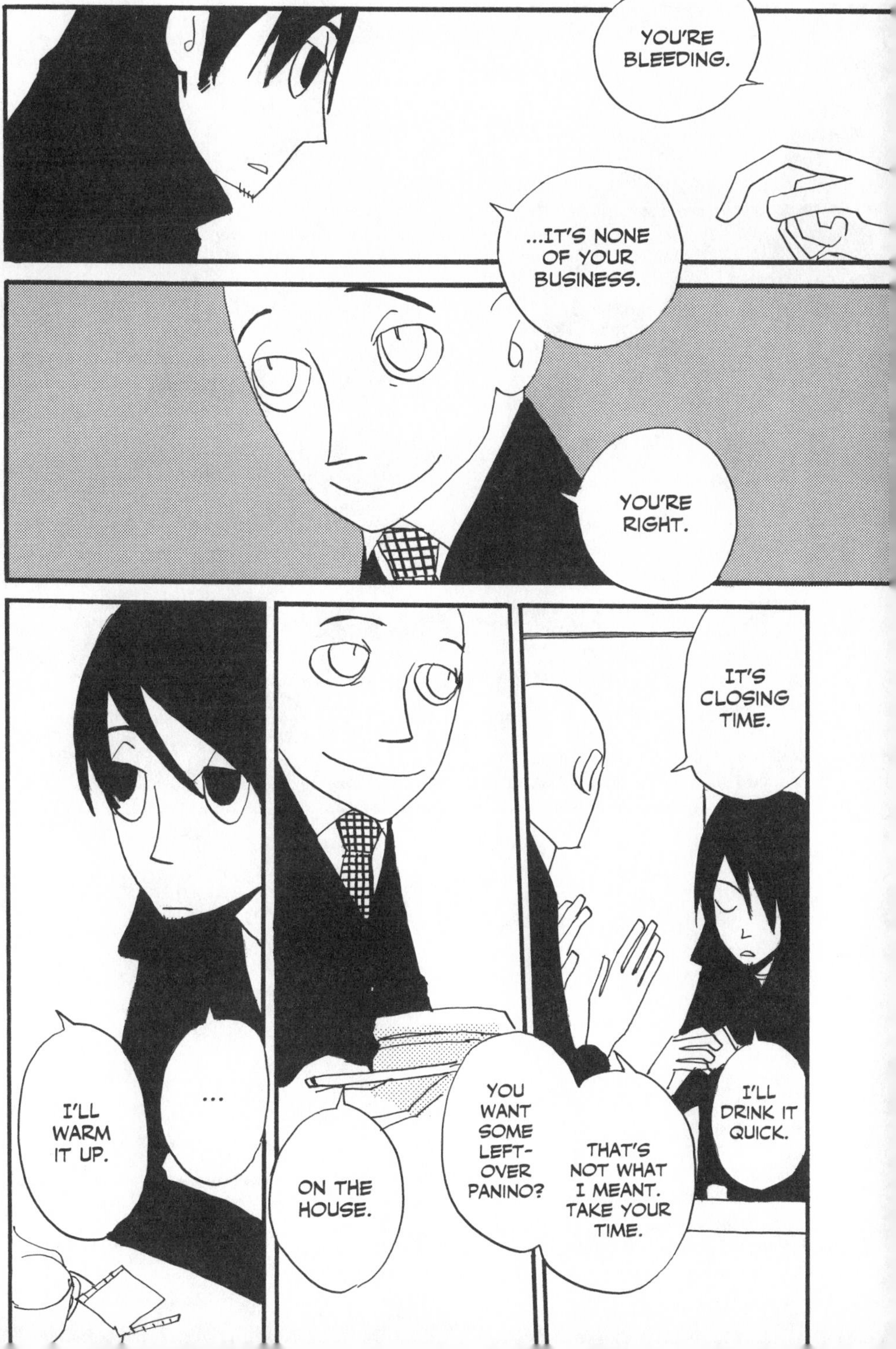
YOU'RE BLEEDING.
...IT'S NONE OF YOUR BUSINESS.
YOU'RE RIGHT.
IT'S CLOSING TIME.
I'LL DRINK IT QUICK.
THAT'S NOT WHAT I MEANT. TAKE YOUR TIME.
YOU WANT SOME LEFT-OVER PANINO?
ON THE HOUSE.
...
I'LL WARM IT UP.

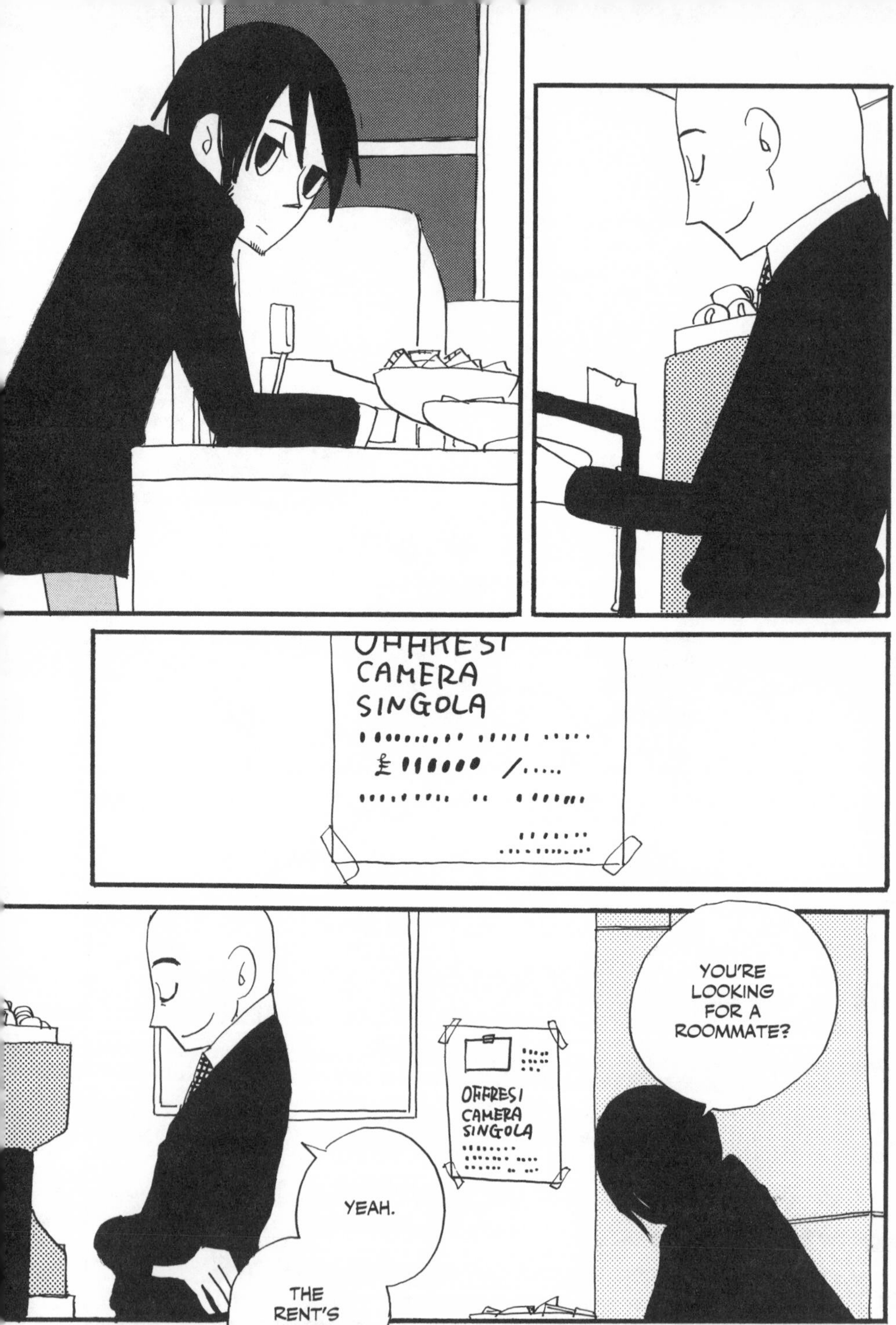
CAMERA
SINGOLA
OFFRESI
CAMERA
SINGOLA
YOU'RE LOOKING FOR A ROOMMATE?
YEAH.
THE RENT'S CHEAP.

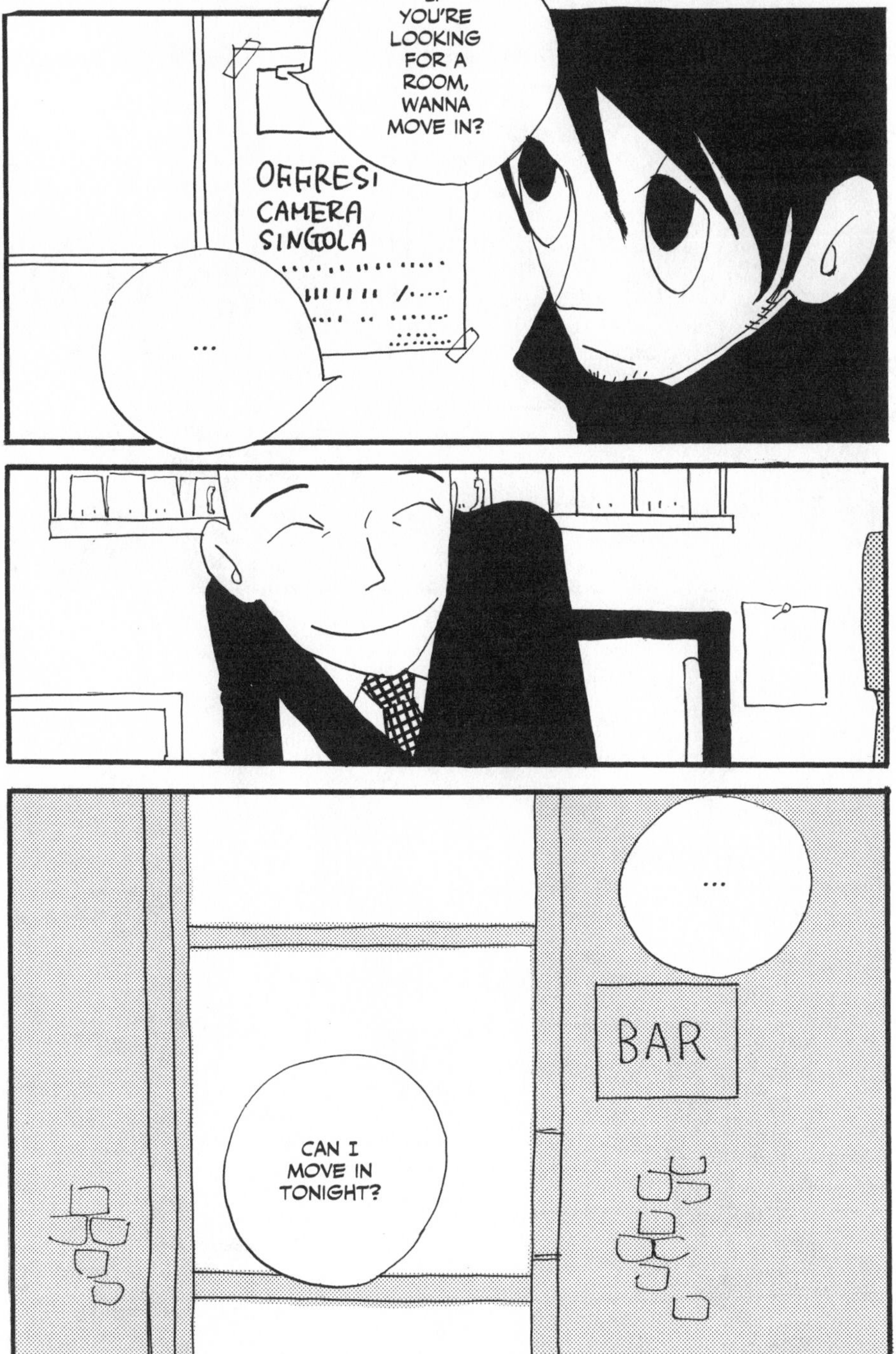
IF YOU'RE LOOKING FOR A ROOM, WANNA MOVE IN?
OFFRESI CAMERA SINGOLA
...
...
BAR
CAN I MOVE IN TONIGHT?

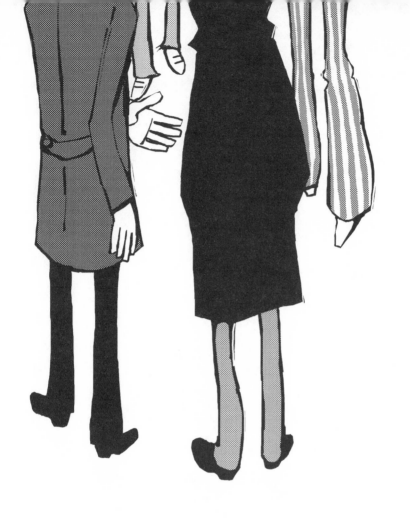

NATALE IN ITALIA

~CHRISTMAS IN ITALY~

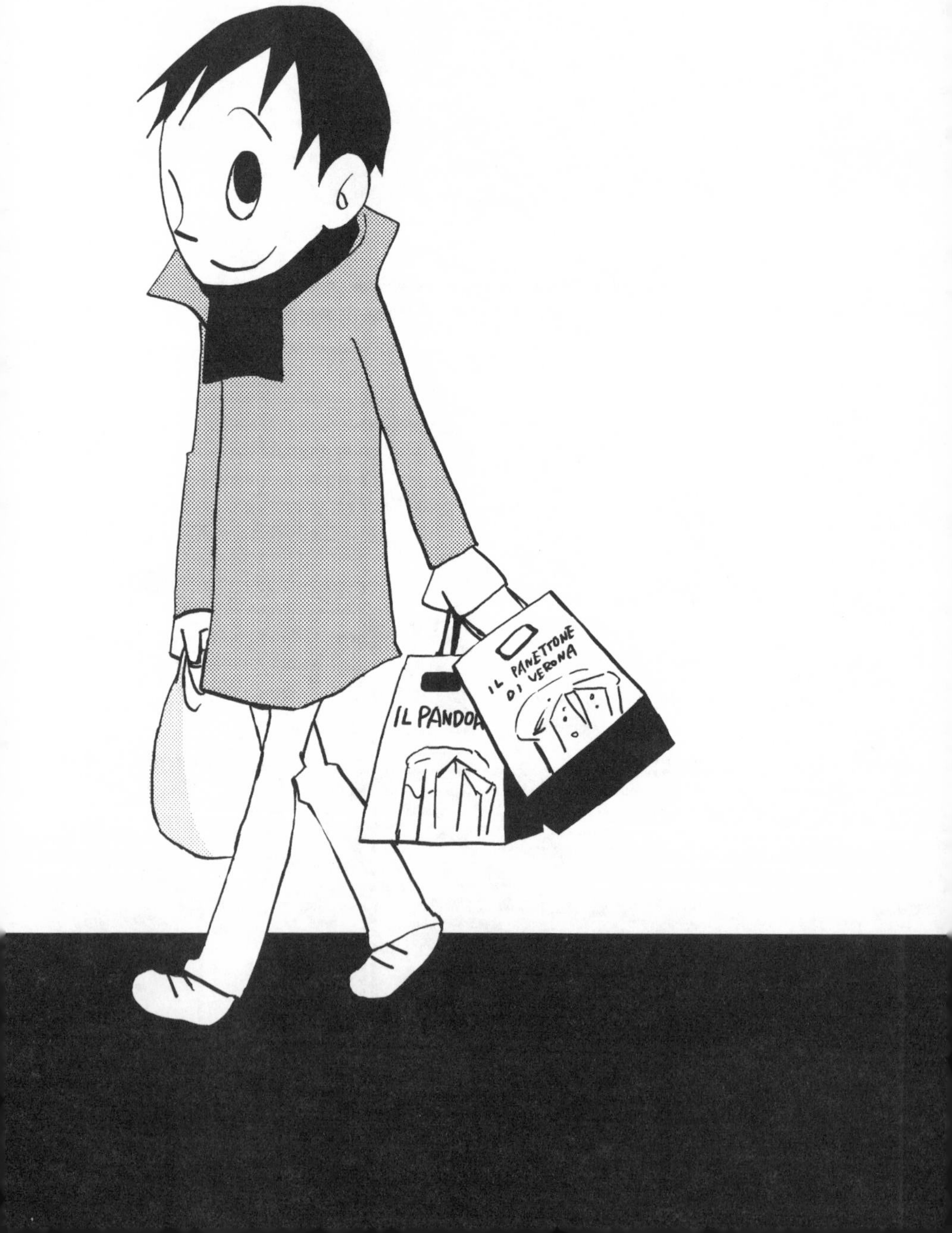
IL PANETTONE
DI VERONA

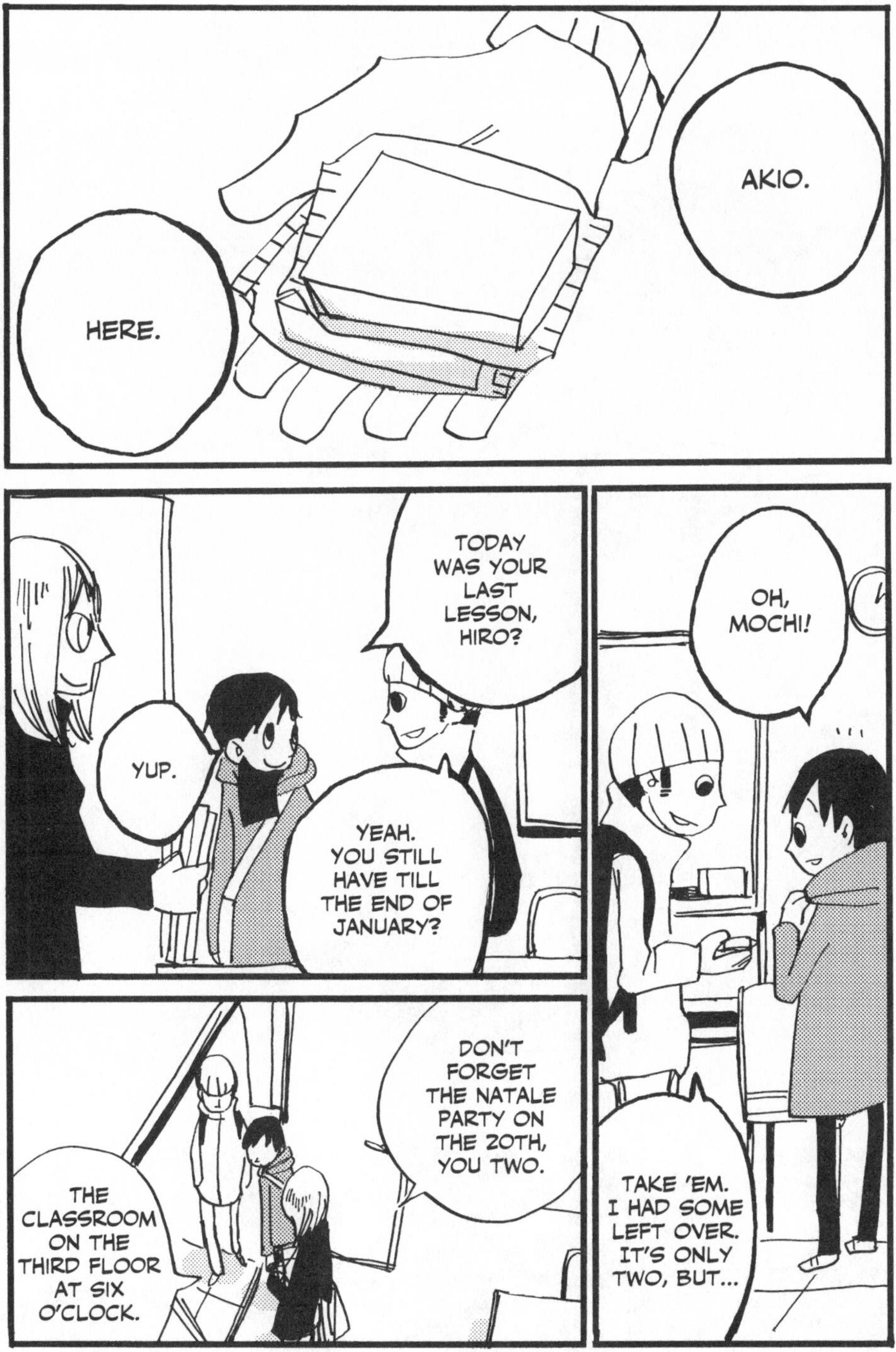
AKIO.
HERE.
OH, MOCHI!
TAKE 'EM. I HAD SOME LEFT OVER. IT'S ONLY TWO, BUT...
TODAY WAS YOUR LAST LESSON, HIRO?
YUP.
YEAH. YOU STILL HAVE TILL THE END OF JANUARY?
DON'T FORGET THE NATALE PARTY ON THE 20TH, YOU TWO.
THE CLASSROOM ON THE THIRD FLOOR AT SIX O'CLOCK.

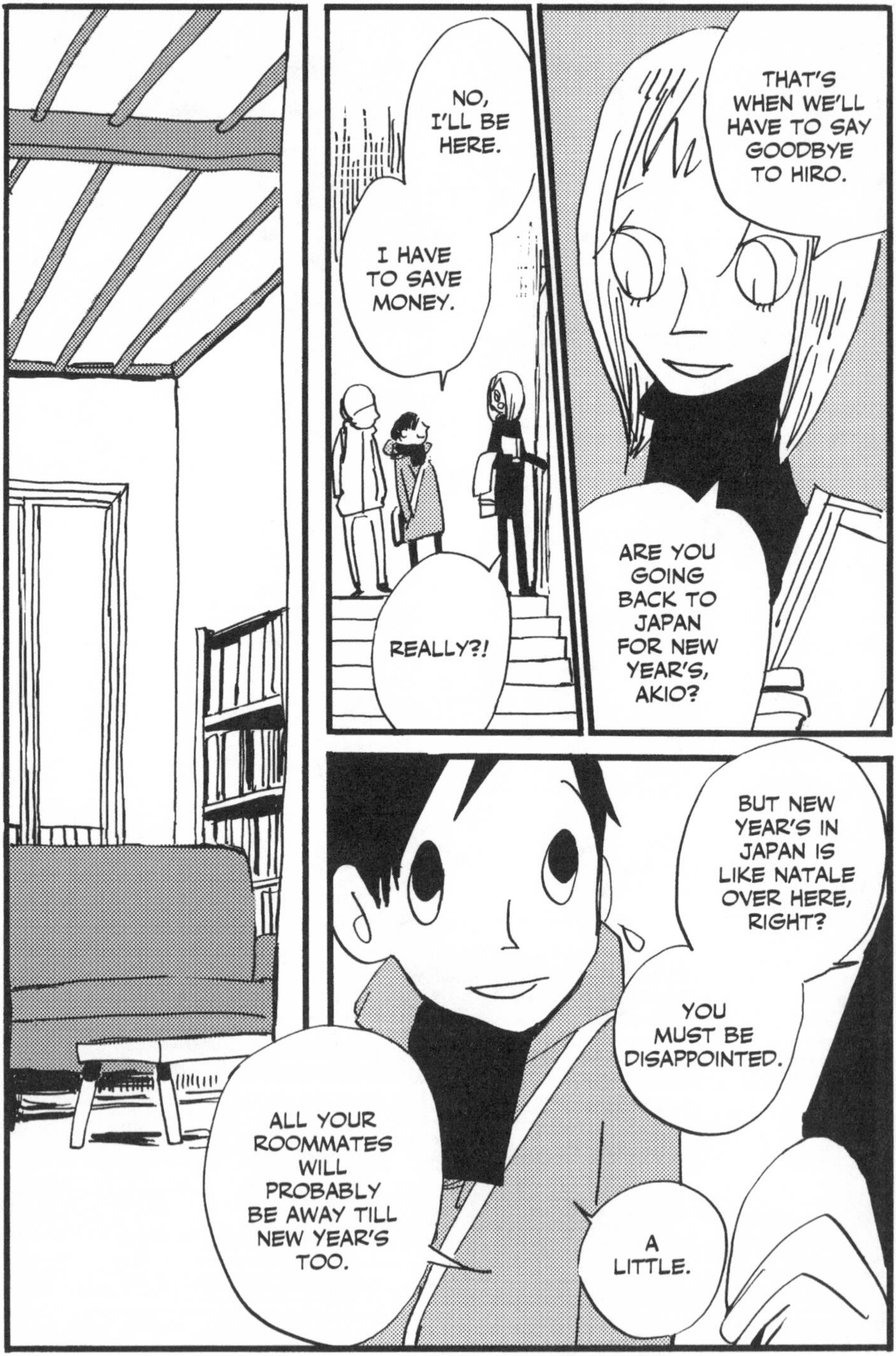
THAT'S WHEN WE'LL HAVE TO SAY GOODBYE TO HIRO.
ARE YOU GOING BACK TO JAPAN FOR NEW YEAR'S, AKIO?
NO, I'LL BE HERE.
I HAVE TO SAVE MONEY.
REALLY?!
BUT NEW YEAR'S IN JAPAN IS LIKE NATALE OVER HERE, RIGHT?
YOU MUST BE DISAPPOINTED.
A LITTLE.
ALL YOUR ROOMMATES WILL PROBABLY BE AWAY TILL NEW YEAR'S TOO.

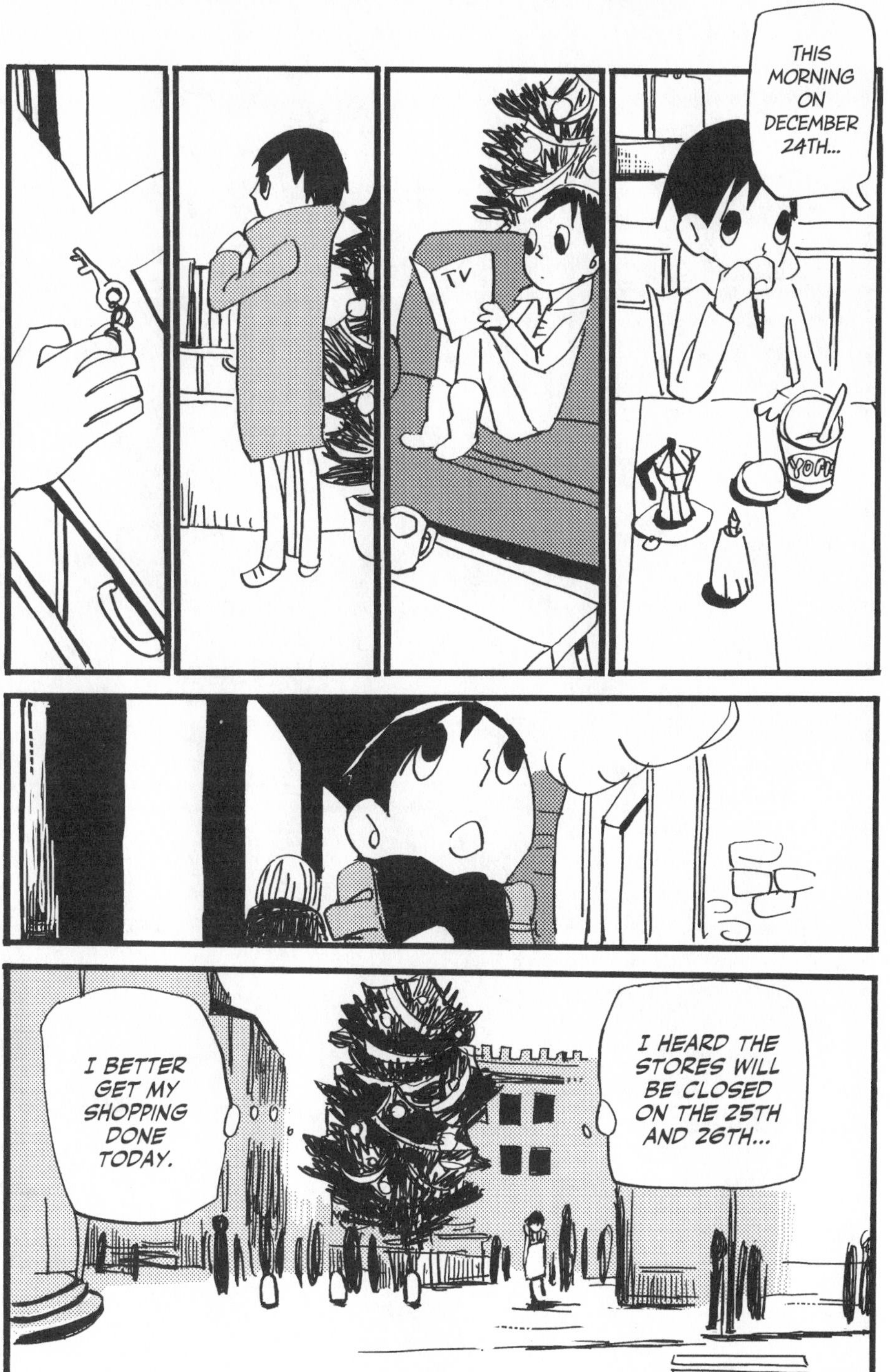
THIS MORNING ON DECEMBER 24TH...
TV
I HEARD THE STORES WILL BE CLOSED ON THE 25TH AND 26TH...
I BETTER GET MY SHOPPING DONE TODAY.

IL PANDORO
IL PANDORO
IL PANETTONE DI VERONA
IL PANETTONE DI VERONA
IL PANETTONE
€6,90
IL PANETTONE DI VERONA
IL PANETTONE DI VERONA
IL PANETTONE DI VERONA

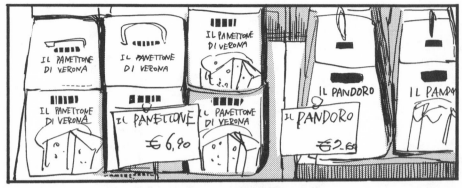

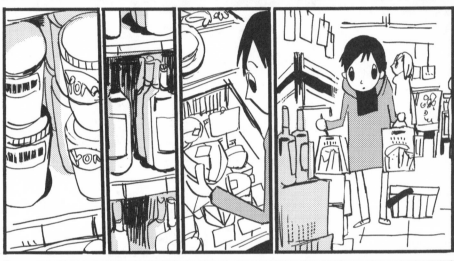

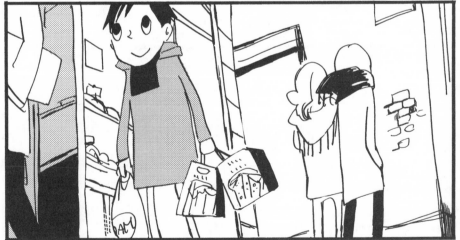

Powdered Sugar

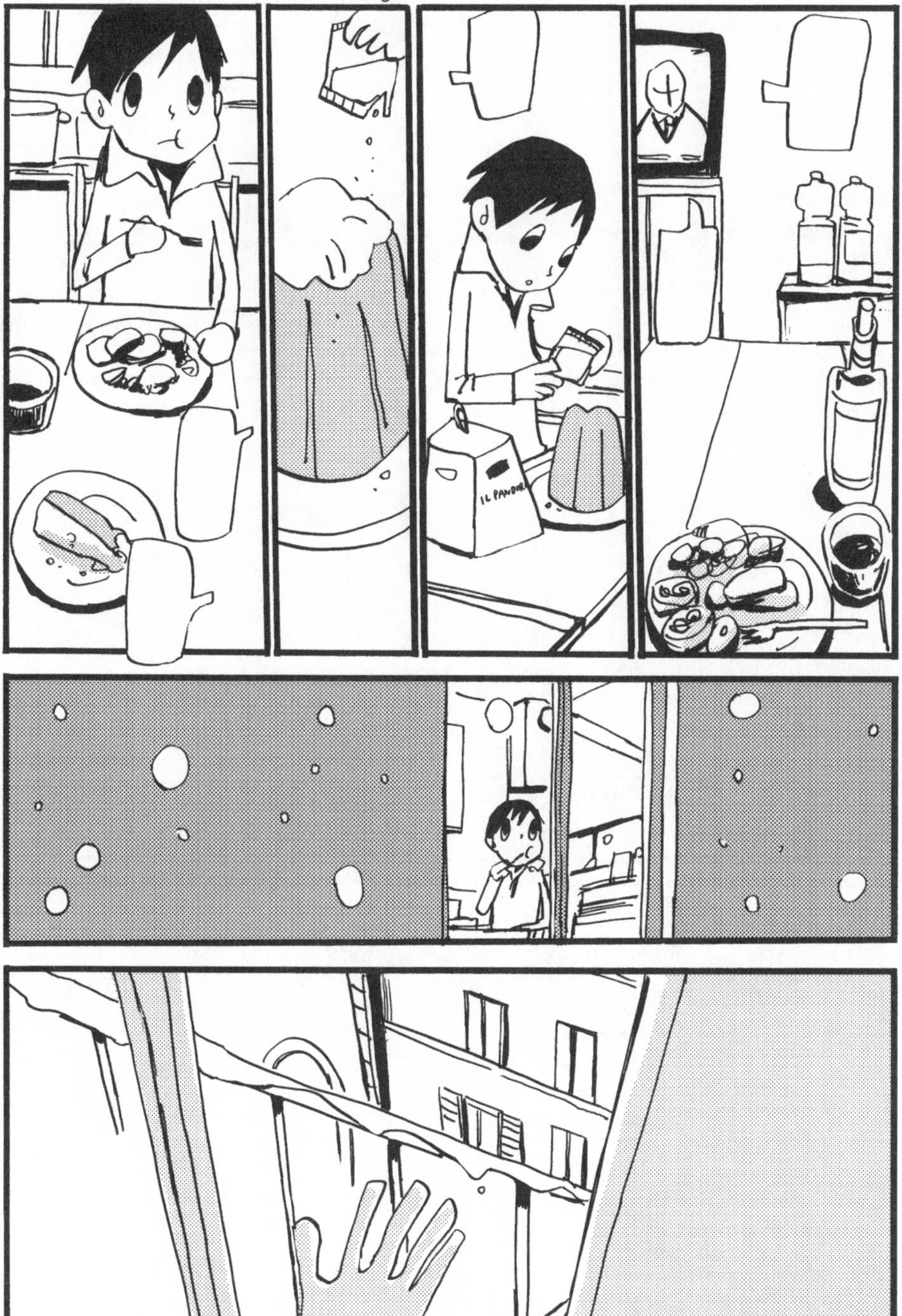
IL PANDOR

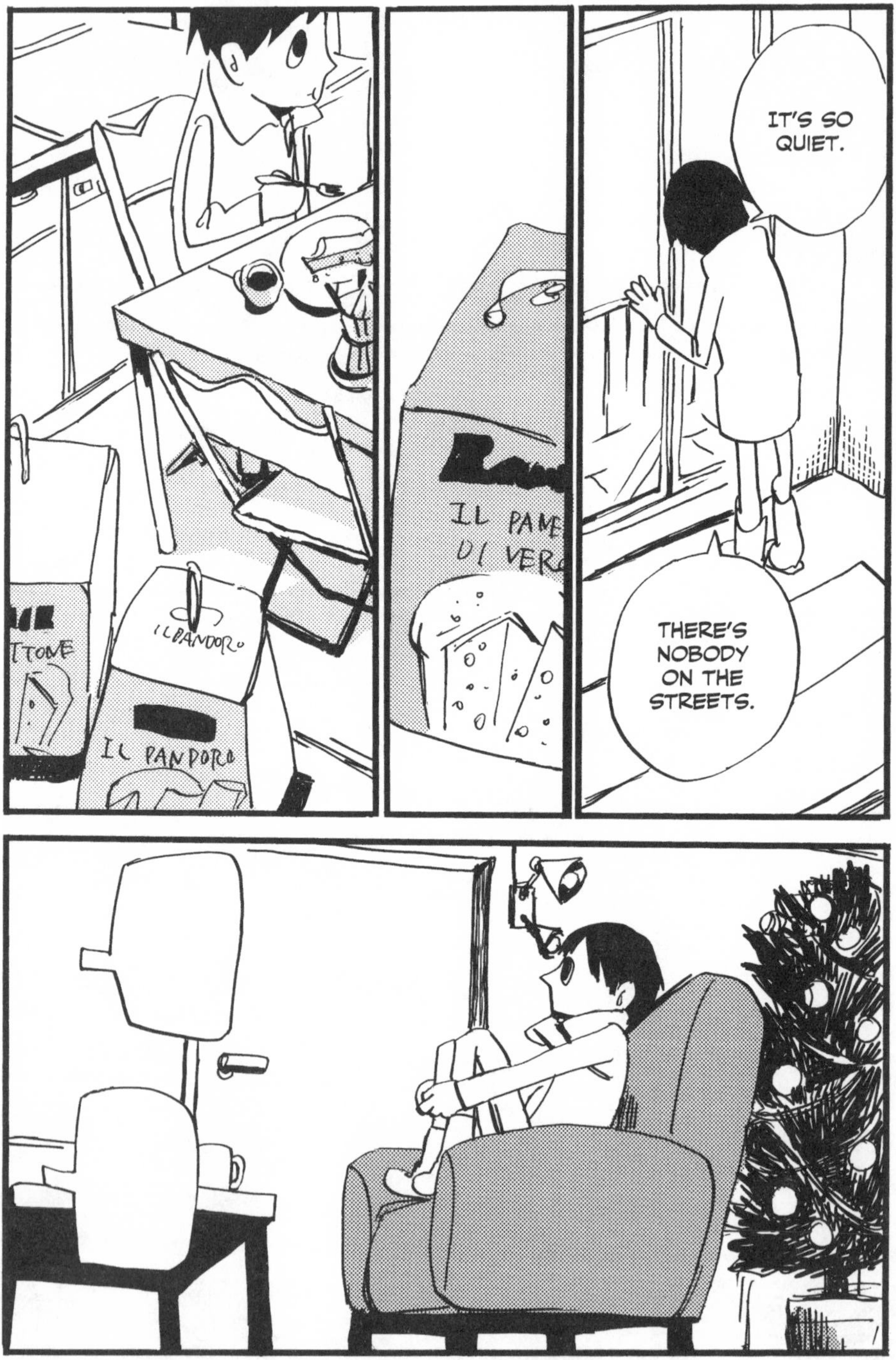
IT'S SO QUIET.
THERE'S NOBODY ON THE STREETS.
IL PANDORO
IL PANDORO

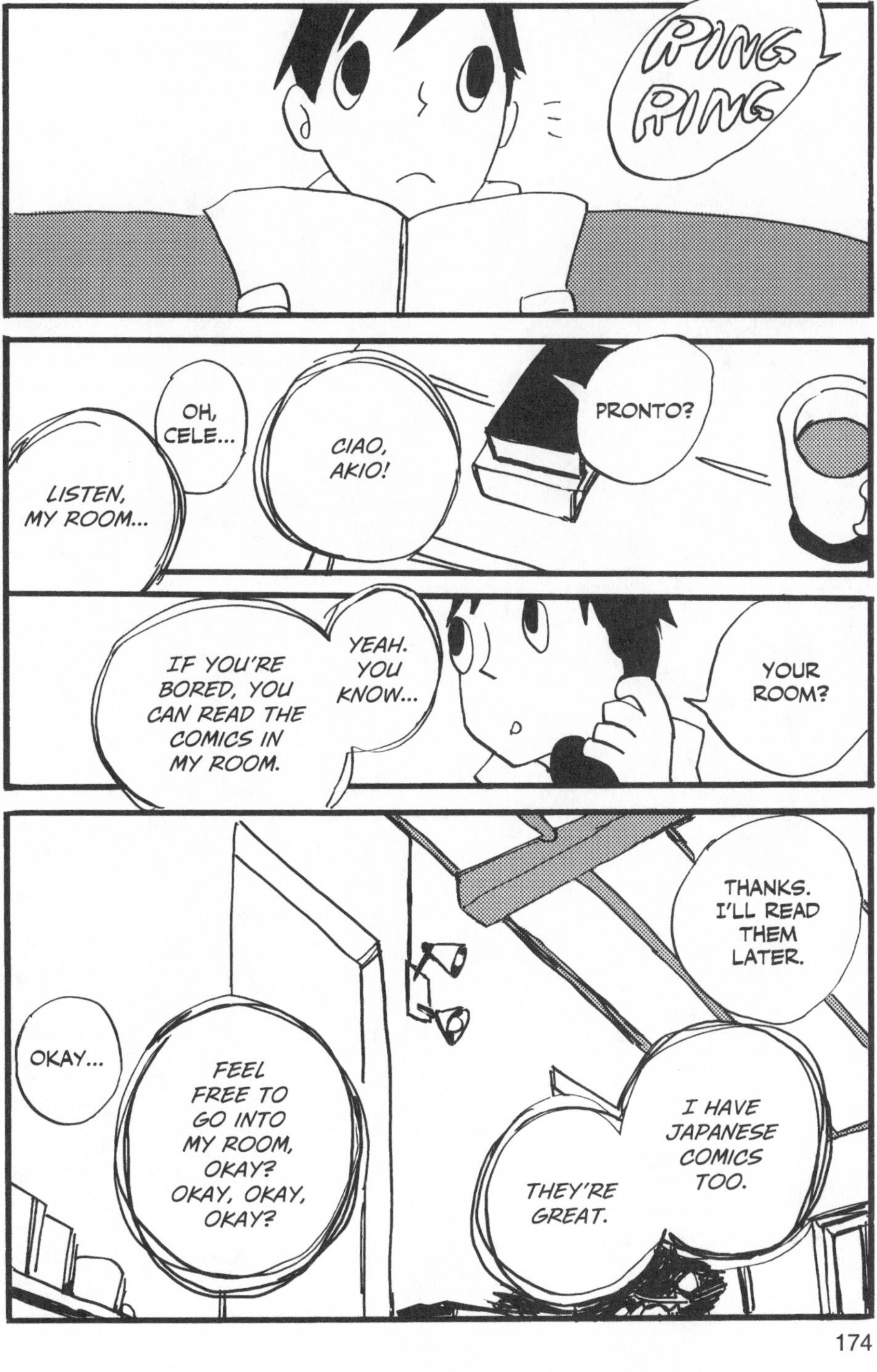
RING RING
PRONTO?
CIAO, AKIO!
OH, CELE...
LISTEN, MY ROOM...
YOUR ROOM?
YEAH. YOU KNOW...
IF YOU'RE BORED, YOU CAN READ THE COMICS IN MY ROOM.
THANKS. I'LL READ THEM LATER.
I HAVE JAPANESE COMICS TOO.
THEY'RE GREAT.
FEEL FREE TO GO INTO MY ROOM, OKAY? OKAY, OKAY, OKAY?
OKAY...

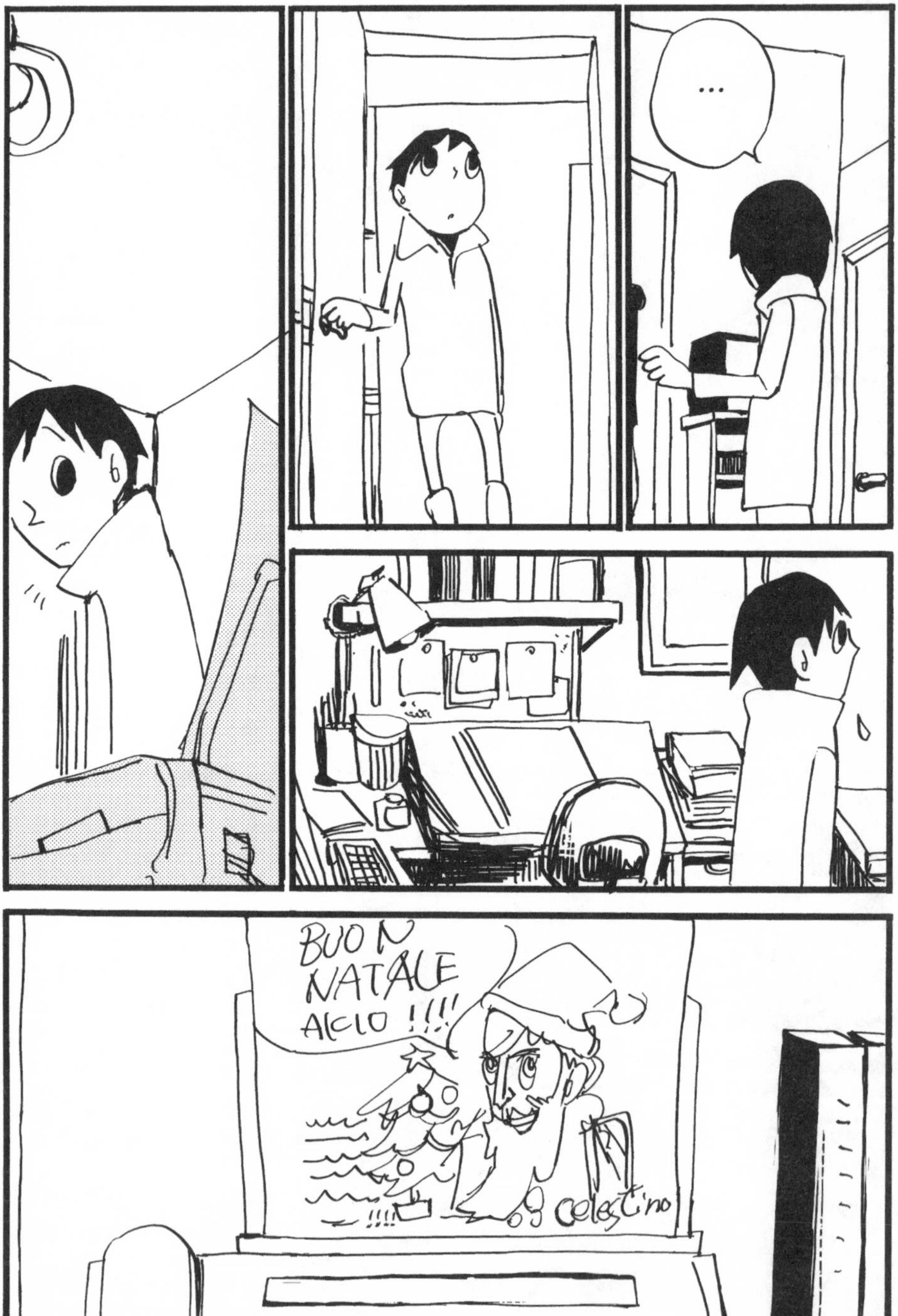
...
BUON NATALE AICLO !!!!
!!!!
Celestino

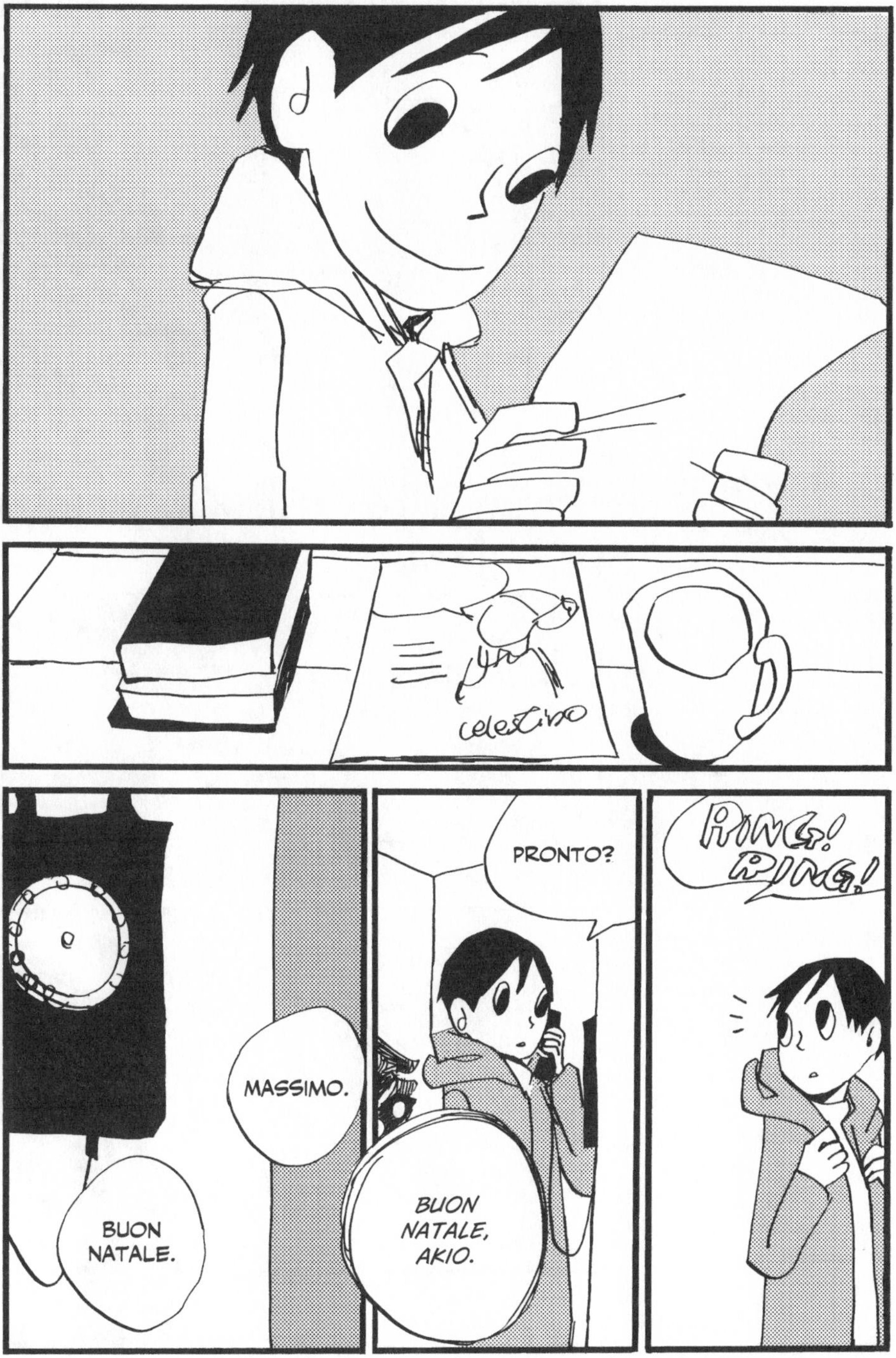
celestino
RING! RING!
PRONTO?
BUON NATALE, AKIO.
MASSIMO.
BUON NATALE.

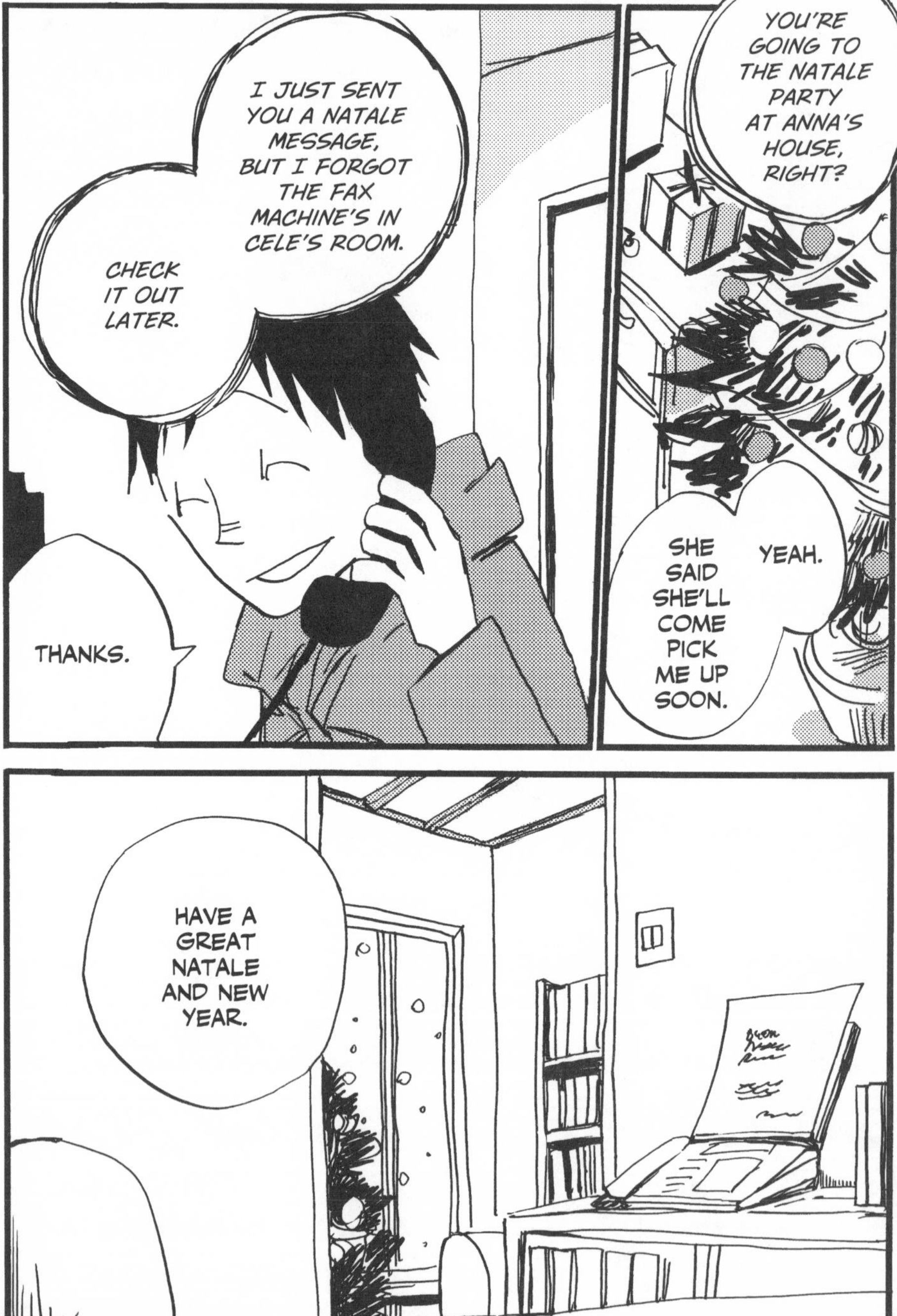
YOU'RE GOING TO THE NATALE PARTY AT ANNA'S HOUSE, RIGHT?
YEAH.
SHE SAID SHE'LL COME PICK ME UP SOON.
I JUST SENT YOU A NATALE MESSAGE, BUT I FORGOT THE FAX MACHINE'S IN CELE'S ROOM.
CHECK IT OUT LATER.
THANKS.
HAVE A GREAT NATALE AND NEW YEAR.

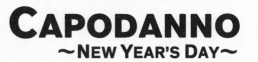

CAPODANNO
~NEW YEAR'S DAY~

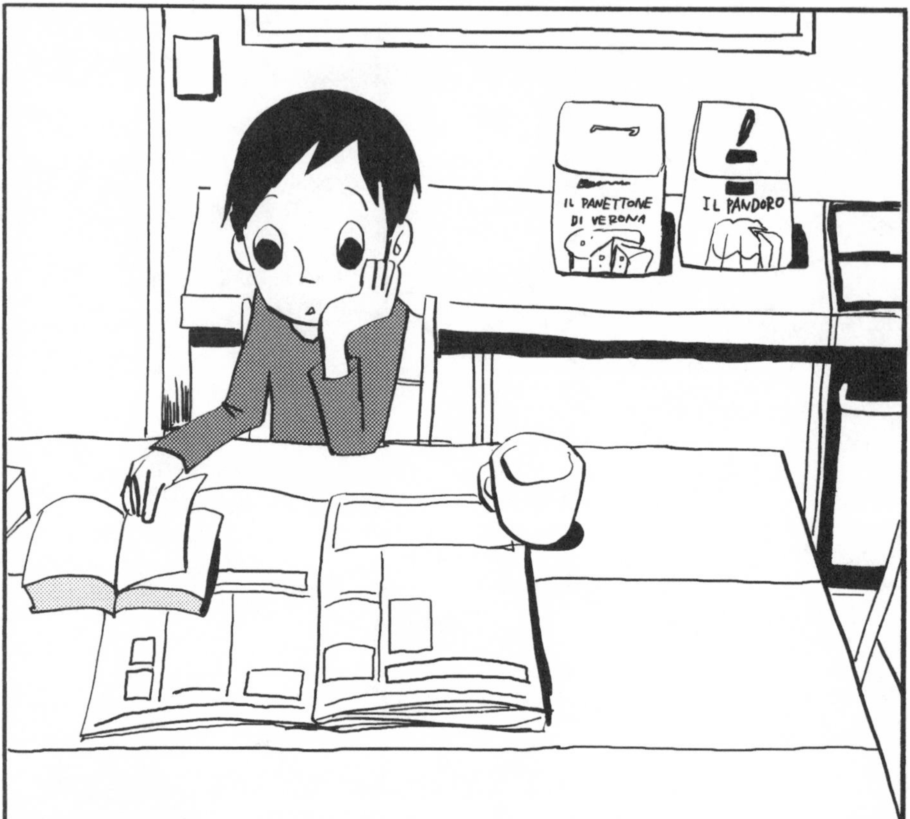
IL PANETTONE DI VERONA
IL PANDORO
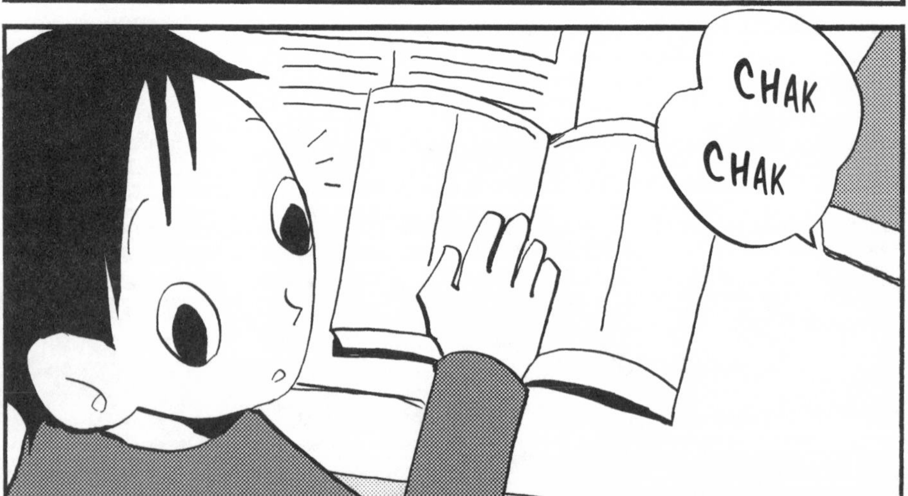
CHAK CHAK

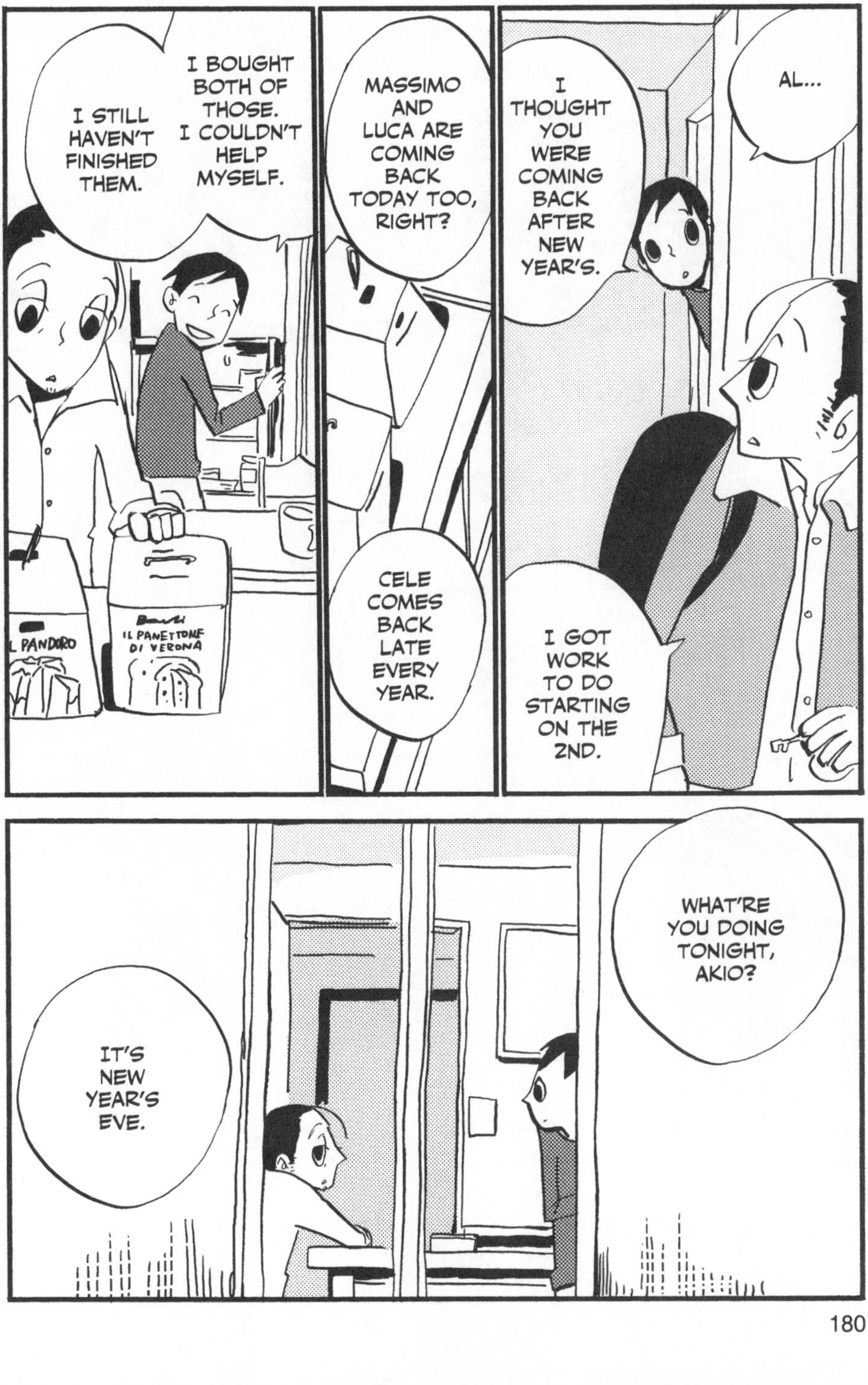
AL...
I THOUGHT YOU WERE COMING BACK AFTER NEW YEAR'S.
I GOT WORK TO DO STARTING ON THE 2ND.
MASSIMO AND LUCA ARE COMING BACK TODAY TOO, RIGHT?
CELE COMES BACK LATE EVERY YEAR.
I BOUGHT BOTH OF THOSE. I COULDN'T HELP MYSELF.
I STILL HAVEN'T FINISHED THEM.
IL PANETTONE DI VERONA
L PANDORO
WHAT'RE YOU DOING TONIGHT, AKIO?
IT'S NEW YEAR'S EVE.

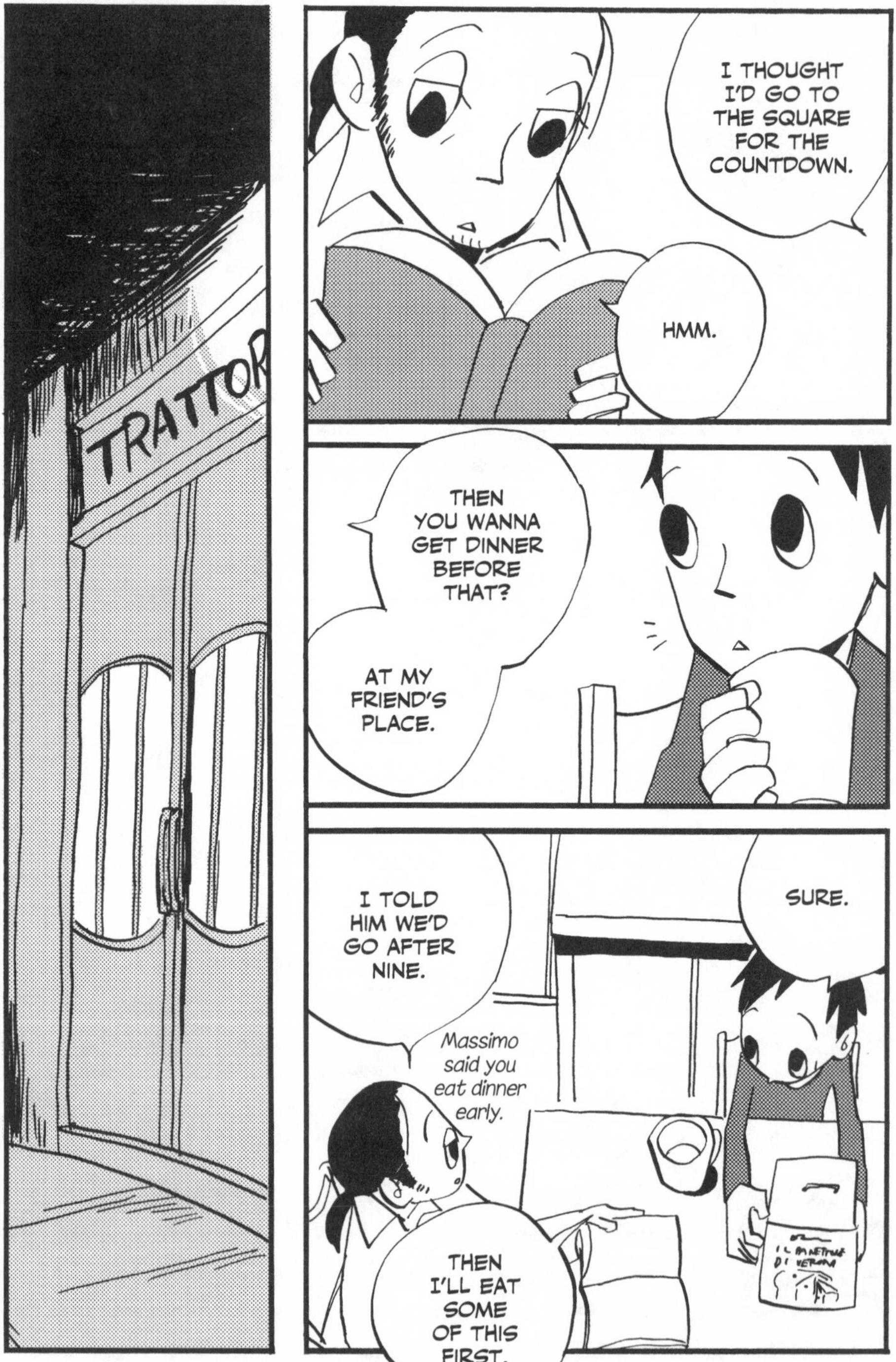
I THOUGHT I'D GO TO THE SQUARE FOR THE COUNTDOWN.
HMM.
THEN YOU WANNA GET DINNER BEFORE THAT?
AT MY FRIEND'S PLACE.
SURE.
I TOLD HIM WE'D GO AFTER NINE.
Massimo said you eat dinner early.
THEN I'LL EAT SOME OF THIS FIRST.
TRATTOR

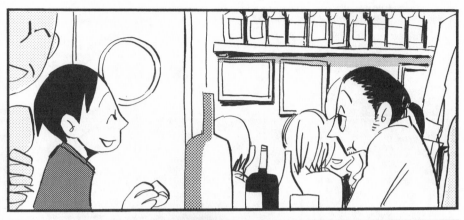

HERE YOU GO.
?
GRAZIE...
OH, IT'S ALMOST 12.
ARE YOU GOING TO RUN TO THE SQUARE?
OH...
STAY HERE FOR THE COUNTDOWN.

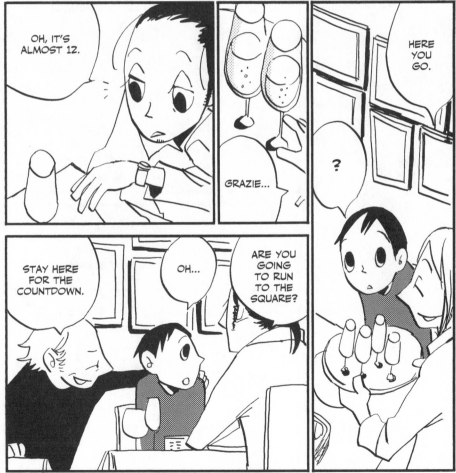

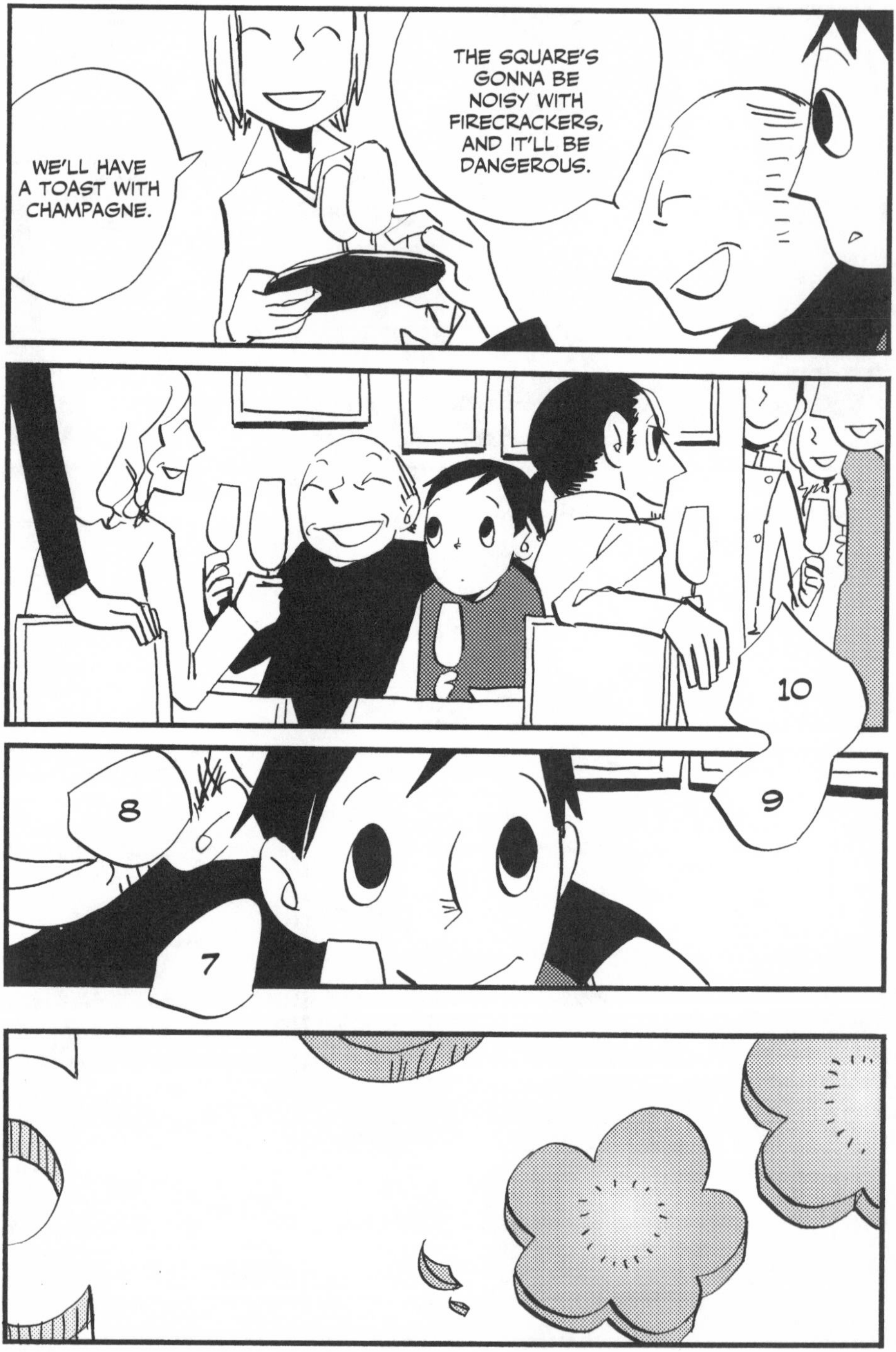
THE SQUARE'S GONNA BE NOISY WITH FIRECRACKERS, AND IT'LL BE DANGEROUS.
WE'LL HAVE A TOAST WITH CHAMPAGNE.
10
9
8
7

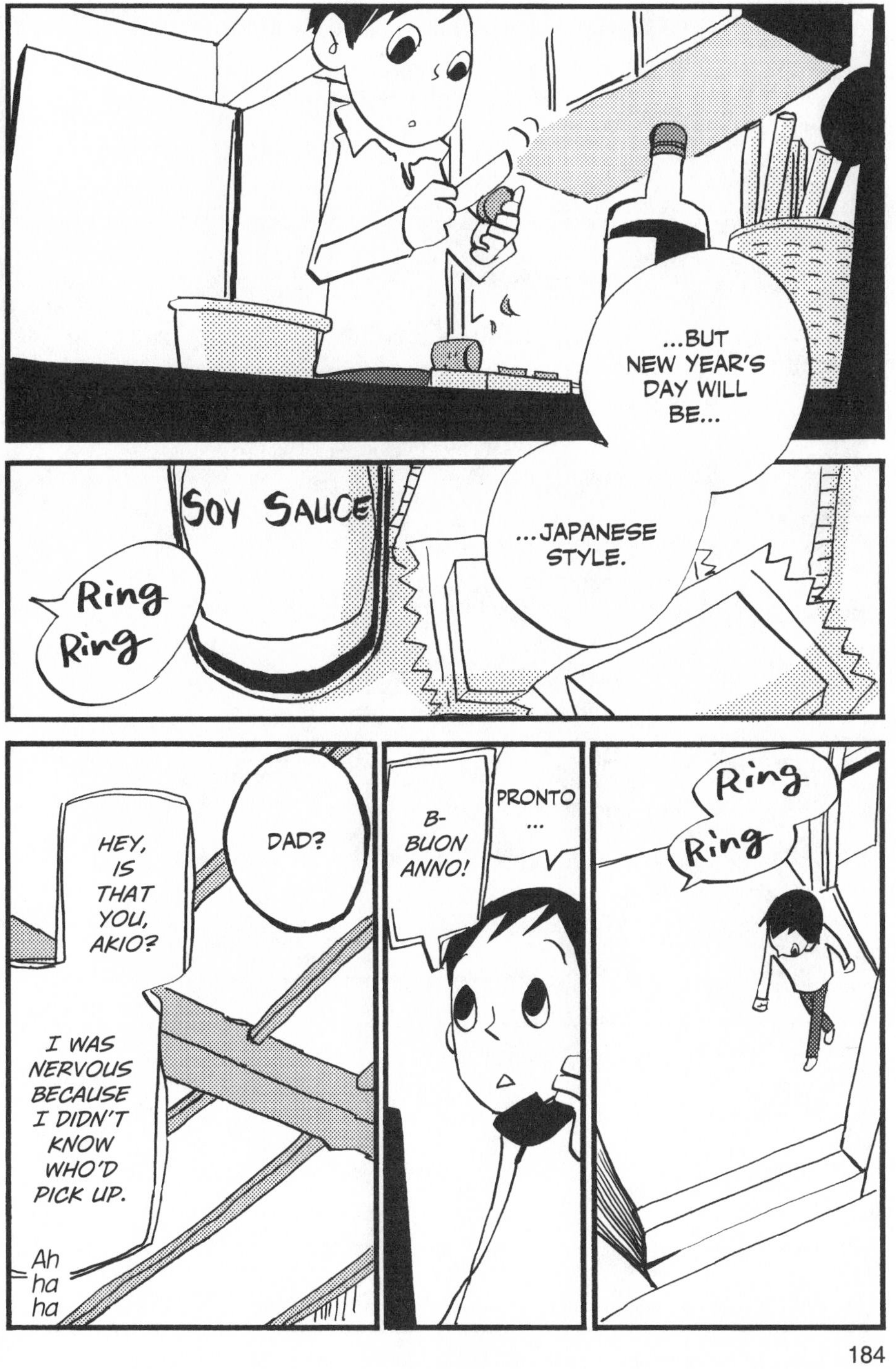
...BUT NEW YEAR'S DAY WILL BE...
...JAPANESE STYLE.
SOY SAUCE
Ring Ring
Ring Ring
PRONTO ...
B-BUON ANNO!
DAD?
HEY, IS THAT YOU, AKIO?
I WAS NERVOUS BECAUSE I DIDN'T KNOW WHO'D PICK UP.
Ah ha ha

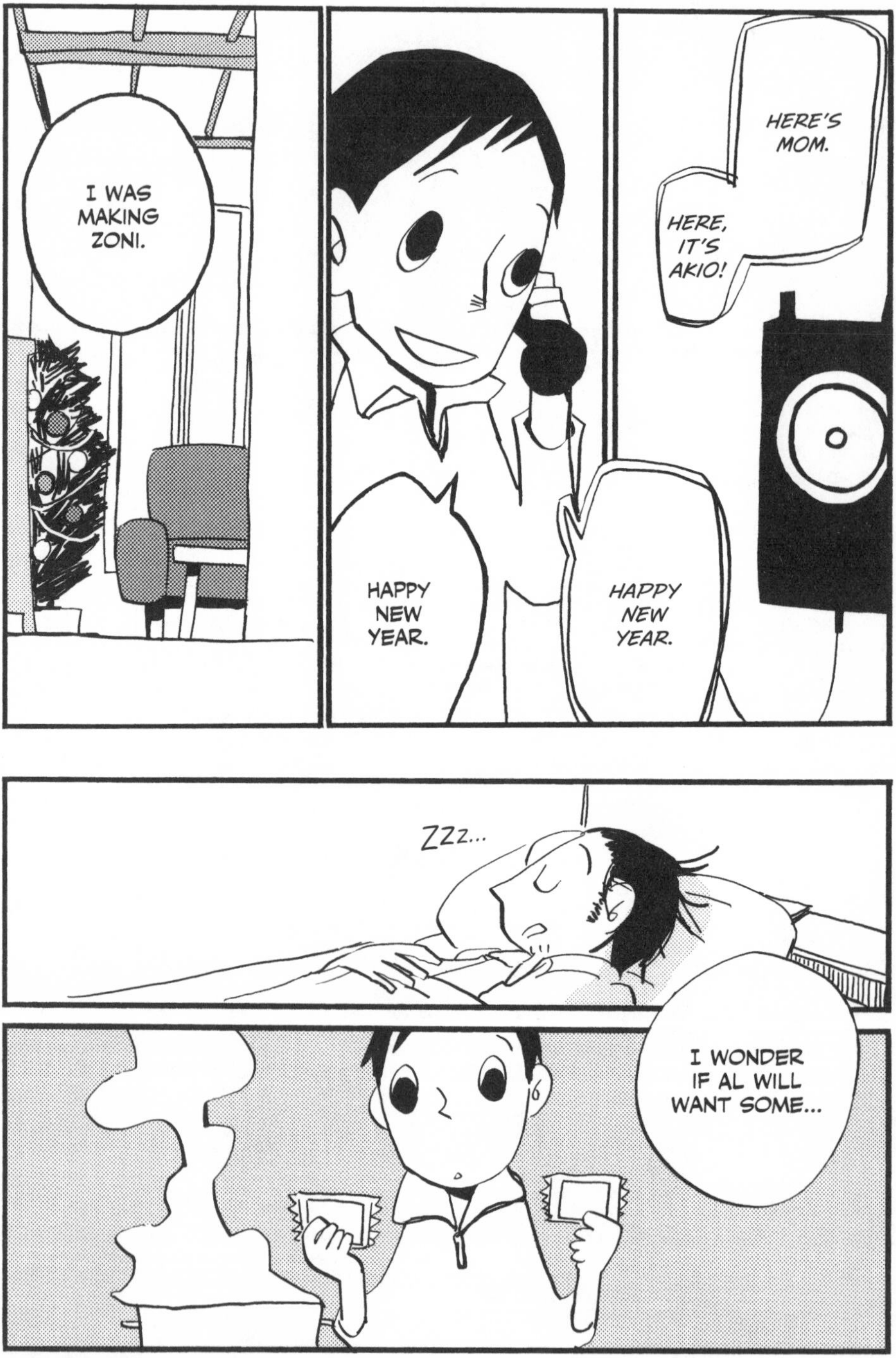

HERE'S MOM.
HERE, IT'S AKIO!
HAPPY NEW YEAR.
HAPPY NEW YEAR.
I WAS MAKING ZONI.
ZZz...
I WONDER IF AL WILL WANT SOME...

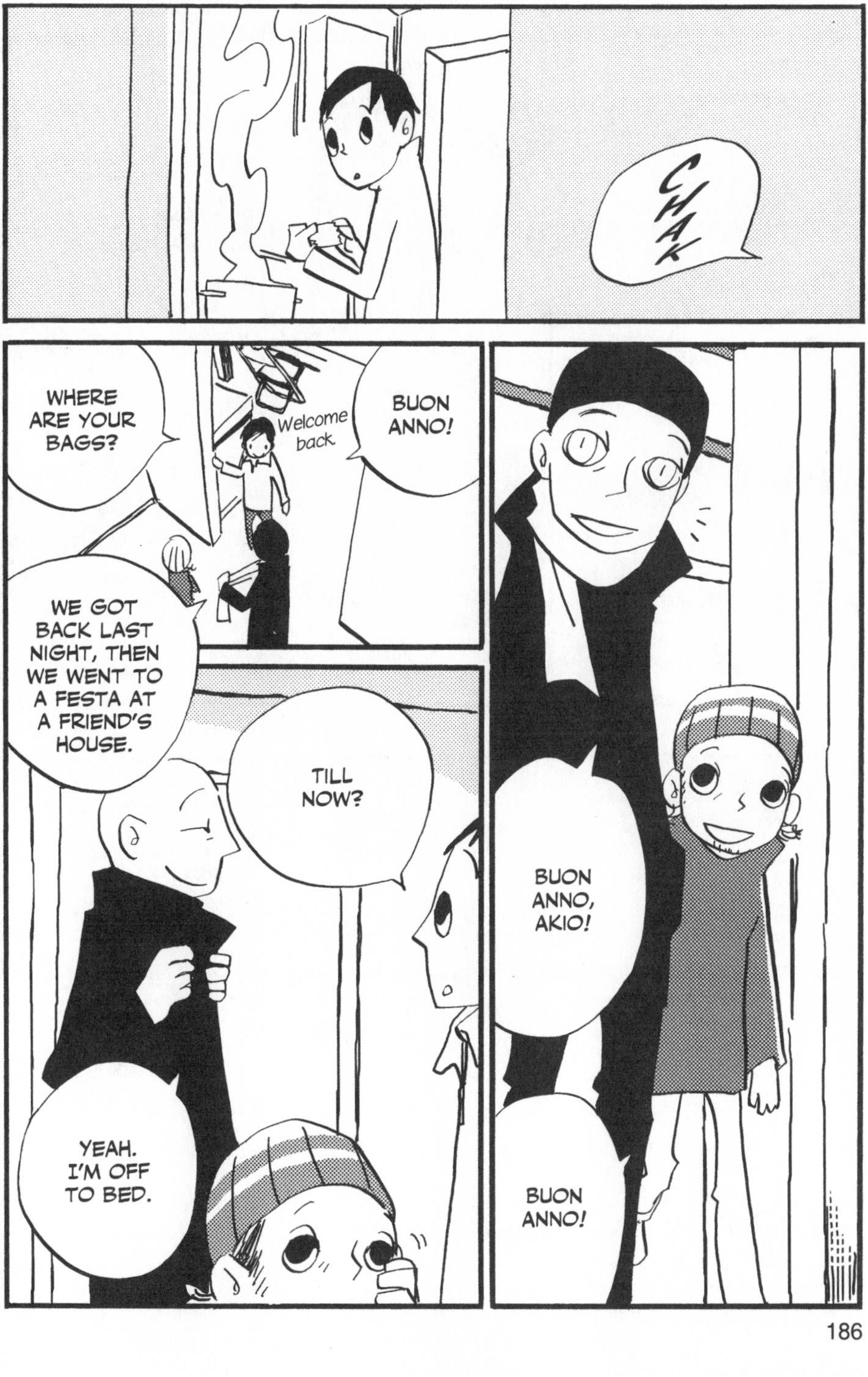
CHAK
BUON ANNO, AKIO!
BUON ANNO!
BUON ANNO!
Welcome back.
WHERE ARE YOUR BAGS?
WE GOT BACK LAST NIGHT, THEN WE WENT TO A FESTA AT A FRIEND'S HOUSE.
TILL NOW?
YEAH. I'M OFF TO BED.

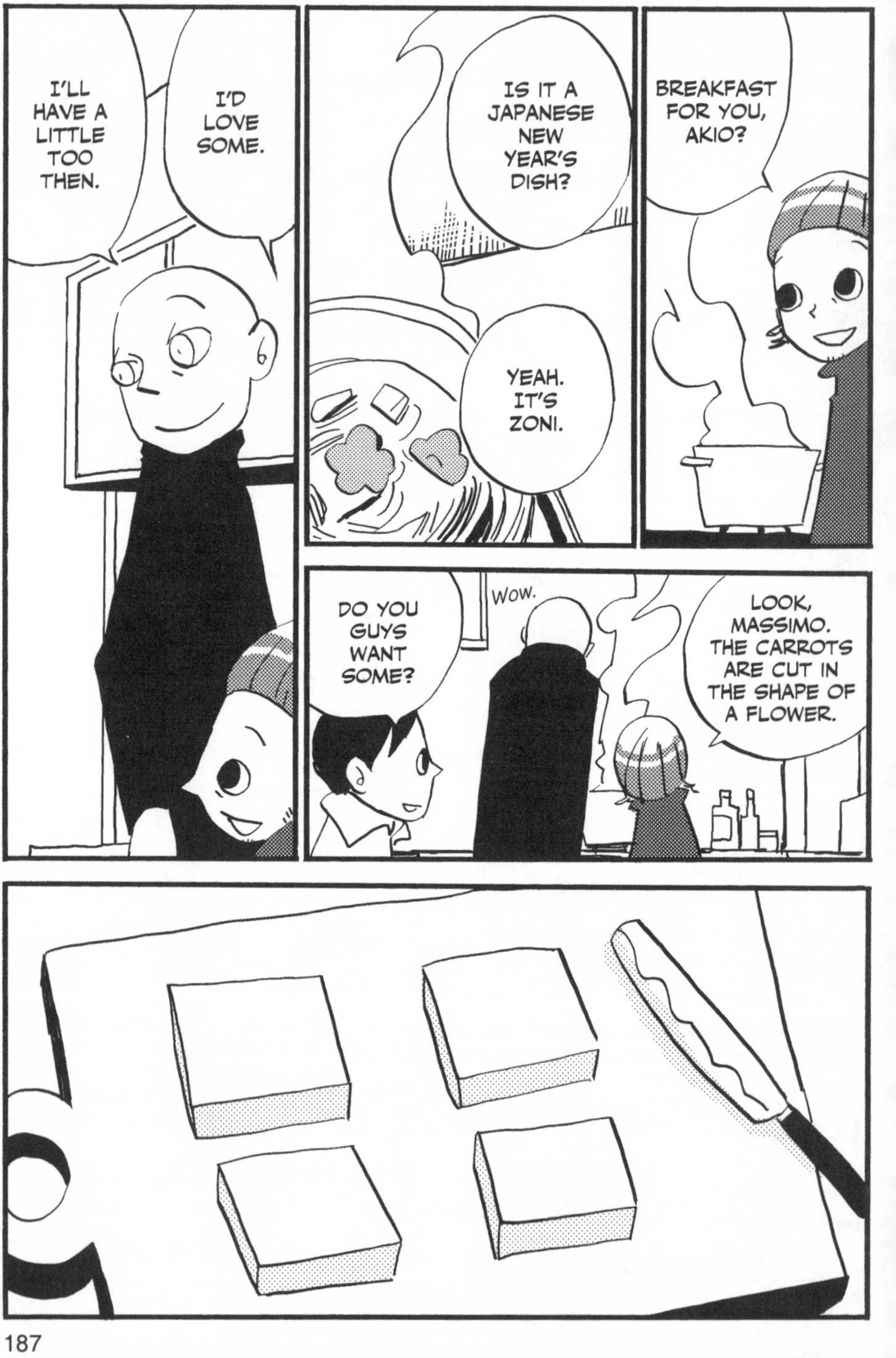
BREAKFAST FOR YOU, AKIO?
IS IT A JAPANESE NEW YEAR'S DISH?
YEAH. IT'S ZONI.
LOOK, MASSIMO. THE CARROTS ARE CUT IN THE SHAPE OF A FLOWER.
WOW.
DO YOU GUYS WANT SOME?
I'D LOVE SOME.
I'LL HAVE A LITTLE TOO THEN.

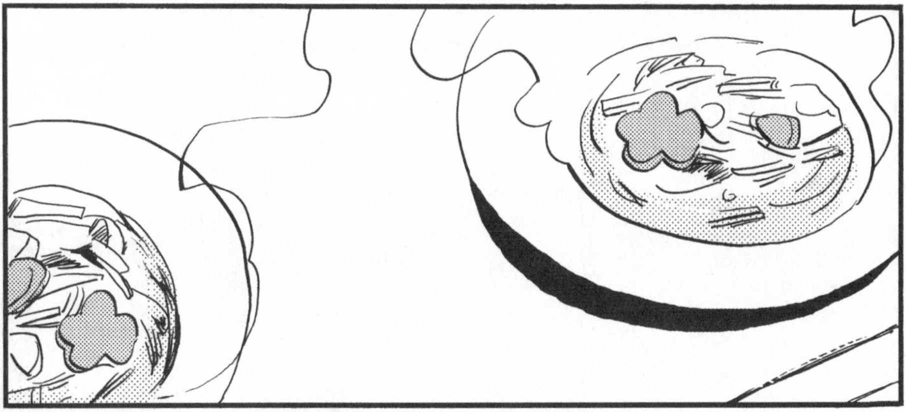

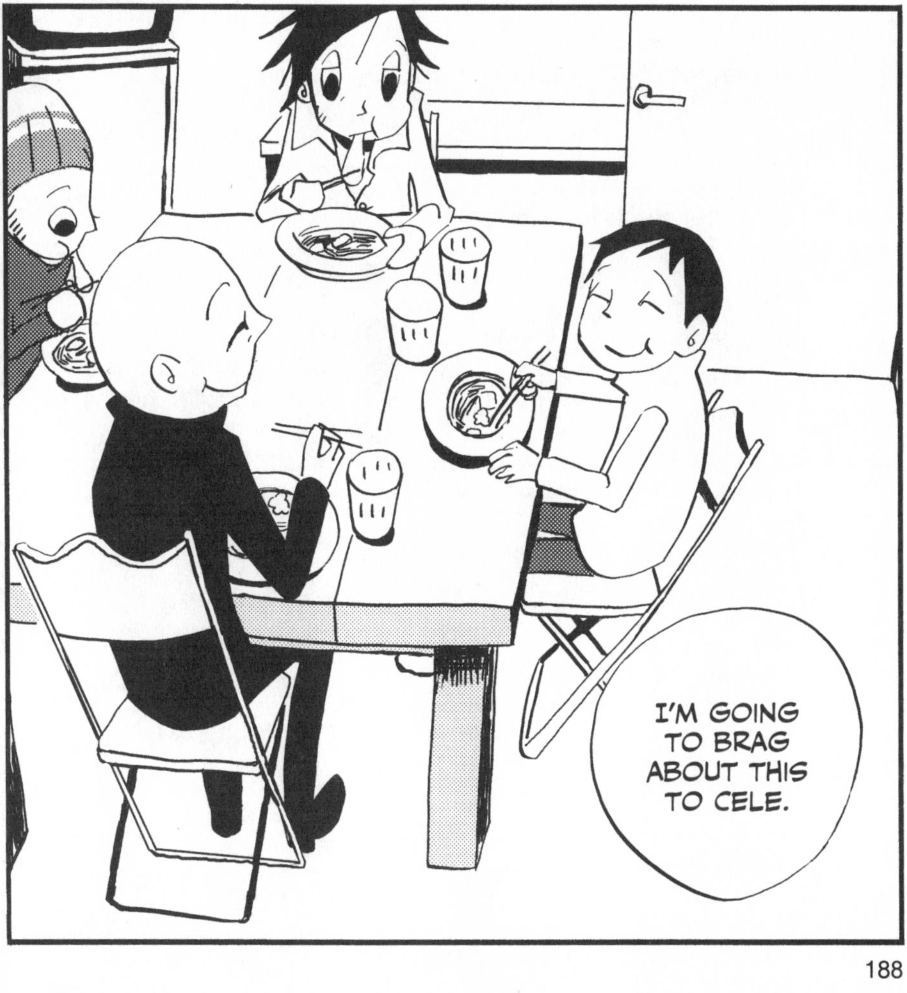
I'M GOING TO BRAG ABOUT THIS TO CELE.

LA QUINTA CAMERA

▪ The Fifth Room ▪

Fine

Also by
**NATSUME
ONO**

House of Five Leaves

not simple

Ristorante Paradiso

Gente

LA QUINTA CAMERA

VIZ Signature Edition

story and art by **NATSUME ONO**

Original Japanese edition "LA QUINTA CAMERA"
published by SHOGAKUKAN Inc.

Original Japanese Cover Design by **chutte**

Translation ▪ **Joe Yamazaki**
Touch-up Art & Lettering ▪ **Gia Cam Luc**
Design ▪ **Fawn Lau**
Editor ▪ **Amy Yu**

Printed in Canada

Published by VIZ Media, LLC
P.O. Box 77010
San Francisco, CA 94107

10 9 8 7 6 5 4 3 2 1
First printing, July 2011

viz media
www.viz.com

RATED T FOR TEEN
PARENTAL ADVISORY
LA QUINTA CAMERA is rated T for Teen and is recommended for ages 13 and up.
ratings.viz.com

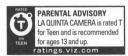

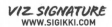

VIZ SIGNATURE
WWW.SIGIKKI.COM